SPECIAL NEEDS, COMMUNITY MUSIC, AND ADULT LEARNING

SPECIAL NEEDS, COMMUNITY MUSIC, AND ADULT LEARNING

AN OXFORD HANDBOOK OF MUSIC EDUCATION

VOLUME 4

Edited by
Gary E. McPherson
and Graham F. Welch

OXFORD
UNIVERSITY PRESS

OXFORD
UNIVERSITY PRESS

Oxford University Press is a department of the University of Oxford. It furthers
the University's objective of excellence in research, scholarship, and education
by publishing worldwide. Oxford is a registered trade mark of Oxford University
Press in the UK and certain other countries.

Published in the United States of America by Oxford University Press
198 Madison Avenue, New York, NY 10016, United States of America.

Library of Congress Cataloging-in-Publication Data
Names: McPherson, Gary E. | Welch, Graham (Graham F.)
Title: Special needs, community music, and adult learning :
an Oxford handbook of music education, Volume 4 /
Edited by Gary E. McPherson and Graham F. Welch.
Description: New York, NY : Oxford University Press, [2018] |
Includes bibliographical references and index.
Identifiers: LCCN 2018002746 | ISBN 9780190674441 (pbk. : alk. paper) |
ISBN 9780190674458 (epub)
Subjects: LCSH: Music—Instruction and study. | Special education. |
Community music—Instruction and study. | Adult education.
Classification: LCC MT1 .O934 2018 | DDC 780.71—dc23
LC record available at https://lccn.loc.gov/2018002746

1 3 5 7 9 8 6 4 2

Printed by WebCom, Inc., Canada

CONTENTS

....

CONTRIBUTORS

Carlos R. Abril holds a PhD in music education from the Ohio State University, an M.M. in performance from Cincinnati College Conservatory of Music, and a B.M. in music education from the University of Miami Frost School of Music. He is professor of music education at the Frost School of Music, University of Miami. Previously, he was associate professor and coordinator of music education at Northwestern University. His research interests include issues surrounding cultural diversity and social justice in music education, music education policy, and music teacher education. He has published his work in a wide array of research and professional journals. He has coedited the books *Teaching General Music: Approaches, Issues* and *Viewpoints* and *Musical Experience in Our Lives*. He serves on a number of editorial boards in Europe and in the Americas, including *Journal of Research in Music Education, Bulletin of the Council for Research in Music Education*, and *Revista Complutense Investigación en Educación Musical*.

Mary Adamek, PhD, MT-BC, is the Director of the Undergraduate Music Therapy Program at The University of Iowa. She is a coauthor of the textbook, *Music in Special Education*, published by the American Music Therapy Association (AMTA) and she has contributed chapters in several music therapy and music education textbooks. She maintains an active leadership role in state, regional, and national music therapy organizations and is a past-president of AMTA. She has extensive professional experience as a music therapist and music educator and is a specialist in the areas of music in special education, full inclusion music education, and supervision of music therapy students in training. She is a recipient of the 2015 Lifetime Achievement Award from the American Music Therapy Association.

Kenneth S. Aigen studied philosophy and psychology at the University of Wisconsin prior to completing master's and doctoral degrees in music therapy at New York University. He is currently an associate professor of music therapy at New York University. His publications focus on Nordoff-Robbins music therapy, qualitative research methodology, music-centered music therapy, the use of groove music in music therapy, and critical examinations of the evolution of music therapy theory and research methods. He was the scientific committee chairman of the Ninth World Congress of Music Therapy and is a past-president of the American Association of Music Therapy. He has been an associate editor for the *Nordic Journal of Music Therapy* and currently is on the editorial board of the *Journal of Music Therapy*. He is also president of the Nordoff-Robbins Music Therapy Foundation (USA) and is a trustee for Nordoff-Robbins International.

Chelcy Bowles is Emerita Professor of music and continuing education in music at the University of Wisconsin–Madison, where she developed, directed, and taught in a year-round program for adult music learners and directed development opportunities for music professionals for more than 20 years. She has taught at all educational levels, and has had a concurrent career as a harpist. Although her research interests and publications have generally paralleled her diverse teaching career, the primary thread has been adult music teaching and learning. She co-founded NAfME's Adult and Community Music Education Special Research Interest Group, and served on the editorial boards of the *International Journal of Community Music*, *Update: Applications of Research in Music Education*, and *American String Teacher*. She holds a bachelor's degree in music education, a master's degree in music theory, and a doctorate of philosophy in music education. She currently serves as a consultant for developing adult music programming.

Mary L. Cohen, PhD, is an Associate Professor and Area Head of Music Education at the University of Iowa. She researches music-making and wellness with respect to prison contexts, writing and songwriting, and collaborative communities. Since 2009, she has led the Oakdale Prison Community Choir, comprised of male inmates and women and men from the community. She facilitates songwriting with choir members. As of August 2016, 107 original songs have been created. Some of these songs, along with the choir newsletters, are available at http://oakdalechoir.lib.uiowa.edu/. Her research is published in venues such as the *International Journal of Research in Choral Singing, Journal of Research in Music Education, Australian Journal of Music Education, Journal of Historical Research in Music Education, Journal of Correctional Education, International Journal of Community Music*, and *International Journal of Music Education*, and numerous book chapters. She is a commissioner for the Community Music Activity Commission of the International Society of Music Education and is Co-Chairing the 2018 CMA Meeting.

William M. Dabback holds an undergraduate degree in music education from West Chester University and received his master of music and doctor of philosophy degrees in music education from the University of Rochester's Eastman School of Music. He is an associate professor in the James Madison University School of Music, where he teaches undergraduate and graduate courses in music education and formed the Harrisonburg New Horizons Band in partnership with the university Lifelong Learning Institute. The primary threads of his scholarship comprise work in adult music learning, sociological issues of music participation, community music, and instrumental music pedagogy. He has presented papers and workshops at international symposia and conferences in the United States, Canada, and Europe, and is a member of the steering committee of the North American Coalition for Community Music.

Alice-Ann Darrow is Irvin Cooper Professor of Music Education and Music Therapy at Florida State University. Her teaching and research interests include teaching music to special populations, inclusive practices for students with disabilities, particularly those with behavior disorders and deaf/hard-of-hearing, and the role of nonverbal communication in the music classroom. Related to these topics, she has published numerous monographs, research articles, and book chapters. Darrow is editor of the text, *Introduction to Approaches in Music Therapy*, and coauthor of *Music in Special Education*, and *Music Therapy with Geriatric Populations: A Handbook for Practicing Music Therapists and Healthcare Professionals*. Darrow has served on the major journal editorial boards in music education and music therapy. She is past chair of the Commission on Music in Special Education for the International Society for Music Education, and presently serves on the NAfME task force for the inclusion of students with disabilities, and as Florida Music Education Association chair for diverse learners.

John Drummond, BA, B.Mus., PhD, is Blair Professor of Music at the University of Otago in New Zealand. He trained in the United Kingdom as a musicologist and composer specializing in opera. In the late 1980s, he became involved in music education, joining the ISME Commission on Community Music Activity, which he chaired 1990–1992. He joined the ISME Board in 1995 and was elected President from 2000 to 2002. From 2002 to 2004 he was on the Steering Group for the International Music Council's project on Musical Diversity, and has been a member of the Cultural Diversity in Music Education Network for many years. He is currently working on a project on the Future of Opera within the *Sustainable Futures for Musical Cultures* international research project.

Cochavit Elefant, PhD, is associate professor of music therapy at the Grieg Academy of the University of Bergen and a researcher at the Grieg Academy Music Therapy Research Centre, Bergen, Norway. She has worked for almost 30 years as a music therapist with children in educational and private settings in the United States and Israel. She is the cofounder of the Israeli National Rett Syndrome Assessment and Evaluation team. Her research interest is in music therapy inclusion and intergroup relations in the community in children with and without special needs. She has also researched communication through songs in population groups with neurological disorders such as children with Rett Syndrome and speech in adults with Parkinson's Disease. She has published several articles, book chapters, and a book *Where Music Helps* (with Stige, Ansdell, & Pavlicevic) in 2010. She serves as an associate editor for the Nordic Journal of Music Therapy.

David J. Elliott is professor of music and music education at New York University. From 1977 to 2002, he was professor of music education at the University of Toronto. He has held visiting professorships at Indiana University, the University of North Texas, Northwestern University, the University of Limerick, and the Puerto Rico Conservatory of Music. His research interests include the philosophy of music and music education, music and emotion, community music, jazz, music composition, and multicultural music education. He is the author of *Music Matters: A New Philosophy of Music Education* (Oxford University Press, 1995), coauthor of *Music Matters: A Philosophy of Music Education*, 2nd edition (Oxford University Press,

2015), editor of *Praxial Music Education: Reflections and Dialogues* (Oxford University Press, 2005/2009), coeditor of *Artistic Citizenship: Artistry, Social Responsibility, and Ethical Praxis* (Oxford University Press, 2016), coeditor of *Community Music Today* (Rowman & Littlefield, 2013), and founder and editor emeritus of the *International Journal of Community Music*. His publications are in English, Spanish, Swedish, Finnish, Greek, German, and Chinese, and he is an award-winning composer/arranger with many works published by Boosey & Hawkes.

Professor Lee Higgins is the Director of the International Centre of Community Music based at York St John University, United Kingdom. He has held previous positions at Boston University, United States, Liverpool Institute for Performing Arts, United Kingdom, and the University of Limerick, Ireland. Lee has been a visiting professor at Ludwig Maximilian University, Munich, Germany, and Westminster Choir College, Princeton, USA. He received his PhD from the Irish Academy of Music and Dance, Ireland, and is the President of International Society of Music Education (2016–2018). As a community musician, he has worked across the education sector as well as within health settings, the prison and probation service, youth and community, adult education, and arts organizations such as orchestras and dance. As a presenter and guest speaker, Lee has worked on four continents in university, school, and nongovernmental organization settings. He is the senior editor for the *International Journal of Community Music* and was author of *Community Music: In Theory and in Practice* (Oxford University Press, 2012), co-author of *Engagement in Community Music* (Routledge, 2017) and coeditor of *The Oxford Handbook of Community Music* (2017).

Valentina Iadeluca graduated in ancient (Greek and Latin) literature at the "La Sapienza" University of Rome in 1993. In 2000, she completed a master's in Cultural Management and Communication at the LUISS Management University of Rome. Since 1996, she has taught in many different nursery and primary schools of Rome. She is a music teacher at CDM–Centro Didattico Musicale of Rome, specializing in singing, girls' choir, creative movement, and singing for children aged 6 to 8, and children groups from 3 to 6 years old. Since 1996, she has taught in many different nursery and primary schools of Rome. All the activities are based on Orff-Schulwerk principles and integrate Edwin Gordon's Music Learning Theory. Iadeluca defines herself as an interpreter of modern music and a jazz singer and has studied singing with different teachers, performing several kinds and styles of music.

Judith A. Jellison is the Mary D. Bold Regents Professor in Music and Human Learning and University Distinguished Teaching Professor in the Sarah and Ernest Butler School of Music at the University of Texas, Austin. Her experiences working with diverse populations in schools and hospitals have shaped her philosophy and research, which focuses on the musical development of children with disabilities and inclusive educational practices. Oxford University Press publishes her book, *Including Everyone: Creating Music Classrooms Where All Children Learn*. She has served on editorial boards of major journals in music education and music therapy and is the recipient of the Senior Researcher Award from MENC: The National Association for Music Education, and the Publications Award from the American Music Therapy Association. She is a member of The University of Texas's Academy of Distinguished Teachers and is a recent recipient of the Outstanding Teaching Award from the University of Texas System Board of Regents.

Janet L. Jensen holds degrees in music education, string development, and flute performance from the University of Wisconsin–Madison, and a doctorate of philosophy in music education from the University of Texas at Austin. Her faculty responsibilities at UW–Madison included undergraduate and graduate coursework in string pedagogy, repertoire, and literature, conducting the All-University String Orchestras, and the master's degree program in String Development. As Associate Director, she oversaw undergraduate recruitment, scholarships and awards, and advising. Her research interests are in curriculum development, lifelong learning, and learning communities linking higher education with other populations, music and arts education policy, and the iconographic history of early bowed instruments. Her outreach activities focus on professional development for teachers, support of school and youth programs, arts and music education advocacy, and she is active as a conductor and clinician of school and amateur orchestras. She currently directs an outreach Progressions Program through the Milwaukee Youth Symphony Orchestra.

Patrick M. Jones received a bachelor of science in music education from West Chester University, a master of arts in conducting from George Mason University, a diploma of fine arts in conducting from the University of Calgary, and a doctor of philosophy in music education from the Pennsylvania State University. He is Assistant Vice President for Academic Partnerships at Drexel University. His scholarly interests include music education theory, history, and policy. He has served in various positions in professional societies and serves on the editorial boards of the *International Journal of Community Music* and *Visions of Research in Music Education*. In addition to his academic career, he is a retired Air Force Colonel who served in military bands for 30 years, concluding his career as Chief of Air National Guard Bands.

Jody L. Kerchner is Professor and Director of Music Education at the Oberlin Conservatory of Music, Ohio, where she is the secondary-school music and choral music education specialist. She is also founder and conductor of the Oberlin College Women's Chorale and the Oberlin Music at Grafton (OMAG) all-male prison choir. Her research interests include children's responses during music listening, choral music education, empathetic leadership, assessment, social justice and musical access, and reflective thinking. She has authored many publications, including her latest books, *Musicianship: Composing in Choir* (GIA, 2016) and *Music Across the Senses: Listening, Learning, & Making Music* (Oxford University Press, 2013).

Thomas W. Langston studied teaching at St. John's College, York (United Kingdom) and received an Associate, Licentiate, and Fellowship in vocal performance through the London College of Music, and a Licentiate in singing teaching through the Royal Academy of Music, London, before completing a bachelor of arts through the Open University (United Kingdom), a master of letters at the University of New England (Australia), and a doctorate of education at the University of Tasmania (Australia). Thomas is an Honorary research associate with the University of Queensland. His research interests are varied. His most important research examines the manifestation of social capital in community music. His earlier research interests were in musicology and in particular the vocal music of the Italian and English Renaissance. He has published in the area of narrative in music education. He is active in community music conducting a number of choirs.

Andreas C. Lehmann holds a master's degree in music education and a PhD in musicology from the Hochschule für Musik und Theater Hannover (Germany). He conducted postdoctoral research in psychology at the Florida State University, Tallahassee. He is currently professor of Systematic Musicology at the Hochschule für Musik Würzburg (Germany). He is associate editor of Musicae Scientiae, on the editorial board of JRME, and vice president of the German society for music psychology. He teaches in the area of music psychology and related topics. His research interests concern the structure and acquisition of high levels of instrumental music performance skill (sight-reading, practice, generative processes), they include historical studies on the development of expertise, and they cover a broad range of topics in music education (e.g., competency modelling, amateur music making, and participation).

Katrina McFerran is Professor and Head of Music Therapy at the University of Melbourne in Australia. She has investigated the role of music for well-being in the lives of young people since 2001, and has published more than 70 articles and 30 book chapters on this topic, along with two books titled *Adolescents, Music and Music Therapy* (2010), and *Creating Music Cultures in the Schools* (2014). Her research and writings focus on the ways that young people use music, emphasizing their agency, and the ways that choices may vary depending on young people's mental health, unconscious associations, and contextual factors. This has led to the development of a tool for understanding "Healthy-unhealthy Uses of Music" (HUMS) which supports adults to ask questions and solicit perspectives about adolescent's music use. Katrina continues to focus her work with young people in schools, with an emphasis on using music to prevent mental health problems.

Gary E. McPherson studied music education at the Sydney Conservatorium of Music, before completing a master of music education at Indiana University, a doctorate of philosophy at the University of Sydney, and a Licentiate and Fellowship in trumpet performance through Trinity College, London. He is the Ormond Professor and Director of the Melbourne Conservatorium of Music at the University of Melbourne, and has served as National President of the Australian Society for Music Education and President of the International Society for Music Education. His research interests are broad and his approach interdisciplinary. His most important research examines the acquisition and development of musical competence, and motivation to engage and participate in music from novice to expert levels. With a particular interest in the acquisition of visual, aural, and creative performance skills, he has attempted to understand more precisely how music students become sufficiently motivated and self-regulated to achieve at the highest level.

David Myers is professor at the University of Minnesota and consulting chair for music at Augsburg College in Minneapolis. A frequent presenter for NASM, he was an inaugural at-large board member for the College Music Society, where he chaired the task force on the undergraduate curriculum. The report is published by Routledge in *Redefining Music Studies in an Age of Change*. He was SOM director at Minnesota for 6 years. He writes and speaks widely on lifespan access and learning, arts collaborations, and curriculum innovation. He was American consultant for the European joint master's degree (NAIP), has been a panelist for the National Endowment for the Arts, and was national evaluator for the League of American Orchestras. Board memberships include MacPhail Center for Music, the American Composers Forum, the St. Paul Chamber Orchestra, and VocalEssence. He serves on several national and international journal editorial boards.

Adam Ockelford studied at the Royal Academy of Music in London, before embarking on a career that has embraced performing, composing, teaching, researching, writing, consultancy, and management. His PhD drew together thinking from music theory and music psychology, in investigating how music intuitively makes sense to us all. Today, his research interests are in music psychology, education, theory and aesthetics—particularly special educational needs and the development of exceptional abilities; learning, memory, and creativity; and the cognition of musical structure and the construction of musical meaning. He has over 100 publications to his name, including 20 books. He is Secretary of the Society for Education, Music and Psychology Research (SEMPRE), Chair of Soundabout, an Oxfordshire-based charity in the United Kingdom that supports music provision for children and young people with complex needs, and founder of The AMBER Trust, a charity that supports visually impaired children in their pursuit of music.

Helen Phelan is Professor of Arts Practice and the founder program director of the PhD in Arts Practice at the Irish World Academy of Music and Dance, University of Limerick, Ireland. Previous to this appointment, she served as course director of the MA Ritual Chant and Song program for 9 years. Her research interests are in the areas of performance studies, ritual studies, ritual song, singing and social inclusion, arts practice research, and music education philosophy. She is co-founder of the female schola, Cantoral, specializing in Irish medieval chant and polyphony. She is founder-director of Sanctuary, a Higher Education Authority initiative supporting the cultural expression of new migrant communities in Ireland and founder of the Anáil Dé/ Breath of God Festival of World Sacred Music. Her administrative roles have included appointments as Academic Coordinator, Irish World Academy (1995–1999), Assistance Dean Academic Affairs, College of Humanities

(2003–2005), Associate Director, Irish World Academy (2009–2013) and Acting Director (2012). In 2012, she was also appointed the Herbert Allen and Donald R. Keough Distinguished Visiting Professor at the University of Notre Dame. She currently runs the Irish Research Council funded research initiative "Singing and Sustainable Social Integration." Her book *Singing the Rite to Belong: Music, Ritual and the New Irish* was published by Oxford University Press in 2017.

Andrea Sangiorgio, PhD, is a music educator, music teacher educator, and educational researcher. He gained a PhD at the University of Exeter, United Kingdom (2016), with a qualitative research study on "Collaborative creativity in music education: Children's interactions in group creative music making." He received a master's degree in ethnomusicology (2006) and piano studies in Italy (1999). He graduated in Music and Movement Education at the Orff-Institute, University "Mozarteum," Salzburg, Austria (1997). Since December 2015, he has held the position of Professor for Elemental Music Education (Elementare Musikpädagogik) at the Hochschule für Musik und Theater in Munich, Germany. Since 1997, he has been the codirector of CDM–Centro Didattico Musicale, a music school in Rome inspired by the Orff approach. In collaboration with Rome University "Tor Vergata" he directs a 1-year Orff-Schulwerk teacher education course. He works as a national and international music teacher educator, mainly on the themes: elemental music and dance education, voice training for children, ensemble music for percussion instruments, group improvisation and musical creativity, and cognitive aspects of music learning.

Laya H. Silber studied music theory and conducting at the Rubin Academy of Music in Jerusalem, Israel, before completing a master of music at the New England Conservatory of Music and a doctorate of music education at Columbia University Teachers' College. She is the assistant chair, director of undergraduate studies, and choral director in the Department of Music of Bar-Ilan University in Ramat Gan, Israel. Her research interests include Yiddish art song, the music of George Gershwin and the American Yiddish theater, performance practice of choral music, and choral singing and well-being. A significant aspect of her research is in the area of choral singing in prisons, with special emphasis on multipart singing and its effects on social skills.

Marissa Silverman studied English literature at New York University before completing a master of fine arts in music at State University of New York (Purchase), a master of teaching at Pace University, and a doctorate of music performance at New York University. She is associate professor and coordinator of undergraduate music education at the John J. Cali School of Music, Montclair State University, New Jersey. A Fulbright scholar, her research interests include philosophy of music and music education, urban music education, interdisciplinary methods of education, and music education and identity. She has published in *Action, Criticism, and Theory for Music Education, International Journal of Music Education, Music Education Research, Research Studies in Music Education,* and *International Journal of Community Music.* She is coauthor of *Music Matters: A Philosophy of Music*

Education, 2nd edition (Oxford University Press, 2015) and coeditor of *Artistic Citizenship: Artistry, Social Responsibility, and Ethical Praxis* (Oxford University Press, 2016) and *Community Music Today* (Rowman & Littlefield, 2013).

Rineke Smilde graduated from the Groningen Conservatory with principal study flute. She holds a master's degree in musicology (contemporary music) from Amsterdam University and a PhD summa cum laude in education from the Georg August University in Goettingen, Germany. She is professor of Lifelong Learning in Music at the Prince Claus Conservatory in Groningen and at the University of Music & Performing Arts in Vienna. She co-leads the international research group "Lifelong Learning in Music" that examines questions about the relationship between musicians and society, and what engaging with new audiences means for the different roles, learning, and leadership of musicians. Rineke's particular research interests are the different learning styles of musicians and the role of biographical learning in the context of lifelong and lifewide learning. She has published widely on different aspects of lifelong learning in (higher) music education and lectures and gives presentations worldwide. She served as vice president of the European Association of Conservatories (AEC) and has led various international research projects for the AEC.

David S. Smith holds a bachelor of music education degree from Greenville College, a master of music education degree from Michigan State University, and a doctor of philosophy in music education and music therapy from Florida State University. Currently, he is professor of music education at Western Michigan University, where he teaches classes in music education methodology, psychology of music, and research at the undergraduate and graduate levels, and supervises short- and long-term practicum experiences in music education and music therapy. His areas of expertise and research interests include diverse learners in inclusive environments, and musical involvement across the age and ability spectrum, particularly adult and older adult individuals. He is a past president of the American Music Therapy Association, charter member of MENC's Adult and Community Music Special Research Interest Group, and founding member of the North American Coalition for Community Music.

Kari K. Veblen holds a bachelor's degree in music from Knox College with coursework from St. Olaf College; followed by masters and doctoral degrees from the University of Wisconsin–Madison. Thus far, her career spans four decades including stints as elementary music teacher, community musician, curriculum consultant to orchestras and schools, faculty member at UW–Stevens Point, visiting scholar (Center for Research in Music Education, University of Toronto, Canada), and research associate (Irish World Music Centre, University of Limerick, Ireland). Currently professor of music education at University of Western Ontario, Canada, she teaches undergraduate and graduate courses such as cultural and Canadian perspectives, music for children, and qualitative research methods. Current work includes 1) a 30-year fascination with the transmission of traditional Irish/Scots/

Celtic/diasporic music, 2) adult music learning in formal, informal, and nonformal contexts, and 3) community music networks and individuals worldwide. Author, coauthor and coeditor of books, peer-reviewed chapters, articles, and conference papers, her latest book project is the *Oxford Handbook of Social Media and Music Learning* (with Janice Waldron & Stephanie Horsley). Veblen has served in various professional capacities, including the International Society for Music Education board.

Dr. Janice Waldron is an Associate Professor of Music Education at the University of Windsor. Her research interests—informal music learning practices, online music communities, social media and music learning, vernacular music, and participatory cultures—are reflected in her book *Oxford Handbook of Social Media and Music Learning* (with Stephanie Horsely & Kari Veblen). Published in *Music Education Research, International Journal of Music Education, Action, Criticism, and Theory in Music Education, Journal of Music, Education, and Technology* and *Philosophy of Music Education Review*, Dr. Waldron also has authored several *Oxford Handbook* chapters in its Music Education series. She serves on the Editorial Boards of *Action, Theory, and Criticism in Music Education, International Journal of Music Education, Journal of Music, Education, and Technology, T.O.P.I.C.S*, and is the website editor of the Mayday Group. She was also named the 2012 "Outstanding Researcher: Emerging Scholar" at the University of Windsor.

Graham F. Welch holds the University College London (UCL) Institute of Education Established Chair of Music Education. He is elected Chair of the internationally based Society for Education, Music and Psychology Research (SEMPRE), a former President of the International Society for Music Education (ISME), and past co-chair of the Research Commission of ISME. Current Visiting Professorships include the Universities of Queensland (Australia), Guildhall School of Music and Drama, and Liverpool (United Kingdom). He is an ex-member of the UK Arts and Humanities Research Council's (AHRC) Review College for music and has been a specialist consultant for Government departments and agencies in the United Kingdom, Italy, Sweden, the United States, Ukraine, the UAE, South Africa, and Argentina. Publications number over 350 and embrace musical development and music education, teacher education, the psychology of music, singing, and voice science, and music in special education and disability. Publications are in English, Spanish, Portuguese, Italian, Swedish, Greek, Japanese, and Chinese.

Introduction to Volume 4

Special Needs, Community Music, and Adult Learning: An Oxford Handbook of Music Education

SINCE 2012, when the *Oxford Handbook of Music Education* (OHME) was first published, it has offered a comprehensive overview of many facets of musical experience in relation to behavior and development within educational or educative contexts, broadly conceived. These contexts may be formal (such as in schools, music studios), nonformal (such as in structured community settings), or informal (such as making music with friends and family), or somewhat incidental to another activity (such as travelling in a car, walking through a shopping mall, watching a television advert, or playing with a toy). Nevertheless, despite this contextual diversity, they are educational in the sense that our myriad sonic experiences accumulate from the earliest months of life to foster our facility for making sense of the sound worlds in which we live.

Special Needs, Community Music, and Adult Learning includes the first three parts of Volume 2 from the original OHME. Importantly, all chapters have been updated and refined to fit the context of this new specialist volume title.

While recognizing that development occurs through many forms, formally and informally, the three parts that comprise this volume focus on issues and topics that help to broaden conceptions of music and musical involvement. Part 1 (*Special Abilities, Special Needs*) opens with the important, but too often neglected, aspect of music education that involves that part of the population who have special abilities and special needs. As explained in Adam Ockelford's commentary for this part, there is an urgent need for quality research to address the serious shortcomings that currently impact on the area. Through research, according to Ockleford, we will be able to move beyond anecdotal accounts of success to more systematic approaches to music education that help us understand some of the pertinent issues that can

promote or hinder learners who share particular characteristics. Through understanding those whose development is not necessarily neurotypical, music educators
will also gain unique and powerful insights into what it means to be musical. And
by developing sound pedagogical approaches that are tailored to take account of all
learners, we will be more able to move from making individual adaptations toward
designing sensitive "universal" solutions.

This same theme underpins Part 2 (*Music in the Community*) where it is
recognized that music is a shared, community experience, and that community
music practice internationally is diverse and consistently evolving to meet the
changing needs of the people it serves. This continual reinvention is an example
of how musicians and music educators are continually reframing, adjusting, combining, integrating, and overlapping existing ways of engaging people to make
music. It is also the essence of how various forms of music making, musical sharing,
and musical caring creates "community."

As is evidenced in Part 3 (*Adult Learning in a Lifespan Context*), the process
of music education can be identified as being located somewhere on a lifelong
continuum that embraces the interweaving of the informal with the formal and
nonformal, dependent in part on the degree of external agency and organization inherent in any given educational experience. An implication of this line of thinking is
the need to encourage music educators to think in terms of a music learning society,
where adult education is not peripheral to the priority of other age groups, but is
seen as an integral piece within a larger vision for the good of society. Such thinking
will open many possibilities for ways in which music education for adults and youth
may be intersecting and complementary, including intergenerational programs,
programs that engage with distinctive dimensions of particular communities,
programs that honor music legacies and traditions, and adult music education as
an assumed piece of a lifelong music education paradigm. Implications that arise
involve the preparation of future music educators who should be encouraged to
believe in the opportunities available within adult music education, as they develop
attitudes and commitments that view adult music education as an integral dimension of all work within the field of music education.

We take this opportunity to thank the various representatives of Oxford
University Press. In particular, we are especially grateful to the OUP Commissioning
Editor, Suzanne Ryan, for her enthusiasm about updating all chapters and pub-
lishing the OHME in five new specialist volumes.

Very special thanks should be attributed to our three Part Editors, Adam
Ockelford (Part 1), David J. Elliott (Part 2), and David E. Myers and Chelcy
L. Bowles (Part 3) who enthusiastically took responsibility for their specialist area of
this volume. We are grateful for their hard work ensuring that each chapter within

their part fits the mission of this volume, which was to help update and redefine music education internationally.

Now that all of the authors can see their contributions in the context of this new volume, we hope that they will agree that our journey together continues to be worthwhile. We hope also, that our readers enjoy the fruits of our labor.

Gary E. McPherson and Graham F. Welch
Chief Editors
March, 2017

SPECIAL NEEDS, COMMUNITY MUSIC, AND ADULT LEARNING

PART 1

SPECIAL
ABILITIES,
SPECIAL NEEDS

Part Editor
ADAM OCKELFORD

CHAPTER 1

....

COMMENTARY:
SPECIAL ABILITIES,
SPECIAL NEEDS

....

ADAM OCKELFORD

Engaging with music variously involves a range of different skills, depending on the nature of the activity concerned—whether listening, composing, performing, improvising, or simply recalling a favorite snatch of melody in your head (Ockelford, 2017). Cognitive abilities, such as the capacity for auditory processing and memory, will inevitably be required; imagination will come into play in acts of creation or re-creation; physical skills will be needed to cause or control sounds; and social and emotional intelligence will be demanded to express oneself and communicate with others. Hence what may be termed "musicality" is not a single skill, but a *profile* of capacities, whose development and actualization will vary according to internal and external motivating forces and opportunities, as Andreas Lehmann and Gary McPherson show in chapter 3.

Although the disposition of musical profiles will inevitably vary between individuals, it appears that some degree of musicality is to all intents and purposes universal, even being present among those with the most profound disabilities (as the "Sounds of Intent" research undertaken by Graham Welch and me that is set out in chapter 2 suggests). Moreover, musical savants—those with advanced musical abilities in the context of intellectual impairments (see, for example, Miller, 1989; Ockelford, 2008b; Treffert, 2000, 2010)—graphically demonstrate the modularity of musical intelligence. For example, it is perfectly conceivable for children to engage in advanced improvised musical dialogues with others, even though their severely delayed global development means that they are unable to communicate verbally (Ockelford & Matawa, 2010; Ockelford, 2011a).

Hence the challenge for policy makers, managers and practitioners is not *whether* to provide appropriate music education for all children and young people, irrespective of their abilities or needs—but *how*, and Judith Jellison (chapter 5), and Alice-Ann Darrow and Mary Adamek (chapter 6) discuss this topic in some depth, and make a number of recommendations. It is clear that educators have a crucial role to play in dismantling the barriers—attitudinal and environmental—that still prevent individuals across the world from being able to engage in a fully inclusive fashion with the musics of their culture. In this regard, it is important to note that music *education* is distinct from music *therapy* (as Katrina McFerran and Cochavit Elefant make clear in chapter 4). All too often, if children or young people have disabilities or other special educational needs, there is an unquestioned assumption that a therapeutic approach will be the most appropriate way for them to access music (in school and beyond), whereas music education and therapy could (and, I believe, should) be complementary, each driven by distinct musical and extra-musical aims (Bruhn, 2000; Robertson, 2000; Ockelford, 2000, 2008a; Markou, 2010). In short, therapy should not be used as a substitute for education, and *vice versa*. The situation is complicated since music education for pupils and students with special needs has two distinct strands: education *in* music (which seeks to advance musical skills, knowledge and understanding) and education *through* music, whose aim is to promote wider learning and development, including cognitive, social and communication skills (Ockelford, 2000).

A key ingredient in moving music education forward for those with special abilities or needs, both in policy and practical terms, is high quality research, and this is where the global music education research community should acknowledge serious shortcomings, as a spur to devoting more resource to this area in the future. By definition, children who are "special" in one way or another will be in the minority, but I believe that, far from being on the periphery, their concerns should lie at the *heart* of music-education research, for three reasons.

First, a commitment to equality of opportunity means that there is an ethical imperative for research to be undertaken that seeks to improve provision for *all* children and young people. There is a real urgency to move beyond anecdotal accounts of success (fascinating and inspiring as these may be) to more systematic approaches that tackle some of the underlying issues that promote or hinder progress for groups of learners who share particular characteristics.

Second, by seeking to understand how people function in exceptional circumstances, we can shed light on how we all think, feel and behave. I have written elsewhere of children with severe or even profound disabilities offering us unique and powerful insights into what it means to be musical, if we can only slough away our prejudices and learn to listen with fresh ears (Lubbock, 2008; Ockelford, 2011b). And the individual profiles of musicality that evolve in what I term "extreme early cognitive environments" ('EECE's)—such as those incurred through congenital blindness or intense autism—can result in such peaks of music-perceptual and cognitive ability that we are able to view these characteristics with unusual clarity. Recognizing the consequences of EECEs can throw the nature/nurture debate into new relief (Ockelford, 2011c). For example, around 40% of children born with little or no sight (and around 5% of those with autism) go on to develop absolute pitch in the first two to three years of life, strongly suggesting an environmental effect operating within a general (though not universal) genetic predisposition (Ockelford, Pring, Welch& Treffert, 2006; Ockelford & Matawa, 2010).

Third, by researching and developing sound pedagogical practices for children with disabilities and other special needs, we will develop approaches that are likely to be good for *everyone*; as Jellison (chapter 5) notes, we need to move from making individual adaptations and move, as far as possible, toward designing "universal" solutions. While continued technological development is likely to play a large part in this process, ultimately, it is people's *attitudes* that count, and it is changing *attitudes* to disability in music education that the research community needs to spearhead.

How will we know when we have arrived? As the demographics of disability change across the world (due to advances in medicine, which tend to eradicate the more straightforward causes of sensory and motor impairment in countries as they develop economically and socially, while leaving a legacy of people surviving with far more complex needs), and as music education itself continues to evolve to reflect the explosion of new musics in fast-changing cultures, inevitably, music-education research in the field of special needs will remain in a state of flux for many years to come. But maybe there is a simpler answer. Maybe, when, in the future, our thinking has advanced to the stage where it is no longer felt to be necessary to have a book dealing with "special" profiles of musical ability and need (as the circumstances of all learners are included and addressed throughout), then we will at least know that the journey to music-educational equality is well under way.

REFERENCES

Bruhn, H. (2000) *Musiktherapie: Geschichte, Theorien, Grundlagen*, Göttingen: Hogrefe.

Markou, K. (2010) *The Relationship between Music Therapy and Music Education in Special School Settings: The Practitioners' Views*, unpublished PhD thesis, Roehampton University, London.

Miller, L. (1989) *Musical Savants; Exceptional Skill in the Mentally Retarded*, Hillsdale, New Jersey: Lawrence Erlbaum Associates.

Lubbock, J. (2008) Foreword in A. Ockelford, *Music for Children and Young People with Complex Needs*, Oxford: Oxford University Press, pp. vii and viii.

Ockelford, A. (2000) "Music in the education of children with severe or profound learning difficulties: Issues in current UK provision, a new conceptual framework, and proposals for research," *Psychology of Music* 28(2): 197–217.

Ockelford, A. (2008a) *Music for Children and Young People with Complex Needs*, Oxford: Oxford University Press.

Ockelford, A. (2008b) *In the Key of Genius: The Extraordinary Life of Derek Paravicini*, London: Arrow Books.

Ockelford, A. (2011a) "Songs without words: exploring how music can serve as a proxy language in social interaction with autistic children who have limited speech, and the potential impact on their wellbeing," in R. MacDonald, G. Kreutz and L. Mitchell, (eds.), *Music, Health and Wellbeing*, Oxford: Oxford University Press, pp. 289–323.

Ockelford, A. (2011b) *Music, Language and Autism*, London: Jessica Kingsley.

Ockelford, A. (2011c) "Through the glass, vividly: the extraordinary musical journeys of some children with autism," in I. Papageorgi and G. Welch, *Advanced Musical Performance: Investigations in Higher Education Learning*, (in the "SEMPRE" series of *Studies in the Psychology of Music*'), Aldershot: Ashgate, pp. 143–168.

Ockelford, A. (2017) *Comparing Notes: How We Make Sense of Music*, London: Profile Books.

Ockelford, A. and Matawa, C. (2010) *Focus on Music 2: Exploring the Musical Interests and Abilities of Blind and Partially-Sighted Children with Retinopathy of Prematurity*, London: Institute of Education.

Ockelford, A. Pring, L., Welch, G., & Treffert, D. (2006) *Focus on Music: Exploring the Musical Interests and Abilities of Blind and Partially-Sighted Children with Septo-Optic Dysplasia*, London: Institute of Education.

Robertson, J. (2000). "An educational model for music therapy: the case for a continuum," *British Journal of Music Therapy*, 14(1), 41–46.

Treffert, D. (2000) *Extraordinary People: Understanding Savant Syndrome*. Lincoln, Nebraska: iUniverse.com. [Originally published 1989 in New York by Harper and Row.]

Treffert, D. (2010) *Islands of Genius: The Bountiful Mind of the Autistic, Acquired, and Sudden Savant*, London: Jessica Kingsley.

CHAPTER 2

MAPPING MUSICAL DEVELOPMENT IN LEARNERS WITH THE MOST COMPLEX NEEDS: THE SOUNDS OF INTENT PROJECT

ADAM OCKELFORD AND
GRAHAM F. WELCH

Children with disabilities are generally under-represented in the music education and music psychology research literatures (Jellison, 2000), notwithstanding the many studies in the field of music therapy (the latter being defined as "the functional use of music to reach non-musical objectives"; Jellison, 2000, p. 236). Where comparative research data exist between able-bodied children and those with disabilities (reported, for example, by Darrow, 1984; Cassidy, 1992; Flowers & Wang, 2002; Stordahl, 2002; Swedberg, 2007), the evidence suggests that the latter demonstrate just as wide a range of musical abilities. Moreover, studies with disabled adults have reported the benefits of sustained musical activity in the improvement of specific musical skills (MacDonald, Davies, & O'Donnell, 1999; O'Donnell, MacDonald, & Davies, 1999).

Nevertheless, it was only at the beginning of the twenty-first century that the first systematic attempts were made to map the musical development of learners with the most complex needs—those with severe learning difficulties (SLD) or profound and multiple learning difficulties (PMLD) who, in global terms, were functioning cognitively, emotionally and socially as though in the first 30 months of "typical" development—and who make up around 0.5% of the school-age population in, for example, the United Kingdom. Indeed, until relatively recently, it was not even known whether such individuals underwent a "natural" process of musical maturation through the usual channels of cultural exposure and (in the case of some individuals) engagement, or whether educational interventions were effective in furthering the acquisition of musical skills (as opposed to the acknowledged therapeutic interventions that used music to promote wider learning, development and well-being).

A position paper by Ockelford (2000) set out the need for research in this area, and a number of initiatives followed, including a survey of the music offered in special schools for pupils with learning difficulties in England (Welch, Ockelford, & Zimmermann, 2001; Ockelford, Welch, & Zimmermann, 2002); a doctoral study by Kyproulla Markou at Roehampton University that examines the relationship between music education and music therapy for children with SLD or PMLD (see Ockelford, 2008, pp. 37–45); and the establishment of the *Sounds of Intent* project, whose aim was to map the musical development of young people with the most complex needs (see, for example, Ockelford, Welch, Zimmermann, & Himonides, 2005; Welch, Ockelford, Carter, Zimmermann, & Himonides, 2009; Cheng, Ockelford, & Welch, 2010; Ockelford & Matawa, 2010; Ockelford, Welch, Jewell-Gore, Cheng, Vogiatzoglou, & Himonides, 2010; Ockelford, 2015). To date, the *Sounds of Intent* project remains unique in its purview; hence it is on this research that we will focus our attention.

The *Sounds of Intent* research team, led by Welch at the Institute of Education, London, and Ockelford at Roehampton University, worked from 2002 with a group of practitioners who were active in the field—music therapists, teachers and others—with the intention of developing accurate descriptions and shared interpretations of the different forms and levels of musical engagement that they observed among children and young people with complex needs. Members of the group held a series of meetings over a two-year period to undertake detailed analysis of video recordings of musical behaviors that were deemed to be "typical," "exceptional" or of particular interest. The children's responses, actions and interactions were encapsulated in short descriptions such as those shown in Table 2.1.

Given these and many similar examples, it became evident that the musical development of these children could not be conceptualized unidimensionally since, for instance, an individual's capacity for attending to sounds may well be more advanced than his or her ability to produce them. Therefore, at least two dimensions were needed: "listening and responding," for which the single term "reactive" ("R") was used, and "causing, creating and controlling," for which the label "proactive" ("P") was adopted. In relation to the examples shown in Table 2.1, descriptions 1, 2,

Table 2.1 Descriptions of musical engagement by children and young people with complex needs.

No.	Observation	R	P	I
1	*A* sits motionless in her chair. Her teacher approaches and plays a cymbal with a soft beater, gently at first, and then more loudly, in front of her and then near to each ear. *A* does not appear to react.	•		
2	*R* is lying in the "Little Room" (a small, resonant environment, with sound-makers suspended within easy reach), vocalizing in an almost constant drone. Occasionally a sudden movement of her right arm knocks her hand against a bell. Each time, she smiles and her vocalizing briefly turns into a laugh.	•	•	
3	*M*'s music therapy session begins—as ever—with the "Hello" song. And as ever, he makes no discernible response.			•
4	*B* startles, then smiles, when a tray of cutlery is dropped in the dining room.	•		
5	*T* brushes her left hand against the strings of guitar. There is a pause and then she raises her hand and brushes the strings again, and then again.		•	
6	*Y* usually makes a rasping sound as he breathes. He seems to be unaware of what he is doing, and the rasping persists, irrespective of external stimulation. His class teacher has tried to see whether *Y* can be made aware of his sounds by making them louder (using a microphone, amplifier and speakers), but so far this approach has met with no response.		•	
7	*G*'s teacher notices that he often turns his head towards her when she sings to him, but she has never noticed him turn towards other sounds.	•		
8	*W* giggles when people repeat patterns of syllables to her such as "ma ma ma ma ma," "da da da da da," or "ba ba ba ba ba."	•		
9	*J*'s short, sharp vocalizations are interpreted by his teachers and carers to mean that he wants someone to vocalize back.			•
10	*K* gets very excited by the regular beat on the school's drum machine.	•		
11	*U* loves "call and response" games and joins in by making his own sounds.			•
12	*C* copies simple patterns of vocalization—imitating the ups and downs of her speech and language therapist's voice.			•

(continued)

Table 2.1 Continued

No.	Observation	R	P	I
13	S waves her hand more and more vigorously through an ultrasonic beam, creating an ever wider range of swirling sounds.		•	
14	N often vocalizes in response to vocal sounds that are made close to him, although he does not seem to copy what he hears.			•
15	Z loves the sound of the bell tree and, when it stops, she rocks in her chair, which staff interpret as a gesture for "more."	•		
16	D has been able to make a wide range of vocal sounds since he started school, but recently he has begun to make more melodious vowel sounds, which he repeats in short sequences.		•	
17	L hums distinct patterns of notes and repeats them. Her favourite pattern sounds rather like a playground chant, and her music teacher notices that she repeats it from one day to the next, though not always using the same notes.		•	
18	F cries when she hears the "goodbye" song. It only takes the first few notes to be played on the keyboard for her to experience a strong emotional reaction.	•		
19	H enjoys copying simple rhythms on an untuned percussion instrument. Now he is started making his own rhythms up too, and he flaps his hands with delight when someone else copies what he is doing.			•
20	E just laughs and laughs when people imitate her vocalizations.			•
21	V vocalizes to get his therapist to make a sound—it does not matter what, he just seems to relish having a vocal response.			•
22	I always gets excited in the middle of the "Slowly/Quickly" song, anticipating the sudden change of pace.	•		
23	O scratches the tambourine, making a range of sounds. Whenever he plays near the rim and the bells jingle, he smiles.	•	•	
24	Q's eye movements intensify when he hears the big band play.	•		
25	X tries to copy high notes and low notes in vocal interaction sessions.			•
26	P has learnt to associate his teacher's jangly bracelet, which she always wears, with her: for him, it seems to be an important part of her identity.	•		

4, 7, 8, 10, 15, 18, 22, 23, 24 and 26 could reasonably be categorized as being predominantly or entirely "reactive," and 2, 5, 6, 13, 16, 17 and 23, "proactive." However, a further group of observations remained (as in examples 3, 9, 11, 12, 14, 19, 20, 21 and 25) in which listening to sounds and making them occurred in the context of engagement with others, and it was decided that this type of activity merited the status of a separate dimension, which was termed "interactive" ("I"). (See table 2.1.) While these dimensions are not conceptually discrete, the significant issue is that they were deemed by practitioners to be *meaningful* and *useful* in terms of categorizing the types of musical engagement that they observed and encouraged.

Having determined the three dimensions that were to be used in the model, the next stage was to attempt to place examples of musical engagement such as those cited in Table 2.1 along them, deriving their relative positions using the notion of contingency—by seeking to identify each behavior as a necessary precursor or possible successor to another or others. For instance, it was evident that an awareness of sound (described in example 2) will invariably come before a differentiated response (as in example 7), which in turn must precede the capacity to anticipate change (example 22). The adoption of a heuristic approach such as this was inevitable, since the available evidence comprised snapshots of different children at various stages of development, rather than longitudinal data on the same individuals as they matured, which would have offered greater certainty as to the nature of developmental change. Treading an exploratory path, though, was deemed to be a valid first step for two reasons: first, as it was not yet known what data would be appropriate to collect; and second, since it was believed that productive longitudinal studies of children with PMLD in particular would be likely to last for several years. However, the research team felt that once a preliminary model was in place, this could subsequently be used to inform longer-term empirical work, as well as being informed by it.

As more data were acquired and analyzed, potential sequences of music-developmental stages emerged. As a way of benchmarking what was being proposed, attempts were made to map the interim findings onto what is known of "typical" early musical development, drawing on the well-established literature in the field, ranging, for example, from Moog, (1968/1976) to Dowling (1982), Hargreaves (1986) and Trehub (1990, 2003); and from Lecanuet (1996) and Papoušek (1996) to Trevarthen (2002) and Welch (2006). Although the emerging data from children with complex needs did not contradict the "mainstream" findings, it was found that there was limited overlap, particularly in relation to pupils with PMLD, whose levels of musical engagement often seemed to correspond to abilities that would typically occur prenatally or, at the latest, in the first few months of life. A further influence was Ockelford's "zygonic" theory of musical-structural understanding (e.g., 2002, 2005, 2009), which seeks to explain how music makes intuitive sense through the (typically nonconscious) recognition of repetition and regularity in the domains of pitch and perceived time. The thinking was that, since such a capacity does not arise in people fully-formed, it must evolve as a strand in musical development, implying that the theory may provide a useful way of conceptualizing stages within the process of musical maturation.

Several attempts were made to draw the three sources of evidence—observations, the findings of "mainstream" child psychology and zygonic theory—into a single coherent music-developmental framework for young people with the most complex needs. Different configurations were proposed and systematically trialed in the field, with practitioners offering qualitative feedback, supplemented with quantitative data gathered by a research assistant. This information enabled the research team iteratively to refine the model, enabling it to capture a wider range of musical behaviors, and enhancing intra- and inter-domain consistency (Welch, Ockelford, Carter, Zimmermann, & Himonides, 2009). Eventually, six fundamental levels of music processing capacity emerged, which seemed to offer both an intuitively satisfying and theoretically coherent scheme. These are set out in Table 2.2.

Extending these six levels across the three identified domains of musical engagement gave rise to the headlines or "level descriptors" of reactivity, proactivity and interactivity shown in Figure 2.1. Visually, these were arranged as 18 segments in six concentric circles, which practitioners on the *Sounds of Intent* research team regarded as being the most appropriate metaphor for children's development, ranging from the center, with its focus on self, outward, to increasingly wider communities of other people.

Table 2.2 The six levels underpinning the *Sounds of Intent* framework (acronym 'CIRCLE').

Level	Description	Acronym	Core cognitive abilities
1	Confusion and Chaos	C	None: no awareness of sound as a distinct perceptual entity
2	Awareness and Intentionality	I	An emerging awareness of sound as a distinct perceptual entity and of the variety that is possible within the domain of sound
3	Relationships, Repetition, Regularity	R	A growing awareness of the possibility and significance of relationships between the basic aspects of sounds
4	Notes Forming Clusters	C	An evolving perception of groups of sounds, and the relationships that may exist between them
5	Deeper Structural Links	L	A growing recognition of whole pieces, and of the frameworks of pitch and perceived time that lie behind them
6	Mature Musical Expression	E	A developing awareness of the culturally determined "emotional syntax" of performance that articulates the "narrative metaphor" of pieces

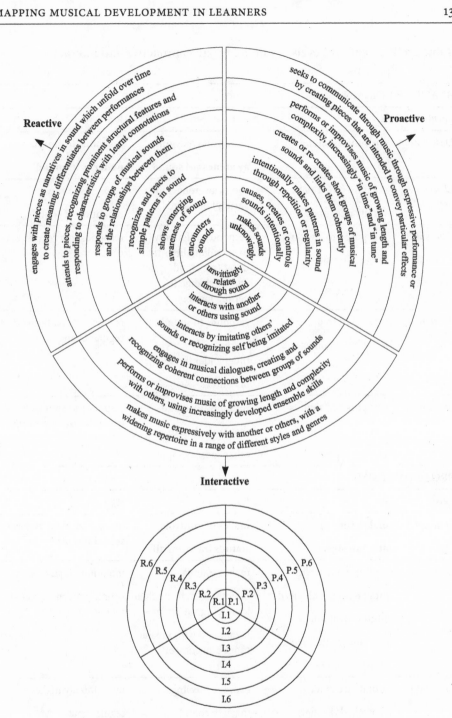

Figure 2.1 Representation of the *Sounds of Intent* framework.

For ease of reference, levels were ranked from 1–6, each of which could be preceded with an "R," a "P" or an "I," to indicate, respectively, reactive, proactive or interactive segments. Each was broken down into four more detailed elements, as the examples in Table 2.3 show.

Table 2.3 Elements at Levels 1–3 in the reactive, proactive and interactive domains.

REACTIVE DOMAIN

Level	R.1	R.2	R.3
Descriptor	**encounters sounds**	**shows an emerging awareness of sound**	**responds to simple patterns in sound**
Element A	is exposed to a rich variety of sounds	shows awareness (of a variety) of sounds	responds to the repetition of sounds
Element B	is exposed to a wide range of music	responds differently to sound qualities that differ (e.g., loud/ quiet), and/or change (e.g., getting louder)	responds to a regular beat
Element C	is exposed to music in different contexts	responds to sounds increasingly independently of context	responds to patterns of regular change
Element D	is exposed to sounds that are linked to other sensory input	responds to sounds that are linked to other sensory input	responds to sounds used to symbolize other things

PROACTIVE DOMAIN

Level	P.1	P.2	P.3
Descriptor	**makes sounds unknowingly**	**makes or controls sounds intentionally**	**makes simple patterns in sound intentionally**
Element A	sounds made by life processes are enhanced and/or involuntary movements are used to make sounds	makes sounds intentionally, through an increasing variety of means and with greater range and control	intentionally makes simple patterns through repetition
Element B	sounds are made or controlled through co-active movements	expresses feelings through sound	intentionally makes a regular beat
Element C	activities to promote sound production occur in a range of contexts	produces sounds intentionally in a range of contexts	intentionally makes patterns through change

Table 2.3 Continued

REACTIVE DOMAIN			
Element D	activities to promote sound production are multisensory in nature	produces sounds as part of multisensory activity	uses sound to symbolize other things

INTERACTIVE DOMAIN			
Level	I.1	I.2	I.3
Descriptor	**relates unwittingly through sound**	**interacts with others using sound**	**interacts imitating others' sounds or through recognizing self being imitated**
Element A	co-workers stimulate interaction by prompting with sounds and responding to any sounds that are made	sounds made by another stimulate a response in sound	imitates the sounds made by another
Element B	co-workers model interaction through sound	sounds are made to stimulate a response in sound	shows awareness of own sounds being imitated
Element C	activity to promote interaction through sound occurs in a range of contexts	interactions occur increasingly independently of context	imitates simple patterns in sound made by another
Element D	some interaction is multisensory in nature	interaction through sound engages other senses too	recognizes own patterns in sound being imitated

The way in which the level descriptors and elements relate to each other within and between the reactive, proactive and interactive domains is complex. Level descriptors form a hierarchy such that, within each domain, achievement at higher levels is dependent on the accomplishment of all those that precede. So, for example, in the interactive domain, I.4, "Engages in musical dialogues, creating and recognizing coherent connections between groups of sounds," could only occur following I.3, "Interacts by imitating other's sounds or recognizing self being imitated" and (therefore) after accomplishing I.2 and I.1. Between domains, there is a broad flow of contingency that runs from reactive to proactive and then to interactive. For instance, in the proactive domain, intentionally making patterns in sound through repetition (P.3) depends on the capacity to recognize simple patterns in sound (R.3); while interacting with another or others using sound (I.2) relies on the ability to cause, create or control sounds intentionally (P.2), which in turn requires an awareness of sound (R.2).

The relationships between the contingencies that link the 72 elements are more convoluted. Although there is sometimes a necessary connection between elements at different levels *within* domains (for example, a child could not engage in intentional repetition, P.3.A, before having the wherewithal to make a variety of sounds, P.2.B) and *between* them (for instance, imitating the sounds made by another, I.3.A, similarly requires functioning at the level of P.2.B), this is not always the case. It is quite conceivable that a child could intentionally make simple patterns through a regular beat, P.3.B, for instance, before using sounds to symbolize particular people, places or activities, P.2.D. However, the research team felt that complexities of this type were an inevitable consequence of the intricate nature of musical development: multilayered and multistranded. At any given time, it was unlikely that the framework would show a pupil as being at a particular *point* on a developmental scale, but, rather, having a music-developmental *profile*, incorporating attainment at different levels in relation to a number of different elements.

Given these complexities, though, how could the framework operate as a practical tool for assessment, enabling practitioners to record pupils' levels of achievement and change, to draw comparisons between the attainment and progress of individuals and groups, and to gauge the potential impact of different music-educational and therapeutic interventions? The first steps in this direction had previously been taken by Fern-Chantele Carter, research officer on Phase 1 of the *Sounds of Intent* project, who showed (using an earlier version of the framework, with only five levels, pertaining solely to pupils with PMLD) that the model could potentially be used to enable developmental trends to be identified (Welch, Ockelford, Carter, Zimmermann and Himonides, 2009). Carter assessed 68 pupils over a period of two terms, making a total of 630 judgments as to where she believed pupils were functioning on the framework in a given session. These levels were mapped onto participants' ages, and although the correlation between the two was weak, ($r = .289$, $p = .018$), older participants did tend to be more highly rated (see fig. 2.2). Despite a very wide range of individual variation, with some young participants functioning at a higher level than their older peers, Carter's work held out the prospect of being able to gauge the musical progress in pupils with the most complex needs using a framework of the type developed by the *Sounds of Intent* team. However, it was evident that refinements to the protocols for gathering and ranking the data were required to enable longitudinal studies of individual children to be made, since, even in a 12-month period, it seemed likely that they would make only tiny increments of progress.

This next step in the *Sounds of Intent* research was taken by Evangeline Cheng, a doctoral student at the Institute of Education, who subsequently joined the research team. She observed six young people with PMLD engaging in weekly music sessions over a period of six months, and continuously assessed them in relation

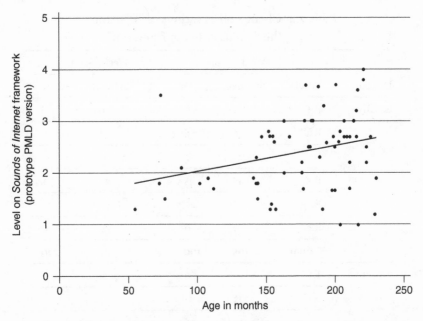

Figure 2.2 The relationship between age and level of musical attainment in pupils with PMLD, gauged using an early version of the *Sounds of Intent* framework.

to the elements set out in Table 2.3 (rather than the level descriptors that Carter had used). This approach allowed her to identify and rate a wider range of musical behaviors than had previously been possible. She also recorded the frequency with which given levels of engagement were seen in each session. Here is an example of an 11-year-old boy, "J."

J had severe learning difficulties, cerebral palsy, visual impairment, a speech, language and communication difficulty, and epilepsy. He was able to say a few single words and the names of some members of staff. He would nod for "yes" and sometimes used a specially designed switch to play prerecorded messages conveyed between home and school. J used a wheelchair, and needed help with life skills including eating, dressing and personal care.

Cheng observed J for a period of 21 weeks, which she divided for the purposes of analysis into two phases. Phase 1 ran from Week 1 to Week 14, and entailed sessions with the school's music teacher, involving songs and musical games to promote socialization and language acquisition, and rhythmic activities with non-tuned percussion instruments. In Phase 2, from Week 15 to Week 21, J's class participated in a music community link project called "Music Makers Sing!," which was staffed by two members of a professional London orchestra and a music technician. During this time, each child had the opportunity to interact more intensively with adults on a one-to-one basis, and switches were introduced to facilitate proactive participation.

Cheng observed a total of 513 instances of musical engagement on J's part: 184 "reactive" (an average 9 occurrences per session), 181 "proactive" (average 9), and 148 "interactive" (average 7). These are summarized, phase by phase, in Table 2.4.

Table 2.4 Cheng's observations of "J," using
the *Sounds of Intent* framework

Domain	Level	Weeks 1–14		Weeks 15–21	
		Frequency	%	Frequency	%
Reactive	R.1	0	0	0	0
	R.2	6	6	0	0
	R.3	23	22	10	12
	R.4	48	45.5	24	30.5
	R.5	28	26.5	45	57
	R.6	0	0	0	0
	Total	105	100	79	100
Proactive	P.1	0	0	0	0
	P.2	12	11	1	1
	P.3	40	36	9	11
	P.4	35	31	20	25
	P.5	25	22	39	48
	P.6	0	0	0	0
	Total	112	100	69	100
Interactive	I.1	0	0	0	0
	I.2	18	22	9	13.5
	I.3	8	10	1	1.5
	I.4	44	53.5	42	63.5
	I.5	12	14.5	14	21.5
	I.6	0	0	0	0
	Total	82	100	66	100

Combining the reactive, proactive and interactive scores for the levels at which J functioned (2, 3, 4 and 5) shows a distinct shift in his global *Sounds of Intent* profile between Phases 1 and 2 of the observation period. This was the first time that the framework had been used to show change in a pupil's musical engagement over time (see fig. 2.3).

In the process of Cheng's analysis, though, it became evident that each element embraced a potential range of behaviors. For example, P.2.B, "creates an increasing diversity of sounds intentionally through an increasing variety of means" could refer to equally a child vocalizing within a limited pitch range and tapping a drum

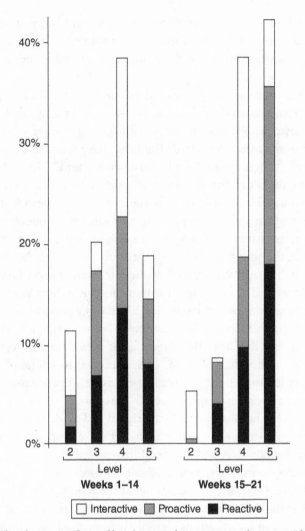

Figure 2.3 The change in J's profile of musical engagement between Phases 1 and 2.

with one finger, and a young person making a wide range of vocal sounds and playing a number of non-tuned percussion instruments. Similarly, I.3.A, "imitates the sounds made by another" could denote a pupil echoing a single vocalization made by his music teacher, or a client copying a variety of vocal and instrumental sounds produced by her music therapist. Hence it became apparent to the research team that the elements themselves should be broken down into different degrees of engagement to enable more subtle intrapersonal changes to be recorded, something that was particularly important for practitioners working in the domain of PMLD. To test this principle out, further empirical work was undertaken.

A cohort of 20 young people with PMLD was identified at a special school in south London. The pupils were grouped into three classes largely according to age (11 years 11 months, to 14 years 3 months; 15 years 1 month, to 17 years 3 months; and 17 years, to 17 years 7 months; M = 15 years, 3 months; SD = 2.03). They came from a wide range of ethnic and cultural backgrounds from across the southeast of England. All had profound levels of global developmental delay; none was verbal and the great majority were wheelchair users; many had some degree of visual impairment.

The materials used for this phase of the *Sounds of Intent* research were taken exclusively from *All Join In!* (Ockelford, 1996)—a set of 24 songs that were designed to offer a framework for making music with young people who had learning difficulties and were visually impaired. The songs have four topics: "self and other," "time and place," "things around" and "music and sound." Throughout, everyday language is used that consciously avoids abstract concepts or metaphor (characteristic of so many children's songs). Important words and phrases are consistently set to the same rhythm and, where possible, melodic shape, opening up the possibility of some musical fragments acquiring symbolic meaning in their own right. In musical terms, the songs conform to what could reasonably be described as the Western popular "musical vernacular" of the late twentieth century, with regular metrical structures and diatonic tonal frameworks. Rhythms are uncomplicated, and melodies are constrained in pitch range. There is a good deal of repetition. In summary, the songs are intended to be as easy to learn and engage with as possible.

Ockelford arranged to take the three classes' weekly music lessons for a six-month period in the first half of 2009. This amounted to a total of 24 sessions of 45 minutes (equating to 18 hours of musical exposure). Every session followed the same format. Each took place in the pupils' classrooms (the environments with which they were most familiar). Every participant had a one-to-one teaching assistant. Staff and pupils sat in a circle that included Ockelford, who had access to an electronic music keyboard. A wide range of instruments and sound-makers, high-technology and low-technology, were available for use.

Lamorna Jewell-Gore, the music teacher at the school, who knew the children very well, participated in all the sessions, largely through supporting the staff. Once a month, however, (on six occasions) Jewell-Gore stepped back from proceedings and purposively observed each of the children and young people in action, noting examples of musical reactivity, proactivity or interactivity for each that appeared to be typical of their engagement in the session concerned. Written comments were supplemented with some video recordings for later reference. Subsequently, Jewell-Gore mapped the behaviors that she had observed and recorded onto the *Sounds of Intent* framework, gauging which element offered the best fit for each description, and grading them as "low" (that is, just achieving the level of engagement that was described), "high" (fulfilling the terms of the descriptor comprehensively), or "medium" (for levels of attainment between the two extremes). (For example, see table 2.5.)

Each subdivided element was assigned a rank on an ordinal scale, according to its position within the *Sounds of Intent* framework, whereby activity at Level 1 (low) was categorized as "1," Level 1 (medium) was classed as "2," Level 1 (high) was allocated "3," and so forth. The results are as follows (see fig. 2.4). Over the course of the sessions, there is movement away from observed musical engagement at Level

Table 2.5 Examples of Jewell-Gore's observations, and their assignment
          to *Sounds of Intent* sub-levels.

Observation	Assessed as
J shows slight reaction to loud noises but no reaction to localized instruments playing. Did not ... change reaction to change in tempo/dynamics.	R.1.A (low)
G laughed each time the tambourine was hit, and responded to sudden chord changes.	R.2.A (medium)
A vocalized throughout songs and changed notes with key change.	I.3.A (low)
B laughed at a particular motif played on the piano.	R.3.A (low)
D listened to sounds made by the other children, sometimes just looking, sometimes smiling, sometimes laughing.	R.2.B (high)
Q laughed a lot when his own made-up musical sounds were imitated (the "wah-wah" song).	I.3.B (high)

1 and an attendant increase in classifications at Level 3—a high degree of variability in the data notwithstanding.

The underlying trend in this changing pattern of observations can be gauged by comparing means of the reported ranks, session by session. This offers a proxy indication of the children's changing perceived level of musical engagement (see fig. 2.5).

This implies a rate of musical development, equivalent to one *Sounds of Intent* level in 18 months, which experience of working with children with PMLD suggests would not be sustainable. Hence it is reasonable to assume that there were exceptional factors at work in the study, which potentially include the young people's growing familiarity with the materials; Ockelford's deepening knowledge of the young people, which may have enabled him to scaffold the young people's interactions more effectively as the sessions progressed; and Jewell-Gore's practice in using the *Sounds of Intent* framework, which may have meant her observations became more pertinent and perceptive over the six months. One way of validating the results is to review the data from the perspectives of individual students, taking the six-month intervention as a relatively narrow window on a broader period of potential longitudinal change. Mapping mean ranks onto chronological ages suggests that, in general terms, progress may often occur at a much slower rate than Jewell-Gore's observations suggest (see fig. 2.6).

This analysis shows a rise of just over one rank in six years, which equates to around 10% of the increase shown longitudinally. This suggests that any or all of the context-specific factors listed above may account for the majority of the rise in the levels of musical engagement that were observed, or it could be that the intervention was particularly effective at engendering musical development, or both influences

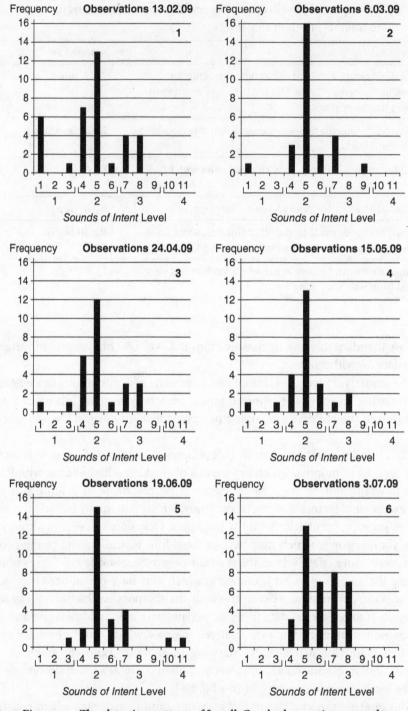

Figure 2.4 The changing pattern of Jewell-Gore's observations over the 6 months of the intervention.

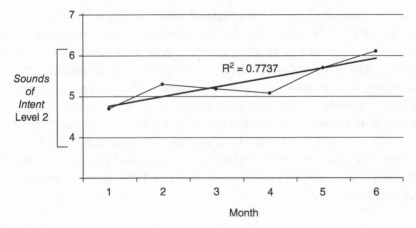

Figure 2.5 The change in the means of ranked observations per session offers a proxy indication of the children's presumed advancing levels of musical engagement.

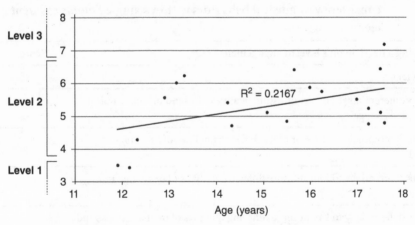

Figure 2.6 Observed level of musical engagement mapped onto age.

may have played a part. Many more data would be required to isolate and quantify the different ingredients in the mix, and to ascertain how they interrelate; the important thing is that this would be possible using the *Sounds of Intent* approach. A further comparison can be drawn, if we compare Jewell-Gore's findings with those obtained by Carter (see fig. 2.2), with the proviso that here an earlier version of the *Sounds of Intent* framework was used, in which Levels 2 and 3 correspond in approximate terms to Level 2 in the later version (Ockelford, 2008, p. 92). Therefore, any comparison should be treated with considerable caution. Nonetheless, Carter's data suggest a rise of around one rank over 10 years, rather lower than Jewell-Gore's findings indicate.

The key thing, though, is that both studies point, in general terms, in the same direction: for pupils with PMLD, music-developmental progress is possible, but will be made in tiny increments, leading to change over a child's school life that, in the absence of sustained, specialist intervention, is likely to be equivalent to between a half and one level on the *Sounds of Intent* framework. Change in musical behavior of this small order of magnitude suggests that, to be sufficiently sensitive for practitioners to chart progress meaningfully over time, observational schedules associated with the *Sounds of Intent* framework will need to be even more fine-grained than the system used by Jewell-Gore. Moreover, the work of Cheng suggests that, whatever protocol is devised, this should take into account not only children's levels of engagement, but consider also the relative frequency with which particular behaviors occur. This suggests a protocol along the following lines may be appropriate, in which both these parameters figure equally (see table 2.6).

Table 2.6   Example of proposed protocol that takes into account the level and consistency of musical behaviors within a single *Sounds of Intent* element.

Gauging a participant's level of engagement	Score
No evidence	0
Reacts differentially to two contrasting qualities of sound or more, and/or to marked change	1
Reacts differentially to three or more differing qualities of or change in sound	2
Reacts differentially to four or more differing qualities of or change in sound	3
Reacts differentially to five or more differing qualities of or change in sound	4
Reacts differentially to six or more differing qualities of or change in sound	5
Gauging consistency	**Score**
Responses are never observed	0
Responses are observed rarely (on around one in eight occasions or fewer)	1
Responses are observed occasionally (on around one in four occasions)	2
Responses are observed regularly (on around one in two occasions)	3
Responses are observed frequently (on around three in four occasions)	4
Responses are observed consistently (on around seven in eight occasions or more)	5

Consolidating the two

Multiply the "level of engagement" score by the "consistency" score. Change can be gauged by comparing scores over a period. The minimum score is 0 (where there is no available evidence or a behavior is never observed) and the maximum score is 25.

Clearly, the issue with such a detailed scheme is its usability from a practitioner's point of view. However, discussions with teachers and therapists on the *Sounds of Intent* research team indicated that such a system would be manageable if it were to be accessed through an appropriate software package that used a touch-screen interface, and trials are currently underway with an interactive web-based version of the framework that can be accessed on a range of mobile devices. This is designed to enable practitioners to record their observations of their pupils' musical behaviors as and when they occur, in the classroom or elsewhere, by selecting options from a series of drop-down menus. All data are processed and stored automatically for later retrieval, permitting teachers and therapists to chart longitudinal changes that may occur, whether or not in response to particular interventions; to offer comparisons within and between specified cohorts; and to record qualitative observations in the form of verbal, video or audio data, in order to build up a profile of a child's experiences and achievements over time.

In conclusion, the notion of "small steps" is often used in relation to pupils with the most complex needs—those with severe, or profound and multiple learning difficulties—and the *Sounds of Intent* research suggests what this may mean in to musical development, in particular by taking into account the levels and frequency of different types of musical engagement. Moreover, making the theoretical framework developed by the *Sounds of Intent* team available through mobile touch-screen technology should make the reality of frequent, fine-grained music-developmental observations a reality in classrooms.

REFLECTIVE QUESTIONS

1. What functions can music fulfil in the education of children with the most complex needs?
2. What are likely to be the main advantages and disadvantages of considering musical development in terms of discrete stages?
3. Can musical development really be quantified?
4. Is it reasonable to use numbers in comparing levels of musical engagement?
5. Should all music teachers have some experience of working with children with complex needs?

KEY SOURCE

Ockelford, A. (2008) *Music for Children and Young People with Complex Needs*, Oxford: Oxford University Press.

REFERENCES

Cassidy, J. (1992) Communication disorders: effects on children's ability to label musical characteristics, *Journal of Music Therapy*, 29(2), 113–124.

Cheng, E., Ockelford, A., & Welch, G. (2009) "Researching and developing music provision in special schools in England for children and young people with complex needs," *Australian Journal of Music Education*, 2, 27–48.

Darrow, A.-A. (1984) "A comparison of rhythmic responsiveness in normal and hearing impaired children and an investigation of the relationship of rhythmic responsiveness to the suprasegmental aspects of speech perception," *Journal of Music Therapy*, 21(2), 48–66.

Dowling, W. J. (1982) "Melodic information processing and its development," in D. Deutsch (ed.), *The Psychology of Music*, New York: Academic Press, pp. 413–429.

Flowers, P. & Wang, C. (2002) "Matching verbal description to music excerpt: the use of language by blind and sighted children," *Journal of Research in Music Education*, 50(3), 202–214.

Hargreaves, D. (1986) *The Developmental Psychology of Music*, Cambridge: Cambridge University Press.

Jellison, J. (2000) "A content analysis of music research with disabled children and youth (1975–1999)" in *Effectiveness of Music Therapy Procedures: Documentation of Research and Clinical Practice*, Silver Spring, MD: The American Music Therapy Association, pp. 199–264.

Lecanuet, J.-P. (1996). "Prenatal auditory experience," in I. Deliège & J. Sloboda (eds), *Musical Beginnings*, Oxford: Oxford University Press, pp. 3–34.

MacDonald, R., Davies, J., & O'Donnell, P. (1999) "Structured music workshops for individuals with learning difficulty: an empirical investigation," *Journal of Applied Research in Intellectual Disabilities*, 12(3) 225–241.

Moog, H. (1968/1976) *The Musical Experiences of the Pre-school Child* (trans. C. Clarke), London: Schott.

Ockelford, A. (1996). *All Join In!: A Framework for Making Music with Children and Young People who are Visually Impaired and Have Learning Disabilities*. London: Royal National Institute for the Blind.

Ockelford, A. (2000) "Music in the education of children with severe or profound learning difficulties: issues in current UK provision, a new conceptual framework and proposals for research," *Psychology of Music*, 28(2), 197–217.

Ockelford, A. (2002) "The magical number two, plus or minus one: some limitations on our capacity for processing musical information," *Musicae Scientiae*, 6, 177–215.

Ockelford, A. (2005) *Repetition in Music: Theoretical and Metatheoretical Perspectives*, London: Ashgate.

Ockelford, A. (2009) "Zygonic theory: introduction, scope, prospects," *Zeitschrift der Gesellschaft für Musiktheorie*, 6(2), 91–172.

Ockelford, A. (2015) "The Sounds of Intent project: modelling musical development in children with learning difficulties," *Tizard Learning Disability Review*, 20(4), 179–194.

Ockelford, A. & Matawa, C. (2010) *Focus on Music 2: Exploring the Musical Interests and Abilities of Blind and Partially-Sighted Children with Retinopathy of Prematurity*, London: Institute of Education.

Ockelford, A., Welch, G., Jewell-Gore, L., Cheng, E., Vogiatzoglou, A., & Himonides, E. (2010) "*Sounds of Intent*, Phase 2: Gauging the Music Development of Children with Complex Needs," *European Journal of Special Education*, 26(2), 177–199.

Ockelford, A., Welch, G., & Zimmermann, S.-A. (2002) "Music education for pupils with severe or profound and multiple difficulties—current provision and future need," *British Journal of Special Education*, 29(4), 178–182.

Ockelford, A., Welch, G., Zimmermann, S.-A., & Himonides, E. (2005) "Sounds of Intent'—mapping, assessing and promoting the musical development of children with profound and multiple learning difficulties," Proceedings of "VISION 2005" Conference, 4–7 April, 2005. *Elsevier: International Congress Series*, 1282, 898–902.

O'Donnell, P., MacDonald, R., & Davies J. (1999) "Video analysis of the effects of structured music workshops for individuals with learning difficulties," in D. Erdonmez & R. Pratt (eds), *Music Therapy and Music Medicine: Expanding Horizons*, Saint Louis: MMB Music, pp. 219–228.

Papoušek, H. (1996) "Musicality in infancy research: biological and cultural origins of early musicality," in I. Deliège & J. Sloboda (eds), *Musical Beginnings*, Oxford: Oxford University Press, pp. 37–55.

Stordahl, J. (2002) "Song recognition and appraisal A comparison of children who use cochlear implants and normally hearing children," *Journal of Music Therapy*, 39(1), 2–19.

Swedberg, O. (2007) *A comparison of Hearing and Deaf/Hard-of-Hearing Students' use of Analytic, Figurative and Temporal Language in Descriptions of Music*, Unpublished Master of Music Education thesis, College of Music, Florida State University.

Trehub, S. (1990). "The perception of musical patterns by human infants: the provision of similar patterns by their parents," in M. Berkley & W. Stebbins (eds), *Comparative Perception; Vol. 1, Mechanisms*, New York: Wiley, pp. 429–459.

Trehub, S. (2003) "Musical predispositions in infancy: an update," in I. Peretz & R. Zatorre (eds), *The Cognitive Neuroscience of Music*, New York: Oxford University Press, pp. 3–20.

Trevarthen, C. (2002) "Origins of musical identity: evidence from infancy for musical social awareness," in R. Macdonald, D. Hargreaves & D. Miell (eds), *Musical Identities*, Oxford: Oxford University Press, pp. 21–38.

Welch, G. (2006) "The musical development and education of young children," in B. Spodek & O. Saracho (eds), *Handbook of Research on the Education of Young Children*, Mahwah, New Jersey: Lawrence Erlbaum Associates, pp. 251–267.

Welch, G., Ockelford, A., & Zimmermann, S-A. (2001) *Provision of Music in Special Education (PROMISE)*, London: RNIB/University of London Institute of Education.

Welch, G., Ockelford, A., Carter, F.-C., Zimmermann, S.-A., & Himonides, E. (2009) "'Sounds of Intent': mapping musical behaviour and development in children and young people with complex needs," *Psychology of Music*, 37(3), 348–370.

....

CHAPTER 3

EXCEPTIONAL MUSICAL ABILITIES: MUSICAL PRODIGIES

....

GARY E. MCPHERSON AND ANDREAS C. LEHMANN

The astonishing achievements of children who show extraordinary talent are of great fascination across the world (McPherson, 2016). This has been the case throughout history, where conceptions of giftedness have moved from a theological view, in which gifted children were regarded as "heavenly"—a gift from God, to a metaphysical phase that emphasized individual aptitudes but also fostered many myths such as the stereotyped "crazed genius," portrayed in many movies. A more contemporary empirical approach is interested in domain-specific training, the interaction of genetic and environmental factors, educational measures and individual differences, and how these differ among cultures (Stoeger, 2009; see also Kopiez & Lehmann, 2016). It does not matter if the young performers are athletes, musicians, academics, or specialize in new skills; their appearances still puzzle and intrigue many in our society who find it difficult to understand the exact nature of their talents or abilities. And since the advent of video-posting on web portals such as YouTube, every precocious youth has a chance to be seen and discovered (Mink & McPherson, 2016).[1]

Prodigies are thought to have emerged as a result of evolutionary processes around 10,000 years ago, when rule-governed knowledge in human culture exploded in size and complexity (Weaver, 2005, cited in Vandervert, 2009a, p. 19; see also, Vandervert, 2009b, 2016a, 2016b). Documented accounts of child musical prodigies, however, only date back to the sixteenth century, and they became a topical issue at the start of the seventeenth century (Stevens, 1982). By the nineteenth century musical prodigies became increasingly recognized and celebrated, with many children touring through European cities to display their musical skills (Kopiez, 2011; Kopiez & Lehmann, 2016). Even today, children such as Tiffany Poon and Niu Niu (piano), Tallan Latz (electric guitar), Igor Falecki (drums), and Nikki Yanofsky (vocal) astound the public with their precocious feats. However, being a musical prodigy does not guarantee either that someone will ultimately succeed as an adult performer or that the very positive feelings we have for them when they are young will carry over to the adult performer (Gagné & McPherson, 2016).

There are descriptions and possible explanations of exceptional achievement in the scholarly literature (see McPherson, 2016 for the most recent and comprehensive account). One of the most famous musical prodigies of all, Wolfgang Amadeus Mozart, was examined in London by Lord Daines Barrington at the age of eight and asked to perform a number of tasks. There are also systematic accounts of the Spanish child composer Pepito Arriola by Stumpf (1909), the child pianist Lucie Stern by Franziska Baumgarten (1930; see Olbertz, 2009), and the pianist-composer Erwin Nyiregyházy by Révész (1916; see Bazzana, 2007). There are case studies of various prodigious children (six by Feldman, 1986; one by Ruthsatz & Detterman, 2003; one by McPherson, 2007; three by Olbertz, 2009; and the "perilous journeys" of musical prodigies by Kenneson, 2002), all of which attest to the scientific interest in the phenomenon. Similarly, there are classical and contemporary studies of savants (e.g., Ockelford, 2007, 2016), including exceptional performers with autism or other disabilities, who excel in one domain, such as music, and constitute another extraordinary form of musical precocity that intrigue us.

Such case studies constitute important milestones in the research literature, but do not always lend themselves to generalization, though some universal mechanisms can be seen at work—for instance, the central role of parents and teachers (McPherson, 2009a), the importance of large amounts of practice (Lehmann, 1997), and the influence of intensive and sustained motivation (see overview by Austin, Renwick, & McPherson, 2006).

This chapter outlines two older static models of exceptional achievement and one more recently elaborated one before moving on to seek explanations about the forces driving the process. We also outline the stages of development and present a supporting case study of a young pianist. Our closing suggestions for parents and teachers attempt to cast the presented empirical literature into practical, everyday advice.

THEORIES OF EXCEPTIONAL ACHIEVEMENT: RENZULLI, MÖNKS, AND GAGNÉ

The existence of prodigies in music demands explanatory theories about their uniqueness and development. While some musicians might consider that music is distinct from other domains of expertise and that high achievement in music should therefore be explicable through a specific music-related cognitive mechanism, recent findings regarding exceptional musical abilities align with or even adapt concepts from general psychology and education (McPherson, 2016). Thinking along these lines suggests that musicians are no different from performers in other domains. Although there is still no general consensus in giftedness research regarding genetic differences, contemporary theories favor interactionist views of genetics and the environment, as discussed by Gagné and McPherson (2016) and in the following summary.

Borrowing a definition of intellectual giftedness, a musically gifted child can be described as one who rapidly and effectively acquires declarative and procedural knowledge, who applies this knowledge adequately in varying situations to solve novel problems, who learns swiftly from experience acquired in new situations, and who recognizes where knowledge can be transferred (generalized) and where not (differentiated) (Rost, Sparfeldt, & Schilling, 2006). Building on previous work by authors such as Feldman, Winner, and his own, Vandervert (2009a, pp. 18–19, 2016a, 2016b) proposed that prodigies possess an earlier-than-normal, accelerated learning progress, self-directed learning, a "rage to master" associated with a strong focus of attention, and visual-spatial precocity. This last norm-referenced definition contrasts with Shavinina's (2009a) criterion for defining child prodigies, namely that they "are usually able to do something that is usually attributed to adults" (p. 233, see also Shavinina, 2016), and more specifically that the difference between a prodigy and very gifted child is that the prodigy is able to demonstrate his or her remarkable talent before the age of 10. This age limit may actually make it difficult to recognize precocious achievement in certain domains such as motor sports or medicine.

One recurrent problem in discussions of exceptional achievement is the dialectic between nature and nurture, and especially how the separate (or reciprocal) influences of the environment and innate dispositions are theoretically dealt with (see McPherson & Hallam, 2009, for a review on musical potential, but also Gagné & McPherson, 2016, on the role of natural abilities in the development of musical prodigies). For this chapter, we will concentrate on the influence of the environment and on individual development, since these have the most direct application and relevance for music education.

The American educator Renzulli (1978, 2005) developed a three-circle model of giftedness comprising intelligence, creativity, and task commitment (see fig. 3.1). The overlap between the circles formed the crucial area, where high intelligence, high creativity, and strong task commitment intersect to allow for exceptional achievement. The important aspect of this model was its elimination of the difference between hidden potential, which can be actualized, and exceptional performance. A few years later, the Dutch researcher Mönks (1981) added the social dimension of family, peer-group, and school to show that individuals are not left to their own devices but require a nurturing environment. These ideas are still valid, because rather than focusing on psychometrically measured factors such as intelligence, they attempt to explain high achievement and how the crucial factors of

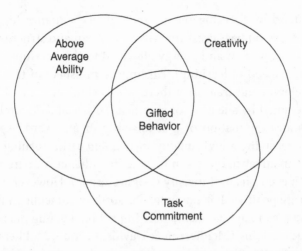

Figure 3.1 Three-circle model adapted from Renzulli (1978).

task commitment (i.e., motivation) and social environment (i.e., social support and early stimulation) impact on development.

The differentiated model of giftedness by Gagné (2009a, 2009b) is the most recent and detailed attempt to define giftedness without giving up the idea of potential and developed skills (see Gagné & McPherson, 2016, for a full account of how the model relates to musical prodigies). It is also of great illustrative value regarding the complexity of the issue, especially in terms of understanding the natural abilities present at or soon after birth that impact on the development of a prodigy. Gagné differentiates between early emerging forms of *giftedness* and *fully developed* forms of *talent*. Within his model, *giftedness* refers to the range of natural abilities or aptitudes that a person possesses, as compared to the *talent* or *talents* that may be developed through developmental processes and exposure to the types of environmental and personal catalysts that he believes impact on development. The ingredients of Gagné's (2009a) model comprise three components: giftedness (G), talent development (D), and talent (T), with the two additional elements intrapersonal catalysts (I) and environmental catalysts (E) completing its structure.

Gifts include a cluster of natural abilities called domains: four related to mental processes (intellectual, creative, social, and perceptual), and two related to physical abilities (muscular and motor control). Each of these natural abilities can be observed in young children and can develop over a person's life. Each seems especially important in different degrees for developing certain talents in music. For example, certain physical attributes involving muscular speed and endurance, plus motor control mechanisms involving agility, coordination, dexterity, and balance, may be essential for some forms of musical talent (such as performing within the Western art music tradition), while not for others (such as improvising or composing).

Gagné (2009a, 2009b) proposed that the talent development process, or the process of acquiring skill and expertise in any area of learning such as music, can be understood by focusing on the individual's *activities* (opportunities to learn to which a person has access in terms of content and structure), *investment* (the extent of time, money, and energy allocated to the developmental process), and *progress* (the speed of learning). An important aspect of this notion is that along any developmental trajectory there will be incidents in which a person's talent might be noted by a teacher or significant other and documented through high grades in an examination or a scholarship or an award (e.g., attending a master class or receiving a high-quality instrument). The ensuing opportunities to engage more in advanced levels in turn act to enhance a desire to pursue personal goals with even greater intensity (Gagné, 2009a). However, not all of these turning points are positive. For example, the death of someone in the family or a marriage breakup can have a considerable impact on a young musician's motivation to continue studying (McPherson & Davidson, 2006; McPherson, Davidson & Faulkner, 2012).

Catalysts of various sorts shape each individual's talent. Gagné (2009a) uses the term *catalysts* because these influences facilitate and accelerate (or alternately impede and decrease) a learner's developmental trajectory. *Intrapersonal catalysts* refer to aspects residing primarily within a person, such as physical and mental traits and goal management. Of course, those intrapersonal catalysts act as a filter for the *environmental catalysts*, consisting of educational input and cultural and social surroundings. For example, living close to a music conservatory or school with a highly developed music program will create opportunities that may not exist for those who do not have access to the expert guidance available within such institutions. The social environment in which a person lives may also impact dramatically on an individual's progress in a certain field, particularly when significant others (parents, family, peers, teachers, mentors) are willing to devote the time and attention needed to scaffold a learner to work at an even higher level. Significant others often make available provisions that enrich and accelerate a learner's progress, or, more broadly, learners may be exposed through enrichment programs that extend far beyond what might normally be offered other individuals (including those of lesser ability). In this light it is not surprising that many exceptional musicians emanate from musical families. In turn, a patient child will be more easily motivated to practice than a restless one, especially when he or she has had particularly positive experiences in music rather than having been confronted with personal musical failures (e.g., a teacher telling a child not to sing in a choir).

One of the more controversial aspects of the Gagné's (2009a, 2009b) model is the inclusion of *chance*. *Chance* may have a role in talent development as "a *qualifier* of *any* causal influence" (Gagné, 2009a, p. 70), particularly as "chance" refers to the accidents of birth and background over which we have no control. Our family and the social environment in which we are raised are but two of the most important ways in which chance impacts our development (see discussion of the model in Gagné & McPherson, 2016, plus McPherson & Williamon, 2016).

The strength of these theoretical explanations is that they isolate the contributing factors and suggest, in the case of Gagné's (2009a) model (see fig. 3.2), some causal relationships. Indeed, in the most recent explanation, Gagné and McPherson (2016) have started to speculate about the relative strength of individual factors, whilst also recognizing that talent formation is also highly individual. We might still ask, however, how strong is the influence of personality when it comes to practicing? Is a supportive home environment a sufficient or only a necessary condition for talent development? Can low creativity hinder giftedness even in the presence of high intelligence and task commitment, and so forth? Therefore, models have merit in that they provide a descriptive explanation of the overall parameters of talent development, but they still do not fully explain the specific magnitude or impact of variables and how each might interact and shape certain forms of talent (see Howe, 1999; also Shavinina, 2009b). An added complication is the large number of contributing factors that make the explanatory value of any individual variable extremely difficulty. Naturally, many of the variables listed in the model have been found to exert *some* influence on the development of exceptional achievement, but their overall explanatory value is unknown.

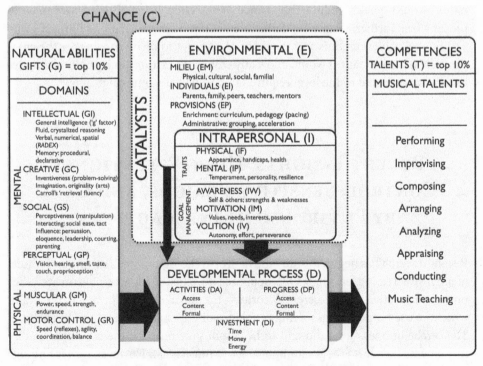

Figure 3.2 Differentiated Model of Giftedness and Talent. Adapted from Gagné (2009a, p. 64).

Prevalence in the Population

The prevalence of extraordinary achievement is interesting and important to educators because many of them do not have a clear idea of how many exceptional students they can expect in a given population of students. Taking the normal distribution as a baseline, one would argue that 2% of students fall to the right of the second standard deviation, which when compared to IQ measures would correspond to a value above 130. This is a standard threshold for the diagnosis of giftedness. However, while intelligence testing is currently the best way to assess intellectual giftedness, music aptitude testing is not well enough developed to enable comparable prognostications to be made (see McPherson & Hallam, 2009). As a consequence, there are only general cutoff values for defining different categories of giftedness and talent. For example, in his various publications, Gagné refers to five hierarchically levels such that a child, when compared to peers of the same age or experience in a domain of learning, could be described as *mildly* (top 10%), *moderately* (top 1%), *highly* (top 0.1%), *exceptionally* (top 0.01%) or *extremely* or *profoundly* (top 0.001%) gifted or talented. We could speculate that the unique and extraordinary development of a true musical prodigy would require the child to be at least in the 99th percentile (top 1%) on all natural abilities, so if the individual dropped down to less than the 99th percentile on any variable, the multiplicative combination would quickly reduce the chance of the child being labelled as a musical prodigy (see further, Gagné & McPherson, 2016). Such calculations illustrate why exceptional achievement is so rare, theoretically, not to mention whether the environmental circumstances would allow any child with extraordinary natural abilities to develop potential to the level required to be labelled a musical prodigy.

Recent Insights: High Attentional Control, Sensitive Periods, and Gene by Environment Interactions

Recent research has begun to study the neuropsychological mechanisms and results of intensive (early) learning. One approach to explain high achievements relies on the interaction of the cerebral cortex—the most modern layer of our brain, which we use for planning, solving problems, or anticipating—and the cerebellum. The cerebellum was long thought to be responsible only for the control of bodily movements (hence it is of great importance to musicians). However, newer findings emphasize the crucial role for the cerebellum in all aspects of working memory (Vandervert, 2007; Vandervert, Schimpf, & Liu, 2007, Vandervert, 2016a, 2016b). This new insight suggests that movement and thought may be similar with regard to how they are processed by the cerebellum. In particular, repetitive mental actions and their solutions from working memory are built into control architectures in the cerebellum and emerge automatically when required. If no ready-made solution is represented, then the next probable one materializes (Wolpert, Doya, & Kawato, 2003; Vandervert, 2007). It is now also thought that exceptional children may develop such control architectures as a result of critical periods when they are highly attentive in an area of learning that they find extremely engaging (Shavinina, 1999, 2009a, 2016). For example, Vandervert (2016a, 2016b) has proposed that collaboration occurs between working memory and the cerebellum, wherein a gifted child's working memory can become extremely sensitive to the unique high-attention emotional thrust that can lead to an accelerated, and more efficient learning of rule-based domains of knowledge and performance.

Immersion of this type can lead to a form of superior, high-attentional memory that is characteristic of exceptional children (Ruthsatz & Detterman, 2003; Shavinina, 1999, 2009a). Cerebellum-mediated thinking also explains how we can understand and imitate other people (Wolpert, Doya, & Kawato, 2003). This process is fundamental to learning in music and other domains, and it is vital for the automatic manipulation of ideas that account for the high-efficiency processing of domain-related material in even young children. In the high accomplishment we see in musical prodigies, linkages are constructed in the cerebellum between the earliest-learned elements of music and symbolic representations pertaining to higher, more abstract levels of understanding. Because of these linkages, running bidirectionally up and down the cerebellum, various thoughts, goals, and circumstances automatically activate entire systems of learned behavior and thought (Vandervert, 2009a, 2016b).

Vandervert (2009a) suggests that through higher level training and education, this automatic sequential-cueing effect can also apply to open symbol systems such as learning to play an instrument. Here, mental and physical skill development combined with the motivational pleasure felt through higher level abstraction results in a two-way circuitry in the cerebrocereballar system that produces a "self-propelling *positive feedback loop* to higher and higher self-directed attentional control, competence and discovery" (p. 26). This proposition is consistent with Winner's (1996) descriptions of the self-directed efforts of child prodigies who "independently invent rules of domain and devise novel, idiosyncratic ways of solving problems" (p. 3).

Shavinina (2010, 2009a, 2016) extends this idea by suggesting that "all prodigies are mental prodigies, because all of them manifest certain intellectually creative performance or/and achievements in various fields of human endeavour" (2009a, p. 234). Her explanation places great emphasis on *sensitive periods*, when unique forms of cognitive representation are formed that accelerate a child's intellectual development. We could imagine that a musical child may suddenly become obsessed with learning how to notate music, by first inventing a personalised notation system, and then mastering the traditional system. Importantly, Shavinina (2009a) stresses that such rapid acceleration of learning may dissipate or even diminish after the end of relevant *sensitive periods*, with the result that the child may lose certain acquisitions when the period ends. This would explain why many gifted children become ordinary adults and why the potential of some children who appear early in life to be gifted is never realized. In many cases, however, these sensitive periods provide the foundation for continuing accelerated development, a "unique intellectual picture of the world" (Shavinina, 2009a, p. 245) and the types of cognitive experiences that provide the psychological basis from which highly gifted children are able to develop their creative, metacognitive, and extracognitive (i.e., feelings, beliefs, intellectual values, intuition) abilities. Back to our notation example: learning notation may allow access to and understanding of complicated scores as well as the writing of complex multivoice pieces that can be communicated and performed. Sensitive periods are therefore best understood not as character-istics, traits or features of a child but rather as "an inner mechanism of prodigious development and the development of the gifted" (p. 234). The question still remains whether any child could acquire these mechanisms or not.

Another important change in thinking comes from recent publications that seemingly contradict commonly held wisdom about genetics, talent, and IQ. For example, Shenk's (2010) widely read synthesis of research takes great pains to show how genes on their own do not determine the physical and character traits of an in-dividual, but interact in a dynamic process with the environment to produce highly distinctive and individual attributes within each individual that Shenk describes as the "G x E dynamic" (i.e., genetic versus environment dynamic). The most com-pelling evidence currently presented stems from animal experiments. In this in-teractionist conception intelligence is not seen as a hardwired, innate aptitude but a living thing (Gardner, 1999) that can be thought of as a "set of competencies in development," of which motivation is at the center, driving the process (Sternberg, 2005, p. 18). Within this conception, talent is not regarded as innate but the result of a long process of maturation and development, with genetic material interacting with environmental stimulation. It is likely that these ideas might in the future have an impact on conceptions about the stability and rigidity of the genetic factor—regarding IQ and musical abilities alike. However, this chapter reviews the currently widespread conceptions of giftedness that stress the importance of environmental influences.

STAGES OR PHASES IN TALENT DEVELOPMENT

After more than five decades of research on musical development, there is no single or unanimous voice that fully explains the phases or stages of musical development; rather, there is a rainbow of opinions. However, progress in thinking about musical development is not so much about working toward consensus as finding ways to refine and focus the debate. This is important because the focus will influence educational premises and ensuing interventions.

The attempt to divide development into discrete stages or phases is problematic since no two learners' progress is the same. Some ideas in sport psychology over recent decades, however, attempt to bring emerging findings into more generalizable models of the many psychological behaviors that appear to underpin people's potential as athletes. Virtually all of these models place a great deal of emphasis on the types of support that learners receive from others, particularly their parents and teachers (in addition to peers and siblings). If there is one conclusive finding from the research that we and others have undertaken, it is that a learner's interest will dissipate or disappear altogether in cases where there is no continuing support.

A model that was originally devised by Abbott and Collins (2004) to outline the role of various psychological behaviors that facilitate development in athletes emphasizes the major transitions that a learner will experience across the phases or stages of learning. Before going further, however, we think it is important to note that one of the more interesting ways sports psychologists have examined development has not been by trying to identify the best performers at any particular moment but rather by identifying the factors that, over time, may inhibit development. Such a notion sits easily with those who believe that musicians are a product of their environment rather than their genetic endowment, because the explanation is focused on how individuals interact with their environment and deal with the opportunities they are given. Abbott and Collins (2004) have transformed a pioneering stage model by Bloom (1985) and other work by Côté (1999) into a more detailed theory that we believe can be adapted to define music talent development across the years of schooling and into the early years of adulthood.

At the heart of Abbott and Collins's model (see fig. 3.3) is the proposition that different forms of training activities each play different roles in the varying stages of development. For example, in the *sampling stage* (which in sport typically occurs between the ages of 6 and 12) practice can be described as "deliberate play"—involving loosely structured activities that are aimed at increasing motivation and enjoyment rather than technical skill. This is followed by the *specialization stage* (approximate ages 13–15), when practice tends to encompass deliberate practice of the skills and techniques provided by specialist coaches, as well as deliberate play where the emphasis is on playing for (social) enjoyment. With increasingly challenging tasks the learner's sense of self-efficacy (can-do attitude) and ability to persist despite obstacles is enhanced. A focus on deliberate practice in the *investment stage* occurs when young athletes are immersed in the sport and are able to set their own goals. The final stage of the model—the *maintenance stage*—typically occurs after the school years and involves sustaining performance at a consistently high level.

Although these four macro stages of development can easily be reworked as a framework for explaining the existing literature in music, it is important to note that the musician's road to musical excellence also involves many micro stages of

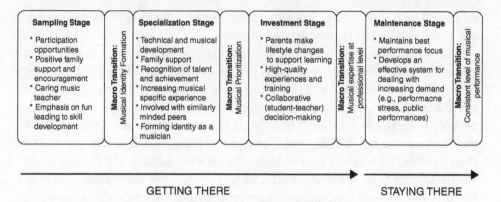

Figure 3.3 Stages for musical development (adapted from sports-related model by Abbott & Collins, 2004).

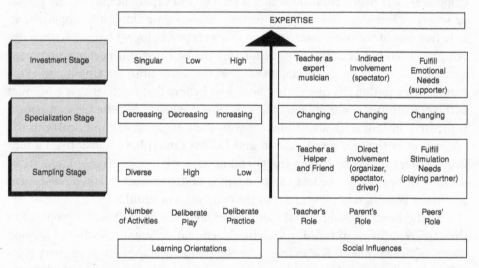

Figure 3.4 Changes in learning orientations and social influences during the sampling, specialization, and investment stages of developing musical expertise (adapted from Côté, Baker, & Abernethy, 2003, p. 98).

development in which he or she encounters challenges, such as the emotionally draining family situations of parents separating, illness, or simply the turmoil of adolescence. Negotiating transitions between stages also involves subtle and not-so-subtle changes to the different quality of support one needs in subsequent stages of development. As Abbott and Collins (2004) suggest, the capacity to initiate and or commit to these changes is vital for learners and their support network of teachers, parents, and peers. As a summary of these ideas, figure 3.4 shows the broad learning orientations and social influences that occur as children make the transition from each of the first three stages outlined in figure 3.3.

Case Study of a Prodigious Pianist

A brief summary of an extensive case study will exemplify the possible path of a prodigy (McPherson, 2007, 2009b). It underscores the interactive, dynamic model in explaining how early exceptional achievements in music develop as a result of environmental forces acting together with innate potential at critical moments in the child's development.

One of the authors (McPherson) has been observing the progress of an extraordinarily talented young female pianist (see www.tiffanypoon.com) for more than 10 years. Unlike most other children investigated to date (see McPherson & Davidson, 2006) this remarkable young pianist was involved in the sampling stage from around age two to five, before moving to the specialization stage between the ages of five and nine, and then moving on to the investment stage from the age of nine—far earlier than ages reported in the general sport psychology literature and far ahead of "typical" children learning to play musical instruments (see McPherson & Davidson, 2006; Faulkner, Davidson, & McPherson, 2010).

Things began at about two years of age, when Tiffany would often sit at a toy piano and try to imitate melodies that she heard on the TV and hi-fi. In preference to going to a toy shop, she would accompany her father to purchase piano recordings which they would listen to on his stereo. At the age of four and a half, Tiffany began taking formal piano lessons, and after three years of learning was practicing up to three or even four hours per day, and capable of performing Grade 8 Associate Board repertoire. During the early stages of development, her mother reports sitting with her daughter and playing games that helped focus the child on repetition and mastery. For example, the mother would challenge Tiffany by saying: "Can you play that scale again five times correctly?" "Can you play it 10 times correctly?" "Now, can you play it 50 times correctly?" These types of activities provided the basis for a playful learning environment in which Tiffany was encouraged to feel special by her mother who would clap and make comments such as "Bravo!" each time she mastered a new task. The loving connection between mother and child also created an emotional climate that helped Tiffany develop the motivation to achieve at a continually higher level. Undertaking long practice sessions was therefore easier for Tiffany, because the emphasis was on playful activities, fun, and mastery of incremental challenges.

At seven years of age, Tiffany's practiced about one or two hours per day, because she had much homework and was also participating in a number of extra curricula activities such as swimming, gymnastics, chorus, jazz dance, drama, English phonics, mathematics and Chinese calligraphy. Around age eight, the parents had difficulty finding a suitable piano teacher so she studied piano by herself.

From the very beginning, there appears to have been a distinct difference between Tiffany's learning agenda and those of her teachers. She displayed superb self-regulatory skills for her age. Over weeks she listened extensively to CD recordings of piano repertoire before choosing those works that she wanted to learn. Most important, before physically attempting to master a work, Tiffany would typically acquire a clear mental image of the piece through repeated hearings of the music (and using various recordings). This strategy is quite different from how most teachers typically proceed, namely from symbol to sound. Her rage to master was not related to the technique of playing the piano but rather what needed to be done in order to master the desired repertoire that she already knew from recordings. Although neither of her parents had received any formal musical training, they supported and encouraged her learning at each stage of her development.

When Tiffany was about nine years old, it became clear that although rapid progress was being made, she deserved to be taught by an exceptional teacher who could help realize her remarkable abilities. This is when enquiries were made regarding the possibility of studying at leading international institutions. As a result, the family then made a lifestyle decision that the mother would move with Tiffany to a large city in the United States where she could take up a scholarship at an internationally renowned music school (here there is a clear parallel to the violinist Midori Goto). In the years since making this decision, Tiffany has continued to make extraordinary progress, evidenced by her invitations to perform with orchestras and internationally, winning competitions, and gaining national media coverage.

Tiffany's mother has made video recordings of her daughter over her entire life, and it is clear from viewing the recordings that the first sensitive period Tiffany might have experienced occurred around two years of age when she would imitate on her toy piano the orchestral and piano recordings she was listening to on her father's stereo system. Her parents report that she did this for many hours each week, which would seem to fit with Shavinina's (2009a, 2016) assertion that such experiences might result in accelerated development, through a cognitive experience that provided the psychological basis for Tiffany to develop at an early age unique feelings, beliefs, intellectual values, and intuitions that helped her once she started formal piano lessons.

IDENTIFYING EXCEPTIONAL ABILITIES

Most exceptionally talented young instrumental musicians are identified first by their parents, who then entrust them to specialists when they feel that they are not capable of supporting their child's learning. Very often considerable investment has already been undertaken in the course of early skill acquisition before the child is considered exceptional by comparison with her peers. In the arts and sports such exceptional achievement is readily observable. Therefore, the benefit of large-scale prognostic screening/testing regarding some "hidden" potential appears questionable on theoretical grounds. When should it be done? What should we look for? Furthermore, since novice performance is subject to large day-to-day variability, one-time testing can be unreliable. Instead, it may be preferable to follow promising children in order to assess their true potential to sustain a demanding educational program. As mentioned, the strong epigenetic environmental impact would suggest focusing on development rather than on disposition.

This may appear contradictory, but large-scale testing or exposing children to learning opportunities in formal settings can be useful in identifying children who have an interest in music-making but no current opportunity to actualize it, due to unfavorable environmental conditions, such as minority backgrounds or low socioeconomic status. It is also important to keep in mind nontraditional musical domains that allow a relatively late start (such as DJ-ing). It may also be difficult to uncover generative abilities related to composition, improvisation, or music production when children are not routinely encouraged to engage in those activities.

Special Needs of the Gifted and Talented

Exceptional early achievers require special care (UNICEF, 2010). Although the numbers of children who abandon their learning along the way are unknown, reports by famous performers who have been prodigies suggest that their childhood was often traumatic, devoid of same-age playmates, and characterized by early specialization at the expense of other domains (Quart, 2006; Bazzana, 2007; Kenneson, 2002). Interestingly, early specialization has been shown *not* to be a prerequisite in sports (Côté, Baker, & Abernethy, 2003). As child-rearing approaches change historically and culturally, it is not easy to state exactly what is ethically appropriate. Perhaps the best way is to suggest educationally proven means that do not stand in conflict with current laws and conventions. For example, in eastern European countries promising children have often been cared for and educated by the state in specialized schools away from their families (Bogunovic, 2008), whereas in Western countries the families carry the burden of responsibility for talent development. The educational implications in both scenarios start with the question of how to nurture such children in ethical ways, and how to support those who do not succeed in the end.

Suggestions for Parents and Teachers

Based on the above, our suggestions for parents and teachers can be grouped into the following six broad categories.

Supporting Sensitive Periods

Parents and teachers need to look out for and support a prodigy's sensitive periods. For example, every effort should be devoted to supporting children's psychological needs when they display the two attributes that seem especially important for rapid musical learning—an intellectual curiosity and emotional engagement with an aspect of the music being learned. These include the need to feel closely related and "connected" to parents and teachers in a nonthreatening learning environment, a sense of competence that results from mastery experiences, sufficient opportunities to demonstrate newly acquired skills (and hence feel "special"), a learning environment that encourages initiative and freedom of choice, and a sense of being personally in charge of one's own behavior and therefore able to cope with difficulties (McPherson, 2009a).

Cooperation between parent, child, and teacher is of special importance when a new sensitive period emerges or when the child confronts difficulties. In particular, teachers and parents need to be clear about their own responsibilities (e.g., who is helping with practice and how?).

Ideally, support systems should be commensurate with the child's needs and the stage of skill development. For example, a warm, caring teacher with whom the child finds it easy to communicate may be preferable in the *sampling stage,* whereas in the *investment stage,* where aspirations soar, the child will need a much more musically demanding teacher.

Self-Regulation and Goal Setting

Involving the child in decision processes shows respect and helps to avoid a sense of helplessness, particularly during challenging and unrewarding periods when learning is frustrating or slow. It is therefore crucial that a teacher (and/or parent) works with the child to set appropriate short-term and longer term goals, and to create high but realistic expectations. All those involved need to be particularly attentive to whose goals are being pursued—the teacher's aspirations, the child's needs, or the parents' unfulfilled desires? Most important, care, love, and attention should not be made contingent on the child's success and obedience, especially regarding practice.

Celebrating the Child's Uniqueness

Exceptional achievers are individuals with unique ability profiles who often show asynchronous development in different domains such as language, motor, cognition, and socialization. Therefore, we should consider the amalgam of children's strengths, weaknesses, and personality and not simply focus on the area in which they are most interested. When the child is old enough to understand that people in our society need a broad base, learning goals can be set to ensure that a general education is incorporated alongside more specialized interests.

Seeking Help

Given the rarity of exceptional students, most teachers will be inexperienced in their guiding of an unusually curious and precocious child. In contrast to sports, where educating athletes is a team effort, the traditional approach in music involves a master-apprentice model that can sometimes stand in the way of the student's needs. Parents should be cautious about entrusting their child to a teacher who has little experience of working with gifted children and lacks an appropriate network in relevant professional circles.

Finding Balance

Even for seasoned performers, mental and physical burnout resulting from over-practice and stress constitute a severe danger to progress and a career. Therefore, exceptionally able children need to be encouraged to find a balance between work and rest and to adopt a healthy, balanced lifestyle.

Changes in Motivation, Attitude, and Learning Style

Bamberger (2016) suggests that the make-or-break "midlife crisis" that many musical prodigies go through during adolescence is due to a cognitive reorganization in representations toward a more structural mental representation of music and music-making. This finding is compatible with neuropsychological research into the changing adolescent brain (e.g., Ernst & Korelitz, 2009). Dramatic changes in performance and attitude need to be accepted and dealt with in adequate ways.

A 20-year follow-up of winners of a German music competition revealed that only half the national-level laureates became professional musicians in some function (Bastian & Koch, 2006). Consequently, having initially identified promising students and educated them to a high level, we might discover that particular students do not fulfil their promise or become disenchanted. In such situations special care needs to be given in identifying alternatives for the young adult that offer viable pathways into meaningful careers. Changes in interest can go along with feelings of failure and guilt on the part of young musicians because of the tremendous energy and financial resources that have been invested in their education.

These negative feelings need to be addressed and managed productively in order to allow a positive outlook later in life. It is therefore important that the student's general education isn't neglected so as to facilitate a switch to another area if needed. A different career may still be possible because many of the skills and knowledge acquired through the learning of music can be transferred to initiate a promising future in another related domain. After all, we also need good amateur musicians!

Coda

Taken together, the emerging neuropsychological models and the interactionist educational concepts form a complex but useful framework for explaining the unique cognitive experience that allows child prodigies to see, understand, and interpret their world and their craft differently from other children (Shavinina, 2010, 2016). At all stages of the process, parents and teachers should be aware that they are fostering a vulnerable child, who has an inner drive to master a domain, and whose "rage to learn" is not necessarily driven by a desire to achieve fame, money, or a possible career. Characteristics that are evident early on may be very different from those required for long-term success. Because of this, exceptional achievers need to be part of the decision-making process and given ongoing encouragement to take responsibility for their actions, so that they can grow up to become autonomous adults who are capable of shaping their own lives.

Reflective Questions

1. In what ways do modern conceptions of exceptional performance differ from everyday or more traditional views?
2. What might be the differences between a very talented middle-school band member and an exceptional young musician of the same age?
3. Think of a famous prodigy. How can the various stages of development be described with regard to this person's life? How do they apply to your own biography?
4. Look at some videos from YouTube (or similar internet platforms) that can be found using the search terms "music" or "musical" and "prodigy." By what standards could or would one call them exceptional?
5. How have your own ideas on giftedness and talent changed after reading this chapter? What parts of the discussion did you find most/least convincing?

KEY SOURCES

....

McPherson, G. E. (ed.) (2006). *The child as musician: A handbook of musical development.* Oxford: Oxford University Press.

McPherson, G. E. (ed.), (2016). *Musical prodigies: Interpretations from psychology, music education, musicology and ethnomusicology.* Oxford: Oxford University Press.

NOTE

....

1. In fact, a search reveals many hits, of which some are only exceptional in the eyes of the child's parents, rather than by any generally accepted standards.

REFERENCES

....

Abbott, A., & Collins, D. (2004). Eliminating the dichotomy between theory and practice in talent identification and development. *Journal of Sports Sciences, 22,* 395–408.

Austin, J., Renwick, J., & McPherson, G. E. (2006). Developing motivation. In G. McPherson (ed.), *The child as musician* (pp. 213–238). Oxford: Oxford University Press.

Bamberger, J. (2016). Growing up prodigies: The midlife crisis. *New Directions for Child and Adolescent Development.* In G. E McPherson (ed.), *Music prodigies: Interpretations from psychology, education, musicology and ethnomusicology* (pp. 294–319). Oxford: Oxford University Press.

Bastian, H. G., & Koch, M. (2006). Karrieretraum und traumkarriere [Career dreams and dream careers]. *Das Orchester, 11,* 8–13.

Bazzana, K. (2007). *Lost genius: The curious and tragic story of an extraordinary musical prodigy.* Philadelphia: Da Capo Press.

Bloom, B. (1985). *Developing talent in young people.* New York: Ballantine Books.

Bogunovic, B. (2008). *Muzicki talenat i uspesnost* [Musical talent and successfulness]. Belgrade: Institut za pedagoska istrazivanja.

Côté, J. (1999). The influence of the family in the development of talent in sports. *Sport Psychologist, 13,* 395–417.

Côté, J., Baker, J., & Abernethy, B. (2003). From play to practice: A developmental framework for the acquisition of expertise in team sports. In J. Starkes & K. A. Ericsson (eds.), *Expert performance in sports: Advances in research in sport expertise* (pp. 89–110). Champaign, IL: Human Kinetics.

Ernst, M., & Korelitz, K. E. (2009). Cerebral maturation in adolescence: Behavioural vulnerability. *Encephale, 35*(suppl. 6), 182–189.

Faulkner, R., Davidson, J. W., & McPherson, G. E. (2010). The value of data mining in music education research and some findings from its application to a study of instrumental learning during childhood. *International Journal of Music Education, 28*(3), 1–18.

Feldman, D. H. (1986). *Nature's gambit: Child prodigies and the development of human potential.* New York: Basic Books.

Gagné, F. (2009a). Building gifts into talents: Detailed overview of the DMGT 2.0. In B. MacFarlane & T. Stambaugh, (eds.), *Leading change in gifted education: The festschrift of Dr. Joyce VanTassel-Baska* (pp. 61–80). Waco, TX: Prufrock Press.

Gagné, F. (2009b). Debating giftedness: Pronat vs. Antinat. In L. V. Shavinina (ed.), *International handbook of giftedness* (pp.155–204). New York: Springer.

Gagné, F., & McPherson, G. E. (2016). *Analyzing musical prodigiousness using Gagné's Integrative Model of Talent Development.* In G. E. McPherson (ed.), *Music prodigies: Interpretations from psychology, education, musicology and ethnomusicology* (pp. 3–114). Oxford: Oxford University Press.

Gardner, H. (1999). *Intelligence reframed: Multiple intelligences for the 21st century.* New York: Basic Books.

Howe, M. J. A. (1999). *The psychology of high abilities.* London: MacMillan.

Kenneson, C. (2002). *Musical prodigies: Perilous journeys, remarkable lives.* Portland, OR: Amadeus Press.

Kopiez, R. (2011). The musical child prodigy (Wunderkind) in music history: A historiometric analysis. In I. Deliège & J. W. Davidson (eds.), *Music and the mind: Essays in honour of John Sloboda* (pp. 225–236). Oxford: Oxford University Press.

Kopiez, R., & Lehmann, A. C. (2016). *Musicological reports of early 20th century musical prodigies: The beginnings of an objective assessment.* In G. E. McPherson (ed.), *Music prodigies: Interpretations from psychology, education, musicology and ethnomusicology* (pp. 168–184). Oxford: Oxford University Press.

Lehmann, A. C. (1997). Acquisition of expertise in music: Efficiency of deliberate practice as a moderating variable in accounting for sub-expert performance. In I. Deliège & J. Sloboda (eds.), *Perception and cognition of music* (pp. 165–191). London: Erlbaum (UK), Taylor & Francis.

McPherson, G. E. (2007). Diary of a child prodigy musician (pp. 213–218). In A. Williamon & D. Coimbra (eds.), *Proceedings of the International Symposium on Performance Science 2007* (pp. 213–218). Association of Européen des Conservatoires, Académies de Musique et Musikhochschulen (AEC), November 22–23, Casa da Música, Porto, Portugal.

McPherson, G. E. (2009a). The role of parents in children's musical development. *Psychology of Music, 37*(1), 91–110.

McPherson, G. E. (2009b, August 12–16). Music in our lives: Rethinking musical development, ability and identity. Unpublished Keynote Address at the European Society for the Cognitive Sciences of Music ESCOM 2009 Conference, University of Jyväskylä, Department of Music, Jyväskylä, Finland.

McPherson, G. E. (ed.), (2016). *Musical prodigies: interpretations from psychology, music education, musicology and ethnomusicology.* Oxford: Oxford University Press.

McPherson, G. E., & Hallam, S. (2009). Musical potential. In S. Hallam, I. Cross, & M. Thaut (eds.), *The Oxford handbook of music psychology* (pp. 255–264). Oxford: Oxford University Press.

McPherson, G. E., & Davidson, J. (2006). Playing an instrument. In G. E. McPherson (ed.), *The child as musician* (pp. 331–352). Oxford: Oxford University Press.

McPherson, G. E., Davidson, J. W., & Faulkner, R. (2012). *Music in our lives: Rethinking musical ability, development and identity.* Oxford: Oxford University Press.

McPherson, G. E., & Williamon, A. (2016). Building gifts into musical talents. In G. E McPherson (ed.), *The child as musician: A handbook of musical development.* (2nd ed.). (pp. 340–360). Oxford: Oxford University Press.

Mink, F., & McPherson, G. E. (2016). Music prodigies within the virtual stage of YouTube. In G. E McPherson (ed.), *Music prodigies: Interpretations from psychology, education, musicology and ethnomusicology* (pp. 424–452). Oxford: Oxford University Press.

Mönks, F. J. (1981). Entwicklungspyscholgische Aspekte der Hochbegabtenforschung [Aspects of developmental psychology in giftedness research]. In W. Wieczerkowski & H. Wagner (eds.), *Das hochbegabte Kind* (pp. 38–51). Düsseldorf: Schwann.

Ockelford, A. (2007). *In the key of genius: The extraordinary life of Derek Paravicini.* Hutchinson: London.

Ockelford, A. (2016). Prodigious musical talent in blind children with autism and learning difficulties. In G. E. McPherson (ed.), *Music prodigies: Interpretations from psychology, education, musicology and ethnomusicology* (pp. 471–495). Oxford: Oxford University Press.

Olbertz, F. (2009). *Musikalische hochbegabung: Frühe erscheingsformen und einflussfaktoren anhand von drei fallstudien* [Exceptional musical abilities: Early symptoms and influences. Three case studies]. Münster, Germany: Lit.

Quart, A. (2006). *Hothouse kids: The dilemma of the gifted child.* London: Penguin.

Renzulli, J. S. (1978). What makes giftedness? Reexamining a definition. *Phi Delta Kappan, 60,* 180–184.

Renzulli, J. (2005). The three-ring conception of giftedness: A developmental model for promoting creative productivity. In R. J. Sternberg & J. E. Davidson (eds.), *Conceptions of giftedness.* (2nd ed.). (pp. 246–279). Cambridge: Cambridge University Press.

Révész, G. (1916). *Erwin Nyiregyházy: Psychologische analyse eines musikalisch hervorragenden Kindes.* Leipzig: Verlag von Veit. Translated as *The psychology of a musical prodigy.* International Library of Psychology, Philosophy, and Scientific Method. New York: Harcourt, Brace & Company, 1925. [Reprints, New York: Blom, 1971; London: Routledge, 1999; Whitefish, MT: Kessinger Publishing, 2007].

Rost, D. H., Sparfeldt, J. R., & Schilling, S.R. (2006). Hochbegabung [Exceptional ability]. In K. Schweizer (ed.), *Leistung und leistungsdiagnostik* (pp. 187–222). Heidelberg: Springer.

Ruthsatz, J., & Detterman, D. K. (2003). An extraordinary memory: The case study of a musical prodigy. *Intelligence, 31,* 509–518.

Shavinina, L. (1999). The psychological essence of the child prodigy phenomenon: Sensitive periods and cognitive experience. *Gifted child quarterly, 43,* 25–38.

Shavinina, L. V. (2009a). A unique type of representation is the essence of giftedness: Towards a cognitive-developmental theory. In L. V. Shavinina (ed.), *International handbook of giftedness* (pp. 231–257). New York: Springer.

Shavinina, L. V. (ed.) (2009b). *International handbook of giftedness.* New York: Springer.

Shavinina, L. V. (2010). What does research on child prodigies tell us about talent development and expertise acquisition? *Talent Development & Excellence, 2*(1), 29–49.

Shavinina, L. V. (2016). On the cognitive-developmental theory of the child prodigy phenomenon. In G. E. McPherson (ed.), *Music prodigies: Interpretations from psychology, education, musicology and ethnomusicology* (pp. 259–278). Oxford: Oxford University Press.

Shenk, D. (2010). *The genius in all of us: Everything you've been told about genetics, talent and IQ is wrong.* New York: Doubleday.

Sternberg, R. J. (2005). Intelligence, competence, and expertise. In A. J. Elliot & C. S. Dweck (eds.), *Handbook of competence and motivation* (pp. 15–30). New York: Guilford Publications.

Stevens, (1982). Das Wunderkind in der Musikgeschichte [The prodigy in music history]. Unpublished diss., University of Münster, Germany.

Stoeger, H. (2009). The history of giftedness research. In L. V. Shavinina (ed.), *International handbook of giftedness* (pp. 17–38). New York: Springer.

Stumpf, C. (1909). Akustische Versuche mit Pepito Arriola. *Beiträge zur Akustik und Musikwissenschaft, 4,* 105–115.

UNICEF (2010). *Fact sheet: A summary of the rights under the Convention on the Rights of the Child.* http://www.unicef.org/crc/files/Rights_overview.pdf [accessed November 22, 2017].

Vandervert, L. R. (2007). Cognitive functions of the cerebellum explain how Ericsson's deliberate practice produces giftedness. *High Ability Studies, 18*(1), 89–92.

Vandervert, L. R. (2009a). The appearance of the child prodigy 10,000 years ago: An evolutionary and developmental explanation. *Journal of Mind and Behavior, 30*(1/2), 12–32.

Vandervert, L. R. (2009b). Working memory, the cognitive functions of the cerebellum and the child prodigy. In L. V. Shavinina (ed.), *International handbook of giftedness* (pp. 295–316). New York: Springer.

Vandervert, L. R. (2016a). Working memory in musical prodigies: A 10,000-year-old story, one million years in the making. In G. E McPherson (ed.), *Music prodigies: Interpretations from psychology, education, musicology and ethnomusicology* (pp. 223–244). Oxford: Oxford University Press.

Vandervert, L. R. (2016b). The brain's rapid encoding of rule-governed domains of knowledge: A case analysis of a musical prodigy. In G. E McPherson (ed.), *Music prodigies: Interpretations from psychology, education, musicology and ethnomusicology* (pp. 245–258). Oxford: Oxford University Press.

Vandervert, L. R., Schimpf, P. H., & Liu, H. (2007). How working memory and the cerebellum collaborate to produce creativity and innovation. *Creativity Research Journal, 19*(1), 1–18.

Winner, E. (1996). *Gifted children: Myths and realities.* New York: Basic Books.

Weaver, A. (2005). Reciprocal evolution in the cerebellum and neocortex in fossil humans. *Proceedings of the National Academy of Sciences, 102,* 3576–3580.

Wolpert, D. M., Doya, K., & Kawato, M. (2003). A unifying computational framework for motor control and social interaction. *Philosophical Transactions of the Royal Society of London B, 358,* 593–602.

CHAPTER 4

A FRESH LOOK AT MUSIC THERAPY IN SPECIAL EDUCATION

KATRINA MCFERRAN AND COCHAVIT ELEFANT

The tradition of music therapy with young people in schools reaches back many years, and some pioneers in the discipline developed models of practice that are still influential today. Research has been conducted to underpin these traditions, and systematic analysis of the literature shows that music therapy can yield significant improvements for young people with behavioral and developmental disorders (Gold, Voracek, & Wigram, 2004), and there is a vast array of descriptions of music therapy addressing social, cognitive, physical, and emotional goals in schools (Hooper, Wigram, Carson, & Lindsay, 2008; Jellison, 2000). A range of active and receptive music therapy methods are used with young people who have various disabilities, with two different interventions typically being employed within each session (McFerran, Lee, Steele, & Bialocerkowski, 2009). Musical improvisation lies at the core of many approaches, whether it is used as a stand-alone method, as is frequently the case in mainland Europe and the United Kingdom (Alvin, 1975; Alvin & Warwick, 1992; Nordoff & Robbins, 2004/1971), or as a creative and flexible influence on the use and adaptation of songs in the therapeutic process, as is more common in North America and Australasia (Wigram, 2004).

Although music therapists have remained loyal to styles of practice that are known to be effective, the winds of change are blowing across the discipline (Ansdell, 2002). The increasing focus on collaborative approaches within the field (Twyford & Parkhouse, 2008) highlights that there is more that music therapists can do, not only within traditional sessions but also before and after them (Stige, 2002, p. 118). Contemporary models of practice in allied fields also offer a wealth of new ideas that are gradually being incorporated into music therapy practice in special education. This chapter details a number of considerations that are beginning to change the face of music therapy in schools and concludes by providing one possible vision for how these changes might be embraced in order to make such changes even more transparent and effective. Although many of the ideas are being adopted in contemporary music therapy, this is the first time that they have been presented coherently together.

A BRIEF OUTLINE OF TRADITIONAL PRACTICE

Illustrative Vignette: Individual Music Therapy

> Steven has been receiving music therapy in his special school for two years. He has profound and multiple disabilities as a result of cerebral palsy and an associated cognitive impairment. His language is pre-intentional, and he uses some sounds to communicate basic affective experiences such as happiness and pain, but all other communication relies on carers to interpret his needs, much as parents do with babies. His teachers and parents are enthusiastic about music therapy. When he is in sessions he uses his voice in an expressive way and often reaches out to access instruments, such as wind chimes and carefully placed percussion, in order to participate in music-making. The music therapist provides musical frameworks that encourage and reflect these contributions during their weekly, individual sessions. The structure is regular, beginning with a personalized hello song that incorporates Steven's favorite sounds and moving through a series of specifically composed songs as well as newly created improvisations that match and mirror the sounds being made on that day, with the intention of affirming the young man's identity and capacity to relate to others through music. Regular evaluation shows that Steven has been using his voice more frequently over time and is increasingly consistent in choice making—edging slowly toward intentional communicative gestures within the music therapy sessions.

This description of a typical session with a child at this level of ability illustrates a number of key influences in traditional music therapy. The regular structure in a consistent space is characteristic of a psychodynamic approach (Darrow, 2008, pp. 79–104). In psychodynamic models of therapy, these features provide containment for the client so that she feels safe to express herself freely within the firm boundaries provided by the therapist and his use of music. Although young people with disabilities are not usually able to talk about their internal struggles, the opportunities to communicate about their feelings to others are afforded them because of their potentially highly expressive musical contributions. Music therapists draw on understandings of protomusicality to make meaning from this dyadic encounter within a framework of communicative musicality (Malloch & Trevarthen, 2008). The use of familiar songs that may have been composed specifically for each child serve a different function. Through repetition, a platform for learning is provided so that the young person is able to predict and contribute to the musical structure—a capacity that many of these children have despite severe brain damage (see Eagle, 1996; Ockelford & Welch, chapter 2). Music is uniquely helpful in this regard because incorporating spontaneous and reflective elements that bring the material alive in each rendition can enliven repetition. These learning strategies reflect aspects of a behavioral approach (Darrow, 2008, pp. 105–128) that is well suited to the school system. The final influence that can be felt in this brief vignette is of a person-centered approach (Rogers, 1951) that draws on the concept of self-actualization (Maslow, 1968). Individual music therapy sessions in special education are likely to be client-led, with the musical contributions of the young person serving as the source of decision-making about "where to from here" throughout the session. In addition, the process is highly affirmative, with acceptance being a central value, even when improvements in ability are being sought. The young person is considered to have inherent potential that needs to be acknowledged rather than taught.

Illustrative Vignette: Group Music Therapy

> The group of young people with autism enter the music therapy room in different ways, reflecting their moods and the severity of their disorders. They sit in the same seats each week, and some rock slightly as they wait for the session to begin. As the session gets under way, the music therapist offers a range of choices—what instrument would you like to play, who would like to play first, who would like to play next? This rehearsal of social skills flows easily now that the group is meeting for the fifteenth time, but it was more difficult initially while the therapist was still learning the individual preferences of the group members and what auditory stimuli they were able to cope with. As the session reaches its peak, the music therapist asks the young people to stand up and choose one of the large instruments available around the room—electric and acoustic guitars, an adapted drum kit, microphones plugged into the PA system. She provides a rhythmic framework using a set of congas and gives a verbal cue to begin. The group plays together, and after a while the music therapist begins to move around the room offering the microphone to different players, who pause to sing or vocalize above the improvised music-making. The theme for the improvisation is "Friends," and the music therapist encourages each member to point to other people in the group and use their names. This activity has only been introduced three weeks ago, and some group members fulfil expectations, while others simply vocalize freely.

Although improvisation still maintains an important role in this group vignette, more structure is required to manage a group music therapy session than the client-led model advocated for individual work. Within a therapeutic context, the purpose of group work is to foster relationships between group members, and the achievement of group cohesion is critical in evaluating the success of the group (Yalom, 1995). This is a psychodynamic premise that underpins the more overt behavioral focus on skill acquisition (in this case, social skills). For a group of young people with autism, social skills are particularly challenging, and therefore group work can provide an important platform for learning. The way the methods are implemented is typically humanistic, and instead of following plans in a systematic way, the music therapist adapts the schedule and focus of the group to the emerging abilities and needs that present in the moment. This dynamic process can sometimes result in apparently chaotic musical experiences, with the music therapist allowing a greater freedom of expression and behavior than is typical in the classroom context. Flexibility and creativity are critical elements of natural human interaction, and these are rehearsed in more improvised music-making. The boundaries are wider but still firmly in place, underpinning a therapeutic rather than educational approach, with an emphasis on group cohesion being equally valued with the achievement of social skills.

The decision to work with young people in individual or group sessions is based on an assessment of needs. Those requiring one-to-one attention are better suited to individual sessions, and those with more socially oriented goals are better suited to groups. These needs often present in a sequence from individual to group work. The model of Creative Music Therapy explicitly promotes this natural progression, using a concept labeled the "music child" to explain the initial need for individual work (Nordoff & Robbins, 1977). The music therapist begins by meeting the young person where he is at and then gradually demanding more reciprocity in the musical relationship. This is then further developed from communication and self-expression into social encounters through music. Nordoff and Robbins's model then progresses to the use of musical plays as a further developmental achievement for the group. Archetypal fairy tales are used as the basis for accessing understandings at the level of the collective unconscious, thereby working with many layers of consciousness simultaneously (Nordoff & Robbins, 1971). The emphasis on performance is rare in the music therapy literature, and acknowledging the role of public engagement has been an important influence on recent movement within music therapy toward more participatory approaches. Sharing performances with other students in the school widens the influence of the music therapy encounter (Pavlicevic & Ansdell, 2004).

Although the progression from individual to private group work and then performance is logical, Karen Goodman (2007) describes the challenges of justifying individual work within a school context in the United States. Decisions are more likely to be dictated by timetabling requirements and teacher/parent advocacy than the professional recommendation of the music therapist. Group work is often advocated by school administrators who prefer music therapists to emulate the role of a music teacher and focus primarily on the development of social skills rather than individual relationships. In contrast, when the music therapist is located within a "well-being" team, individual sessions with a psychodynamic orientation are prioritized. Studies of administrators' perceptions of music therapy (Booth, 2004;

Ropp, Caldwell, Dixon, Angell, & Vogt, 2006) reveal that the majority of school leaders do not have experience or knowledge of professional music therapy practice. Since the music therapy treatment process (Davis, Gfeller, & Thaut, 1999) does not progress in the same way that curriculum-based teaching does, this may lead to less than optimal allocation of music therapy time within the timetable, influenced by factors such as funding models, seniority of the individual therapist, or the number of students to be offered a service. Teachers and administrators naturally draw upon models that are familiar to them during the creation of positions and timetables.

Descriptions of individual and group music therapy in special education vary around the globe and across the street. However, the core features of practice described above are present to a greater or lesser degree in a range of contexts. In the remainder of this chapter new influences on music therapy practice will be outlined that are less consistently applied, although increasingly prominent. Despite the success of music therapy in meeting the interpersonal and creative needs of young people with a range of disabilities, the special education context continues to evolve, as does our awareness of the potential of musical encounters.

MEETING NEW EXPECTATIONS

A powerful influence on music therapy practice in special education is the requirements of evidence-based practice. This paradigm has become dominant in the field of education because it segues neatly out of the emphasis on applied behavioral analysis as the gold standard in the field (McFerran & Stephenson, 2007). The framework of evidence-based practice is specific about what types of research are required in order for services to be approved (Pavlicevic, Ansdell, Procter, & Hickey, 2009). Music therapists have traditionally relied on studies that suggest the effect of music as a motivator within a behavioral framework (Standley, 1996) in which music has repeatedly been shown to increase or decrease particular behaviors when systematically applied (Jellison, 2000). Efficacy studies should closely reflect music therapy practice, however, and the blend of humanistic, psychodynamic, and behavioral influences that are typically enacted within a single music therapy session (described above) can make this challenging. Doctoral investigations in Europe provide examples of how these standards can be met by emphasizing skill development whilst also privileging the therapeutic relationship (Elefant & Wigram, 2005; Kim, Wigram, & Gold, 2008), but it is debatable whether the accurately measured interventions reflect everyday music therapy practice.

The strict demands of evidence-based practice provide an opportunity for the music therapy discipline to reflect on the specific role of music therapy in schools, particularly in relation to music education and classroom-based uses of music. Whether skill acquisition is the most valuable contribution made by music therapists in the lives of students with intellectual, physical, or learning disabilities becomes an important question. As described above, learning outcomes are only one part of what happens in music therapy in special education. Sometimes music therapists will be influenced by person-centered approaches to adopt a stance of acceptance within the therapy session, where they listen and respond and spend time being creative with the young person concerned. At other times they will be influenced by psychodynamic theory to seek greater understanding of students through monitoring indications of personality traits, drives, and resources. Promoting the development of communication and fostering social, cognitive and physical skills is only one part of the picture. Perhaps more important, newer models of contemporary music therapy highlight that we could be doing even more. The opportunity to reflect rigorously on what we do also suggests what more we could be doing.

In the following discussion, four contemporary influences on music therapy will be discussed:

1. The importance of titrating the dosage of music therapy
2. An emphasis on the transfer of skills beyond the music therapy room
3. Looking beyond the school environment
4. Collaborating with young people as active participants

TITRATING THE DOSE

Psychotherapists have been increasingly interested in evidence that suggests long-term, ongoing work is not the most effective way to offer therapy services. Titration is emerging as a possible alternative to ongoing psychotherapy and means adjusting the dose of the intervention, usually aiming toward greater independence from therapy. The concept is based on psychopharmaceutic principles and is informed by the same kind of consumer orientation. It questions whether therapy can become addictive by fostering dependence. It also investigates how much time and resources should be required in order to expect noticeable improvements. Meta-analyses by the "common factors" school (Hubble, Duncan, & Miller, 1999) have charted the time trajectory of therapeutic benefit and have repeatedly found that it can be plotted similarly to a standard growth curve (see fig. 4.1 for a visual representation). They cite evidence to suggest that if positive outcomes have not been achieved in the first three to five sessions of psychotherapy, it is unlikely that they ever will be. They also document a plateau in outcomes after approximately 12 sessions and suggest the dosage of therapy should be altered to reflect this change. After initial outcomes have been achieved, less regular sessions should be offered. This does not mean ceasing services, but rather changing the dosage to ensure an efficient and effective sustenance of outcomes. Continued but less frequent contact ensures the strength of the therapeutic relationship so that a return to high dosage levels can be instigated in response to difficult periods in the future.

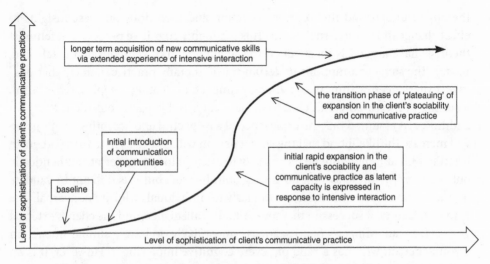

Figure 4.1 The "Dual Aspect Process Model" of Intensive Interaction
(adapted from Firth, 2008).

Psychotherapists are not the only allied professionals to be highlighting these kinds of temporal considerations. Researchers in the emerging field of Intensive Interaction are also pointing to the growth trajectory as a useful framework for intervention (Firth, 2008). Intensive Interaction is a model of communication with people who have severe and profound disabilities that has many similar features to music therapy (Hewett & Nind, 1998). The temporal axis of the growth trajectories identified by Graham Firth's research is longer than 12 sessions because it takes into account the profound nature of cognitive impairment of clients with multiple and profound disabilities. Instead of 12 sessions as an estimation of effective treatment length, they quote research evidence to suggest 12 months as an approximate time frame for effective, sustained communication improvements (see Ockelford & Welch, chapter 2).

The adaptation of Firth's chart in Figure 4.1 reflects a rapid initial period of communicative interaction, where a shared language is developed between the individual and the therapist. This is then seen to plateau, and there is a changing emphasis from an initial achievement of social inclusiveness that is utilized to work toward sustained behavioral change. The second emphasis is expected to extend behaviors that have spontaneously emerged in the initial encounters and to cement them as a part of the individual's communicative repertoire.

TRANSFER OF ACHIEVEMENTS

The expectation that achievements from within a closed therapy session will extend into the broader arena of the young person's world is, once again, based on premises informed by psychodynamic theory. In psychotherapy, clients utilize personal therapy to understand their current situation and then draw on these insights to effect change in their external world. This is a highly cognitive process that feminist theorists have argued is most suited to the affluent and well-educated (McLellan, 1995a). The same assumptions underpin music therapy practice, namely that positive experiences within music therapy impact on young people's self-esteem, resulting in increased confidence to achieve their full capacity outside therapy. In addition, it is assumed that the experience of a respectful and accepting relationship will increase the likelihood that the young person will take risks in trusting others to listen to him and therefore be more likely to attempt to communicate authentically outside therapy. These assumptions may both be true, but it is difficult to validate internal processes such as these, particularly for individuals who are nonverbal. The common factors of successful therapy—alliance, allegiance, and the client's external world (Duncan, Miller, & Sparks, 2004)—most likely do have a similar impact on a young person who has a mild or severe cognitive impairment. However, it is an assumption that could be further investigated.

Speech and language therapists, who also address the development of communication in the special education context, often choose to approach practice differently. Over the past two decades they have moved away from a predominantly individual approach and explored the value of collaborative consultation (Coufal, 1993). Speech therapists use lengthy assessment periods to develop a baseline understanding of a young person's communicative level for further evaluation (Frattali, 1998). This occurs in both private and public settings, so that they see the full range of communicative strategies used by the young person concerned. They aim to feed this information to all those involved in the care of the young person and introduce augmentative communication strategies that are designated as suitable to the individual's level of development. They promote the idea that if young people are approached consistently they will have the best chance of understanding the possibilities for interaction (Elksnin, 1997). Music therapists often reinforce the strategies proposed by speech therapists within their sessions, although it is less common to adopt a consultancy model because of the emphasis on relationships as the basis of therapeutic growth.

Physiotherapists and occupational therapists also tend to take more consultative roles in special education rather than providing regular and ongoing individual service (Rainforth, York, & MacDonald, 1991). They focus on providing strategies for improvement to all those involved in the care of the young person (Lacey & Ouvry, 1998). This service may be in the form of stretches and exercises from physiotherapists, or adapted utensils and equipment from occupational therapists. In both cases, there is no doubt that ongoing one-to-one work may foster more significant skill acquisition, but these professionals do not see this as realistic. Allied health assistants are sometimes employed to carry out some of the repetitive interventions that are considered helpful on a daily basis, but more commonly, teachers and parents are engaged in the practice of these skills. These professionals actively avoid dependence on their services in a way that is distinct from traditional music therapy services with the same kinds of young people. Consultancy models are beginning to be investigated in the music therapy doctoral research, such as Kern's research in early intervention in the United States (2004) and Rickson's (2008) rich examination of the promise of music therapy consultancy in isolated communities in New Zealand.

LOOKING BEYOND THE SCHOOL ENVIRONMENT

Beyond special education, other allied health professionals have moved toward even grander visions for engaging clients as active participants in their growth and health. Community models of music education are documented in this book, as well as being commonplace in social work and increasingly popular in psychology (Rappaport, 1987). Kenneth Bruscia (1998) first explained "ecological music therapy" as focusing on health and social change in addition to personal achievements, whereas conventional models of music therapy tend to maintain an individualistic focus, even within group work. Music therapists have traditionally been very interested in individuals and what they might be able to achieve. However, there is increasing acknowledgment of the importance of looking beyond individuals and considering how actively they participate in their extended context, at the levels of family, community, and culture.

This change of emphasis also impacts on the frameworks that are used to understand the role of music therapy in special education. Instead of emphasizing intersubjective communication founded on parent-infant interaction theory (such as: Stern, 2000; Trevarthen & Malloch, 2000), a participatory orientation focuses on the young person as working toward independence. There is an increased consciousness of where the young person is heading instead of a focus on being in the moment, which is in keeping with a humanistic orientation. More years of individual or group therapy may be valuable but this is not necessarily the only suitable context for music therapy.

An "outward and around" focus (Stige, Ansdell, Elefant, & Pavlicevic, 2010, p. 282) suggests that the music therapist consider if there are other ways that music could be used to achieve different kinds of outcomes. Elefant describes a case where long-standing friendships are developed between young people with and without disabilities when the music therapist responds to the group's desire to engage in music in the mainstream school (in Stige, Ansdell, Elefant, & Pavlicevic, 2010; also detailed by Aigen, chapter 10). She envisages the role music might play not just within the special school but also outside it. Elefant provides an accepting environment where the young people gradually display their potential to one another after a preparatory period where these skills are developed. She cultivates an actively reflective attitude in the group, through which all the young people gradually increase their understandings of one another's abilities and limitations. In response to these features, the group actively participates in taking control of their own destiny, making suggestions about how to further their friendships in a way that ultimately attracts the attention of their community. This is one documented example of how music therapy could expand in the special education context.

An explanatory model for this kind of development can be found in the work of Mercedes Pavlicevic and Gary Ansdell (2009). They explain musical-social development as a tri-leveled progression starting with the theory of communicative musicality in which the dyadic musical experience between the client and the therapist is central. The progression then follows through a stage of social development of collaborative musicing and performance, reminiscent of the early ideas of music therapy pioneers Nordoff and Robbins (1977). The levels of musical development are explained in an inverted pyramid scheme as musicality, musicianship, and musicing, suggesting that the person can progress from one level to the other. This model gives a broader perspective and inspires new possibilities for thinking about the young person from a more ecological perspective.

COLLABORATION WITH THE YOUNG PEOPLE AS ACTIVE PARTICIPANTS

The final, and most challenging, influence to be considered by music therapists highlights a more empowering approach than that adopted traditionally. Some critics consider psychotherapeutic approaches to be disempowering and advocate for a better balance of power between client and therapist (McLellan, 1995b). This perspective has been expounded by Randi Rolvsjord (2010) in relation to models of music therapy with people institutionalized for mental health concerns. Music therapists in Europe have traditionally emphasized improvisation as central to practice, whereas Rolsjvord emphasizes an expansion of practice that aligns with the interests of the participant, such as learning instruments or using preferred songs. School-based music therapists are more familiar with these methods, but reconsiderations of expertise continue to be valuable. "What do you want?" may be a critical question for young people involved in music therapy who can be assisted to find their own voices to express desires about therapy. Although choice making is an inherent part of conventional practice, ranging from choices of instruments and preferred repertoire, to levels of participation, this can be further expanded to involvement in decisions about what kind of music therapy—individual, group, classroom-based, or performance-oriented. Although a high degree of cognitive impairment can make the answer challenging for the therapist to understand, it is not impossible. Typically, however, the student's own voice regarding her musical life is often lost or left unheard among the clamor of different professional discourses. Educational and clinical discourses govern a great part of the daily lives of children with disabilities, affecting their time in the school system and their development toward adulthood. Including the student in decision-making is a worthy possibility that should be considered.

CONCLUSION

This chapter began with illustrations of traditional music therapy practice in special education accompanied by explanations of the underpinning theoretical frameworks that have shaped practice. This was followed by discussion of a number of exciting new developments in practice that will potentially impact on music therapy in special education into the future. A blend of theoretical influences will continue to inform music therapists, but with an increased emphasis on collaboration and empowerment with a consciousness of the young person's life context. The importance of "titrating" dosage suggests not just ongoing evaluation of clinical work, but a more deeply reflexive consideration of how much therapy is helpful and for how long. This alliance with psychodynamic theory can be supplemented by behavioral influences adopted from allied health emphasizing observable achievements that transfer beyond the therapeutic encounter. The transfer of skills can also be understood in an ecological framework, further challenging the music therapist to think beyond functional achievements that transfer to the classroom, and to focus on expansion of the musical relationship to peers, families, and community members. Finally, we have suggested that this actively reflexive approach to program planning should move beyond flexibility on the part of the therapist, and toward a more empowering model that seeks the young person's opinions and desires to inform the changing nature of musical relationships. These suggestions move music therapists out of an established model of practice and into a constantly challenging but exciting approach that demands not only musical and therapeutic skills but also critical thinking. An actively reflexive stance has been advocated by community music therapy theory (Stige, Ansdell, Elefant, & Pavlicevic, 2010) and obliges the music therapist to consider possibilities beyond what is already in place.

As illustrated throughout this volume, understandings of how music can be used to foster education and growth are expanding rapidly. Despite an increasingly restrictive approach to research being adopted by institutional review boards in some countries (Lincoln, 2005), practice on the ground is increasingly health oriented. Music has always played an important role in shaping culture—both reflecting and anticipating cultural change. Aigen (chapter 10) provides an elegant summary of the emerging force of community music therapy as one expression of this within music therapy, while Darrow and Adamek (chapter 6) describe the ways that music therapists and educators use music in public schools to support children with special needs. McFerran's commentary (volume 1, chapter 29) contextualizes these contemporary practices from a cultural perspective, highlighting political influences that have led to the inclusion of music programs in public schools for young people with psychosocial, as well as physical and intellectual, challenges. A number of important considerations have been highlighted, alongside the changing face of music practice described from other disciplinary perspectives. Prescriptive, traditional models are being replaced by active, reflexive approaches that focus on individual's desires both within and beyond the therapy room. This change of emphasis should inevitably incorporate many of the features of conventional practice, but deepen and question them, rather than accept and apply them. The result will be even better quality musical support for young people with disabilities within the special school system.

REFLECTIVE QUESTIONS

1. What are likely to be some of the key challenges for therapists working within the special education system?
2. What strategies are likely to be helpful in maximizing the effectiveness of therapists and educators working together?
3. How can practitioners ensure that children's voices are heard in the decisions concerning therapeutic input?
4. Given finite resources, what criteria should be used for prioritizing which children receive music-therapeutic input?

KEY SOURCE

McFerran, K., Lee, J. Y., Steele, M., & Bialocerkowski, A. (2009). A descriptive review of the literature (1990–2006) addressing music therapy with people who have disabilities. *Musica Humana*, 1(1), 45–80.

REFERENCES

Alvin, J. (1975). *Music therapy*. London: Hutchinson.
Alvin, J., & Warwick, A. (1992). *Music therapy for the autistic child*. Oxford: Oxford University Press.
Ansdell, G. (2002). Community music therapy and the winds of change. *Voices: A world forum for music therapy*, 2(2). http://www.voices.no/mainissues/Voices2(2)ansdell.html.

Booth, R. (2004). Current practice and understanding of music therapy in Victorian special schools. *Australian Journal of Music Therapy, 14*, 64–75.

Bruscia, K. (1998). *Defining music therapy*. Gilsum, NH: Barcelona Publishers.

Coufal, K. L. (1993). Collaborative consultation for speech-language pathologists. *Topics in Language Disorders, 14*(1), 1–14.

Darrow, A.-A. (ed.). (2008). *Introduction to approaches in music therapy* (2nd ed.). Silver Spring, MD: American Music Therapy Association.

Davis, W. B., Gfeller, K. E., & Thaut, M. H. (1999). *An introduction to music therapy: Theory and practice* (2nd ed.). Boston: McGraw-Hill.

Duncan, B. L., Miller, S. D., & Sparks, J. (2004). *The heroic client: A revolutionary way to improve effectiveness through client-directed, outcome-informed therapy* (rev. ed.). San Francisco: Jossey-Bass.

Eagle, C. T. (1996). An introductory perspective on music psychology. In D. Hodges (ed.), *Handbook of music psychology* (2nd ed.) (pp. 1–28). San Antonio, TX: IMR Press.

Elefant, C., & Wigram, T. (2005). Learning ability in children with Rett syndrome. *Brain and Development, 27*(Suppl.1), 97–101.

Elksnin, L. (1997). Collaborative speech and language services for students with learning disabilities. *Journal of Learning Disabilities, 30*(4), 414–426.

Firth, G. (2008). A dual aspect process model of intensive interaction. *British Journal of Learning Disabilities, 37*, 43–49.

Frattali, C. (ed.) (1998). *Measuring outcomes in speech-language pathology*. New York: Thieme.

Gold, C., Voracek, M., & Wigram, T. (2004). Effects of music therapy for children and adolescents with psychopathology: A meta-analysis. *Journal of Child Psychology and Psychiatry, 45*(6), 1054–1059.

Goodman, K. (2007). *Music therapy groupwork with special needs children: The evolving process*. Springfield, IL: C. C. Thomas Publishers.

Hewett, D., & Nind, M. (eds.). (1998). *Interaction in action: Reflections on the use of intensive interaction*. London: David Fulton.

Hooper, J., Wigram, T., Carson, D., & Lindsay, B. (2008). A review of the music and intellectual disability literature (1943–2006). *Music Therapy Perspectives, 26*(2), 66–94.

Hubble, M. A., Duncan, B. L., & Miller, S. D. (1999). *The heart and soul of change: What works in therapy*. Washington, DC: American Psychological Association.

Jellison, J. (2000). A content analysis of music research with disabled children and youth (1975–1999): Applications in special education. In *Effectiveness of music therapy procedures. Documentation of research and clinical practice* (pp. 199–264). Silver Spring, MD: American Music Therapy Association.

Kern, P. (2004). Using a music therapy collaborative consultative approach for the inclusion of young children with Autism in a childcare program. Doctoral diss., Universität Witten/Herdecke, Germany.

Kim, J., Wigram, T., & Gold, C. (2008). The effects of improvisational music therapy on joint attention behaviors in Autistic children: A randomized controlled study. *Journal of Autism and Developmental Disorders, 38*(9), 1758–1766.

Lacey, P., & Ouvry, C. (eds.) (1998). *People with profound and multiple learning disabilities: A collaborative approach to meeting complex needs*. London: David Fulton Publishers.

Lincoln, Y. S. (2005). Institutional review boards and methodological conservatism: The challenges to and from phenomelogical paradigms. In N. K. Denzin & Y. S. Lincoln (eds.), *The Sage Handbook of Qualitative Research* (3rd ed.). London: Sage.

Malloch, S., & Trevarthen, C. (2008). *Communicative Musicality: Exploring the Basis of Human Companionship*. Oxford: Oxford University Press.

Maslow, A. (1968). *Toward a psychology of being*. New York: John Wiley & Sons.

McFerran, K., & Stephenson, J. (2007). Music therapy in special education: Do we need more evidence? *British Journal of Music Therapy*, 20(2), 121–128.

McLellan, B. (1995a). *Beyond psychoppression*. North Melbourne, Australia: Spinifex Press.

McLellan, B. (1995b). *Beyond psychoppression: A feminist alternative therapy*. Melbourne, Australia: Spinifex Press.

Nordoff, P., & Robbins, C. (1977). *Creative music therapy: Individualised treatment for the handicapped child*. New York: John Day Company.

Nordoff, P., & Robbins, C. E. (1971). *Music therapy in special education*. New York: John Day Company.

Nordoff, P., & Robbins, C. E. (1977). *Creative music therapy: Individualized treatment for the handicapped child*. New York: John Day Company.

Nordoff, P., & Robbins, C. E. (2004/1971). *Therapy in music for handicapped children*. Gilsum, NH: Barcelona Publishers.

Pavlicevic, M., & Ansdell, G. (eds.) (2004). *Community music therapy*. London: Jessica Kingsley Publishers.

Pavlicevic, M., Ansdell, G., Procter, S., & Hickey, S. (2009). *Presenting the evidence* (2nd ed.). London: Nordoff-Robbins Music Therapy.

Rainforth, B., York, J., & MacDonald, C. (1991). *Collaborative teams for students with severe disabilities: Integrating therapy and educational services*. Baltimore: Paul Brooks Publishing Company.

Rappaport, J. (1987). Terms of empowerment/exemplars of prevention: Toward a theory for community psychology. *American Journal of Community Psychology*, 15(2), 121–148.

Rickson, D. J. (2008). The potential role of music in special education (The PROMISE): New Zealand music therapists consider collaborative consultation. *New Zealand Journal of Music Therapy*, 6, 76–97.

Rogers, C. (1951). *Client-centered therapy: Its current practice, implications and theory*. London: Constable.

Rolvsjord, R. (2010). *Resource oriented music therapy in mental health care*. Gilsum, NH: Barcelona Publishers.

Ropp, C. R., Caldwell, J. E., Dixon, A. M., Angell, M. E., & Vogt, W. P. (2006). Special education administrators' perceptions of music therapy in special education programs. *Music Therapy Perspectives*, 24(2), 87–93.

Standley, J. M. (1996). A meta-analysis on the effects of music as reinforcement for education/therapy objectives. *Journal of Research in Music Education*, 44(2), 105–133.

Stern, D. (2000). *The interpersonal world of the infant*. New York: Basic Books.

Stige, B. (2002). *Culture-centered music therapy*. Gilsum, NH: Barcelona Publishers.

Stige, B., Ansdell, G., Elefant, C., & Pavlicevic, M. (2010). *Where music helps: Community music therapy in action and reflection*. Surrey, UK: Ashgate.

Trevarthen, C., & Malloch, S. (2000). The dance of wellbeing: Defining the musical therapeutic effect. *Nordic Journal of Music Therapy*, 9(2), 3–17.

Twyford, K., & Parkhouse, C. (2008). Collaborative working in a special needs setting. In K. Twyford & T. Watson (eds.), *Integrated team working: Music therapy as part of transdisciplinary and collaborative approaches* (pp. 62–67).

Wigram, T. (2004). *Improvisation: Methods and techniques for music therapy clinicians, educators and students*. London: Jessica Kingsley Publishers.

Yalom, I. (1995). *The theory and practise of group psychotherapy* (4th ed.). New York: Basic Books.

CHAPTER 5

INCLUSIVE MUSIC CLASSROOMS AND PROGRAMS

JUDITH A. JELLISON

Inclusion as a broad educational policy is not new. The global history of inclusion can be traced in the conventions, declarations, and recommendations of UNESCO, beginning with the establishment of the Universal Declaration of Human Rights by the United Nations (1948), and more recently, UNESCO's Policy Guidelines on Inclusion in Education (2009). In these and other UNESCO documents, inclusion refers to the rights of diverse groups of children to a comprehensive education, including an arts education and cultural experiences (UNESCO, 2006).

UNESCO addresses "special needs education" for the first time in a report from the World Conference on Special Needs Education: Access and Quality (UNESCO, 1994) held in Salamanca, Spain. In the report, *The Salamanca Statement*, the delegates describe the conference as providing "a platform to affirm the principle of Education for All and to discuss the practice of ensuring that children and young people with special educational needs are included in all such initiatives and take their rightful place in a learning society," and state that conference documents were informed "by the principle of 'inclusion', recognizing the need to work towards schools for all" (p. 3). In a call for the education of children who had previously been excluded from regular schools, delegates urge governments to "adopt as a matter of law or policy the principle of inclusive education, enrolling all children in regular schools, unless there are compelling reasons for doing otherwise" (p. 10).

UNESCO's Policy Guidelines on Inclusion in Education (2009) identify areas for deliberations by policy-makers (e.g., attitudes, curricula, teacher education) and call for "further clarification of the term 'inclusive education'" (p. 17). In these guidelines, the definition of inclusion also concerns diverse groups of learners, stating:

> Inclusion is thus seen as a process addressing and responding to the diversity
> of needs of all children, youth and adults through increasing participation
> in learning, cultures and communities, and reducing and eliminating
> exclusion within and from education. It involves changes and modifications
> in content, approaches, structures and strategies with a common vision that
> covers all children of the appropriate age range and a conviction that it is
> the responsibility of the regular system to education all children. (UNESCO,
> 2009, pp. 8–9)

Deliberations among and within countries regarding definitions and practices largely concern the extent to which students with disabilities are to be educated with students without disabilities in regular school and community experiences. Other issues concern the reality of adopting Western models of inclusion in developing countries (Winzer & Mazurek, 2009) and the lack of scientific studies examining inclusive practices (e.g., Kalambouka, Farrell, Dyson, & Kaplan, 2007; Lindsay, 2007). Even as each country clarifies inclusive education in its laws and educational policies, the fundamental premise of inclusion—equity of educational opportunity for children with disabilities—is supported worldwide.

This chapter will not attempt to examine the complex, controversial policy issues concerning educational placements of students with disabilities, but will focus instead on those students who *are* in inclusive music settings and their musical development. The purpose of this chapter is to introduce five broad guidelines for inclusive music programs. Inclusive programs in this chapter are those where (1) students with disabilities attend regular music classrooms in their schools, and are not isolated from their peers without disabilities; (2) students with disabilities interact with their same-age, typically developing peers and participate with them in regular music classes and other age-appropriate school music activities; (3) music and music-related goals are flexible and individualized and instruction is not solely based on disability categories; (4) progress is assessed in a variety of contexts; and (5) music teachers, professionals, and parents collaborate in determining what is important for students to learn and ways to incorporate special supports and services into age-appropriate school, home, and community music activities and experiences. From this perspective, the ultimate goal for inclusive music programs is the development of learning environments where students with and students without disabilities participate successfully and happily in meaningful music experiences.

GUIDELINES FOR INCLUSIVE MUSIC PROGRAMS

Children with disabilities in special schools develop musically when programs are designed and implemented by competent music teachers, but inclusive settings present additional challenges for teachers. What is required for students with disabilities to develop musically in inclusive classrooms? Although there is scant information from the music research literature to answer this question, applications can be made from the vast amount of knowledge from other disciplines. Guidelines in this chapter are grounded in research from theories and research in psychology, special education, and music education, and are adapted specifically from ideas on inclusion presented by Jellison (2015). The guidelines are not mutually exclusive, although the placement of the first guideline in the list below is intentional; all other guidelines contribute to its successful implementation.

Emerging guidelines from empirical, theoretical, and pedagogical sources suggest that the musical lives of children with disabilities can be improved when:

- A meaningful music curriculum is designed to be flexible and accessible, instructional practices are effective, individual adaptations are only as "specialized" as they need to be, and student progress is assessed.
- Culturally normative music experiences and participation in socially valued roles and socially valued activities with typically developing children are part of the routine of daily life.
- Self-determination is fostered in music environments where children feel safe and secure, and where they experience autonomy, demonstrate competence, and make decisions about music, music-making, and other music activities in their lives.
- Interactions with same-age "typical" peers in inclusive music environments are frequent, positive, and reciprocal.
- The design, implementation, and evaluation of an individualized music education program involves collaboration and coordinated efforts among parents/guardians, professionals, other significant individuals in the child's life, and the child (when appropriate).

ACCESS TO MUSIC LEARNING
AND ADAPTATIONS

Historically, goals for many students with disabilities in regular music classrooms were frequently functional (e.g., social, behavioral, daily living), and music participation consisted primarily of listening to music, or occasionally playing a rhythm instrument. However, with increasing pressure from parents whose children were denied access to the general education curriculum offered to "typically developing" students, laws in the United States were revised. The Individuals with Disabilities Education Improvement Act of 2004 required that students have both academic and functional performance goals and assessment of progress. Implications of these new requirements may be interpreted to include music learning goals as well as social and functional goals for children with disabilities in inclusive music classrooms.

The regular music curriculum offered to "typically developing" students will be as accessible as possible to students with disabilities when it is designed to be flexible and adaptations meet students' needs. Although the pedagogical literature in music education and music therapy provides examples of adaptations and strategies for students with disabilities (e.g., Adamek & Darrow, 2005), the systematic study of teaching practices, adaptations, and music learning in inclusive music classrooms is limited to a few research reports as shown in Brown and Jellison 2015) and Jellison and Draper (2015). What is known about the music capabilities of students with disabilities and their music learning has largely come from anecdotal reports and systematic observations of *isolated* skills of individual students in separate settings.

Although research reports provide some evidence of students' learning specific music skills and knowledge, students' musical development has not been systematically studied until recently. Based on survey results showing a lack of music curricula and instruction in special schools in England (Ockelford, Welch, & Zimmerman, 2002), Ockelford (2008) set about developing and implementing a music curriculum for students defined as having complex needs (profound and multiple learning difficulties). Ockelford reports students' musical and nonmusical (e.g., social, communication) development, and his work forms the basis for a framework mapping the musical and nonmusical development of students in the special school sector (first year results are reported in Welch, Ockelford, Carter, Zimmerman, & Himonides, 2009; see also Ockelford & Welch, chapter 2). Since classroom music teachers see the same students for several years, systematic study of the musical development of students in special schools may inform practices related to students with disabilities in inclusive music classrooms.

Curricular Decisions

Meaningful music curricula include both short- and long-term goals that improve the quality of students' lives now and in the future. Parents, guardians, and teachers who know individual children's strengths and needs can help identify appropriate music goals by considering the following: (1) a child's interest and the context for instruction; (2) the number of skills and the kind of knowledge to be learned in the time allotted; (3) whether frequent opportunities will be available to practice using the skills and knowledge in meaningful ways; and (4) whether the skills and knowledge will be used to participate independently, if not fully, in music activities in their schools, homes, and communities, alone and with others.

Music goals form the basis for all school music programs regardless of students' abilities or disabilities, but social goals are also an important part of the music curriculum as they relate to music learning. In some cases, social goals in music settings are similar to goals identified in students' general education programs. In these cases, students will have opportunities to practice applying skills and knowledge in different contexts. In his book *Intelligent Music Teaching*, Duke (2015) proposes a comprehensive list of music and social behaviors that can be performed by musicians at all levels of experience and expertise. Several behaviors selected from this list are presented below:

- Music goals. Skills and knowledge needed for accurate and expressive music performance and successful participation in a variety of music activities (e.g., keep a steady pulse in body movement and musical performance, change dynamic levels and tempo following verbal and nonverbal cues, perform independent part coordinating pulse and dynamic level with ensemble, assume appropriate posture for singing and playing instruments, read and notate music, identify melodic/rhythmic motifs in written and performed music).
- Social goals. Skills and knowledge needed for successful interactions and participation in music classrooms with others (e.g., follow rules and routines, work cooperatively with others, practice self-control, express preferences and interests, compliment performers, evaluate one's own performance and feelings).

Inclusive classrooms are highly complex in that teachers must choose appropriate goals and flexible effective instructional methods for children with varying abilities and disabilities. Music learning activities provide flexibility for teachers to select appropriate goals that meet individual student's needs and to design and implement methods with adaptations necessary for students to reach those goals.

Universal Design

Adaptations of all types (e.g., curricular, instructional, pertaining to materials or the physical environment) have traditionally been individual, in that only the student with a disability is considered in designing the adaptations. Numerous descriptions of adaptations and their applications are found in the literature, and they will not be discussed here. In a more recent approach, individual needs of a student with a disability serve as a catalyst for changes made to the teaching of all students, including typical students. This "universal" approach has as its central premise the design of lessons that are flexible and that allow students with varied abilities and disabilities to be successful and progress in the same curriculum, to the extent appropriate.

The concept of a universal approach comes from the field of architecture and the universal design movement, an outcome of advocacy and legislation for accessibility to buildings and public spaces for persons with mobility impairments. This movement led to the design of environments and products (e.g., ramps, curb cuts to sidewalks, wider doors) that can be used to the greatest extent by all people. Universal design has inspired classroom applications and the development of a framework for designing educational environments. Known as Universal Design for Learning (UDL), this approach is grounded in research on learner differences, effective practices and assessment, and new developments in technology and media (Center for Applied Special Technology, http://www.cast.org/udl; Rose & Meyer, 2006).

UDL views students with disabilities not as a separate group of learners, but as members of a continuum that includes all learners in the classroom. The following principles form the framework to accommodate the wide variety of learning differences that can be found in inclusive classrooms:

- Provide multiple, flexible methods of *presentation*. Give learners various ways to acquire information and knowledge.
- Provide multiple, flexible methods of *expression* and apprenticeship. Offer students alternatives for demonstrating what they know and can do.
- Provide multiple, flexible options for *engagement* in order to help learners get interested, be challenged, and stay motivated (Rose & Meyer, 2006, p. ix).

Although UDL is prominent in special education practices, it is relatively new to music education. Music lessons, however, can be designed to be accessible, equitable, and flexible and reflect principles of a universal approach (Jellison, 2015, 2016). When principles of presentation, expression, and engagement are applied in a universal approach to music education: (1) students with and without disabilities are engaged in a meaningful music activity or task; (2) activities and tasks include multiple ways to participate; (3) important learning goals are not compromised for any student; and (4) the progress of each student is assessed. Consider the following examples where students with disabilities in classrooms may have influenced curricular and instructional decisions:

- A classroom movement activity also includes singing and playing instruments.
- Rehearsals have two short breaks rather than one long break.
- Students work in small groups to develop accompaniments or arrangements using computers or manuscript paper.
- On occasion, students evaluate their performance and set goals for improvement.
- Clear written instructions (rather than spoken only) are distributed for important announcements, and the order of classroom activities/music is written on the board.

Because a universal approach focuses first on the regular curriculum, activities, and routines, it guards against the tendency to "overspecialize" individual adaptations or exclude a student with a disability from a particular classroom activity or task. To increase music achievement in the same types of activities performed by typical classmates, students with disabilities can also participate partially.

Partial participation can be used effectively in a universally designed activity for those students who may not be able to perform all of the goals, activities, or tasks performed by most of their classmates. In some cases, students may even perform an alternative or supplementary goal similar to the overall activity "theme" (arrange pictures of key song words in order with an aide or classmate while the class sings). Although the term "partial participation" was coined several decades ago (Baumgart, Brown, Pumpian, Nisbet, Ford, Sweet, Messina, & Schroeder, 1982), partial participation is now common practice in inclusive classroom settings, and the term has entered the special education lexicon.

In observations of classroom teachers using partial participation, Ferguson and Baumgart (1991) identified common errors that can also occur in inclusive music classrooms when partial participation (1) is limited to one activity (child plays only simple percussion instruments; only listens as classmates perform music); (2) is limited to one small part of the activity (starts the CD player, then watches others engage in an activity); (3) does not include extracurricular music activities (participates in class but does not attend field trips to concerts with classmates); (4) requires a high degree of assistance from other adults or students; (5) occurs only in the presence of the teacher and has no application to other music contexts (activities with typical peers outside school, or parents and siblings in the home); (6) involves an activity that is not valued, respected, or preferred by peers; and (7) requires changes in the activity in such a way that the activity loses its musical or educational value for other students in the class.

Partial participation, and adaptations in general, can increase a student's level of participation and access to the curriculum; however, choices of curricular goals and types of adaptations to reach those goals must be made with a clear understanding of the breadth of implications concerning not only the student's learning (academic, social, and emotional) but also the learning and attitudes of "typical" classmates. These issues are discussed more fully in the next four guidelines.

CULTURALLY NORMATIVE MUSIC EXPERIENCES AND SOCIALLY VALUED ROLES

When students with disabilities in inclusive music settings are, to the extent that is possible, having the same types of experiences as their typical classmates, their experiences are culturally normative. Normalization focuses on how persons with disabilities live and are treated, and is based on the notion that overt differences can be minimized when people with disabilities live and participate in mainstream society. The principle of normalization broadly proposes that culturally normative experiences and activities should be part of daily routines of persons with disabilities, regardless of the severity of the disability (Wolfensberger, 1972). Because of its broad application, the principle of normalization remains an influential concept in disability policies and practices worldwide.

The most influential individuals associated with the development of the principle of normalization are Neils E. Bank-Mikkelsen, Bengt Nirje, and Wolf Wolfensberger (see reprinted original papers in Flynn & Nitsch, 1980). The normalization movement began in Scandinavia in 1959, when Bank-Mikkelsen, then head of the Danish Mental Retardation Service, had a principle written into Danish law "to create an existence for the mentally retarded as close to normal living conditions as possible." Actions in Denmark influenced the Swedish disability advocate Bengt Nirje, who, at the time was secretary general of the Parents Association for Persons with Mental Retardation. Nirje was the first to coin the term "normalization" and clarify its application to the normalization of life's conditions and not the normalization of a person. Nirje was a strong advocate for normalization practices in Europe and the United States, where he influenced educator and scholar Wolf Wolfensberger, best known as an advocate for the normalization principle in the United States.

Living in a community and participating with typical peers in music classes in a neighborhood school are important steps toward normalization; however, normalization practices do not ensure social inclusion and positive social interactions. Wolfensberger (1983) broadened the principle of normalization and formulated a second principle he called social valorization—valuing people with disabilities as a result of their social role. He contends that when an individual with a disability performs roles that are valued, the individual's social image or value will be enhanced. When applied to students in inclusive music settings, it would be expected that negative stereotyping among classmates will decrease and positive perceptions, attitudes, and behaviors will increase when students with disabilities have roles in music activities that are valued by their typical peers (perhaps successfully playing an instrument or singing, or leading a group in a music activity). Knowledge of the effects of socially valued roles on classmates' attitudes is useful when teachers are prioritizing curricular goals for students with disabilities.

FOSTERING SELF-DETERMINATION

The deinstitutionalization and inclusion movements sensitized parents, teachers, advocacy groups, and self-advocates to the need for programs to facilitate the transition of students with disabilities into adult life. This fact is vividly made clear by adults with disabilities who received their education as children in restrictive environments (e.g., institutions), and who lack skills for employment, domestic living, and independence to the maximum extent possible. These problems are being remedied in schools where goals associated with self-determination are included in educational programs and in transition plans for adult life.

Whether self-determination per se can be taught as a curricular goal is questionable. There is, however, a general consensus among professionals that skills *associated* with self-determination (e.g., choice making, self-regulation, problem solving) can be taught, and that these skills can result in positive outcomes for life. Ryan and Deci (2000) propose "relatedness" (feeling safe and secure in interpersonal settings), competence (feeling a sense of achievement), and autonomy (feeling in control) as psychological needs for self-determination. Choices, decisions, preferences, solutions to problems, goals, evaluation, advocacy, and accomplishments not only need to be personal but also *feel* personal.

In a comprehensive curriculum to foster self-determination, students of all ages and with different types and levels of disabilities can experience a degree of autonomy by learning how to ask and respond to questions related to goals, actions, and outcomes (Wehmeyer, 2007; Wehmeyer, Palmer, Agran, Mithaug, & Martin, 2000). To the extent necessary and as appropriate, teachers and classmates offer support throughout this process to help students set goals and develop and evaluate plans. When applied to music instruction, students can ask and answer questions such as "What music do I want to learn?" "What can I play/sing now?" "What must change for me to improve?" "What can I do to make this happen?" "Do I see progress?" With the guidance of music teachers and parents, students can learn to consider options and make decisions about their music experiences. Students can learn the music skills that will increase their competence and confidence, and thus give them more opportunities to make real decisions about their music participation throughout life.

Adults and children who are unaware of the importance of autonomy and choice can diminish important music learning opportunities when they engage in inappropriate assistance and prompting of students with disabilities. In a study of proximity of typical peers to classmates with disabilities, Jellison (2002) observed typical peers unnecessarily assisting, prompting, and interacting. Observations showed individual differences among the "typical" children—a few children were able to refrain from unnecessary helping and remain attentive to the music instruction even when seated close to their peers with disabilities; other typical students were distracted and inattentive when seated close to the same children. Close proximity of *some* classmates can be counterproductive to students' learning and their sense of autonomy and individual achievement. No child's musical development should be hindered as a result of inclusion. Every child must learn to remain attentive to academic instruction and learn when, how, and under what conditions their social interactions and good intentions to help classmates with disabilities will be beneficial.

INTERACTIONS WITH PEERS

As children participate in meaningful music experiences in roles valued by their peers, and as they experience autonomy, demonstrate competence, and make personal choices in inclusive classrooms, so must they learn how to interact positively with their classmates. Many academic and social goals in the music curriculum require cooperation and communication.

Positive peer interactions influence more than social development. Several noted theorists have identified social ecology as a powerful influence on learning outcomes—cognitive, emotional, and social—and research that is grounded in these theories has led to effective educational practices for children with a wide range of abilities and disabilities. Albert Bandura (1977) proposed that learning is closely tied to the environment created by others in the group. Research and practices in education related to observational learning and modeling are directly tied to his theories. One of the more striking examples of modeling can be observed by comparing separate (disabilities only) and inclusive classrooms. With few exceptions, positive models for academic and social behaviors are abundant in regular classrooms, a benefit of inclusive experiences for students with disabilities. Developmental theorist Lev Vygotsky (1935/1978) suggested that social interactions are necessary for overall cognitive development. He emphasized cooperation among peers as a way to build new skills and acquire new knowledge valued by a culture. Vygotsky's ideas led to a practice that is widely recognized among professionals in psychology and education: the practice of cooperative learning.

A large body of research evidence in educational psychology supports the use of cooperative learning strategies. Based on the early work of Maller (1929), Slavin (1980) and Johnson and Johnson (1987) developed explicit protocols and strategies for teachers. Children teaching children, whether through structured small groups or peer tutoring, is an idea that has gained wide acceptance among parents and professionals. The inclination for children to teach and learn from one other is thought to enable the socialization of children into their culture and is viewed as a distinctly human characteristic (Tomasello, 1999). In an early meta-analysis of hundreds of studies examining peer-assisted learning interventions in elementary classrooms, Rohrbeck, Ginsburg-Block, Fantuzzo, and Miller (2003) found positive outcomes related to peer interaction variables (i.e., peer tutoring, small cooperative groups), findings that continue in more recent reviews (e.g., Pai, Sears, & Maeda, 2015). Although students of various ages and abilities can benefit academically from specifically structured peer interactions, these types of interventions are particularly effective for vulnerable students (students in the lower elementary grades, minority students, students at risk, students with disabilities).

Achievement outcomes are related to peer interaction variables, but there are also dramatic outcomes regarding attitudes, attitude formation, and attitude change. Theories on the nature of prejudice (e.g., Allport, 1954) led to hundreds of studies examining the question of whether intergroup contact (face-to-face interactions between members of clearly defined groups—racial, ethnic, disability, elderly, other) reduces prejudice. In a meta-analysis to test intergroup contact theory, Pettigrew and Tropp (2006) found that intergroup contact not only reduced prejudice, but attitude changes generalized to other members outside the group. When teachers structure extended direct positive interactions between students with and students without disabilities, research predicts that negative attitudes toward classmates with disabilities not only will decrease but also will generalize to other children with similar characteristics.

The literature on peer relationships and friendships is too expansive to discuss in detail here, but the effects of these relationships on a child's well-being and success in school are well known. We know that relationships among children, unlike children's relationships with adults, are more open, spontaneous, and in many ways more creative because children develop their own rules, solve their own problems, and construct how and why things work the way they do. Children develop cognitively and socially when they can learn from each other and engage in intimate, constructive conversations. Although other variables can influence success in school, the significance of positive peer relationships is unarguably one of the most powerful.

Music has been used as a strategy to teach social goals (e.g., following instructions, self-regulation) in the field of music therapy and are common variables in music therapy research (Brown & Jellison, 2015). Less prominent in the music research literature is the study of peer interactions and peer-assisted learning strategies between groups of students with and students without disabilities and the effects of these interactions on behaviors and attitudes.

A review of available music research on the topic of attitudes toward individuals with disabilities (Jellison & Taylor, 2007) shows that direct contact, either through small groups or peer-tutoring, increases positive interactions between students with and students without disabilities and improves verbally reported attitudes from typically developing students. Teachers and parents should not assume that positive attitudes and interactions occur naturally, just because music is a part of the environment. Music activities alone will not necessarily result in interactions among children with and children without disabilities (e.g., Jellison, Brooks, & Huck, 1984; Kern & Aldridge, 2006). If a culture of inclusion is to be promoted in the classroom, then teachers must specifically structure positive interactions among students.

Although music research specific to peer interactions is infrequent, music teachers can feel confident in developing strategies for inclusive classrooms that are grounded in theories and research from psychology and special education (Jellison, Brown, & Draper, 2015). Music instruction in inclusive classrooms provides a multitude of opportunities for positive social interactions (e.g., short face-to-face interactions with a stand partner; discussion groups to plan performances or tours; small groups to create improvisations; peer tutoring on individual parts). In a classroom that fosters mutual respect and understanding through positive group interactions, problem solving regarding participation by a student with a disability will occur naturally among the student's classmates. Many teachers have inspiring stories about their students' interactions (Scott, Jellison, Chappell, & Standridge, 2007). Children learn best in a positive classroom environment, and children, learning together, vividly remind us of this fact.

COLLABORATION AND COORDINATED EFFORTS

Competent music teachers independently learn about their students' characteristics, skills, and interests during the course of instruction. However, when students with disabilities are included in music classes, teachers will need to collaborate and coordinate their efforts with other individuals to increase the probability of their students' success.

Collaboration is more than communication. It is a conscious effort on the part of individuals with different areas of expertise to coordinate their efforts to improve the educational experiences of children. Whether through formal or informal discussions, an exchange of information among parents, special educators, music therapists, and other professionals is critical to the curricular and instructional decision-making process. Students with disabilities can contribute their own ideas about their interests, preferences, choices, and ways they can successfully reach goals and participate in activities.

In communication with others about students' needs, music teachers have opportunities to relate information that might otherwise be unavailable. Research in music psychology and music therapy provides evidence substantiating the positive effects of music on physical, emotional, and behavioral responses (e.g., attention, motivation, memory, learning). It is safe to assume that because of the unique nature of music and music activities, music teachers will observe behaviors in their students that may not be observed in environments without music.

Collaboration and coordinated efforts among individuals are understandably prominent ideas in the pedagogical and research literature. Much of the literature on this topic in special education concerns parents (or guardians in the role of parents) and paraprofessionals.

Parents/Guardians

When asked about goals for their children, many parents talk about their children having happy adult lives—enjoying good health, employment, a residence as an adult with some material comforts, and a social life that includes pleasurable activities and friends. Parents' conception of participation concerns not only their children taking part in activities but also that participation contributes to their children's well-being (Eriksson & Granlund, 2004). Parents want their children to have a sense of belonging and self-worth, and they want more than a functional curriculum for their children; they also don't want to feel alienated by their children's schools (Soodak & Erwin, 1995).

Given the many concerns that accompany parenting a child with a disability, parents may not attend to their child's musical development. Parents and special education teachers may recommend music education as a part of their child's educational program solely for social inclusion and development. Music teachers can inform parents of their child's musical achievements, interests, and realistic possibilities— opportunities for music participation not only during school years, but music participation for recreation and leisure outside of school and throughout life. We can expect parents of a child with disabilities, like most parents, to be delighted to hear about their child's music achievements, and this information will also reinforce the idea that music is an important academic subject in their child's educational program.

Paraprofessionals

Paraprofessionals (classroom aides) often have frequent contact with students and teachers in inclusive classes. Giangreco and his colleagues have published extensively on the role of paraprofessionals in inclusive classrooms and have reviewed the literature on this topic (Giangreco, Suter, & Doyle, 2010). Observations show that paraprofessionals can offer effective personal supports for students, but their presence can also be detrimental when roles and duties are not defined. Paraprofessionals can impede students' musical and social development by assuming the role of a music teacher (determining when and how the student will participate), thus limiting students' opportunities for choice, independent performance, and interactions with their music teacher and classmates. Music teachers can encourage paraprofessionals to work more creatively and productively in inclusive music settings. Although they may assist with music instruction (with supervision), the musical development of students must remain the responsibility of music teachers. When roles have been clearly established, music teachers and paraprofessionals are in positions to collaborate and develop effective, efficient, and meaningful ways for students to participate and progress musically.

CLOSING

Continuing efforts of the global community to uphold children's rights to education and cultural participation, and national special education laws and policies, are changing the lives of children with disabilities. Increasing numbers of children with disabilities now have access to the curricula offered to "typically developing" children in inclusive classrooms and programs. In the absence of music research to inform curricular and instructional decisions for inclusive music settings, music teachers can use guidelines that emerge from empirical, theoretical, and pedagogical sources in special education and psychology. Guidelines for inclusive music classes and programs focus on the musical development of children with disabilities in accessible music programs, their social and emotional development, and the importance of collaboration for the development of meaningful music experiences in school and music participation throughout life. Denied educational opportunities for decades, children with disabilities are now learning alongside their classmates without disabilities, interacting with them, developing musically, and becoming independent, competent, and self-confident. By doing so, they are more fully enjoying the varied and rich musical experiences that life has to offer.

REFLECTIVE QUESTIONS

1. What are likely to be the main barriers to successful inclusion in music education in different countries, states, and even different schools?
2. Given that educational policies affect the lives of children who struggle academically and socially in school, what can any individual music teacher do to facilitate successful inclusion practices and improve the quality of children's musical lives?
3. What are the likely benefits and challenges for children without disabilities in music classrooms with classmates with disabilities?
4. Looking to the future, what skills, knowledge, and experiences are essential for the preparation of music teachers who will meet a variety of challenges in classrooms with children who vary considerably in capabilities, interests, and levels of motivation?

KEY SOURCE

Jellison, J. A. (2015). *Including everyone: 'Creating music classrooms where all children learn.* New York: Oxford University Press.

REFERENCES

Adamek, M. S., & Darrow, A. A. (2005). *Music in special education.* Silver Spring, MD: American Music Therapy Association.
Allport, G. W. (1954). *The nature of prejudice.* Reading, MA: Addison Wesley.

Bandura, A. (1977). *Social learning theory*. Englewood Cliffs, NJ: Prentice Hall.

Baumgart, D., Brown, L., Pumpian, I., Nisbet, J., Ford, A., Sweet, M., . . . Schroeder, J. (1982). Principle of partial participation and individualized adaptations in educational programs for severely handicapped students. *Journal of the Association for Persons with Severe Handicaps, 7*, 17–27.

Brown, L. S. & Jellison, J. A. (2015). Music research with children and youth with disabilities and typically developing peers: A systematic review. *Journal of Music Therapy, 49*, 335–364.

Center for Applied Special Technology. *Summary of universal design for learning concepts*. http://www.cast.org/udl [accessed November 22, 2017].

Duke, R. A. (2015). *Intelligent music teaching*. Austin, TX: Learning and Behavior Resources.

Eriksson, L., & Granlund, M. (2004). Conceptions of participation in students with disabilities and persons in their close environment. *Journal of Developmental and Physical Disabilities, 16*, 229–245.

Ferguson, D. L., & Baumgart, D. (1991). Partial participation revisited. *Journal of the Association for Persons with Severe Handicaps, 16*, 218–227.

Flynn, R. J., & Nitsch, K. (eds.) (1980). *Normalization, social integration, and community services*. Baltimore: University Park Press.

Giangreco, M. F., Suter, J. C., & Doyle, M. B. (2010). Paraprofessionals in inclusive schools: A review of the literature. *Journal of Educational and Psychological Consultation, 20*, 41–57.

Jellison, J. A. (2002). On-task participation of typical students close to and away from classmates with disabilities in an elementary music classroom. *Journal of Research in Music Education, 32*, 228–247.

Jellison, J. A. (2015). *Including everyone: Creating music classrooms where all children learn*. New York: Oxford University Press.

Jellison, J. A. (2016). Including everyone: A universal approach. In G. E. McPherson (ed.), *The child as musician* (2nd ed.) (pp. 361–372). New York: Oxford University Press.

Jellison, J. A., Brooks, B., & Huck, A. M. (1984). Structuring small groups and music re-inforcement to facilitate positive interactions and acceptance of severely handicapped students in the regular music classroom. *Journal of Research in Music Education, 32*, 243–264.

Jellison, J. A., Brown, L. S., & Draper, E. A. (2015). Peer assisted learning and interactions in inclusive music classrooms: Benefits, research, and applications. *General Music Today*, 1–5.

Jellison, J. A., & Draper, E. A. (2015). Music research in inclusive schools settings: 1975–2013. *Journal of Research in Music Education, 62*, 325–331.

Jellison, J. A., & Taylor, D. M. (2007). Students with disabilities, inclusion, and attitudes: A review of music research (1975–2005). *Bulletin of the Council for Research in Music Education, 172*, 9–23.

Johnson, D. W., & Johnson, R T. (1987). *Learning together and alone: Cooperative, competitive, and individualistic learning* (13th ed.). Englewood Cliffs, NJ: Prentice-Hall.

Kalambouka, A., Farrell, A. D., & Kaplan, I. (2007). The impact of placing pupils with special educational needs in mainstream schools on the achievement of their peers. *Educational Research, 49*, 365–382.

Kern, P., & Aldridge, D. (2006). Using embedded music therapy interventions to support outdoor play of young children with autism in an inclusive community-based child care program. *Journal of Music Therapy, 43*, 270–294.

Lindsay, G. (2007). Educational psychology and the effectiveness of inclusive education/mainstreaming. *British Journal of Educational Psychology, 77*, 1–24.

Maller, J. B. (1929). *Cooperation and competition*. New York: Teachers College, Columbia University.

Ockelford, A. (2008). *Music for children and young people with complex needs.* New York: Oxford University Press.

Ockelford, A., Welch, G. F., & Zimmerman, S. A. (2002). Music education for pupils with severe or profound and multiple difficulties—current provision and future need. *British Journal of Special Education, 29,* 178–182.

Pai, H., Sears, D. A., & Maeda, Y. (2015). Effects of small-group learning on transfer: A meta-analysis. *Educational Psychology Review, 27,* 79–102.

Pettigrew, T. F., & Tropp, L. R. (2006). Interpersonal relations and group processes. *Journal of Personality and Social Psychology, 90,* 751–783.

Rose, D. H., & Meyer, A. (2006) (eds.). *A practical reader in universal design for learning.* Cambridge, MA: Harvard University Press.

Rohrbeck, C. A., Ginsburg-Block, M. D., Fantuzzo, J. W., & Miller, T. R. (2003). Peer-assisted learning interventions with elementary school students: A meta-analytic review. *Journal of Educational Psychology, 95,* 240–257.

Ryan, R. M. and Deci, E. L. (2000). Self-determination theory and the facilitation of intrinsic motivation, social development, and well-being. *American Psychologist, 55,* 68–78.

Scott, L. A., Jellison, J. A., Chappell, E. W., & Standridge, A. A. (2007). Talking with teachers about inclusion: Perceptions, opinions and experiences. *Journal of Music Therapy, 54,* 38–56.

Slavin, R. E. (1980). Cooperative learning. *Review of Educational Research, 50,* 315–342.

Soodak, L. C., & Erwin, E. J. (1995). Parents, professionals, and inclusive education: A call for collaboration. *Journal of Educational & Psychological Consultation, 6,* 257–276.

Tomasello, M. (1999). *The cultural origins of human cognition.* Cambridge, MA: Harvard University Press.

UNESCO. (1994). *World conference on special needs education: Access and quality.* http://unesdoc.unesco.org/images/0009/000984/098427eo.pdf.

UNESCO. (2006). *Road Map for Arts Education.* Paris: UNESCO. http://unesdoc.unesco.org/images/0017/001778/177849e.pdf

UNESCO. (2009). *Policy guidelines on inclusion in education.* Paris: UNESCO. http://unesdoc.unesco.org/images/0017/001778/177849e.pdf

United Nations (1948). The universal declaration of human rights. http://www.un.org/en/universal-declaration-human-rights/index.html [accessed November 22, 2017].

Vygotsky, L. (1935/1978). *Mind in society: The development of higher psychological processes.* Cambridge, MA: Harvard University Press.

Wehmeyer, M. L. (2007). *Self-determination: Instructional and assessment strategies.* Thousand Oaks, CA: Corwin Press.

Wehmeyer, M. L., Palmer, S. B., Agran, M., Mithaug, D. E., & Martin, J. E. (2000). Promoting causal agency: The self-determined model of instruction. *Exceptional Children, 66,* 439–453.

Welch, G., Ockelford, A., Carter, F-C., Zimmerman, S. and Himonides, E. (2009). "Sounds of Intent": Mapping musical behaviour and development in children and young people with complex needs. *Psychology of Music, 37,* 348–370.

Wolfensberger, W. (1972). *The principle of normalization in human services.* Toronto: National Institute on Mental Retardation.

Wolfensberger, W. (1983). Social role valorization: A proposed new term for the principle of normalization. *Mental Retardation, 21,* 234–239.

Winzer, M., & Mazurek, K. (2009). Inclusive schooling; Global ideals and national realities. *Journal of International Special Needs Education, 12,* 1–9.

CHAPTER 6

PREPARING FOR THE FUTURE: MUSIC STUDENTS WITH SPECIAL EDUCATION NEEDS IN SCHOOL AND COMMUNITY LIFE

ALICE-ANN DARROW AND MARY S. ADAMEK

Students with disabilities entering school and community life today will find greater acceptance and accessibility than students in the not-so-distant past. Due to antidiscrimination laws such as the Americans with Disabilities Act of 1990 in the United States and the Disability Discrimination Act in the United Kingdom (1995, extended in 2005), life in general is easier for many individuals with disabilities. Nevertheless, our work as educators of and advocates for persons with disabilities is not complete. Many challenges remain ahead for those who wish to see full access to school and community life for individuals with disabilities. These challenges encompass all facets of life: educational, social, medical, vocational, and financial. The purpose of this chapter, however, is to describe the present status of music education for students with disabilities, and to provide recommendations for the future regarding the musical lives of students with disabilities.

A Note about the Disability-Related Terminology Used in this Chapter

The American Psychological Association's style manual (American Psychological Association, 2009) states that when identifying a person with a disability, the person's name or pronoun should come first, and descriptions of the disability should be used so that the disability is identified, but is not modifying the person. A similar kind of "people first" terminology is also used in the United Kingdom, but more often in the form "people with impairments" with impairments referring to a medical or health condition. In the United Kingdom, the term "disabled people" is generally preferred to "people with disabilities" (Glasgow Centre for Inclusive Living, 2008). It is argued under the social model of disability (Davis, 1996) that "disability" is something created by external societal factors, such as physical or organizational barriers, or negative or exclusive attitudes (whether intended or inadvertent), and it is these that are the ultimate factors defining who is disabled in any particular society. The term "disabled people" is also widely used by international organizations, such as Disabled Peoples' International. It is important for professionals in the field of disability to understand and to respect all views concerning terminology; however, due to the writing and language habits of the authors, this chapter will follow the American Psychological Association's style manual regarding terminology.

As authors of this chapter, we have attempted to be as geographically inclusive as possible; however, our primary frame of reference is the United States, and that should be noted. We acknowledge that some countries may be more forward thinking than the United States, and others less so, regarding educational services for students with disabilities. Consequently, we have attempted to moderate our professional assertions without negating the purposes of this chapter, which is to provide status summaries and proposals for the future regarding the profession of music education.

The Present Status of Music Education for Students with Disabilities

The music classroom has long served as a typical placement for students with disabilities. Music educators were pioneers in the movement to integrate students with disabilities into the regular classroom (Atterbury, 1990; Graham & Beer, 1980). Music has been a component of some special education programs as far back as the early 1800s, when Jean-Marc-Gaspard Itard (1775–1838) and others utilized music in the diagnosis and treatment of speech and hearing problems. In addition, music was found to be effective to teach auditory and speech skills to students with cognitive impairments (Solomon, 1980). In the early years, there were few expectations for students with disabilities in terms of their musical growth. Their placements in music classrooms were primarily for therapeutic and social integration purposes. In the past 25–30 years, increasingly greater emphasis has been placed on providing them with opportunities to become competent musicians (Adamek & Darrow, 2010). Educators have come to realize that it is possible for many students with disabilities to develop music skills commensurate with their peers if they are provided the necessary instructional support (Veenman & Elshout, 1995; Yaman, Nerbel, & Bayrhuber, 2008). Music educators today are responsible for providing all students with opportunities to sing, play, listen, read, and create music, as well as to learn about its history and cultural contexts (NAfME, 2014).

Beyond changes in the purposes of music instruction for students with disabilities, current practices in both music and general education have evolved from focusing on the students' cognitive, physical, or sensory deficits to minimizing these deficits and maximizing their strengths. Students with disabilities have come a long way from the days when they were hidden away behind the doors of institutions or special education classrooms. These students now have access to public education, and—with that—all areas of arts education. There are a number of basic philosophical principles that provided the foundation for this evolution in the education of students with disabilities (Jellison, 1999; Kochhar, West, & Taymans, 2000):

1. The *human potential movement* is based on the belief that all people have the desire to develop in positive ways. This philosophy promotes a society that provides basic rights and equal opportunities for all individuals, including educational and social service opportunities. These educational opportunities and support services must be appropriate to the individual's developmental level and needs. Additional supports may be required to compensate for a person's disabilities.

2. The *general system theory* is based on the premise that educators must examine the student as a whole person and collaborate with others to provide an integrated approach to the individual's education. Individuals are viewed as more than the sum of their parts. All aspects of a student, the student's environment, and resulting interactions must be addressed. Using this educational approach, the teacher assesses the various needs of students and the impact of environment on their behavior and learning.

3. The *principle of normalization* reflects the belief that individuals with disabilities should have experiences as close as possible to those of their typical-developing peers. This principle provided the foundation of the civil rights movement for persons with disabilities. The principle of normalization has many implications for the classroom and school settings. With normalized life experiences, students with disabilities have opportunities for increased community integration and social interactions with peers, and ultimately, improved quality of life.

4. The *self-determination movement* promotes students' and families' empowerment and their decision-making rights regarding services impacting the future. Characteristics such as assertiveness, creativity, flexibility, and self-esteem, and skills such as problem solving and decision-making, are developed throughout the student's education to promote self-determination as an adult.

As a result of the inclusion movement in education, the number of students with disabilities in music classrooms has increased dramatically over the past 20 years (Adamek & Darrow, 2010). Consequently, some school districts have hired music therapists to provide services to students with the most severe disabilities. According to the *AMTA Sourcebook* (AMTA,2013), one of the largest client populations in music therapy is public school children with disabilities. Though their educational objectives generally differ, both music educators and music therapists play important roles in the musical lives of students with disabilities.

THE ROLE OF MUSIC EDUCATORS AND THERAPISTS IN RELATION TO STUDENTS WITH DISABILITIES

While both music educators and music therapists engage students in music-making experiences, the goals for each discipline are different. There is overlap in the two professions, as both are concerned with students' musical growth and development. The primary difference, however, is the type of goals targeted by each discipline. Music educators specialize in the acquisition of musical knowledge, skills, and appreciation, while music therapists use music primarily to achieve nonmusic goals, such as physical, social, and emotional goals (Adamek & Darrow, 2010; Daveson & Edwards, 1998; McFerran & Elefant, chapter 4). Below are examples of the variety of roles music educators and music therapists play in schools. Any of these roles might be combined for music educators or music therapists, depending on their professional certifications, licensures, and experiences.

Music Educator as the Primary Service Provider for Adapted Music Classes

In addition to teaching students in standard inclusive music classes (general music, band, chorus, orchestra, etc.), some music educators teach "adapted music" or "special music education" classes with students who have severe disabilities. These students are typically educated in self-contained classrooms and are not usually included in the general education music class, due to the severe nature of their disabilities or the lack of appropriate inclusive music classes. For example, a high school may have several performing groups for students, including chorus, band, and orchestra. The students who do not have the prerequisite skills for a performance group but enjoy music participation are educated in a special "adapted music" class taught by the music educator. The students learn about music through engaging in music-making activities such as singing, listening, instrument playing, and movement experiences at their level of ability. Performance is not a focus of this class; however, the students may perform for their peers in a "reverse mainstreaming" situation.

Primary instructional focus: provides opportunities for students to participate in music experiences with others and to learn basic music skills at a developmentally appropriate level.

Music Therapist as the Primary Service Provider for Adapted Music Classes

In another district, a music therapist who is trained to work with students with disabilities facilitates this type of "adapted music" class or "special music education" class, while the music educators teach the regular education inclusive classes. The school uses a music therapist to deliver the instruction because of the therapist's education and experience with children and youth who have disabilities. Adapted music classes can be offered at all age levels, from very young children through to young adults.

Primary instructional focus: provides opportunities for students to participate in music experiences with others and to learn basic music skills at a developmentally appropriate level. Therapist also structures music experiences to address students' Individual Education Plan (IEP) goals.

Collaboration between the Music Educator and Music Therapist to Teach Music Classes for Students with Disabilities

A music therapist coteaches with a music educator in general music classes, in ensembles, and/or in self-contained special education classrooms. The music therapist adapts the instruction of the music educator for students with disabilities. The music therapist might also serve as a consultant to the music educator to help with various adaptations necessary for students' musical growth.

Primary instructional focus: provides opportunities for students to participate in music experiences with others and to learn basic music skills in an inclusive classroom setting. In addition, the music therapist assists the music educator in adapting music, instruments, or other instructional materials to meet the abilities and educational needs of students with disabilities.

Music Therapist Providing Music Therapy Services to Students with Disabilities

The music therapist provides district-wide music therapy services for students in special education, including sessions based on students' Individual Education Plan (IEP) goals. In this situation, the music therapist usually travels to several schools to provide services only to students with disabilities. The music therapy sessions focus on students' general IEP goals, such as increased attention to task, improved socialization, or improved academic skills. For some students, these sessions are in addition to their inclusive music education class, or take the place of the inclusive experience. The music therapist might also provide one-to-one sessions for students who qualify for music therapy as a related service. In order for schools to provide music therapy as a related service, the music therapist assesses a student for eligibility to determine if music therapy is necessary for the student to make progress toward IEP goals. If music therapy as a related service is recommended, the intervention team (commonly called the Individual Education Plan or IEP team in the American. education system) will decide if the service is viable, and if so, in what type of setting (direct services—either one-to-one or group, or only consultative services). The music therapy services in this instance are focused specifically on the student's IEP goals.

Primary instructional focus: using music for development in non-music areas such as increased communication skills, or improved attainment or behavior. Using music to assist individual students' progress on IEP goals.

The Role of Community Music Educators

Music education and music therapy positions are often targeted for budget cuts during difficult economic times. When there is no school music program, community music educators become the sole providers of students' music education. Community music educators are those who teach music privately, or who conduct music groups such as church and civic choirs or other public music ensembles. Even when school music programs are available, many students with disabilities wish to participate in such programs. Community music educators, such as private piano teachers or church choir directors, often have limited training in working with young people who have disabilities. Such coursework is not usually a part of church music or piano degree programs. Fortunately, many community music teachers have shared their experiences and provided a type of peer education by publishing articles in their professional journals (Barss, Marrion, Haroutounian, & Benham, 1999; Gougoux et al., 2004).

Beyond training, the primary difference between the practices of public school music educators or therapists and community educators is their legal obligation to teach students with disabilities. Community music educators may consider it their moral obligation to teach students with disabilities; however, they may also choose their students, and if they wish, exclude certain students. There are no laws known (to the authors) that govern the practices of private music teachers. In contrast, there are laws that govern the public education of students with disabilities in many countries.

LAWS GOVERNING MUSIC EDUCATION
AND MUSIC THERAPY SERVICES

One of the most notable pieces of legislation in the United States was P.L. 94–142 (1975), the Education for All Handicapped Children Act, later renamed Individuals with Disabilities Education Act (1990), and revised and reauthorized as the Individuals with Disabilities Education Improvement Act 2004 (IDEA 2004). Six basic underlying principles for special education services in public education were established through this important legislation (Rothstein, 2000; Turnbull & Turnbull, 2000):

1. Zero reject, free and appropriate public education must be provided for all children with disabilities.
2. Nondiscriminatory evaluations must be used to determine eligibility and need for services.
3. Educational services must be provided in the least restrictive environment.
4. Services must be individualized to meet the needs of the student;
5. Parents have the right to be included and involved in the development of their child's educational program.
6. Procedural protections must ensure that the requirements of the law are met.

Based on these principles, no child can be denied a free and appropriate public education, and that includes access to music education, and music therapy services as well if it is determined these services are necessary to meet the goals of a student's education plan. Music educators and music therapists who work in inclusive music classrooms are required (Adamek & Darrow, 2008) to:

1. Know the impact of students' disability on their ability to participate and to learn in the music classroom
2. Be able to implement instructional accommodations and modifications that will assist students in achieving the highest academic level or level of musicianship possible
3. Be able to evaluate students' progress appropriately
4. Create opportunities for positive interactions between students with and without disabilities

TYPICAL PATTERNS OF SERVICE PROVISION FOR LEARNERS WITH SPECIAL NEEDS

Various approaches to providing music education and music therapy services to students with disabilities were listed earlier in this chapter. In summary, where music education is the primary focus, music educators typically teach students with disabilities included in the regular education music class, or in a smaller self-contained classroom consisting of only students with disabilities. It is important to note there are numerous ways to provide additional support to students with disabilities in both types of settings. Teachers can make modifications to the standard music curriculum, construct an alternative music curriculum, adjust their instructional styles, provide additional peer or adult support, alter musical goals and corresponding assessments, provide alternative ways to deliver instruction (visually, tactually, aurally, etc.) and for students to respond to instruction (orally, manually, technologically, etc.), adjust the difficulty of musical tasks or the time allotted to learn new tasks, and finally, alter or modify the classroom environment. The purpose of all of these supports is to create more successful learning experiences for students with disabilities (Adamek & Darrow, 2010). Music educators often find that these types of instructional adaptations benefit students without disabilities as well.

STRENGTHS AND WEAKNESSES OF CURRENT SERVICE PROVISIONS

Teachers, administrators, and parents, and sometimes the student, are the primary decision-makers in determining how educational services are delivered to students with disabilities. Settings and services can be tailored to a student's specific educational needs. Nevertheless, each of the various services and settings may provide educational and social benefits or incur educational and social barriers.

Benefits of Inclusive Music Class Instruction:

- Typically developing peers often provide positive models for behavior and music skills.
- Students with disabilities have increased opportunities for normalized peer interactions.
- Students have access to typical music education curriculum and performance opportunities.
- Students are able to demonstrate a talent or skill in music that might have gone undetected due to focus on students' disability.

Challenges of Inclusive Music Class Instruction

- Students with disabilities might not be able to keep up or to access the information and materials without extensive modifications by the teacher.
- Teachers may not have the expertise or the time necessary to prepare adapted instructional materials.
- Students with disabilities may unwittingly be ignored because music educators do not have training or experience with students who have disabilities and thus feel unprepared and lack the confidence to teach them.

Benefits of Separate Music Classes:

- More attention can be given to the specific learning needs of students.
- Students may have better access to materials and information through modifications to curriculum and instructional adaptations made by the teacher.
- Students with disabilities are more likely to have opportunities to take leadership roles.
- Generally, separate music classes have fewer students.

Challenges of Separate Music Classes:

- Students with disabilities lack positive peer role models and social interaction with "typically developing" peers.
- "Typically developing" students do not learn acceptance of others who may be different.
- Because of their smaller size, special education classes are often combined for music education instruction—resulting in a wide range of student disabilities or behavioral issues that make it difficult for teachers to adapt instruction and to modify teaching materials.

RECOMMENDATIONS FOR THE FUTURE

All students are capable of music learning (see Ockelford & Welch, chapter 2). It is music educators who must determine if they are capable of instructing all students. Inclusive music education is like many other ideals—the premise is readily accepted, but its implementation is often difficult. The challenge for the future is to prepare a new generation of music educators who are not only confident and competent but also eager to teach students with a wide range of abilities. University faculties in music education may wish to take the following suggestions into consideration as they prepare future teachers.

Increased monitoring to determine the extent to which students with disabilities participate in music education programs. "What was old is new again" is often and unfortunately a maxim in educational "reform." Educators must be mindful that inclusive educational practices remain an option, and that "special classes" for "special students" are not reintroduced as the sole strategy for educating students with disabilities. Questions that music educators might ask are: What are the patterns of participation in music by students with disabilities? Do students participate more at one level than another (primary versus secondary) or in certain types of music classes than others (general music classes versus ensembles)? Do their patterns of participation differ from those of students without disabilities? If so, what might be the reasons? Are patterns of exclusion evident? For example, do students with disabilities participate significantly less in auditioned or advanced ensembles than do their typical-developing peers?

Incorporation of universal design instruction. For many years, the term "special education" was used to denote the education of students with disabilities in either segregated or mainstreamed classrooms. The term "special education" is swiftly fading from the lexicon of academia. In today's schools, all education is considered to be "special." Educational reformers are embracing the concept of universal design, whereby instruction is equitable, and flexible enough to be applicable to all students regardless of their abilities or differences (Burgstahler, 2007a, 2007b). Universal design is sometimes referred to as inclusive design, or design-for-all. The principles of universal design were first applied to architectural models with the goal of providing individuals with barrier-free structures—such as wide interior doorways or lever doorknobs. The same principles of parity are now being applied to academic instruction. Universal design instruction (UDI) operates on the premise that the planning and delivery of instruction, as well as the evaluation of student learning, can incorporate inclusive attributes that accommodate learner differences without excluding learners, and without compromising academic standards (Bowe, 2000; Rose & Meyer, 2006). Examples of UDI are real-time captioning of lectures for students with hearing losses, use of text-to-speech technology, or tactile graphs and maps for students with vision losses. Applying the principles of universal design necessitates flexible goals, instructional methods, materials, and assessments that can accommodate all students.

Increased inclusion of students with disabilities as participants in music education research. A considerable body of music research exists relating to students who have disabilities (Jellison & Draper, 2015); however, students with disabilities are often excluded as participants in music education research in order to develop a standard or profile of the "norm." Inclusive classrooms, which include students with disabilities, should now be considered the "norm"; therefore, students with disabilities should be included in music education research, regardless of their sensory, cognitive, or physical disabilities. The principles of universal design can be applied to educational research as well as to educational instruction. Below is a brief summary of the seven universal design principles (Connell et al., 1997) and how they might be applied to research with all students. Not all of the principles will apply to all research in music education; however, researchers' understanding and application of these principles will broaden the usefulness of their research findings, and ultimately the implementation of their findings into practice.

Seven Principles of Universal Design

1. *Equitable use*—the research findings are applicable to students with diverse abilities.
2. *Flexibility in use*—the research procedures are appropriate for a wide range of student abilities.
3. *Simple and intuitive use*—procedures are easily understood, regardless of participants' experience, knowledge, language skills, or concentration level.
4. *Perceptible information*—the researcher communicates necessary information effectively to participants, regardless of ambient conditions or participants' sensory disabilities or cognitive functioning.
5. *Tolerance of error*—the researcher minimizes hazards and adverse consequences of participants' accidental or unintended actions.
6. *Low physical effort*—procedures can be efficiently and comfortably carried out with minimal participant fatigue.
7. *Size and space for approach and use*—research setting and equipment are accessible for participant approach, reach, manipulation, and use, regardless of participant size, posture, or mobility.

Increased use of evidence-based practice in music education. Evidence-based practice in education refers to the use of research and scientific studies as a basis for determining the best educational practices. The basic premise of evidence-based practice is to provide transparency and to assure administrators, parents, and other concerned individuals that educational techniques and interventions will provide the best possible outcomes. The use of evidence-based practices requires that music educators read their professional journals, particularly research journals, understand the results of the research as it is reported, and attempt to implement the findings into their teaching practices.

Increased use of technology and adapted equipment to meet the music education needs of students with disabilities. The musical learning of students with disabilities can be greatly enhanced by using, managing, and creating adaptive music instruments and other technological devices or processes. Educational and music technologies include, but are not limited to, software, hardware, and internet applications and activities. Using such adaptive materials requires staying informed as to the availability of appropriate technology, training in how to use it, and often obtaining grants or special funds to purchase such equipment. Teachers often find that such adaptive materials are useful to all their students, not just those with disabilities.

Increased representation of students with disabilities in music leadership roles. Historically, persons with disabilities have been viewed as weak and not competent to assume leadership roles (Gallagher, 1999). For this reason, one of the world's most famous leaders, Franklin Delano Roosevelt, went to great lengths to conceal his disability. For many years, there were no known pictures of Franklin Delano Roosevelt in his wheelchair; consequently, most Americans were unaware of the extent of his disability. Today, educational laws such as IDEA encourage the empowerment of students with disabilities. Leadership potential in students with disabilities needs to be recognized and promoted in order for these students to truly maximize their capabilities. Music classrooms, ensembles in particular, provide many opportunities for students to exercise leadership skills. Roles such as band officer, section leader, music librarian, or equipment captain all provide leadership opportunities for students with varying degrees of organizational and musical skills.

Promotion of positive portrayals of individuals with disabilities in the arts. The media have incredible power to influence our perceptions of others, particularly those with whom we have little contact. The arts, television, film, and theatre in particular continue to be one of the major public information sources about disabilities. Darrow (2011) in "What's So Wicked about *Wicked*?" identified a number of negative stereotypes about persons with disabilities in the popular Broadway musical *Wicked*. She also identified similar negative stereotypes in *Glee*, a popular television series about a high school glee club, which won the 2009 Golden Globe for best television musical or comedy (Darrow, 2009). The scripts for the episodes reinforce many common misperceptions about persons with disabilities. It is likely that both film and television scripts will continue to be written by persons who have little experience with disability, and disability roles will continue to be played by actors without disabilities; and thus it is likely the popular media will continue to perpetuate stereotypic portrayals of people with disabilities. It is imperative that educators challenge stereotypic views of disability played out in schools and the media, and that they not propagate such stereotypes in their own teaching. One way to avoid common stereotypes is to use appropriate terminology when referring to students with disabilities.

Use of appropriate terminology when referring to students with disabilities. Who decides what disability-related terminology is appropriate? As with any term used to describe a group of people, deference is usually given to those individuals being described (American Psychological Association, 2009). For example, the evolution of terms used to describe individuals based on race and/or sexual orientation is well known. This evolution was a result of public education and the self-advocacy by these groups. A disability should not be used as the primary adjective used to identify an individual, such as "the deaf student in my class." A disability is not the most important descriptor of any individual. Defining persons by their disabilities often isolates or segregates people and, more important, fails to recognize their humanness that goes well beyond their disabilities. What words would be used to describe the individual if he did not have a disability? Interesting? Boring? Funny? Dull? There are other inappropriate disability-related terms that create negative stereotypes (Darrow, 2013; and consequently may devalue persons with disabilities. Terms such as "afflicted with," "suffers from," or "is a victim of" create an image of helplessness and incompetence. Employing preferred terminology signifies acknowledgment of and respect for persons with disabilities.

Assisting in the transition of students with disabilities from school music programs to community music programs. Much of the attraction to participating in school music programs is the socialization that occurs at rehearsals, on performance trips, and just hanging out in the music room before and after school. Music educators can assist in the social development of students with disabilities by providing opportunities for interpersonal interactions, and encouraging and monitoring such interactions. They can also do much to encourage the continued musical and social growth of students with disabilities by presenting opportunities for music-making in the community, both before and after graduation. Community ensembles, church choirs, open mic night at various venues, and civic concerts are opportunities for music-making and listening that are generally open to all individuals, regardless of musical skills or disabilities. Participation in such organizations or performance events may make the transition from school to community life more rewarding and less threatening for students with disabilities, and indeed for all students.

Conclusion

Music has long played a role in special education programs for students with disabilities; however, due to inclusive practices in schools today, music educators carry greater accountability than ever before in the education of their students. Though instructional roles may differ, music educators frequently work with students who are along the continuum of abilities from gifted to those with the most severe disabilities. The knowledge base required to work effectively with such a broad range of student abilities increases each year. Music educators can prepare themselves by engaging in continued education, collaborative, and consultative efforts with other school personnel, and by keeping abreast of appropriate readings in professional journals. The educational rights of students with disabilities should be unquestioned. As music educators, our challenge is to put our inclusive ideals into practice by exploring new and innovative instructional strategies, and by serving as models of acceptance and appreciation for student diversity.

REFLECTIVE QUESTIONS

1. What are some of the challenges and benefits faced by music educators in inclusive music education classes and ensembles?
2. What are some of the challenges and benefits faced by students with disabilities who are educated in inclusive music education classes?
3. What are some of the challenges and benefits to students who are typically developing who are educated in inclusive music classrooms?
4. How do funding sources influence who provides services for students with disabilities?
5. Who determines how students with disabilities will be musically educated?
6. What is fair and equitable in music education? Who should be able to participate in music education classes and ensembles?
7. How might participation in music education promote a more inclusive society?
8. What can teachers and students without disabilities learn from students who have disabilities?
9. How can pre-service music educators prepare themselves to teach diverse student populations?
10. How do the media influence our perceptions of persons who are different (regarding ethnicity, race, sexual orientation, gender, or abilities/disabilities)?

CLASS ASSIGNMENTS

1. Identify examples of universal design present in classroom architecture, environment, and instruction.
2. Identify examples of appropriate and inappropriate terminology used in the media regarding persons with disabilities.

KEY SOURCE

Adamek, M., & Darrow, A. A. (2010). *Music in special education*, (2nd ed.) Silver Spring, MD: American Music Therapy Association.

REFERENCES

American Music Therapy Association. (2013). *AMTA Member Sourcebook*. Silver Spring, MD: AMTA.

American Psychological Association. (2009). *Publication manual of the American Psychological Association* (6th ed.). Washington, DC: American Psychological Association.

Atterbury, B. W. (1990). *Mainstreaming exceptional learners in music*. Englewood Cliffs, NJ: Prentice-Hall, Inc.

Barss, F., Marrion, M., Haroutounian, J., & Benham, K. (1999). Learning from Kara: Reflections of three friends. *American Music Teacher, 48*, 15–21.

Bowe, F. G. (2000). Universal design in education: Teaching nontraditional students. Westport, CT: Bergin & Garvey.

Burgstahler, S. (2007a). Universal designing of instruction (UDI): Definition, principles guidelines, and examples. Seattle: DO-IT, University of Washington. http://www.washington.edu/doit//Brochures/Academics/instruction.html.

Burgstahler, S. (2007b). *Equal access: Universal design of instruction*. Seattle: DO-IT, University of Washington. http://www.washington.edu/doit/Brochures/Academics/equal_access_udi.html

Connell, B. R., Jones, M., Mace, R., Mueller, J., Mullick, A., Ostroff, E., & Vanderheiden, G. (1997). *Principles of universal design*. Raleigh: North Carolina State University, Center for Universal Design. https://design.ncsu.edu.

Darrow, A. A. (2011). What's so wicked about Wicked? *Florida Music Director, 64*(6), 14–18.

Darrow, A. A. (2009, January). Arts and disability: The media's influence on perceptions of persons with disabilities. Course lecture, Florida State University, Tallahassee.

Darrow, A. A. (2013). What's in a name? Referring to students with disabilities. *Orff Echo, 45*(3), 11–14.

Daveson, B., & Edwards, J. (1998). A role of music therapy in special education. *International Journal of Disability, Development and Education, 45*, 449–457.

Davis, K. (1996). The social model of disability: Setting the terms of a new debate. Glasgow, Scotland, UK: Glasgow Centre on Independent Living.

Gallagher, H. G. (1999). *FDR's splendid deception*. St. Petersburg, FL: Vandamere Press.

Adamek, M., & Darrow, A. A. (2008). Music therapy in schools. In W. Davis, K. Gfeller, & M. Thaut (eds.), *Introduction to Music Therapy: Theory and Practice* (pp. 405–426) (3rd ed.). Silver Spring, MD: American Music Therapy Association.

Glasgow Centre for Inclusive Living. (2008). *Factsheet: The social model of disability and its implications for language use*. Glasgow, Scotland, UK: Glasgow Centre on Independent Living.

Gougoux, F., Lepore, F., Lassonde, M., Voss, P., Zatorre, R. J., & Belin, R. (2004). Pitch discrimination in the early blind: People blinded in infancy have sharper listening skills than those who lost their sight later. *Nature, 430*, 309.

Graham, R. M., & Beer, A. S. (1980). *Teaching music to the exceptional child.* Englewood Cliffs, NJ: Prentice-Hall, Inc.

Jellison, J. A., & Draper, E. A., (2015). Music research in inclusive school settings 1975–2013. *Journal of Research in Music Education, 62*(4), 325–331.

Jellison, J. A. (1999). Life beyond the Jingle Stick: Real music in a real world. *Update: Applications of Research in Music Education, 17*(2),13–19.

Kochhar, C., West, L., & Taymans, J. (2000). *Successful inclusion. Practical strategies for a shared responsibility.* Upper Saddle River, NJ: Prentice-Hall.

National Association for Music Education. (2014). *National Standards for Music Education.* Reston, VA: MENC.

Rose, D. H., & Meyer, A. (eds.) (2006). *A practical reader in universal design for learning.* Cambridge, MA: Harvard University Press.

Rothstein, L. F. (2000). *Special education law* (3rd ed.). New York: Longman.

Solomon, A. (1980). Music in special education before 1930: Hearing and speech development. *Journal of Research in Music Education, 28,* 236–242.

Turnbull, H. R., & Turnbull, A. P. (2000). *Free appropriate public education: The law and children with disabilities* (6th ed.). Denver: Love.

Veenman, M. V. J., & Elshout, J. J. (1995). Differential effects of instructional support on learning in simulation environments. *Instructional Science, 22,* 363–383.

Yaman, M., Nerbel, C., & Bayrhuber, H. (2008). Effects of instructional supports and learner interests when learning using computer simulations. *Computers & Education, 51,* 1784–1794.

PART 2

MUSIC IN THE COMMUNITY

Part Editor

DAVID J. ELLIOTT

CHAPTER 7

COMMENTARY: MUSIC IN THE COMMUNITY

DAVID J. ELLIOTT

What is "community music"? To many in our profession this term may signal a new idea or practice within "music education." Actually, it's the reverse. In the broadest sense, community music predates institutionalized school music education by thousands of years. For as many people know, archeological evidence indicates that humans have been making music for at least 50,000 years (Schneider, 1997). If so, then humans have also been engaged in passing on, transmitting, or "teaching and learning" music in their communities for an equally long period of time. Otherwise, music would not exist. In short, wherever there is something people identify as "music," there is something we would reasonably recognize as community music: making, hearing, and learning how "to music."

As it turns out, then, the basic problem that puzzles many people about community music (CM) is not "music" but "community." With this in mind, a good starting point for what follows in this section is John Dewey's (1927) thoughts on the relationship between the "goods" (values, benefits) of some kind of activity and the nature of "community."

> Wherever there is conjoint activity whose consequences are appreciated as good
> by all singular persons who take part in it, and where the realization of the good
> is such as to effect an energetic desire and effort to sustain it in being just because
> it is a good shared by all, there is in so far a community. (p. 149)

Dewey's thinking allows us to make an important leap: if people engaged in music making value their participation for "the good(s)" it provides, then the means by which they learn the skills and understandings required to participate in these goods is also a means of creating and sustaining "community" in all beneficial senses of this term. Moreover, the means of teaching and learning a community's music may also be a "good" in itself.

Peter Dykema, a central figure in the early development of American music education and community music, believed strongly in Dewey's thoughts and values. Dykema (1916) argued that towns and cities across the United States should ensure that citizens of all ages have access to musical groups, competent teachers, and performance venues of all kinds. He urged also that teachers should focus on fostering students' love of music so they would continue playing and singing after compulsory lessons and classes ended. Dykema's writings not only precede and affirm the thoughts of many contemporary music educators and community music workers; it is also noteworthy that he, too, grappled with the meaning of community music: "Community music is a term that has obtained great vogue the past three years and yet so far as I know it has never been defined" (p. 218). That said, Dykema proceeded to articulate an essential principle of the contemporary theory and practice: "community music is not the name of a new type of music nor even of a musical endeavor. . . . It is not so much the designation of a new thing as a new point of view . . . community music is socialized music . . . music for the people, of the people, and by the people" (p. 218).

Contemporary concepts of CM echo the values articulated by Dewey and Dykema, but they have broadened and deepened dramatically, due to (1) expanding ways of making, accessing, and experiencing music, (2) new understandings about the plethora of "goods" that musical "participation" affords people of all ages and dispositions, and (3) a surge in published research on the nature and values of community music. This last point requires elaboration.

Research papers about various aspects of CM worldwide have been a major feature of the biennial meetings of the Community Music Activity Commission of ISME since the 1980s and a recent feature of other professional meetings (e.g., NAfME, North American Coalition for Community Music). Otherwise, CM practitioners and scholars have had few formal vehicles (outside doctoral dissertations and a few national music education journals) for the dissemination of their research. To answer this need, David J. Elliott and Kari K. Veblen launched in 2004 the *International Journal of Community Music*, which is currently edited by Lee Higgins. It has emerged as a central repository of qualitative, philosophical, descriptive, and historical research on CM, as well as powerful motivating force for new and more diverse forms of CM activity (see Veblen, Messenger, Silverman, & Elliott, 2013).

Conceptually speaking, Veblen and Olsson (2002) see the core of CM as consisting of "people making music" (p. 730) in/through many forms of musicing, musical styles, locations, and social-musical relationships. Other characteristics of CM activity that Veblen and Olsson highlight and celebrate include multiple forms of teacher-facilitator configurations; a commitment to lifelong musical learning (p. 731) and participants' social and personal growth; and a deep concern that all people have access to musical participation, including immigrants, children with physical and mental challenges, disenfranchised cultural groups, and children of low-income families (p. 731). In addition, scholars and practitioners note the tendency of CM organizations to assist school music educators whenever appropriate and possible.

The authors in this part of this volume of the handbook provide varying perspectives on all of the above, as well as other aspects and concepts of the natures and values of CM. In the opening chapter, Higgins argues that the term "community" is incomplete without an awareness that community, properly conceived, is a matter of ethical interactions and "hospitality." After a deep conceptual analysis of these themes, Higgins traces the application of community-as-hospitality in three contrasting sites of CM: Bambini al Centro (Rome); East Hill Singers (Kansas); and the Music Academy of Gauteng (Benoni, South Africa).

"Reciprocity" is a key theme in the second chapter in this part of the volume, where Jones and Langston unpack the concept of CM as/for social capital. They note that social capital can be understood as any product of community interactions, including social networking, collective problem solving, and improvements in the quality of communal life. They suggest that while there is a wide body of research on social issues and CM, there is little research on the intersections and the gains in these areas. The authors ask: How do music, music education, and CM affect social capital? And what relationships exist between trust, social connectedness, social capital, and musical enjoyment? The authors explain a number of practical ways to foster "life-wide and lifelong musicing" and the development of social capital by addressing issues of curriculum, pedagogy, teacher education, enhancing musical opportunities that already exist within a community, and helping students organize their own musical experiences.

Scholars and practitioners of CM remain unresolved about whether music therapy, as a discipline, fits within it. Aigen suggests, however, that the aims and practices of CM therapy (CoMT) are in fact aligned with many of music therapy's premises and practices. To explore the nature of CoMT, Aigen explains its aims, both theoretically and practically. He highlights a number of CoMT examples in a variety of contexts, including a residential rehabilitation facility in New York City; a site in Raanana, Israel, where practitioners work with children with special needs; and the Centre for the Treatment of Torture Victims in Berlin, where political refugees receive help.

Silverman's chapter integrates philosophical reflections on CM with analyses of two neglected concepts and practices in music education and CM: love-as-action and social justice. Through the integration of theory and practice, she explains ways CM may adopt, adapt, and benefit from the practices of community facilitators working in various circumstances. Silverman then proceeds to discuss some prerequisites for, and dimensions of, these concepts in the context of Western societies generally and the United States particularly. The last section of Silverman's discussion connects the concept of love-as-social-justice to a practical example in New York City's urban environment.

Phelan argues that the phenomenon of global migration has tremendous import for the theory and practice of CM. She provides examples of migration in

Ireland and explains how migration and globalization affect the work of community musicians in Limerick. In the process, Phelan emphasizes that "hospitality" is both a condition and a central component of CM and conceptualizes this component through the lenses of space and place. In addition, she suggests that we think of musical sounds as perceivable means for hospitality: "humanly embodied sound becomes, not just a source of musical knowledge but of musical hospitality, in its ability of 'invite' and evoke 'missing' cultural landscapes." When CM practitioners work in spaces of migration, sonic hospitality becomes an important aspect of the landscape of welcoming "the Other."

Cohen, Silber, Sangiorgio, and Iadeluca discuss how CM practices interact with at-risk youth. The authors explain the concept of "at-risk" youth, as this phenomenon is neither universally understood nor easily classified. They then proceed to explain the importance of Noddings's "ethics of care" for community musicians' work with at-risk youth. They propose also that "the nature of 'music' as a lived experience" is rooted in caring relationships. In other words, if people are participating in musical activities, they are (or should be) engaged in caring relationships. If so, then musical activities are extremely adept at ameliorating the personal/social challenges faced by at-risk youth. Cohen, Silber, Sangiorgio, and Iadeluca use a number of CM programs as examples. They trace the ethics of caring in diverse CM settings, such as Portugal, the United Kingdom, Israel, Venezuela, and the United States.

Finally, Veblen and Waldron probe future possibilities for CM. They begin by examining the aims and values of "communitas" and how these values shape and enhance aspects of practice. In grounding CM in its function as "communitas," Veblen and Waldron prepare the way for understanding current and potential relationships between CM and (for example) face-to-face social networks and computer-mediated musical-social networks, including online music education research communities, online music composition, and music trading online.

As we see from the above, the very idea of "community music" raises many conceptual and practical issues large and small, which in turn lead to many fascinating sub-questions. As Veblen (2007) explains, many people address questions about CM through highly refined concepts, or from an "on the ground," grassroots perspective—from the viewpoint of CM "workers" or "facilitators" involved in some variation of "teaching and learning music" that's related to but outside traditional music schools. Others think and work in relation to problem-solving strategies they create and deploy to address the immediate needs and circumstances of the people they serve; in the process, they think and rethink the "who-why-what-when-and-where" of CM.

In summary, it is highly unlikely—and in fact highly desirable—that there will ever be a fixed concept or "how-to" of CM. For however and wherever CM is conceived and practiced, this elusive phenomenon continues to evolve and diversify locally and internationally to meet the changing needs of the people it serves today and those it will serve tomorrow; it reinvents itself continuously in relation to the musics and technologies its practitioners and clients desire and appropriate; and, of course, CM matures constantly as CM facilitators deploy their creativity to reframe, adjust, combine, integrate, and overlap existing ways of empowering people to make music for the realization of its many "goods" and the many ways that music making, musical sharing, and musical caring creates "community."

REFERENCES

Dewey, J. (1927). *The public and its problems.* Athens, OH: Swallow Press.

Dykema, P. W. (1916). The spread of community music. *The annals of the American academy of political social science 67,* 218–221.

Schneider, A. (1997). Archaeology of music in Europe: An overview. In Hans-Werner Heister (ed.), *Music/revolution. Festschrift for Georg Knepler 90th Birthday, 1* (pp. 39–66). Hamburg: Bockel of-Verlag, 1997. [Abridged version in T. Rice, J. Porter, & C. Goertzen (eds.), *The Garland Encyclopedia of World Music,* vol. 8: *Europe* (pp. 34–45). New York: Garland Publishing 2000.]

Veblen, K., & Olsson, B. (2002). Community music: Toward an international perspective. In R. Colwell & C. Richardson (eds.), *The new handbook of research on music teaching and learning* (pp. 730–753). New York: Oxford University Press.

Veblen, K. (2007). The many ways of community music. *International Journal of Community Music, 1*(1), 5–21. Intellect Press. https://www.intellectbooks.co.uk.

Veblen, K., Messenger, S., Silverman, M., & Elliott, D. J. (eds.) (2013). *Community music today.* New York: Rowman & Littlefield Publishers, Inc.

CHAPTER 8

··

THE COMMUNITY
WITHIN
COMMUNITY MUSIC

··

LEE HIGGINS

Although the term *community music* (CM) has gained considerable popularity in recent years, its meaning is still unclear to many. This is understandable, because many who have thought about the term (or, indeed, practiced community music) have resisted the temptation to reduce it to a simple definition on the belief that doing so will do a serious injustice to the endeavor. The argument often put forth is that activities deemed community music are just too diverse, complex, multifaceted, and contextual to be captured in one universal statement. Following this train of thought, community musicians have been critical of the power dynamics of naming, pointing out that there is a danger in assuming scholarly definitions are somehow superior to more operational definitions, which community music facilitators use on a daily basis (Gonzalez Ben, 2016).

Those engaged in the field of community music practice and research have concluded that the best way to understand community music is through what it *does* rather than what it *is*.

The purpose of this chapter is to put forward an explanation of the concept "community" as it relates to the larger concept of "community music." After an etymologic analysis of the concept, I suggest that the "community" in "community music" is best understood as "hospitality," as initially articulated by Jacques Derrida (1999, 2000, 2001). My proposition is that "hospitality" encompasses the central characteristics of community music practice, broadly understood as people, participation, places, inclusivity, and diversity. I do not mean that hospitality should replace the term "community," but that "hospitality" evokes the practical meaning of "community" in that which is named "community music." From this perspective, I am proposing that "community" conceived actively as "an act of hospitality" runs deeply through the practice of community music, and that an acute awareness of hospitality will expose the distinctiveness of community music within the field of music education.

I will use two questions to guide my explorations: (1) How can the concept of community be understood in practices named community music? and (2) How is community made manifest through community music? I will address these questions in four sections: (1) an etymological consideration of the word "community"; (2) community in the twenty-first century; (3) rethinking the status of community music as a hospitable act of reciprocal call and the welcome; and (4) illustrations of practice. The chapter concludes by suggesting that it is the act of hospitality, a welcome to would-be music participants evoked by their call, that gives community music its distinction.

COMMUNITY

As a contested concept, "community" is both problematic and powerful. The term became particularly important to nineteenth-century social theorists, including Ferdinand Tönnies (2001[1887]), Max Weber (1947), and Emile Durkheim (1984[1893]). At this time, society was caught up in rapid changes of industrialization and urban development, and sociologists were concerned with the potential disintegration of traditional ways of living. Cultural upheavals that include the French and American revolutions, industrialization from the nineteenth century, and most recently the onslaught of globalization have produced changes in the ways people live together and communicate. This may account for why the word "community," and its associated concepts and meanings, has been popular.

The etymology of the word "community" can be understood from several perspectives. In an analysis of the German word *gemeinschaft*, often translated as meaning "community," Kant (1998) makes a distinction in Latin between *communio*, an exclusive sharing space protected from the outside, and *commercium*, the processes of exchange and communication. Following Kant, Tönnies, who was perhaps the first to clearly describe the term, explores *gemeinschaft* (community) in relation to *gesellschaft* (society), suggesting that both terms are different forms of associated living brought about by human will. His influential conclusions suggested that modern societies have replaced *gemeinschaft*, the site of traditional cultural values, with *gesellschaft*, an expression of modernity, as the primary focus for social relations. William Corlett (1995) considers the word "community" from a slightly different standpoint: first *Communis, com + munis*, meaning common and defense, as in "with oneness or unity," favored by the communitarian theorists, and second *communes, com + munnus*, meaning having common duties or functions, emphasizing the doing of one's duty, "with gifts or services."[1]

In the field of anthropology, the term has been usefully isolated with three broad variants: (1) common interests between people; (2) a common ecology and locality; and (3) a common social system or structure (Rapport & Overing, 2006). More specifically, in *The Ritual Process*, Victor Turner (1969) begins his analysis of the word "community" with *communitas*, the Latin expression for belonging, which is irreducible to any social or political arrangement. Philip Alperson's (2002) description of community articulates the most general etymological understanding: community as a state of being held in common. Alperson advocates that both ontologically and structurally, community refers to a relation between things.

Charting the term's changing patterns of application and understanding, the field of anthropology and sociology provide a variety of perspectives. These include community as loss and recovery (Gutek & Gutek, 1998; Rousseau, 1993); belonging (Block, 2008); communitarianism (Christodoulidis, 1998; Etzioni, Volmert, & Rothschild, 2004; Lehman, 2000; Stone, 2000); citizenship (Beiner, 2002; Demaine & Entwistle, 1996); multiculturalism (Giroux, 1993; Kernerman, 2005; Nagle, 2008); symbolic structure (Cohen, 1985); globalization (Adams & Goldbard, 2002; Rupp, 2006); diaspora (Angelo, 1997; Brah, 1996; Matsuoka & Sorenson, 2001; Najam, 2006); nationalism (Bhabha, 1990; Vincent, 2002; Williams & Kofman, 1989), and the imagined (Anderson, 2016). A review of this literature serves to remind us that the concept of community is constantly changing, functioning differently depending on the context of its use.

Given the above, it is unsurprising that different uses and applications of the term "community" are in some ways unavoidable. This is so because the root of the word designates a social phenomenon and a sense of belonging and identity, both of which are context bound and are always in a state of flux. In the next section I reflect on contemporary interpretations of the word. One might think of these ideas as contesting "community," because they challenge our most comfortable notions of what is meant by the term.

COMMUNITY IN THE TWENTY-FIRST CENTURY

Recent anthropological discussions have tended to emphasize "difference" as a guiding idea in exploring tensions found between fixed social and political relations within communal frames, and the considerable pressures toward individuation, fragmentation, and border identities (Amit & Rapport, 2002; Barber, 1996; Brah, 1996; Childs, 2003; Donnan & Wilson, 2001; Hannerz, 1996; Olthuis, 2000; Vila, 2005; Wilson & Donnan, 1998). Understood through postmodernism's critique of modernity, this perspective maintains that communities are not static or bounded but rather, organic and plural.[2] Illustrative of a contemporary perspective, Gerald

Delanty (2009) suggests four categories in which one might reconsider community in the twenty-first century:

1. Collective identities: Considered as bursts of time, such as dropping the children off or picking them up from school, or the hours spent with work colleagues in the office.
2. Contextual fellowship: Understood as times of emergency or grief, the terrorist attacks on the World Trade Center or the death of Princess Diane for instance. Contextual fellowship can also be said to have taken place in times of travel delay or cancellation. It is during these times that people find a common bond that momentarily links them together.
3. Liminal communities: A sense of the transitional, those "in-between" spaces that have importance in people's lives. For example, the ritualistic morning coffee in Starbucks, the train journey to and from work, or the Saturday morning yoga class. These moments have a consciousness of communality.
4. Virtual communities: Most often associated with technologically mediated communities such as Facebook, YouTube, Instagram, LinkedIn, or eBay.

When the term "community" is thought about in these ways, the phrase "community *without* unity" seems appropriate. From a line of thought that has a trajectory from Georges Bataille (1988), Maurice Blanchot (1988), Jean Luc-Nancy (1991), and Jacques Derrida (1997), this formulation has a resistance to one unified and authoritative identity. This is so because the communality at the heart of community provides internal contradictions. The very concept of the "common" (*commun*) and the "as-one" (*comme-un*) becomes a problem for the politics of pluralism. Community without unity is then a descriptive attempt to recognize the importance of diversity in the modern space of communal relationships (Brent, 1997).[3]

As a contemporary music practice, I suggest that the general use of the term "community" is a ratification of community musics' participatory ethos; an emphasis on creative endeavors toward music-making through workable agreements and open and honest sharing. In short, community musicians strive for understanding among individuals with common (albeit diverse) goals despite cultural, class, gender, economic, and political differences. The work community musicians do attempts to provoke discourse, stimulate active participation, and enable a sense of voice, both for individuals and those complicit groups or communities of which they are part. As a pursuit of socially conscious music-making experiences, the traditional notion of community can often be at odds with the practice of community music. From the perspective of western European history, the word "community" can be seen as dangerously advocating a group consensus that has historically fed into visions of fascism, fundamentalism, discord, and war (Derrida, 1995).

It is clear that the word "community" has a complex etymology and an equally complex and diverse usage. When the word "community" is used in conjunction with the word music, its meaning is open to many interpretations. One might argue that broad interpretations of the word community have helped both its growth and development. Community music seminars, such as the International Soceity of Music Education's (ISME) Commission for Community Music Activity, have witnessed a wide gamut of projects presented under a community music banner reported in McCarthy (2008) and experienced through subsequent meetings. This serves to support this point. However, open definitions are not always satisfactory. Huib Schippers (2009) reinforces this sentiment by noting that one of the contributing factors to the confusion surrounding the definition of community music is a tendency "to mix descriptions of specific practices with organization, artistic and pedagogical approaches, and sets of beliefs underlying the activities" (p. 93). Unlike Andrew Peggie (2003), who suggests that we take the C-word out of community music, or Anthony Everitt (1997), who states "it is time to ditch the term [community music] and replace it with 'participatory music'" (p. 160), I am not advocating a rejection of the word, but I do find aspects of its historical use problematic and out of sync with contemporary community music practice. Brydie-Leigh Bartleet and myself attempt to come to terms with this in our Introduction to the *Oxford Handbook of Community Music* (2017) noting that as the field matures, we expect practitioners and theorist alike to critically examine, reflect, and (re)define how the range of conceptual understandings relate to their own community music practice.

In the next section, I suggest that the term "hospitality" might best articulate the meaning behind the prefix "community." With a conceptual arrival at this point through the notion of "community without unity," an idea that recognizes that community is as much about struggle as it is about unity, this is an attempt to "reload" the word "community" in order to give a stronger sense of meaning to the named practice. My key point is that hospitality acts as a verb that describes the actions and desires of community musicians.

COMMUNITY AS HOSPITALITY

Hospitality begins with a welcome.[4] As a preparatory thought and consequential gesture, the welcome becomes an invitation: the making of time for another and the invitation to become included. It is an ethical action toward a relationship to another person.[5] This type of hospitality suggests unconditionality, a welcome without reservation, without previous calculation, and in the context of community music, an unlimited display of reception towards a potential music participant. As such, unconditionality approaches a transcendental idea, one toward which we should aspire, even though inaccessible. However, the transcendental nature of this unconditionality can itself prove problematic. How can we possibly unconditionally welcome all comers into our various bands, choirs, and orchestras, regardless of their abilities and skills? How could we "give place" to them all without entering into a reciprocal agreement that includes being punctual, practicing, and extending a generosity of spirit toward other group members?

Ordinarily, unconditional refers to a situation not limited by conditions. Within this context, there is a break from the Kantian idea that describes the unconditional as an absolute, a sovereign instance, or an archetype, a supreme, preeminent, or indisputable something. Kant's (1998, p. A 567/B 597) sovereign instance is removed from time and space and completely given to itself, a logic that suggests fixity. In the context used here, unconditionality is accepted as residing at the very origin of the seminal concepts that give the West its history, politics and culture (Wortham, 2010). The unconditional is therefore always entwined with what is conditional and must be recalled in order to rethink and transform commonly accepted ideas and concepts. The unconditional is not therefore sovereign and becomes intrinsically linked to a future that is unforeseeable.

For example, a community musician may have prepared a series of workshops for a local arts center. Meticulously planned, the content of the session has been defined by knowledge of who and how many will come. An hour before the first session is due to start, the community music facilitator (See Higgins & Bartleet, volume 2, chapter 18) finds the expected group of music participants will now additionally include five young asylum seekers who have been relocated to the area and have shown interest in music. The unexpected change takes the community musician by surprise and requires the ability to augment current plans and make room for another possibility. The determined future has been disrupted and shattered by a future that was unforeseeable. In resonance with traits that distinguish community musicians—a commitment to people, participation, places, inclusivity, and diversity—the facilitator must embrace the notion of unconditional hospitality in order to run the workshop successfully.[6]

A disposition with unconditional hospitality at its core infiltrates the community musicians' approach to music-making. Community musicians place a heavy emphasis on improvisation and invention, both of which require a type of unconditionality. This can be described as an openness to a future that is different from that which is predictable. Indeed, the inventive process looks toward a future that is also unknown and unpredictable. This vision of a nonstatic and nonfixed future generates something new and different from what has come before, and can prove conducive to opportunities through which to generate a creative music-making experience. Creativity, as both a process and a way of being, builds on this ability to engage in the development of original, inventive, and imaginative future things. Thus, having an imaginative capacity fosters the ability to look at things differently, as if they could be something other than they typically are. Although community musicians often celebrate in "new" musical findings, it must be noted that these inventions also happen with relationship to other participants, accomplishments, contexts, and histories.

The open invitation given through the welcome is a genuinely human expression and an ethical moment that community music facilitators and/or the participants can generate, and that results in an experience of a greater sense of connectivity among and between participants, and between participants and the music (Higgins, 2016). From the community musicians' perspective, it is through the initial hospitable welcome that participants are encouraged toward creative music-making that can produce events that leave a lasting impression on both community musician and participants. This hospitable welcome is vital in every socially interactive musical experience, in every context. It is the unconditional acceptance of everyone into the musical events and workshops.

The implication of the sign of a hospitable "community" within "community music" is a refusal of any interpretation of community that privileges "gathering" over "dislocation."[7] It follows that any privilege granted to unity conjures up the homogenized whole, and can become a threat for responsibility, for decision, for ethics, and for politics (Derrida, 1997).[8] Maintaining such a position is difficult because no matter how complex our world gets, the need for human connectedness and belonging is paramount. In short, there is an irrepressible desire for a "community" to form. As a practice, I would suggest that those invested in community music might like to reimagine the term "community" in its name. The "community" in "community music" is a "community-to-come," a generous welcoming toward the music participants "always *coming*, endlessly, at the heart of every collectivity" (Nancy, 1991, p. 71). As an act of unconditional hospitality, the "community" in "community music" is a promise to the welcome, a commitment to a "community *without* unity," a chance to say "yes" without discrimination to any potential music participant.[9]

What follows are three illustrations that I believe demonstrate acts of hospitable music-making. I have chosen these to illustrate work in three very different places and in three very different contexts. Rather than describing the conditions from which these data have been collected, I have created a textual framework to support the idea of hospitality as a verb that describes the actions and desires of community musicians and the importance of the welcome.

ILLUSTRATIONS OF PRACTICE

Bambini al Centro

Across Europe there are many music projects that form a vital role in combating the modern challenge of social exclusion. Bambini al Centro (literally: Children in the Center) represents an example of this aspect of community music. The data used for this illustration consists of a composite from personal observations and interviews during three trips to Rome in conjunction with an ethnographic account carried out by the directors and presented at the 2006 ISME community music seminar in Rome (Iadeluca & Sangiorgio, 2008).

Andrea Sangiorgio and Valentina Iadeluca are community musicians who maintain that "hospitality" is central in their practice. They had always imagined a place where children in poor or difficult situations could use music as a language to

express themselves, to create, to get in contact with others, to learn to play respect-
fully, and to cooperate for a common end. This would be a place where children,
parents, and grandparents could encounter music and dance together.

In 1999, Bambini al Centro opened its doors with money from a national fund
that supports work with young people. Its two directors, Sangiorgio and Iadeluca,
had created a recreational musical space devoted to children from birth to 12 years
and their families. The principal goal of the center was to provide an opportunity
for encounters, relationships, sharing, and personal growth with, and through,
music and dance. Housed within a public elementary school in Rome's northeastern
suburbs known for its economic difficulties, Bambini al Centro hosts between 120–
160 children and their families each year. At the heart of its service was the aim to
promote the well-being of children and their parents through the experience of
making music in groups. After 10 years of activity, the service was so well known
in the local area that the requests largely exceed the possibility of reception. This
growth was a surprise: the project exceeded the founders' expectations. Many people
came to the center through personal contacts. Many others were referred through
the center's social services network and the nursery and primary schools of the area.
Often social workers or class teachers directed the attention of the center to specific
cases of children with difficulties or problems. These children were welcomed and
treated as the most important users of the center rather than being overlooked and
put on a waiting list. Although maintaining this openness was sometimes difficult,
given the practical realities of running an operation that had limited space, personnel, and resources, the center held fast to its policy of hospitality.

Hospitality could paradoxically mean both "host" and "stranger," its root
common to both "host" and "hostile." It is between such a paradox that Bambini
al Centro operated, advocating an "open" door policy but within a structure that
ensured that the staff maintain "control." One of the center's key services was the
"playroom." This supported families in organizing their children's leisure time after
school and offered children a suitable alternative to loneliness, television, computer
games, or wandering around the streets. Activities included early childhood music,
for parents and children birth–36 months; music and play, for ages 4–6 years,
incorporating active music-making with Orff instruments; music-making for older
children, ages 7–8 years, utilizing voice and percussion instruments; and music
theatre, for ages 9–12 years, including both parents and children. The demand was
high and pushed the limits of the resources. As described above, the use of the
word "community" most often evokes a sense of closure, a bounding of a group that
defines who is included and who is excluded. The hospitality of the center exceeded
this, but there was always a chance they would have to refuse someone because the
practicalities demand it.

The center's vision exemplifies hospitality as they push back at customary
definitions of community boundaries. Over the years many people have reported
how important Bambini al Centro has become in their everyday lives; it is a trust-
worthy place where they could take their children, knowing they will be respected
as human beings and encouraged to develop their skills. Maintaining this openness

was difficult given the practical realties of running a business with limited space, personnel, and resources, the center held fast to its policy of hospitality until the lack of government funds forced its temporary closure.

East Hill Singers

Recently, there has been a growing interest in prison choir programs (Cohen, 2007a, 2007b, 2008; Cohen & Silverman, 2013, Silber, 2005).[10] It is here that the hospitable welcome can contribute to reducing the tensions felt by the prison population, both between each other and between themselves and those on the "outside." Drawn from data collected and presented by Mary Cohen (2010), this story of the hospitality offered by musician Elvera Voth serves as an example of the power of the welcome.

In 1995, Voth volunteered to conduct a secular prison choir in Lansing, Kansas. Voth, a native Kansan, had worked as a choral music educator in Alaska for over 30 years, prepared choruses for Robert Shaw, and founded numerous musical organizations, including the Department of Music Education at the University of Alaska, the Anchorage Boys' Choir, and the Alaska Chamber Singers. On retirement she returned to Kansas with the intention of putting her considerable music skills to use within an area of need. During a reunion of a Mennonite men's chorus, she shared her vision of working within the criminal justice system with her former student Janeal Krehbiel. Krehbiel's brother-in-law, a deputy warden of Lansing Correctional Facility, arranged a meeting between Voth and David McKune, the warden. McKune granted Voth permission to begin a men's chorus at the minimum-security unit called the East Unit. The chorus took its name, East Hill Singers, from the unit's name.

Voth posted a sign inside the Facility advertising the choir, stating simply "Forming a Singing Group." There was no exclusive parameter, merely an open invitation. This was her act of unconditional hospitality, a gesture toward a future that was unknown. The limits of her welcome were tested immediately when the prisoners asked if they could form a rap group. Perhaps not surprisingly, this was something Voth could not facilitate. However, the openness of the initial call enabled a level of communication that formed the beginnings of a fruitful and relevant music-making experience. It was Voth's ability to allow herself to be exposed to an unforeseeable future that enabled the subsequent prison singing programs to happen.

Voth's programming consisted of predominantly sacred and classic choral works. The number of prisoners in the choir fluctuated between 15 and 25 per concert season. In order to enrich their choral sound, Voth realized that the inmates would benefit from vocal support. This provided an opportunity for the inmates to work together with "outside" volunteers. To find additional volunteer singers, she recruited men from Kansas City's Lyric Opera Chorus and the Rainbow Mennonite Church choir to sing with the inmates. The volunteers met monthly outside the prison to practice. Anywhere from 2–12 came into the prison to rehearse with the inmates. Sometimes Voth had them come once per month; other times a few came every week. The chorus performs two public concerts at the culmination of each concert season.

Voth's hospitality is often challenged by the conditional realities of working within the criminal justice system. Inmates must be at level 3 on a three-level behavioral incentive system in order to leave the facility for public concerts. If they do not maintain this behavioral level, they cannot go out into the community with the group to perform.

During the public concerts, many inmates offer personal narratives as part of the concerts. According to Voth and volunteer singers, these narratives are a key element of any concert. The narratives explain details about the choral selections and describe how singing in the chorus is meaningful to the inmate singers. They describe the "hospitality" and "welcome" that is needed to enable the choir to function.

After a short time working with the East Hill Singers, Voth realized the immense benefits of this musical experience in a prison context for the singers. She wanted to offer the opportunity to other prisoners to sing in a choir. In 1999, Voth began the West Wall Singers, a chorus at the maximum-security unit in Lansing. For four years she has traveled twice and sometimes three times per week to Lansing, located about 40 minutes from her home in Kansas City. In 2002, she turned the maximum-security chorus over to two other volunteers.

Music Academy of Gauteng

The final illustration centers on the Music Academy of Gauteng (MAG) in Benoni, South Africa. This case is particularly poignant for me because it served as the impetus for my exploration of hospitality.

Operating on a shoestring budget, an assortment of donated instruments, and inadequate rehearsal spaces, MAG is in some ways typical of many community music programs throughout the world. Founded in 1994 by jazz trumpeter Johnny Mekoa, MAG aims to create opportunities for young people in Benoni to play music together in a safe and supportive environment.[11] Known by locals as "Johnny's Place," MAG's main purpose is to offer both full-time and part-time jazz education opportunities for the township's large youth population. The music project aspires to provide a stepping-stone for young people into tertiary education or the music industry, MAG presents a career in music as an alternative to "hanging around" on the streets and getting absorbed into gangster activity. Classes are available for a nominal cost, as the project's population is designated as disadvantaged by local government agencies.

Children who live the majority of their lives on the streets have always been particularly welcomed in the academy. Sensitive to local needs, Johnny has always considered his school a sanctuary for some of Benoni's disenfranchised and troubled youth. Although music can be seen as its central purpose, MAG provides an invaluable escape from the many hostilities of street life. Young people can find refuge within its compound through a hospitable atmosphere and a commitment to a policy of equality of opportunity. The "welcome" shown to the local people is at the heart of MAG's mission; as at Bambini al Centro, there are always tensions between what is desired and what can be achieved within the political real-ties. Community music's hospitality is, then, a "welcome" to the participant while always remaining mindful of responsibilities inherent in any leadership role, for example, providing a safe space physically, mentally, and spiritually.

Through artists such as Jonas Gwangwa, Hugh Masekela, and Abdullah Ibrahim, South African jazz has established itself an identifiable sound and a marketable product both at home and abroad. It is because of this that young people from the MAG project view music as a possible and legitimate escape from a life of poverty and little opportunity. While visiting the MAG, Johnny explained that for many young people in his program, music is seen as one of the few escape routes from the social traumas of township life. Johnny's community is built on "hospitality" and provides a genuine "welcome" to those in the surrounding area. Its unconditionality is always penetrated by the political, social, and economic realties of post-apartheid South Africa. However, those who are able to cross the threshold are exposed to concrete experiences that include tuition in music theory, instrumental classes, and ensemble playing. The music participation takes place through a generosity of spirit and a sacrifice of personal wishes. This is done for the good of the groups and is given momentum by the welcoming call and passion of Johnny Mekoa and the determination of its young players.

CONCLUSION

Communities can be based on ethnicity, religion, class, gender, or politics. They can be located in villages, towns, cities, or cyberspace. Communities can be large or small, local or global, traditional, modern, or postmodern. However, this "warmly persuasive word" has at its heart the search for human belonging (Williams, 1985, p. 76). Creating opportunities for music-making that were not already established, the projects presented above illustrate how community musicians "welcome" potential participants through acts of "hospitality." It is through the embrace of unconditional hospitality that musicians Andrea Sangiorgio, Valentina Iadeluca, Elvera Voth, and Johnny Mekoa can make a "welcome" that fertilizes a network of shared relationships, creating what is generally understood as a sense of community. As Maurice Blanchot (1988) suggests: "this sharing refers back to the community and is exposed in it" (p. 19). Such networks echo Emmanuel Levinas's (1981) notion that "the community with him begins in my obligation to him" (p. 11). Blanchot (1988) reinforces this sentiment by stating: "if I want my life to have meaning for

myself, it must have meaning *for someone else*" (p. 11). With the help of community musicians, participants of the Bambini al Centro, the East Hill Singers, and the
Music Academy of Gauteng are constantly preparing themselves for the arrival of
new music participants. In this way their community-making is one that is porous,
permeable, and open-ended.

This chapter has proposed that the concept of "community" in community music
resides as an act of "hospitality," a "welcome" (given by those who name themselves
community musicians) to those that want and "call" to participate in active musical
doing. The welcome and the call are instrinsically linked and work as a reciprocal
structure. While resisting the temptation to define community music on the grounds
that doing so ignores the power dynamics in the act of naming, I have attempted
to conceptualize its distinctive characteristics on the basis of an understanding of
the act of hospitality. This perspective implies that the strength of the term "community" within "community music" lies in the hospitable welcome it extends to
participants, rather than in any other codification of the word. It becomes an open-
door policy, a greeting to strangers, extended in advance and without full knowledge of its consequences. New participants do not simply cross a threshold with
the intention of joining a community music project: any new "welcome" is always a
direct challenge to what has been currently constituted. This challenge surprises and
calls into question prior group identity and predetermined community borders. One
might say that the promise of the "welcome" constantly puts the "inside" in doubt—
and this can be scary for both the group leader and the participants. According to
this formulation the "outside," or the excluded, affects and determines the "inside," or
included. However, if community musicians can acknowledge a desire for unconditional hospitality this may prevent the closure that is characteristic of a determinate
community and thus provide an enhanced ability to say "Yes, please join in."

Community musicians concerned with creating accessible and diverse music-
making opportunities (and music educators more generally) might take another
look at their policy for inclusion and ask: "Do I create an environment of unconditional hospitality?" "Am I open to new and different possibilities?" "How
welcoming is my music program?" If community musicians can think beyond comfortable understandings of what usually constitutes community, then they may be
more successful in providing increased and richer opportunities for the "voices" of
participants to be heard.

REFLECTIVE QUESTIONS

1. Consider community music projects in your locality: How might you
   understand their vision of community?
2. When confronted with a new class or group, how might you create an
   atmosphere that is open and hospitable?

3. What mechanisms of practice enable a "welcome" toward potential music participants?
4. How might school music education adapt and use a concept of hospitality? What are the tensions inherent in this approach and what strategies might be employed to meet the challenges?

KEY SOURCES

Bartleet, B.-L., & Higgins, L. (eds.). (2017). *The Oxford Handbook of Community Music*. New York: Oxford University Press.

Delanty, G. (2009). *Community*. 2nd ed. London: Routledge.

Derrida, J. (2000). *Of Hospitality* (R. Bowlby, Trans.). California: Stanford University Press.

Higgins, L. (2012). *Community Music: In Theory and in Practice*. New York: Oxford University Press.

Higgins, L., & Willingham, L. (2017). *Engagement in Community Music: An introduction*. New York: Routledge.

NOTES

1. For a detailed account of the word "community," see the first chapter in Roberto Esposito's book *Communitas: The Origin and Destiny of Community* (2010).
2. Wayne Bowman (2009) argues this point, stating that "who 'we' are, and with whom we identify most strongly are open questions whose answers are plural, fluid and grounded in patterns of influence" (p. 111).
3. In this formulation, the *without* can be understood as a reminder that the act of welcoming is an ethical responsibility.
4. Hospitality derives meaning from the Greek word *philoxenia*, meaning "love of stranger."
5. This philosophical position draws from the thought of Emmanuel Levinas. Levinas would describe this as a humanism of the other, according to which being-for-the-other takes precedence over being-for-itself (Levinas, 2006).
6. In this formulation, the unconditional implies a sense of "violence" toward that which is stable, fixed, and comfortable. Used here, violence operates as the "machinery of exclusion" and implies an essential impropriety that does not allow anything to be sheltered from risk, failure, and forgetting (Hägglund, 2008).
7. In this sense, the concurrence of harmonization through collective gatherings is understood as a limiting process. Dislocation, however, requires continuous negotiation, and in these situations new rules and idioms must be found on which to phrase disputes or conversation (Lyotard, 1988).
8. These sentiments do not advocate the destruction of unity. Instead the challenge is to notions of "pure" unity and "absolute" totality, as these ideas significantly reduce negotiation, conversation, and movement. One might say that unity couched in terms of purity becomes a synonym of death.

9. Helen Phelan (2007) interrogates Derrida's (2000) expression "Let us say yes . . ." with her analysis of Sanctuary, an Irish initiative to promote greater access to education through the pursuit of cultural activities. (See also chapter 12 in this volume).

10. In April 2010, the *International Journal of Community Music* published a special focused edition on community music and the criminal justice system.

11. See the MAG's website, https://www.musicinafrica.net/directory/music-academy-gauteng.

REFERENCES

Adams, D., & Goldbard, A. (2002). *Community, culture and globalization*. New York: Rockefeller Foundation.

Alperson, P. (ed.). (2002). *Diversity and community: An interdisciplinary reader*. Oxford: Blackwell Publishing.

Amit, V., & Rapport, N. (2002). *The trouble with community: Anthropological reflections on movement, identity and collectivity*. London: Pluto Press.

Anderson, B. (2016). *Imagined communities*. New York: Verso.

Angelo, M. (1997). *The Sikh diaspora: Tradition and change in an immigrant community*. New York: Garland Publishing.

Barber, B. R. (1996). Multiculturalism between individuality and community: Chasm or bridge? In A. Sarat & D. R. Villa (eds.), *Liberal modernism and democratic individuality: George Kateb and the practices of politics* (pp. 133–146). Princeton, NJ: Princeton University Press.

Bartleet, B.-L., & Higgins, L. (eds.). (2017). *The Oxford Handbook of Community Music*. New York: Oxford University Press.

Bataille, G. (1988). *Inner experience*. New York: SUNY Press.

Beiner, R. (2002). *Liberalism, nationalism, citizenship essays on the problem of political community*. Vancouver: University of British Columbia Press.

Bhabha, H. K. (1990). *Nation and narration*. London: Routledge.

Blanchot, M. (1988). *The unavowable community* (P. Joris, Trans.). New York: Station Hill Press.

Block, P. (2008). *Community: The structure of belonging*. San Francisco: Berrett-Koehler.

Bowman, W. (2009). The community in music. *International Journal of Community Music*, 2(2 & 3), 109–128.

Brah, A. (1996). *Cartographies of diaspora: Contesting identities*. London: Routledge.

Brent, J. (1997). Community without unity. In P. Hoggett (ed.), *Contested communities: Experiences, struggles, policies* (pp. 68–83). Bristol, UK: Policy Press.

Childs, J. B. (2003). *Transcommunality: From the politics of conversion to the ethics of respect*. Philadelphia: Temple University Press.

Christodoulidis, E. A. (1998). *Communitarianism and citizenship*. Aldershot, Hants, UK: Ashgate.

Cohen, A. P. (1985). *The symbolic construction of community*. London: Tavistock Publications.

Cohen, M. L. (2007a). Explorations of inmate and volunteer choral experiences in a prison-based choir. *Australian Journal of Music Education*, 61–72.

Cohen, M. L. (2007b). Hallelujah!—prison choirs: Studying a unique phenomenon. *Choral Journal*, 48(5), 47–50.

Cohen, M. L. (2008). Conductors' perspectives of Kansas prison choirs. *International Journal of Community Music*, 1(3), 319–333.

Cohen, M. L., & Silverman, M. (2013). Personal Growth through Music: Oakdale Prison's Community Choir and community Music for Homeless Populations in New York City. In K. Veblen, S. J. Messenger, M. Silverman, & D. J. Elliott (eds.), *Community Music Today* (pp. 199–216). Landham, MD: Rowman and Littlefield.

Cohen, M. L. (2010). Risk taker extraordinaire: An interview with Elvera Voth. *International Journal of Community Music*, 3(1), 151–156.

Corlett, W. (1995). *Community without unity: A politics of Derridian extravagance*. Durham, NC: Duke University Press. Durham

Delanty, G. (2009). *Community*. 2nd ed. London: Routledge.

Demaine, J., & Entwistle, H. (1996). *Beyond communitarianism: Citizenship, politics, and education*. New York: St. Martin's Press.

Derrida, J. (1995). A "madness" must watch over thinking. In E. Weber (ed.), *Points . . . Interviews, 1974–1994* (pp. 327–338). Stanford, CA: Stanford University Press.

Derrida, J. (1997). The Villanova roundtable. In J. D. Caputo (ed.), *Deconstruction in a Nutshell: A Conversation with Jacques Derrida* (pp. 1–28). New York: Fordham University Press.

Derrida, J. (1999). *Adieu: To Emmanuel Levinas* (P. A. Brault & M. Naas, Trans.). Stanford, CA: Stanford University Press.

Derrida, J. (2000). *Of hospitality* (R. Bowlby, Trans.). Stanford, CA: Stanford University Press.

Derrida, J. (2001). *On cosmopolitanism and forgiveness* (M. Dooley & M. Hughes, Trans.). London: Routledge.

Donnan, H., & Wilson, T. M. (2001). *Borders: Frontiers of identity, nation and state*. Oxford: Berg.

Durkheim, E. (1984/1893). *The division of labor in society* (2nd ed.). New York: Free Press.

Esposito, R. (2010). *Communitas: The origin and destiny of community* (T. Campbell, Trans.). Stanford, CA: Stanford University Press.

Etzioni, A., Volmert, D., & Rothschild, E. (2004). *The communitarian reader: Beyond the essentials*. Lanham, MD: Rowman & Littlefield Publishers.

Everitt, A. (1997). *JDining in: An investigation into participatory music*. London: Calouste Gulbenkian Foundation.

Gonzalez Ben, A. (2016). In Dialogue: Response to Alexandra Kertz-Welzel, "Daring to Question: A Philosophical Critique of Community Music." *Philosophy of Music Education Review*, 24(2), 220–224.

Giroux, H. A. (1993). *Living dangerously: Multiculturalism and the politics of difference*. New York: P. Lang.

Gutek, G. L., & Gutek, P. (1998). *Visiting utopian communities: A guide to the Shakers, Moravians, and others*. Columbia: University of South Carolina Press.

Hägglund, M. (2008). *Radical atheism: Derrida and the time of life*. Stanford, CA: Stanford University Press.

Hannerz, U. (1996). *Transnational connections: Culture, people, places*. London: Routledge.

Higgins, L. (2016). My Voice is Important Too: Non-Formal Music Experiences and Young People. In G. E. McPherson (ed.), *The Child as Musician* (2nd ed., pp. 594–605). New York: Oxford University Press.

Iadeluca, V., & Sangiorgio, A. (2008). Bambini al Centro: Music as a means to promote wellbeing. Birth and configuration of an experience. *International Journal of Community Music*, 1(3), 311–318.

Kant, I. 1998. *Critique of pure reason*. (P. Guyer & A. W. Wood, Trans.) Cambridge: Cambridge University Press.

Kernerman, G. P. (2005). *Multicultural nationalism: Civilizing difference, constituting community*. Vancouver: University of British Columbia Press.

Lehman, E. W. (2000). *Autonomy and order: A communitarian anthology*. Lanham, MD: Rowman & Littlefield Publishers.

Levinas, E. (1981). *Otherwise than being or beyond essence* (A. Lingis, Trans.). The Hague: Martinus Nijhoff.

Levinas, E. (2006). *Humanism of the other* (N. Poller, Trans.). Urbana: University of Illinois Press.

Lyotard, J. F. (1988). *The differend: Phases in dispute* (G. V. D. Abeele, Trans.). Manchester: Manchester University Press.

Matsuoka, A. K., & Sorenson, J. (2001). *Ghosts and shadows: Construction of identity and community in an African diaspora*. Toronto: University of Toronto Press.

McCarthy, M. (2008). The community music activity commission of ISME 1982–2007: A forum for global dialogue and institutional formation. *International Journal of Community Music, 1*(1), 49–61.

Nagle, J. (2008). Multiculturalism's double bind: Creating inclusivity, difference and cross-community alliances with the London-Irish. *Ethnicities 8*, 19–36.

Najam, A. (2006). *Portrait of a giving community: Philanthropy by the Pakistani-American diaspora*. Cambridge, MA: Harvard University Press.

Nancy, J. L. (1991). *The inoperative community*. Minneapolis: University of Minnesota Press.

Olthuis, J. H. (2000). *Towards an ethics of community negotiations of difference in a pluralist society*. Waterloo, Ontario: Canadian Corporation for Studies in Religion.

Peggie, A. (2003). Let's take the c-word out of community music. *Sounding Board* (Autumn), 9.

Phelan, H. (2007). "Let us say *yes* . . ." Music, the stranger and hospitality. *Public Voices, 9*(1), 113–124.

Rapport, N., & Overing, J. (2006). *Social and cultural anthropology: The key concepts*. 2nd Edition. London: Routledge.

Rousseau, J. J. (1993). *The social contract and discourses*. London: Everyman.

Rupp, G. (2006). *Globalization challenged: Conviction, conflict, community*. New York: Columbia University Press.

Schippers, H. (2009). *Facing the music: Shaping music education from a global perspective*. New York: Oxford University Press.

Silber, L. (2005). Bars behind bars: The impact of a women's prison choir on social harmony. *Music Education Research, 7*(2), 251–271.

Stone, B. L. (2000). *Robert Nisbet: Communitarian traditionalist*. Wilmington, DE: ISI Books.

Tönnies, F. (2001[1887]). *Community and civil society*. Cambridge: Cambridge University Press.

Turner, V. W. (1969). *The ritual process: Structure and anti-structure*. New York: Penguin Books.

Vila, P. (2005). *Border identifications: Narratives of religion, gender, and class on the U.S.-Mexico border*. Austin: University of Texas Press.

Vincent, A. (2002). *Nationalism and particularity*. Cambridge: Cambridge University Press.

Weber, M. (1947). *The theory of social and economic organization*. New York: Oxford University Press.

Williams, C. H., & Kofman, E. (1989). *Community conflict, partition and nationalism*. New York: Routledge.

Williams, R. (1985). *Keywords: A vocabulary of culture and society*. New York: Oxford University Press.

Wilson, T. M., & Donnan, H. (1998). *Border identities: Nation and state at international frontiers*. Cambridge: Cambridge University Press.

Wortham, S. M. (2010). *The derrida dictionary*. New York: Continuum.

CHAPTER 9

COMMUNITY MUSIC AND SOCIAL CAPITAL

PATRICK M. JONES AND THOMAS W. LANGSTON

Musicing in community serves many purposes. Such purposes determine the emphases of ensemble leaders and members. Music education occurs in many settings, both in and out of school buildings and through formal and informal means. At first it might appear that music education serves completely different purposes than community music (CM). We argue to the contrary, that music educators serve CM functions and CM facilitators serve music education functions. Articulating a comprehensive list of such functions is beyond the scope of this chapter. For our purposes, we will be content with defining that a key community role of music educators is to help students develop the musical skills, knowledge, habits, and dispositions to engage musically throughout life, and that a key music education role of CM facilitators is to help musicians in CM settings develop similar attributes, as well as fostering the types of ensembles and musical experiences in which people of various ages and social and economic strata can engage.

To accomplish these purposes requires the rejection of two narrow approaches to musicing in both school and community settings—music strictly as an independent sonic event and music strictly as sociocultural expression.

Independent sonic event. The first narrow approach treats music as an independent sonic event (Langer, 1942; Meyer, 1956; Reimer, 2003). Music is understood as consisting of sounds occurring during a fixed period of time. This is a musical version of "art for art's sake," even if the music being performed does not meet "artistic" standards as defined in the Western tradition and/or is serving a utilitarian purpose, such as a marching band at a football game. A purpose for musicing from this perspective could be conceived as developing facility with sonic materials such as tone and rhythm, and knowledge of sonic products such as compositions, recordings, and live performances absent contemporary social context. The greatest limitation of this approach is its narrow conception of music as an event or object consisting merely of sounds. It can result in a sonic-centric understanding of music.

Sociocultural expression. The other approach treats music as a form of sociocultural expression (Blacking, 1973; Nettl, 2005; Regelski, 2004; Small, 1998). Musics are understood as expressions of various groups and cultures from which they come. This approach is informed by ethnomusicology and has resulted in a movement known as multicultural music education. A purpose for musicing from this perspective could be conceived as developing skills, knowledge, and understanding of various types of musics as vehicles to understanding the cultures from which they come, including Western cultures. One risk of this approach is that it can still treat musics as decontextualized objects and events, and performances can often amount to mere pastiches or uninformed imitations. Even when issues of cultural context are addressed, the cultures from which the musics come can be treated as "others" subject to analysis by and disconnected from the lived experiences of the performers themselves. The greatest limitation of this approach is that it can result in an overly intellectualized and superficial understanding of music's relationship to culture.

While both of these approaches are based on essences and aspects of music—its sonic sphere and cultural contexts—each one can result in a narrow understanding and experience in and of music that fails to address music's inherently social nature, which can help people engage positively in the world and strengthen individuals and communities through the development of social capital (Putnam, 1993a, 1993b; Stern & Seifert, 2002; Coffman & Adamek, 2001, 2006; Ernst, 2005; Pitts, 2005; Dabback, 2007; Langston, 2005).

This chapter is built on three premises previously articulated by Jones (2010). First, that globalization has made the development of intercultural understanding and civic engagement some of the most crucial things people must develop for our era and the foreseeable future. Second, that social capital is the stuff from which such understandings and engagement emanate. And third, that community musicing and music education can foster the development of such social capital through music's organic practices and inherently social nature.

Explanation of Theoretical Framework and Key Principles

While recent researchers have explored social capital (Putnam, 2000) and CM (Coffman, 2006), there has been little exploration of the nexus between the two.

Social capital is variously defined, with most authors tending to discuss social capital in terms of its application to individuals and communities, origin, benefits or otherwise, and ways of determining its presence. Social capital is generally understood to be a product of community attributes such as networks, social norms and values, and trust between individuals and between and within community organizations. Such attributes hinge on interactions between individuals and organizations and help to generate coordination, cooperation, and interactions that may be of mutual benefit to those involved.

The importance of social capital to communities is such that it is often regarded as the glue that holds communities together and even as the basis of a truly civil society. The concept of social capital as a measure of civic involvement has gained in significance since the work of early scholars such as Bourdieu (1986) and Coleman (1988). Social capital has produced a mass of literature and a wide range of "definitions" and descriptions in an attempt to explain it.

What Is Social Capital and What Does It Do?

For Bourdieu (1986) social capital was made up of social obligations that under certain conditions could be converted into economic capital (p. 243). Bourdieu also considered social capital to be the sum or aggregate of actual or virtual resources that are linked to the possession of a durable network of relationships of mutual acquaintance or recognition (p. 248).

Coleman (1988) considers social capital a property of individuals. Further he suggests that social capital should be defined by its function (p. S98). He thinks that social capital inheres in the structure of relationships between and among people and facilitates actions between individuals. For Coleman (1988) social capital also greatly enhanced an individual's perceived quality of life (p. S118). It is clear, then, that without interactions between individuals and organizations there can be no social capital created or used.

Putnam (2000, p. 19) also views social capital in terms of connections among people and the social networks, norms of reciprocity and obligations, and the trustworthiness that arise from these connections. Putnam (2000) suggests social capital is a group phenomenon that involves people working together rather than doing things for others. Such social capital producing/harnessing activities provide the wherewithal to facilitate collective problem solving and community advancement by enhancing and creating opportunities for information sharing, goal achievement, and wealth creation, and, in passing, improving people's lives. Moreover, Putnam regarded trust as a norm arising from social networks and associationism.

FORMS OF SOCIAL CAPITAL

Social capital is understood as consisting of three basic forms: bonding, bridging, and linking. Bonding social capital is found in homogeneous groups such as families and close-knit community-of-purpose groups. Bonding social capital has been characterized as "sociological superglue" (Putnam, 2000, p. 23), which helps create (and is created by) strong ties between group members. The loyalty shown by group members to the group itself may, as a consequence, exclude others who do not fit the social norms and values that the group values. Bridging social capital, a "sociological lubricant" (p. 23), helps facilitate and enhance interactions between other individuals and groups. Such bridging between individuals and groups enhances opportunities to form networks and create opportunities for reciprocal actions to be performed. Linking social capital is characterized by relationships that are created between groups and individuals from different social strata or power levels (Woolcock & Sweetser, 2003, p. 2). It facilitates access to resources belonging to individuals and groups that exist outside the organization and the normal social networks that the organization may use.

INDICATORS OF SOCIAL CAPITAL

Various indicators for the presence of social capital within community organizations have been identified. As indicated, social capital develops from the interactions of individuals and groups. It follows, therefore, that participation in a group is an important component of social capital because it provides opportunities for many of the other indicators to be created, such as presence of networks and connections, trust, shared norms and values, reciprocity, and formal and informal learning.

Langston (2009) argues that an individual's upbringing and history may lead to a propensity to participate and interact with others and the development of personal and community social capital is facilitated through these interactions. Participation should be active rather than passive for social capital to be enhanced in individuals and organizations. For example, social capital may be created as a by-product through active participation in community organizations such as choirs and bands.

Participation by individuals in community groups fosters the development of social capital in the individuals themselves and in the organizations of which they are members. Putnam (1993a, 1993b) suggests that the very act of singing in a choral society may strengthen a community's social fabric. Participation creates opportunities for the individuals to forge links with others, develop networks, and gain knowledge about the community group, its members and their networks, and the wider community within which the organization sits. Participation further strengthens social capital development by providing a basis for inclusion, the enhancement of information flow, and the using and sharing of community resources. Such involvement leads to a greater awareness of others and what attributes they have to offer. Through this awareness there is the potential for growth of knowledge and trust. The more that people know of the activities, skills, knowledge, and networks of others, the easier it is to create opportunities for further community and civic activities.

Networks formed by individuals through interaction with others are a core component of social capital. Putnam (1993a, 1993b) suggests that networks of civic engagement foster and facilitate norms of generalized reciprocity (p. 3). Stone (2001) considers that the structural elements of social capital are networks and that the "content" of the networks are the norms of trust and reciprocity. For Stone (2001, p. 7) networks and the trust and reciprocity arising from them are the measurable components of social capital.

For many CM organizations, rehearsals and performances form the major part of their active life. Rehearsals provide opportunities for shared experiences and the creation of many of the facets of social capital. In such CM organizations social capital is manifested by overt actions of members and via stated beliefs. Trust in a variety of forms is created through participation and interaction in CM and civic and community involvement. Cooperation and collaboration and the development of networks and connections are fostered along with leadership, knowledge and identity resources, caring for and valuing others, obligation and reciprocity, faith-based engagement, shared norms and values, learning, and fellowship (notably, fellowship is a social capital indicator that has been largely ignored in the literature).

There has been much discussion about trust and social capital. Trust in this case is understood as mutual expectations of behavior based on shared norms and values. Debate is ongoing about whether trust causes social capital or is created by social capital. Early views of the trust/social capital link, for example Coleman (1988), Putnam (1993a, 1993b), and Fukuyama (1995), considered that trust was a fundamental component of social capital. Later Woolcock (2001) suggested that trust was a product of social capital. What appears to be clear is that trust cannot exist in a relationship without social capital and that social capital needs trust in order to be created and develop.

For organizations to prosper there is a need for the members of those organizations to possess a degree of common understanding, acceptance, and sharing of norms of action and values along with a belief, a trust if you will, that these actions will be reciprocated by other members of the organization. Organizations such as faith-based organizations, choirs, and other voluntary organizations provide opportunities for caring and valuing others. Opportunities for leadership, social interaction, and extra-organizational group activities often occur, and shared norms and values become "institutionalized." The shared norms and values provide for informal control as they regulate group and individual behaviors, and provide the basis for a shared understanding of the common practices of the organization. To this extent, the actions and behaviors that meet the norms and values of an organization will engender reciprocal behaviors on the part of other members of the organization. Sharing the norms, values, knowledge, information, and understandings of an organization engenders a feeling of belonging and inclusion.

Within community organizations such as choirs, trust manifests itself in various ways. Members show loyalty to the organization, commitment to the ongoing activities and norms and values of the group, and are reliable in terms of attendance, knowing the music. They will be supportive of the other members and the choir as a whole. Trust builds as members become aware of the nature of others in the organization, their skills and attitudes, likes and dislikes, and willingness to voice opinions. Gaining confidence through participation and trust in their own abilities and the abilities of others and the willing support given by others is important to all members. This kind of support builds bonding social capital through the development of internal support networks. Trust underpins the quality of interactions of individuals, providing an arena of commonality, a mutual awareness and understanding of the state of the community.

Within CM organizations such as choirs or bands, trust is detected in the interactions between individuals that rely on trust. These interactions produce expectations, feelings of obligation and reciprocation, commitment, loyalty, norms and values relating to behavior, and community attitudes and beliefs. Trust appears to be important for the development of mutuality: the concept that what happens within a community group, which is rich in social capital, happens for the benefit of the group as well as for the benefit of the individual.

A CM organization such as a choir forms a network within itself. This network may provide bonding social capital support for individuals in their attempts to improve their performance abilities, provides an induction into the choir, and facilitates feelings of comfort and belonging within that organization. Members of musical organizations are often members of other groups, each of which has its own networks. Involvement with organizations such as churches can encourage interaction between the organizations. The bridging social capital that is created helps facilitate opportunities for collaborative music-making and enhances the weaving of the social fabric for mutual benefit.

Shared norms and values are the internal and informal rules and practices that are adopted by CM organizations and help to develop that feeling of belonging, unity, and, binding together that is a hallmark of bonding social capital. Indicators of social capital (networks formed within the organization and with organizations in the community, acceptance of and willingness to adopt the norms and values of the organization, trust in others, community and civic involvement) are some of the social capital norms and values indicators that demonstrate that social capital is present within any organization. Indicators of shared norms and values may be as diverse as norms of attendance, the organization as a whole celebrating good performances by the group and individuals within it, soloists and rank-and-file members striving to improve, and positive comments made by participants about other participants. Such positive emphases act as informal sanctions on members and encourage further positive attitudes and comments. Shared experiences contribute to the development of shared language and shared understanding. Successful performances and rehearsals create a willingness to do more together, which may in turn develop the fellowship within the group.

Fellowship as a social capital indicator has largely been ignored in recent literature. Langston and Barrett (2008) suggest that fellowship appears to facilitate informal networking, the sharing of knowledge, caring, and the development of feelings of trust. Within organizations, fellowship may evolve from friendship and, in turn, facilitate friendship, mutual support, working together, and the development of relationships. Fellowship may lead to the creation of a mechanism for informal networking, knowledge sharing, caring, and developing feelings of trust between the individual members of a CM organization. Fellowship may also provide an opportunity to learn about other members. By learning about others, members appear to forge a bond with them, to the mutual benefit of the organization as a whole and of the members themselves.

SITES OF COMMUNITY MUSIC OF AND FOR SOCIAL CAPITAL

There is considerable debate in the literature as to what constitutes "community music." Often CM may be characterized by professional intervention within community music-making settings. Frequently CM may be characterized by music-making that arises from "grassroots" activity in and by the community. While both forms and sites of CM can generate social capital, Langston suggests that the social capital generated by "grassroots" activity, in and by the community, is more sustainable. The "grassroots" approach to music-making largely focuses on activities primarily intended to meet local interests and to give pleasure to the participants. "Grassroots" music groups, such as community choirs and bands, build on *Gemeinschaft* and use the bonds formed within the group to further their own ends. Tönnies (2001, 2002) identified a *Gemeinschaft* community as the archetypal bonding social capital community that is primarily kinship based. In such a community, Tönnies (2001) suggests, friendship and comradeship grow from similarities of opinion, work, artistic sympathy, or creative purpose (2001, p. 29). Veblen (2002), comparing systems of CM, describes *Gemeinschaft* as having personal and deep interactions. In such *Gemeinschaft* communities, relationships are enduring and where relationships are homogenous and small scale; church and family are significant factors (p. 1).

Literature on social capital suggests that it is important to participate and to support participation for a number of reasons. Communities that have high community participation rates enhance social capital and community well-being. Community choirs, bands, dance groups, rehearsals, performances, and other group activities provide opportunities for groups and individuals to interact with others. The social capital developed through such activities helps to build communities. In addition to fostering musical skills development, such organizations create opportunities for reciprocity and obligations, empower participants to develop networks and maintain or improve their community connectedness, and create shared norms, values, and trust.

FUTURE DIRECTIONS

Future directions for social capital and CM are somewhat difficult to predict, as little is overtly done at present to enhance communities through either social capital or CM development.

Putnam (2000) suggests that there is a link between poor social capital and communities with high unemployment, high crime, and low trust. If that is indeed the case then it could be in the interests of local, state, and federal governments to provide funding to further the activities of CM organizations, be they of an interventionist or grassroots nature. Such support could provide the mechanism to bring various marginalized sectors of the community together, as in the "Choir of Hard Knocks."

Social capital development could be a deliberate aim of CM organizations. Organized and financially and socially welcoming, music activities could provide opportunities for successful participation and interactions with others; enhance the knowledge of individuals about their communities and others in them; create networks of communities of common interest; create positive shared norms and values; and encourage trust, reciprocity of actions, and mutuality of obligations.

LEARNING AND TEACHING PRINCIPLES
AND APPROACHES

In order to foster the development of social capital, music educators and CM facilitators should consider social capital when developing musical offerings, designing curricula, and selecting pedagogical approaches. All three forms of social capital can be fostered in traditional school and community ensembles. However, two of the forms require doing more than simply having people participate as musical members.

Bonding. Bonding social capital, the "sociological superglue," is found in homogeneous groups and groups with a unified purpose. As such, any type of musical group that meets repeatedly can foster the development of this type of social capital. It might be argued that traditional school and community ensembles have been excellent venues for the development of bonding social capital. The implication for music education is to continue developing the types of close-knit and focused ensembles that have been successful in school and community settings while expanding genres and ensembles that invite participation by people with a wide range of musical skills and interests.

Bridging. Bridging social capital, as a "sociological lubricant," helps facilitate and enhance interactions between individuals and groups. In order to foster musical interactions, music educators must help students develop the kinds of musicianship skills, knowledge, habits, and dispositions needed to perform with others in musical settings that are ad hoc in nature, such as jam sessions, pickup groups, or short-term ensembles such as pit orchestras for musical theatre productions.

Linking. Linking social capital relates to relationships between groups and individuals from different social strata or power levels. This form of social capital can be developed through ensembles and musical opportunities that are intergenerational and include members from different social and economic strata, hoping it develops naturally through individual interactions. Intentionally fostering the development of linking social capital in individuals might be accomplished by including members with different experiences on the same committees or small ensembles, and assigning musical and non-musical leadership roles to individuals with less life experience or from lower social or economic levels in order to help them become comfortable interacting with those with more life experience and from upper social strata or income levels. Skocpol (2003) addresses this in her study of community organizations and their contributions to helping individuals of different social and economic classes learn to interact democratically.

Whereas developing bonding social capital may be more about group and ensemble participation, fostering bridging and linking social capital requires more emphasis on the development of individual skills. Bridging social capital, developed musically, appears to require the development of transportable musicianship skills, and linking social capital appears to require the development of musical and nonmusical interaction skills. Focusing on musicianship, fostering the development of social capital requires helping students develop the skills, knowledge, habits, and dispositions they need to engage musically with others as amateurs throughout life. This requires learning and teaching principles and approaches oriented toward this goal, and will also require changes in the professional education offered to music teachers and CM facilitators.

Music education occurs in a variety of settings. Bodilly et al. (2008) describe this by stating "the arts education ecology comprises multiple providers of and influencers of arts education" (p. 73). They identify four groups of arts education providers: schools, cultural organizations, community-based providers, and out-of-school-time (OST) providers. Some such efforts, however, are merely aimed at audience development for the professional arts industry as opposed to the development of musicianship for lifelong musicing (McCarthy, Ondaatje, & Novak, 2007). It is also true that music education practices vary from country to country. Bearing all that in mind, and considering the audience for this volume and that school-based music educators are the one body exclusively focused on music education for students' musical development as its primary enterprise, we will focus on school-based music education practices that can foster the development of social capital and engagement in CM.

School-Based Offerings

School-based music offerings can foster both life-wide and lifelong musicing. Jones (2009) has argued that doing so will require school curricula to be reconceptualized to focus on life-wide musicing that can foster lifelong musical participation. In order to do so, school offerings should be created with developing social capital in mind in terms of curriculum and pedagogy.

Curriculum. Curriculum should connect students to the musical ecology in which the school is situated. It should foster development of musicianship skills, knowledge, habits, and dispositions needed for students to engage musically in the community while still in school and throughout their lives. This contains implications for styles and ensembles. In order to do so, curricular decisions must consider three things:

1. The student as the locus of curriculum. This contrasts practices that focus on courses, ensembles, specific genres, or, in some countries, national or state standards.
2. The local musical ecology in which the school is based, particularly the musical opportunities available to students throughout their lives.
3. The musical activities in which students engage outside schools.

There is no "one size fits all" curriculum; all curricula are local. No two schools can have the same music curriculum because no two schools have the same students, serve the same communities, and exist within the exact same musical ecology. A relevant music curriculum will empower students for personal musical agency and improve the community, not simply impart a list of predetermined content. Since schools exist within musical ecologies, the first stage in curriculum design is to discover the musical ecology that surrounds the school. A variety of research techniques can be used to determine the musical ecology of a community, such as conducting computer searches for places where one can go as an audience member or dancer as well as participatory musicing such as community performing ensembles and reviewing media products such as broadcast media notices, newspapers, fliers, community bulletins, and advertisements of musical offerings on bulletin boards in supermarkets, coffeeshops, and so on in the communities to search for musical offerings. You might also include broadcast media. One should ask people about music and musicing. Get them talking about music, their musical interests and activities, and the musical offerings they know of in the community. Ask them to recommend other people you can ask about music. Interview as many informants as possible from various backgrounds and with a variety of musical interests and involvements. Finally, survey students (not just those in music classes) to take the pulse of their musical interests and activities. Once the musical ecology and student musical interests and activities are known, a curriculum can be designed that connects students to musical opportunities that already exist in the community, creates musical opportunities within the community, and helps students develop the expertise to organize their own musical experiences.

Connect students to musical opportunities that already exist in the community. There are very obvious opportunities in many communities, such as community bands, choirs, and orchestras, as well as groups in churches and synagogues, that are easily accessible for our students, utilizing the musical skills they currently develop in school. There may be other opportunities in the community that we have not been addressing in our curricula, such as handbell choirs in churches or community African drumming ensembles. In such cases one would want to start offering handbells and African drumming in school to prepare students for musical participation in the community. One simply needs to find out what opportunities are available in the community and begin orienting curricular offerings to them.

Create musical opportunities within the community. School music teachers possess the expertise to organize community groups such as bands, choirs, orchestras, jazz bands, and so on. One could also offer seasonal opportunities for musicing that don't require sustained involvement, such as a community theater musical production, a community performance of *Messiah*, periodic group singing events, or coffeeshop singer-songwriter nights.

Help students develop the expertise to organize their own musical experiences. This is the long-term solution to fostering sustained community musicing. It would be a neo-Renaissance movement where people pursue musicing in informal social settings as a hobby. The various types of traditional ensembles—concert bands, choirs, orchestras, and other types of ensembles—could continue. Schools can offer an enlarged repertoire that includes musics and instruments of many genres and styles; specifically, those found in the school's local musical ecology, and pop and world musics. Performances will utilize appropriate repertoire and instrumentation based on the event and venue. They could include pep bands, marching bands, jazz bands, and so on. Particular emphasis should be placed on small ensembles that are not dependent on professionally educated musicians to lead them. These would consist of groups of four to five musicians, which is a manageable size for people to gather regularly for recreational musicing. Anything larger would be more difficult for busy students and working adults to schedule on a regular basis. The genres would have to be such that people would actually be interested in participating and sharing their music with their families and friends. We must be visionary in this effort and open to such ensembles consisting of singing, acoustic instruments, electronic instruments, and digital audio technology. The genres can vary from madrigals to barbershop and string quartets to bluegrass. All genres that foster people making music together as a hobby should be considered.

In addition to performing, students will fill a multitude of musicianly roles such as songwriter, composer, transcriber, arranger, director, sound and recording engineer. They learn to make music that is contextually relevant by composing, arranging, and selecting repertoire for use in various settings, such as school assemblies and sporting events, that create ambience and promote intended opinions and emotions among attendees. They learn to arrange and compose music based on certain historical models or various cultural genres, and use existing sound samples in electronic and live formats to target various demographic segments of the population and portray various emotions.

They also need to develop nonmusical skills needed to organize their own musicing throughout life by organizing events, coordinating public relations and marketing, writing programs and marketing materials, securing venues, coordinating logistics, and so on.

Pedagogy. Pedagogical approaches should foster development of skills in musical leadership in a variety of roles such as conducting, rehearsing, and arranging, thus enabling students to create their own ensembles in a variety of settings and for a variety of purposes. To accomplish this, school music ensembles and classes function less as a fixed ensemble with specific instrumentation and more like a "musicians collective" from which musicians are drawn to perform a variety of musics in various ensembles. Instead of the teacher serving as maestro/conductor, rehearsals would function like lab science, visual arts, and creative writing classes, where teachers design project parameters and provide instruction as needed but the students work alone and in small groups to solve the problems and meet the parameters of the project. The pedagogical approach will be focused on developing student musicianship, creativity, and musical expression, with small ensembles performing primarily student compositions, and arrangements being rehearsed, directed, recorded, edited, and produced by students. The teacher will alternate between providing instruction, setting parameters, coaching, and leading analysis, critique, and assessment activities.

Small ensembles are the most viable outlets for continued musicing for busy students and working adults. Such ensembles are also best suited for developing students' musical collaboration and leadership skills. What we lack as a profession is a model of how to facilitate this in a room filled with large numbers of students. We recommend adopting a lab science approach. Just as in a lab science or visual art classes, one can have several groups around the room working simultaneously, with the teacher moving among them monitoring their work, answering questions, and providing coaching. Students can be composing, rehearsing, recording, and editing simultaneously. Teachers can periodically pull them together for a lecture, demonstration, assignment, or group critiques, and then send them back to work in their small groups. The key is to allow the students to be in charge of the ensembles, choose the repertoire, work musically among themselves, and make the musical decisions.

This is counter to the traditional pedagogical model where the teacher directs students at all times. Research into what has come to be called informal music learning indicates that young people are perfectly capable of forming musical ensembles and making musical decisions even without the guidance of teachers (Campbell, 1995; Green 2002, 2008; Souza et al., 2003; Jaffurs, 2004; Allsup, 2002; Davis, 2005). These studies should allay concerns that students cannot work independently while the teacher circulates among them. While we are not advocating the strict incorporation of informal learning as it exists in the literature, we cite this research to support our recommendation that teachers needn't always be directing the students. Teachers have an important role in helping students develop musicianship skills, knowledge, habits, and dispositions and in expanding their musical horizons beyond what they already know and to which they are immediately attracted.

Teacher education. Jones (2008) has argued that music teacher education must be changed in order to equip music teachers to offer curricula and employ pedagogical approaches that foster the development of social capital. Music teacher education must expand the genres and instruments teachers learn as well as equip them to teach songwriting and arranging. Since not all genres and instruments can be learned while at university, music teachers must also know how to learn new genres and instruments on their own. There are two complementary approaches to doing this. One is to gain expertise via lessons, workshops, attending concerts and festivals, reading books and articles, and listening to recordings. The second approach is to bring experts into schools as clinicians and "artists-in-residence" to work with teachers and students in developing various offerings. In addition, many students bring musical expertise to school from their out-of-school musical experiences. These students are "culture bearers" and possess expertise that teachers can tap into to broaden and enrich their own abilities and curricular offerings.

EXAMPLES

There are several examples of social capital development related to involvement in music. Several researchers have studied the development of social capital through participation in music ensembles in particular (Coffman & Adamek, 2001, 2006; Dabback, 2007; Ernst, 2005; Langston, 2005). Other researchers have linked musical participation to improved social conditions, thus indicating that social capital is developed through participation (Pitts, 2005; Putnam, 1993a, 1993b; Stern & Seifert, 2002).

Summary of the Key Principles and Approaches

Music in community organizations such as choirs, bands, and school performance ensembles provides fertile ground for the creation and development of social capital that benefits all members of the musical community and has implications, both financial and social, for the general community in which these organizations exist. Self-organized, self-motivated, and self-owned "grassroots" organizations develop sustainable social capital and facilitate the formation of sustainable community. The bonding and bridging social capital created through the joining together of people and communities of common purpose foster an environment of mutual cooperation, friendship, fellowship, and goodwill.

Participation in musical activities and especially participation with others boosts intracommunity and intercommunity networking and mental and social stimulation and creates friendship-making opportunities. There has been much written about how participating with others and being involved in activities that keep the mind active benefits older people especially, but has benefits for all to some extent (Bygren, Konlaan, & Johansson, 1996; Johansson, Konlaan, & Bygren, 2001). Many CM groups such as choirs and New Horizons bands appeal to predominantly older, retired people. These activities provide a supportive environment for older people to use the talents and competencies (such as leadership skills) that they have developed throughout many years of work and community involvement. The literature suggests that people who participate in community activities keep their minds and bodies active, live longer, and stay healthier than those who do not (Bygren, Konlaan, & Johansson., 1996; Johansson, Konlaan, & Bygren, 2001, 2001). It may follow, then, that participation in CM may have particular significance for government policy in terms of addressing the health and well-being of an aging population. It may be suggested that local, state, and federal support of activities that boost social capital and provide opportunities for older people to become involved and interact with others while keeping their minds active might be financially cheaper than providing community health funding at its current levels.

Music educators can foster the development of social capital by connecting students to musical opportunities that already exist within the community, creating musical opportunities within the community, and helping students develop the expertise to organize their own musical experiences. They can focus on the students as the nexus of learning and help them develop the kinds of musicianship skills, knowledge, habits, and dispositions necessary to engage in a variety of musical settings outside school throughout life. Such settings include not only organized large ensembles but also ad hoc groups such as jam sessions, pickup groups, or short-term ensembles such as pit orchestras for musical theatre productions.

Finally, formal and informal music education may help to provide a common base of rich musical experiences, volunteering, and community and civic involvement from childhood through to adulthood. In this way music education may positively develop social capital in individuals and in the communities in which the education takes place.

REFLECTIVE QUESTIONS

1. Is it possible to determine an individual's social connectedness (i.e., social capital) from both his or her personal characteristics and his or her neighbors' characteristics (age, race, geographic mobility, etc.) (Putnam, 2007, p. 151)? Within this single question lie two questions, one relating to the individual's personal characteristics and the other to characteristics of the individual's neighbors. If the answer to the question relating to the individual is yes, should formal and informal music education in schools and communities be social-capital-biased in order to foster the development of "communities of common histories" (Langston, 2005), in which individuals can be "primed to participate" in activities with others, and by doing so develop their connectedness and individual and community social capital?
2. Can bonding social capital create social stratification (Putnam, 2000, p. 358) and disadvantage individuals who are excluded from membership of the organizations for one reason or another? If so, how might music teachers and CM facilitators mitigate against such social stratification while still fostering the development of bonding social capital?
3. How might music teachers and CM facilitators foster the development of bridging capital for individuals and groups of musicians?
4. Can schools and communities organize classes, seminars, and courses to enable individuals and groups to develop linking social capital skills to enable them to create connections with "higher" bodies such as funding organizations and local government in order to enhance opportunities for their bands, choirs, and so on? If so, what might such offerings include?

KEY SOURCES

International Journal of Community Music. http://www.intellectbooks.co.uk/journals/view-Journal,id=149/.

Putnam, R. D. (2000). *Bowling alone: The collapse and revival of American community.* New York: Simon & Schuster.

Skocpol, T. (2003). *Diminished democracy: From membership to management in American civic life*. Norman: University of Oklahoma Press.

WESTSITES

....

A New Framework for Building Participation in the Arts. Presents the findings of a RAND study to better understand the process by which individuals become involved in the arts and to identify how arts institutions can most effectively influence this process. http://www.rand.org/publications/MR/MR1323/MR1323.pdf.

The Social Capital Community Benchmark Survey. Examined the civic engagement and connectedness of 30,000 Americans beginning in 2001. Administered by the Saguaro Seminar. www.cfsv.org/communitysurvey/index.html.

The Social Impact of the Arts Project. A research center at the University of Pennsylvania. Its researchers have focused on developing empirical methods to study links between cultural engagement and community well-being since 1994. http://www.sp2.upenn.edu/SIAP.

REFERENCES

....

Allsup, R. E. (2002). Crossing over: Mutual learning and democratic action in instrumental music education. Unpublished Ed.D. diss., Teachers College, Columbia University, New York.

Blacking, J. (1973). *How musical is man?* Seattle: University of Washington Press.

Bodilly, S. J., Augustine, C. H., Zakaras, L., & Wallace Foundation. (2008). *Revitalizing arts education through community-wide coordination*. Santa Monica, CA: RAND Research in the Arts.

Bourdieu, P. (1986). The forms of capital. In J. Richardson (ed.), *Handbook of theory and research for the sociology of education* (pp. 241–258). Westport, CT: Greenwood Press.

Bygren, L., Konlaan, B. & Johansson, S. (1996). Attendance at cultural events, reading books or periodicals, and making music or singing in a choir as determinants for survival: Swedish interview survey of living conditions. *British Medical Journal, 7072*, 313. Retrieved January 27, 2010, from http://bmj.bmjjournals.com/archive/7072ud2.htm.

Campbell, P. S. (1995). Of garage bands and song-getting: The musical development of young rock musicians. *Research Studies in Music Education, 4*, 12–20.

Coffman, D. D. (2006). Voices of experience: Interviews of adult community band members in Launceston, Tasmania, Australia. *International Journal of Community Music, D*. Retrieved April 16, 2006, from http://www.intljcm.com/articles/Volume%204/Coffman/Coffman.pdf.

Coffman, D. D., & Adamek, M. S. (2001). Perceived social support of New Horizons Band participants. *Contributions to Music Education 28*(1), 27–40.

Coleman, J. S. (1988). Social capital in the creation of human capital. *American Journal of Sociology, 94*, (suppl.), S95–120.

Dabback, W. (2007). Toward a model of adult music learning as a socially-embedded phenomenon. Unpublished PhD diss., Eastman School of Music, University of Rochester, NY.

Davis, S. G. (2005). "That thing you do!": Compositional Processes of a Rock Band. *International Journal of Education and the Arts, 6*(16).

Ernst, R. (2005). Music for life: Improving the quality of life and wellness for adults. *International Journal of Community Music, 8*(1).

Fukuyama, F. (1995). *Trust: The social values and the creation of prosperity.* New York: Free Press.

Green, L. (2002). *How popular musicians learn: A way ahead for music education.* Hampshire, UK: Ashgate Publishing Limited.

Green, L. (2008). *Music, informal learning and the school: A new classroom pedagogy.* Hampshire, UK: Ashgate Publishing Limited.

Jaffurs, S. E. (2004). The impact of informal music learning practices in the classroom, or how I learned how to teach from a garage band. *International Journal of Music Education, 22*(3), 189–200.

Johansson, S. E., Konlaan, B. B., & Bygren, L. A. (2001). Sustaining habits of attending cultural events and maintenance of health: A longitudinal study. *Health Promotion International, 16*(3), 229–234.

Jones, P. M. (2008). Preparing music teachers for change: Broadening instrument class offerings to foster life wide and lifelong musicing. *Visions of Research in Music Education, 12.* http://www.rider.edu/~vrme/.

Jones, P. M. (2009). Life wide as well as lifelong: Broadening primary and secondary school music education's service to students' musical needs. *International Journal of Community Music, 2*(2& 3), 201–214.

Jones, P. M. (2010). Developing social capital: A role for music education and community music in fostering civic engagement and intercultural understanding. *International Journal of Community Music, 3*(2), 291–302.

Langer, S. K. (1942). *Philosophy in a new key: A study in the symbolism of reason, rite, and art.* Cambridge, MA: Harvard University Press.

Langston, T. W. (2005). Capitalizing on community music: A case study of the manifestation of social capital in a community choir. Unpublished Ed.D. diss., University of Tasmania.

Langston, T. W. (2009). The importance of being Henry. In M. S. Barrett & S. L. Stauffer (eds.), *Narrative inquiry in music education* (pp. 63–80). Springer Science & Business Media B.V.

Langston, T. W., & Barrett, M. S. (2008). Capitalizing on community music: A case study of the manifestation of social capital in a community choir. *Research Studies in Music Education 30*(2), 118–138.

McCarthy, K. F., Ondaatje, E. H., & Novak, J. L. (2007). *Arts and culture in the metropolis: Strategies for sustainability.* Santa Monica, CA: RAND Corporation.

Meyer, L. B. (1956). *Emotion and meaning in music.* Chicago: University of Chicago Press.

Nettl, B. (2005). *The study of ethnomusicology: Thirty-one issues and concepts* (new ed.). Urbana: University of Illinois Press.

Pitts, S. (2005). *Valuing musical participation.* Hampshire, UK: Ashgate Publishing Limited.

Putnam, R. D. (1993a). *Making democracy work: Civic traditions in modern Italy.* Princeton, NJ: Princeton University Press.

Putnam, R. D. (1993b). The prosperous community: Social capital and public life. *American Prospect 13.* http://xroads.virginia.edu/~HYPER/DETOC/assoc/13putn.html.

Putnam, R. D. (2000). *Bowling alone: The collapse and revival of American community.* New York: Simon & Schuster.

Putnam, R. D. (2007). *E pluribus unum: Diversity and community in the twenty-first century.* 2006 Johan Skytte Prize Lecture. *Scandinavian Political Studies, 30*(2), 137–174.

Regelski, T. A. (2004). *Teaching general music in grades 4–8: A musicianship approach*. New York: Oxford University Press.

Reimer, B. (2003). *A philosophy of music education: Advancing the vision* (3rd ed.). Upper Saddle River, NJ: Pearson.

Skocpol, T. (2003). *Diminished democracy: From membership to management in American civic life*. Norman: University of Oklahoma Press.

Small, C. (1998). *Musicking: The meanings of performing and listening*. Hanover, NH: Wesleyan University Press.

Souza, J., Hentschke, L., Bozzetto, A., Cunha, E., & Cunha Bonilla, K. (2003). Praticás de aprendizagem musical em três bandas de rock. *Per Musi, 7*, 68–75.

Stern, M., & Seifert, S. (2002). *Culture builds community: Evaluation summary report*. Philadelphia: Social Impact of the Arts Project, University of Pennsylvania School of Social Work.

Stone, W. (2001). *Measuring social capital: Towards a theoretically informed measurement framework for researching social capital in family and community life*. Research paper, 24. Melbourne: Australian Institute of Family Studies.

Tönnies, F. (2001). Community and civil society. In J. Harris (ed.), R. Geuss & Q. Skinner (series eds.), & M. Hollis (trans.), *Cambridge texts in the history of political thought*. Cambridge: Cambridge University Press.

Tönnies, F. (2002). *Community and society*. Mineola, NY: Dover Publications.

Veblen, K. (2002). *Apples and oranges, solar systems and galaxies: Comparing systems of community music*. Retrieved November 28, 2009, from http://www.worldmusiccentre.com/uploads/cma/veblen.pdf.

Woolcock, M. (2001). *The place of social capital in understanding social and economic outcomes*. Retrieved December 31, 2009, from http://homepages.wmich.edu/~jbiles/woolcock.pdf.

Woolcock, M., & Sweetser, A. T. (2003). *Social capital: The bonds that connect*. Asian Development Bank. https://www.adb.org

CHAPTER 10

COMMUNITY MUSIC THERAPY

KENNETH S. AIGEN

This chapter will introduce community music therapy (CoMT) and place it in the context of contemporary music therapy practice. Its origins and development within the profession will be traced, and its basic premises and practices will be highlighted by focusing on a variety of contemporary international projects. The relationship of CoMT to conventional music therapy practice and to community music (CM) will also be discussed.

CoMT is neither a model nor a method of music therapy. Its adherents do not claim a unified theoretical framework or a set of practice guidelines. Instead, it is best considered "a broad perspective exploring relationships between the individual, community, and society in relation to music and health" (Stige, Ansdell, Elefant, & Pavlicevic, 2010, pp. 15–16). Consequently, a brief review such as this one is necessarily selective, and the choice of ideas and practices to highlight reflects as much on the interests of this author as on the phenomenon of study.

OVERVIEW OF MUSIC THERAPY

Music therapy is a profession that is practiced globally, with organizations devoted to its advancement throughout North America, South America, Europe, Asia, and Australia. In the Middle East and Africa there are fewer countries with a professional and educational infrastructure for music therapy—with important exceptions, such as Israel in the former and the Republic of South Africa in the latter—but there are efforts to expand professional music therapy into other nations throughout these two regions.

It is in the United States that music therapy has the longest tradition as an organized, autonomous profession. The first university training program in music therapy was established in 1944, and the first national organization devoted to its advancement was created in 1950. Ansdell's (2002) description of the origins of music therapy in the United Kingdom from the 1890s through the 1940s is an accurate portrait of what occurred in the United States as well. Ansdell (2002) describes these proto-music-therapy forms in medical and psychiatric hospitals as primarily non-participatory: music was generally played to patients but not with them. The work was conceptualized as being medical or recreational in nature as "large hospital communities attempted to mirror the 'outside world,' with recorded music, hospital choirs and bands, performances for patients, or sometimes by patients" (p. 1).

In the 1940s, the development of the profession was driven by large numbers of veterans of World War II who suffered emotional and physical injury and were populating hospitals and clinics. Volunteer musicians noted anecdotal benefits, thus stimulating the need for academic education and professional regulation. As music therapy became a recognized profession, Ansdell (2002) notes that it took on five characteristics that distinguished it from the practice that had developed during the first half of the twentieth century: (1) a change from exclusively receptive methods to participatory ones, (2) a use of improvisation to allow spontaneous joint music-making, (3) an emphasis on the relationship between therapist and client that was modeled after other forms of therapy, (4) emphasis on individual sessions, and (5) allying with extrinsic medical and therapeutic theory for both explanatory and legitimizing purposes.

Music therapists have engaged in an ongoing struggle to have the depth, potency, and professionalism of their work recognized. Music therapists whose training orients them to developing individualized treatment plans have traditionally preferred to work with individuals, small groups, and in private spaces. Administrators in health-related institutions who believe that music therapy is only a recreational or adjunctive treatment medium have imposed restrictions on the activity of music therapists—such as requiring them to service large numbers of people, work in public areas of an institution, or organize nonclinical shows and music events—that do not recognize its potential as a primary mode of treatment. It is important to consider these conflicting visions of how music therapy is viewed internally and externally to fully understand the place of CoMT in the profession because some of the practices that constitute CoMT recall those activities that reflect a lack of awareness of the ability of music therapy to function as an in-depth, primary treatment modality.

ORIGINS AND FOUNDATIONS OF
COMMUNITY MUSIC THERAPY

The concept of CoMT is relatively new. It was introduced by Bruscia (1998), who placed it within the "ecological" area of practice, defined as follows:

> included are any efforts to form, build, or sustain communities through music therapy. Thus, this area of practice expands the notion of "client" to include a community, environment, ecological context, or individual whose health problem is ecological in nature. . . . Helping an individual to become healthier is not viewed as a separate enterprise from improving the health of the ecological context within which the individual lives; conversely, helping any ecological context to become healthier is not a separate enterprise from improving the health of its members; and helping individual and ecology to relate to one another harmoniously makes both healthier. (p. 229)

CoMT received its first detailed expositions in Ansdell (2002) and Stige (2002). The impetus for its elaboration came from two sources. Primarily, a number of clinicians internationally were engaged in practices with their clients—such as public performances and creating recordings—that could not be easily subsumed into existing clinical theory. Secondarily, the broader turn in academia to constructivist epistemologies and social theories that emphasized the role of culture and context was primarily manifest in music therapy through the writings on culture-centered music therapy and CoMT (Stige, 2002). It is somewhat ironic that while music therapists have advocated for individualized treatment, small groups, and closed environments in which to work, the natural modes of relating to music favored by clients have led in the opposite direction, eventually bringing the profession full circle through the introduction of CoMT. Thus, in the 1990s, when many music therapists found themselves working in different contexts and with different goals, these changes were just as much a return to the origins of music therapy as they were a reaction to an imbalance in trends that emphasized individualized, intrapsychic work over more communal focuses. Ansdell (2002) described the conditions that led music therapists to seek a more inclusive treatment framework that could incorporate their work:

- Therapists working with clients from very different cultures and who may not have had a concept of therapy (such as indigenous peoples in Australia and South Africa)
- Therapists working with clients whose most pressing need was for connection to the outside community
- Therapists who work in emotionally demanding settings—such as hospice care—who found that their work addressed the needs of family members, clinical staff, and other workers
- Therapists working with traumatized war refugees, where the treatment issues had social and political dimensions

- Therapists whose clinical work incorporated performance and/or recordings

In meeting the needs of these clients, some music therapists came into conflict with conventional ethical and professional guidelines. There clearly was a need for an expansion of existing theoretical, conceptual, professional frameworks to accommodate these practices. The precepts of CoMT were developed in response to this need:

> *Community Music Therapy* is an approach to working musically with people *in context*: acknowledging the social and cultural factors of their health, illness, relationships, and musics. It reflects the essentially communal reality of musicing and is a response both to overly individualized treatment models and to the isolation people often experience within society. (Ansdell, 2002, p. 1)

The goal of CoMT is to help clients access opportunities for musicing and to accompany them from individualized therapy to social contexts of musicing. CoMT involves a conceptual expansion of music therapy, not just taking existing rationales and approaches into communal settings but instead rethinking the relationship between clinical practices and communal contexts. Music is considered to be a natural agent of health promotion, and CoMT practices are built on this belief.

An example of a CoMT framework is Wood's (2006) "matrix model" of music therapy. The traditional view of music therapy has a nested structure that includes individual work at the core that can move out to group work with the establishment of community connections on the periphery of the music therapist's concerns. In contrast, Wood offers a model where clients have the potential to make use of a vast range of musical life, best represented as a matrix. In addition to the individual and group music therapy sessions characterizing the traditional model, the matrix model consists of a number of additional options in terms of the client's participation in music, including learning an instrument, participating in ensembles, and engaging in performances. In this model the forms of musical experience are arranged in a nonhierarchical way, people can develop by taking advantage of what different musical experiences offer, and the system can accommodate to each step in client development with the individual remaining at the core.

Three aspects of Wood's model are particularly important in understanding the novel developments characterizing CoMT. First, Wood includes activities typically considered outside the realm of music therapy, such as concert going and music for special occasions. Second, the model is not hierarchical in the sense that individualized activities are not considered more essential than are community-related activities. Third, there is no sequential organization implied such that individualized activities necessarily precede community-related activities.[1]

Ansdell (2002) has outlined four fundamental ways CoMT differs from traditional music therapy.

Basic aims. In traditional music therapy, individual clients are supported in exploring their inner emotional lives. The purpose is to develop personal insight through musical experience. Music is considered a psychological phenomenon, not a sociocultural one, and the focus is on inner change. In contrast, CoMT recognizes that musicing leads people inward and outward—internal exploration is not the sole focus of the music therapist. The drive to commune with others through music is as important as the drive to self-expression and self-knowledge. Therefore, community music therapists support their clients' desires in both directions.

This notion is based on a characteristic of music that Pavlicevic and Ansdell (2004) have termed the *ripple effect*, something that they identify as being essential to CoMT. They observe that music naturally radiates outward, defying any efforts at containment: it calls to people and binds communities together. Music leads people from an inward to an outward focus as one follows its resonance. Therefore, the practices and precepts of CoMT follow the naturalistic essence of music.

Mode of intervention. In the traditional conceptualization, music therapy is distinguished from other music domains—such as education, performance, and music appreciation—not just by goals but by means as well. Activities such as learning an instrument, composing, or performing are minimized. In CoMT, clinical and non-clinical musicing are considered to be quite similar, as music therapy can involve musicing formats that are similar to those outside of therapy. These natural modes of relating to music are encouraged.

Professional identity and role. The traditional role of a music therapist is clearly different from that of a music educator or performer. The nearest role model is that of a psychotherapist, who has insight into clients and can decode symbolic meanings. In the CoMT perspective, the music therapist's expertise is primarily musical rather than being primarily psychotherapeutic or health-related. The goal is to promote music and musicing for individuals and milieus by removing obstacles. Ansdell describes this role as a "therapeutic musician in residence," a formulation that challenges more traditional hierarchical roles and relationships.

Location and boundaries of therapy processes. In the traditional approach, music therapy occurs in protected, private spaces to ensure confidentiality. The work is primarily intrapersonal, and its main context is the therapeutic relationship, either between client and therapist or among clients in group settings. Extratherapy activities occurring outside the session are generally not taken up. In CoMT, the music therapist takes her musicianship wherever it is needed: this could be in a private room, or it might be in more public spaces such as corridors, waiting rooms, or shared group recreational spaces. In contrast to the traditional approach, in CoMT the therapeutic frame—incorporating the ethical and practical aspects of clinical work—is more fluid and permeable. The therapist's job is to work with the entire context of a client's life, with the overall goal of increasing the musical spirit of a community and enhancing the quality of life of its individual members.

The concept of *community* has multiple referents in CoMT: it can refer to a curative factor or a clinical goal, such as when feelings of musical community are invoked as either the target of one's work or as an explanation for why particular individuals were able to better move toward health within a CoMT program; it can refer to the identified client, as when a therapist asserts as a goal improving the well-being of the community; it can refer to the locale where the activity occurs, such as when the residents of a circumstantial community participate in a performance in the wider, geographically defined community; and it can refer to the therapy process, as is the case when clinical goals refer to the integration of clients into the broader community.

THE SPECTRUM OF COMMUNITY MUSIC THERAPY PRACTICE

In traditional music therapy, clients engage with music through a range of receptive and active forms: they may listen to, play, or compose music. If they are playing music, they may engage in improvisation or the recreation of composed materials. These materials might be of any conventional origin, or they may be composed for use in therapy. If clients are playing music, they might sing, they may use instruments in which they have some prior experience and/or proficiency, or they may use instruments that they have never played previously. Many music therapists will offer clients a wide range of instruments that do not require prior skills, but that still offer the means to achieve expressively rewarding experiences, such as various pitched percussion instruments, drums, cymbals, gongs, keyboards, and so on.

In spite of this great variety, there are some common elements that typify traditional music therapy practice: the work generally takes place in a closed space; it is targeted at a specific, nonmusical health concerns (e.g., increasing self-esteem, enhancing immune system response, increasing the range of motion of a damaged limb);[2] the process of the therapy and its nonmusical results (rather than the creation of a particular musical product or outcome) are considered the only legitimate rationales; the activities comprising the therapy do not usually extend overtly into the world outside the therapy room. A number of features of CoMT practice distinguish it from these elements of traditional music therapy.

CREATING MUSIC OUTSIDE OF A CLOSED THERAPY ROOM

At times, music therapists work in spaces that do not provide privacy because such a room is not available. This might include a waiting room or a shared recreational space in a medical or social services facility. However, when music therapists choose to work in nonprivate spaces by intention, this is an example of CoMT. Such applications can be considered examples of environmental music therapy, defined as "a systematic process of using music to promote health in a specified environment inside or outside of institutions" (Aasgaard, 1999, p. 34). A basic premise of this type of work is that physical, social, and symbolic environments can be healthy or unhealthy and that the health-musicing skills developed by music therapists can make a unique contribution to the well-being of these various environments.

Aasgaard (2004) details a number of music therapy activities that fall into this category. In one, Aasgaard functions as a "Pied Piper" as he regularly leads a musical parade through the corridors of a pediatric hospital:

> The participants are first of all the patients: some in wheelchairs, some in beds, many with infusion pumps. But also relatives, students (of various kinds) and people working in the hospital—altogether 20 or 30 persons—may be present. Sometimes a dozen (young and old) start the event by marching (or rolling) through the corridors playing and singing. In front, walks the music therapist in top hat, blowing his trombone or recorder. As a rule, more and more participants join the line of musicians as the procession slowly proceeds from the 8th floor to the 4th floor. (p. 147)

The clinical purposes of such an activity are varied and embedded within it are goals common to traditional therapy as well as ones that appear unique to CoMT. As an example of the former, consider how—for the time period of the music— hospitalized children are able to feel enlivened, engaged with life, and have their overall mood lifted, all of which are important goals in a pediatric setting. As an example of the latter, consider the effect on the life of the institution to regularly have costumed staff, medical doctors, patients, family members, and other random visitors parading through the halls while creating live music. Such an inclusive ritual can eliminate the rigid distinctions among people that can create feelings of isolation, alleviate the constant stress and fear endemic to a hospital environment, and remind everyone (participants and those who only observe the parade) of another world "dominated by play, fantasy, and pleasurable social interactions" (Aasgaard, 2004, p. 147).

PERFORMING WITH CLIENTS

There are different, often contradictory thoughts about the ethics and clinical value of music therapists performing with their clients. Turry (2001) suggests a number of potential risks, although they are basically of two types: therapists might be unconsciously meeting their own needs for professional recognition, or they may perform with clients to meet their own creative, expressive needs. In these instances, Turry raises the important rhetorical question Who, then, is looking out for the client's best interests?

On the one hand, performance can be beneficial for clients in overcoming the inner obstacles to performing; this can be such a significant accomplishment that Turry has likened it to the "hero's journey," as described by Joseph Campbell. The preparations for, and successful realization of, a public performance can lead to a significant change in one's sense of self-worth. Yet Turry also considers the opposite view about performing embodied in the traditional psychoanalytic perspective that the need to perform can be driven by unresolved psychological conflicts. In this view performance is considered inauthentic, something that conflicts with the value that therapy should be focused on helping clients to "get more insight into their 'real' self" (Ansdell, 2010, p. 173).

In contrast to the psychoanalytic view, practitioners of CoMT draw on more contemporary forms of personality theory that suggest that the self "is a socially and culturally constructed entity, whose nature is indeed performative" (Ansdell, 2010, p. 173). In this perspective, the public display of knowledge, skill, and self-hood embodied in performance is an essential human need, and as something that promotes the inner development of the client's self, it is a legitimate activity in which music therapists should engage with their clients.

Performing in an Institutional Setting

Music therapists have participated in performances within institutional settings since the origin of the profession, although these types of activities were likely considered to be outside the realm of their clinical duties. CoMT is providing new theoretical rationales for performance that construe it as a vital aspect of a clinician's responsibilities rather than as something apart from them. Many of these rationales reflect the fact that these events are structured such that performance generally includes all the members of a community, not just its identified clients.

One such example of how performance can improve the health of a circumstantial community is the Happy Hour,[3] developed by David Ramsey at Beth Abraham Health Services, a residential rehabilitation facility in New York City. During this time, residential patients are allowed two alcoholic drinks; doctors and nurses function as wait staff; and music therapists, patients, family members, and any other employee can take to a stage to perform. Many community-building and individual health-related goals are addressed through this structure.

The most important of these goals is related to enhancing and normalizing the social interactions and perspectives of the community members. For example, as the only time when alcohol consumption is permitted in the institution, Happy Hour allows the patients to be treated as the adults that they are. Having professional staff (such as doctors) functioning as waiters serves to equalize the human relationships in the community, making them more mutual. Providing an opportunity for everyone to perform—whether patient, doctor, therapist, or janitor—serves to reinforce the common humanity shared by all members of the community, a commonality that is all too often lost in the interactions that characterize institutional hierarchies. Because of the disabilities of the patients, it is really only through the expressive, interactive medium of music that this common level of humanity can be realized. And perhaps most important, through the vehicle of musical performance, health workers who care for individuals who may not be able to take responsibility for any of their most personal physical functions are allowed to see these people in a new light:

> What happens for patients during performances is that the perception of being an invalid is almost instantly changed because you're on stage doing something that is culturally idealized. And so if the [people] that bathe you [are] watching you up on a stage singing, the next time they bathe you and tend to your personal hygiene, they're going to think of you differently. It instantly and forever changes that relationship. (David Ramsey, quoted in Aigen, 2004, p. 190)

For Ramsey, part of the rationale for including performance as a clinical vehicle is the idea that performance is an extension of everyday social interactions, rather than something fundamentally different from them. For example, one way that people in everyday life assert their sense of agency and create a view of themselves as competent is through the simple act of taking control of a conversation while speaking to a group of people. However, this simple act is not available to clients with severe disabilities in the areas of motor function, neurological function, and functional communication skills. However, as Ramsey asserts, "when you've got somebody who can't raise their hand or raise their voice, you have to artificially give them the stage to do that. Or else it won't happen" (Aigen, 2004, p. 191). In sum, in CoMT, the desire for public performance is considered to be reflective of a positive desire to interact with one's social world rather than as a symptom of a psychological conflict.

Performing Outside of an Institutional Setting

When performance becomes a vehicle for music therapy processes, it can occur completely within an institution, as was just described, it can involve individuals belonging to a common institution performing in other institutions (see Jampel, 2006), and it can involve performing in public squares or theaters with no particular institutional affiliation. For example, beginning in the mid-1990s, Danish music therapist Sten Roer organized a band of individuals with psychiatric illnesses and performed rock and jazz music in outdoor, public spaces—he even brought the band on an international visit to the United States. And Maria Logis wrote a theater piece with music about her experience as a music therapy client with therapist Alan Turry that was performed at the New York International Fringe Festival, a collection of shows and concerts occurring across a two-week period in New York City (see Aigen, 2004).

Logis's piece is particularly interesting because of the way it originated and how it simultaneously told the story of her therapy while acting as an extension of it. Logis was a corporate executive who contracted cancer and who was reluctant to follow the standard therapies prescribed by her doctors. Something within her told her to sing, but she did not know how or why to do this or how it related to her medical issues. She tried vocal lessons but felt that she needed more. Through a chance comment to her dentist she learned about music therapy and thus began her experience, which took place over many years. Her therapy process involved the spontaneous expression of thoughts and feelings accompanied by Turry's improvisations on the piano. These improvisations gradually evolved into songs, and Logis began performing this music: first live for friends, then for professional audiences. Eventually a CD was recorded with professional musicians, and ultimately the theater piece was created. While Turry supported this work as an example of CoMT, his active participation in the public presentations of it gradually stopped as Logis took these efforts on independently. The performances in the community were conceived as logical consequences of her therapy work and reflected the personal changes that took place there.

Although it did not include public performances such as those engaged in by Roer and Logis, Anna Maratos (2004) describes a dramatic project in a setting for adults with chronic mental illness that did include performance outside the institution in which it was conceived. This work is particularly interesting due to its illustration of the way performance-oriented music therapy can stimulate changes in the way power is wielded by the medical staff.

This project entailed the creation, rehearsal, and performance of an operetta, called *The Teaching of Edward*, which details "a fictional account of the English composer, Edward Elgar's 'discovery' of music therapy through being persuaded by the patients at the asylum where he was employed to go beyond his usual musician's role of performing to patients" (Maratos, 2004, p. 136). In the story, Elgar is unsuccessful in generating interest in performing his music, yet when he inadvertently begins a spontaneous composition with the patients, they participate enthusiastically and with a confidence that belies their psychological difficulties. The song is called "Take Us Where the Music Goes," and in its sentiment it could serve as an official anthem of CoMT.

The dynamics of rehearsal and performance offered a unique way of examining the roles and interpersonal dynamics of the patients and staff. Maratos describes how the psychiatrist who was the play's author also adopted the role of director. One of the patients approached him asking if she could play the narrator in addition to the role of patient. While this desire to portray a healthy, "sane" character was certainly a positive one and should have been responded to affirmatively by the author-director-psychiatrist, he instead replied that there was someone else he was thinking of for the part. In this interaction, Maratos notes the same destructive interpersonal dynamics that typify life in a psychiatric institution. The passive patient assumes a position of weakness and defers to the more powerful psychiatrist. The psychiatrist's response reinforces the inequality and lack of mutuality in their relationship.

However, reflecting on such interactions helped the participants to gain insight into their unconscious and destructive nature. In fact, the patient went on to play both roles and the psychiatrist-author became less controlling in the process, while gaining insight into how his role was perceived: "I had not realised quite how much consultant psychiatrists (with their powers of compulsory detention) were regarded with a combination of fear and loathing. It also helped me to realise how much of what goes in formal ward reviews is totally phoney [sic]" (Maratos, 2004, p. 142). In their professional role, psychiatrists control access into and out of the institution. Patients who are working to rejoin their external communities must convince psychiatrists of their ability to do so. Analyzing this example of performance in CoMT demonstrates how this power imbalance might serve to encourage supplicating and less autonomous behaviors in patients—in order to curry the favor of psychiatrists—that actually serve to impede their ability to function outside of the institutional community.

CONCEIVING OF A COMMUNITY AS THE CLIENT

Practitioners of CoMT have enlarged the conception of the client to include the various types of communities discussed previously. The community is not just a place in which therapy occurs; it is also an entity on which the clinical work is focused.

Cochavit Elefant (2010) has described a CoMT project in Raanana, Israel, in which two groups of children—one with special needs and one without them—were joined in the creation of music therapy group. Although this project had benefits for both groups of children, its rewards did not stop there and extended into the broader social networks of the community. Because of the extensive ripple effect of this project, it makes for an apt illustration of CoMT.

Elefant (2010) notes that although these two groups of children inhabited a common community, they lived quite separately, and many of the children without disabilities had never even met a child with special needs. Her intent was to facilitate the establishment of relationships between the two groups with the idea that "music could become the connecting 'bridge' for the purpose of uniting the groups" (p. 66). Initial activities included singing songs, engaging in instrumental music play, and participating in movement activities that included the use of scarves and parachutes with supportive music. In discussions after each group meeting, the elementary school children initially focused on their similarities with the children with special needs, stating things such as "the special children are just like us, they laugh and cry, they sing and play, they look normal" (p. 69).

After a few months, in the postsession meetings these children began asking about their differences with the special needs children: "Why aren't they speaking? Why are some of the children doing weird movements with their hands? Why are some drooling? Why does it look like some have diapers?" While the educational staff members seemed uncomfortable with such queries, Elefant's therapy expertise helped her to see these concerns as part of the typical process that occurs when groups of people from different backgrounds first get acquainted.

Because Elefant understood these questions as reflective of the desire to come closer to the children with special needs and to better understand them, she allowed these concerns into the therapy groups as part of the natural process of developing intimacy. Starting with the idea that they are "just like us," the difficult differences emerged, and the elementary school children eventually began to realize that the special needs children were indeed different from them in some fundamental respects. It was only after these differences could be honestly and sensitively expressed and explored that the elementary school children could establish a real sense of comfort in the group.

For their part, the children with special needs indicated that they felt the warmth and concern that emanated from the other children. Elefant describes this stage of the group process as being quite moving for her as the children changed "from being two separate groups . . . to have become one whole unit with many different parts" (2010, p. 71). Again, this process of establishing a stronger sense of identity and cohesion after some difficult feelings can be expressed and worked through is also typical of most theories of group therapy.

Approximately six months into the project, progress had been made, and significant goals were achieved. The children from the two groups became close: absences were noted by expressions of regret; feelings of respect and caring for each other were expressed verbally by the elementary school children and through pointing, body language, and assistive communicative devices by the special needs children. The group members began bringing in their own favored musical activities to supplement those suggested by the therapist, and they expressed their affection for, and comfort with, each other through appropriate physical contact, such as holding hands while singing and dancing and sharing hugs at the beginning and end of sessions. The goals achieved in this group were as important for the elementary school children as they were for the special needs children. For example, several of the elementary school children observed that "the children with special needs had taught them about love and friendships" (p. 72). And being in a social environment with children without special needs helped the special needs children in important ways. Many of them "stopped their nonsocial or stereotypical behaviors such as spitting, hitting or pinching" (p. 72) and instead developed more functional ways to communicate with others.

In implementing this group over a period of four years, Elefant was determined to include not just the children but to reach out to many of the social networks that surrounded them, such as their parents, teaching staff, organization leaders, and representatives of local government. The project extended to the whole community, as the changes in the children rippled out into these other spheres. Elefant reports that many other such music groups were developed as a result, and because of the success of the initial efforts, it became easier to establish such groups. Important goals that were achieved in the community included an enhanced level of tolerance for the special needs population and increased funding for such services. The ultimate success of the project was reflected in the fact that the special needs children achieved "inclusion in a community that until then had not given many opportunities for their special residents" (2010, p. 73).

Elefant's work highlights one important aspect of CoMT that distinguishes it from traditional music therapy. As clinicians, music therapists have the responsibility to establish specific treatment goals for clients and to document progress toward these goals. In contrast to this focus on individual change, Elefant notes that in intergroup work the focus is more on the meeting and coming together of two diverse groups of people where the focus is on learning to perceive and accept various types of similarities and, more important, differences. Individual change can occur, but it appears more as a by-product of the intergroup interactions than as something that is directly and overtly targeted as an area of change.

BROADENING THE SCOPE OF LEGITIMATE THERAPY GOALS

In addition to broadening notions of what constitutes a client, CoMT also encompasses an expanded notion of legitimate focuses of clinical work to include things such as empowerment and social justice. Two brief examples of CoMT work with nontraditional goals will be described here, one in a Western context and one that takes place in a non-Western context.

Community Music Therapy with Political Refugees in Berlin

Oksana Zharinova-Sanderson's (2004) work with traumatized refugees in Berlin at the Centre for the Treatment of Torture Victims is just one of many projects with victims of political violence. She notes that although integration into Berlin society can be highly problematic for refugees, it is essential for both the well-being of the individual as well as the health of the local culture because these refugees are "symbols of the new society's attitude to foreign ideas and its capacity to integrate these ideas" (p. 235) into the construction of the new capital of Germany.

Clients at the Centre experienced a range of music therapy activities and interventions. In individual sessions, Zharinova-Sanderson describes percussion improvisations and the active engagement of clients in playing and singing songs from their home culture. In addition, performance was used as an extension of work from individual sessions. Also, music-making with the entire therapeutic community took place at social gatherings such as parties, with one example described by Zharinova-Sanderson as consisting of large group chanting.

Zharinova-Sanderson reports that the focus in CoMT on resources and client strengths conflicted with the existing treatment model of the host center. However, the fact that Zharinova-Sanderson elected a treatment focus that did not involve direct targeting of the clients' trauma does fit in with more progressive views that emphasize the whole person as opposed to a preoccupation with the trauma. Interestingly, while the clients in this program came from extremely diverse backgrounds—including Kurdish political activists, widowed women from Africa, and orphans from Kosovo—what united them was not their shared trauma but their common challenges in the present, such as insecure residential status, the lack of material resources, and fears of East German neo-Nazis.

Music therapy in this context helped clients to contact their inner resources for growth, and by using their own cultural music it allowed them to be more present in their new culture as whole human beings. Performance opportunities that originated from clinical processes allowed audience members to see past "the concept of a 'traumatised refugee' into a real person with real feelings" (Zharinova-Sanderson, 2004, p. 240) for whom empathy can be generated. Two of the most prominent issues faced by traumatized refugees include a lack of trust in humanity and social isolation. One of the primary benefits of CoMT in this context is the way that it can intervene with these issues and disrupt their mutually reinforcing cycle. Individuals who do not trust others tend to avoid social interaction; the resulting paucity of interaction reinforces the lack of trust. In changing the way refugees feel about themselves and are perceived by their new communities, Zharinova-Sanderson asserts that music can become a "force for change" (p. 245) as the act of communal musicing acquires sociopolitical import.

Community Music Therapy with Young Girls in Sierra Leone

Sierra Leone suffered a civil war during the 1990s that devastated the country and its people. Children were enlisted as soldiers, and the role of girls was especially complex, because even though they were abducted, they were forced to fight and serve as spies, soldier-wives, and camp followers (Gonsalves, 2010). The extensive role that girls played in the war was not fully recognized—consequently, they did not receive adequate government resources, and there was no formal demobilization, as whenever possible, they just instinctively assimilated back into their communities (Gonsalves, 2010).

Maria Gonsalves worked as a music therapist with a team of four health professionals to assess and assist in meeting the psychosocial needs of these former girl soldiers when they attempted the difficult process of reentering their communities. The team enlisted individuals to act as allies in the various social entities that comprised the community where they worked. This included the local tribal chief; the chief of police; teachers, local child protection officers, traditional healers, leaders of the women's secret society, traditional birth attendants, and other elders, families; guardians, and the girls themselves (2010). Their meetings included the girls with their mothers or babies, girls without their family or those integrated into new communities, working in commercial sex trade, or in skills programs (2010). Their translator was a teacher who was born and lived in the community.

In the group meetings Gonsalves discovered that song was the natural mode of communication in this culture, and it was through song that the girls communicated their emotional and material needs, their histories and fears, and the nature of their present difficulties. Her work showed her that increased under-standing, re-engagement and connections with others and promotion of healing (2010) are all facilitated through creative musical interaction. Gonsalves makes the point that for traumatized victims of social, political, and gender-based violence, creativity is especially important as it represents a refusal to remain a helpless victim. In this context, creative expression is an act of resistance as it restores the humanity that the various forms of oppression attempt to erase. In this project, music therapy functioned to restore connection and engagement with others. The case vignettes that Gonsalves (2010) reports on demonstrate the capacity of music to achieve many human benefits, including the creation of social solidarity and ac-tivism for peaceful coexistence, which, in turn, works to block forces of oppression and abuse.

CONCLUDING THOUGHTS: BOUNDARIES OF PROFESSIONAL PRACTICE

A number of authors who have been exploring the notion of CoMT have considered its relationship with both traditional music therapy and CM (Ansdell, 2002; O'Grady & McFerran, 2007). I would like to extend this spectrum so that it comprises a con-tinuum of four related areas of practice: (1) traditional music therapy, (2) commu-nity music therapy, (3) therapeutic community music, and (4) CM. I am adding (3) in light of the increasing numbers of musicians who are not professional music therapists but who are working in health-related contexts that music therapists tra-ditionally inhabit, such as hospitals and hospices.

It can be difficult to distinguish the work that occurs as one moves across this spectrum, especially when working at the boundaries of two related areas. As music therapists increasingly move into the domain traditionally inhabited by community musicians and take on more political and social goals, and as community musicians increasingly move into the health-related domains traditionally inhabited by music therapists to focus on work with individuals with illnesses and disabilities, there is a risk that each group will develop new forms of practice without taking advantage of the knowledge that has been gained by their musician colleagues. Equally, there is a danger that lack of awareness of each other's professions will lead to unneces-sary battles for professional legitimacy as each group strives to protect its respective areas of professional practice.

Of course, it is important to proceed with a cognizance of these boundaries because they exist to protect the clients of both groups. However, what should not be lost is that all musicians—whether therapists or not, whether working in institutions or in the outside community—are all engaged in following where music leads (Ansdell, 2010) in order to promote human well-being. It is the enhancement of human lives through music that binds together all music professions: teacher, therapist, community musician, and performer. Constantly hewing to this value will enable the practitioners in these various professions to negotiate the establishment of their shared boundaries in ways that are in the best interests of all members of the community.

REFLECTIVE QUESTIONS

1. What practices and focuses distinguish community music therapy from therapeutic community music?
2. In what ways can community music therapy practices challenge traditional ethical guidelines?
3. In what ways does community music therapy expand the professional obligations of practitioners?

NOTES

1. Although in Wood, Verney, and Atkinson (2004) the authors do propose a model where clients move from individual music therapy sessions to group sessions to community contexts, this sequence is based on the needs of a particular client group (individuals undergoing neurological rehabilitation) rather than on fundamental notions of how music therapy works, in general.
2. One exception is music-centered music therapy (Aigen, 2005), which articulates a view in which the medium of musical experience assumes more prominence than any other extrinsic, nonmusical, goal.
3. For readers who may be unfamiliar with the term, a "happy hour" is a promotional device employed by bars to encourage customers to patronize the bar in the hours between the end of the work day and before dinner (typically, 5:00–7:00 p.m.), by offering discounted drinks and snacks. This program is described in detail in Aigen (2004).

REFERENCES

Aasgaard, T. (1999). Music therapy as milieu in the hospice and paediatric oncology ward. In D. Aldridge (ed.), *Music therapy in palliative care: New voices* (pp. 29–42). London: Jessica Kingsley.

Aasgaard, T. (2004). A pied piper among white coats and infusion pumps: Community music therapy in a paediatric hospital setting. In M. Pavlicevic & G. Ansdell (eds.), *Community music therapy* (pp. 147–163). London: Jessica Kingsley.

Aigen, K. (2004). Conversations on creating community: Performance as music therapy in New York City. In M. Pavlicevic & G. Ansdell (eds.), *Community music therapy* (pp. 186–213). London: Jessica Kingsley.

Aigen, K. (2005). *Music-centered music therapy*. Gilsum, NH: Barcelona.

Ansdell, G. (2002). Community music therapy and the winds of change. *Voices: A World Forum for Music Therapy*, 2(2). https://normt.uib.no/index.php/voices/article/viewArticle/83/65.

Ansdell, G. (2010). Where performing helps: Processes and affordances of performance in community music therapy. In B. Stige, G. Ansdell, C. Elefant, & M. Pavlicevic, *Where music helps: Community music therapy in action and reflection* (pp. 161–186). Farnham, UK: Ashgate.

Bruscia, K. (1998). *Defining music therapy* (2nd ed.). Gilsum, NH: Barcelona.

Elefant, C. (2010). Must we really end? Community integration of children in Raanana, Israel. In B. Stige, G. Ansdell, C. Elefant, & M. Pavlicevic, *Where music helps: Community music therapy in action and reflection* (pp. 65–73). Farnham, UK: Ashgate.

Gonsalves, M. (2010). Restoring connection and personal capacities for healing: music therapy in Sierra Leone. In Elavie Ndura-Ouedraogo, M. Meyer & Judith Atiri (eds.), *Seeds taking root: Pan-African peace action for the twenty-first century*. Lawrenceville, NJ: Africa World Press.

Jampel, P. (2006). Performance in music therapy with mentally ill adults. Doctoral diss., New York University, 2006.

Maratos, A. (2004). Whatever next? Community music therapy for the institution. In M. Pavlicevic & G. Ansdell (eds.), *Community music therapy* (pp. 131–146). London: Jessica Kingsley.

O'Grady, L., & McFerran, K. (2007). Community music therapy and its relationship to community music: Where does it end? *Nordic Journal of Music Therapy*, 16(1), 14–26.

Pavlicevic, M., & Ansdell, G. (eds.) (2004). *Community music therapy*. London: Jessica Kingsley.

Stige, B. (2002). *Culture-centered music therapy*. Gilsum, NH: Barcelona.

Stige, B., Ansdell, G., Elefant, C., & Pavlicevic, M. (2010). *Where music helps: Community music therapy in action and reflection*. Farnham, UK: Ashgate.

Turry, A. (2001). Performance and product: Implications for the music therapist. http://musictherapyworld.net/ [accessed November 23, 2017].

Wood, S. (2006). Interdependence and emergence: Core concepts in community music therapy? *Voices: A World Forum for Music Therapy*. http://www.voices.no/discussions/discm51_02.html [accessed November 23, 2017].

Wood, S., Verney, R., & Atkinson, J. (2004). From therapy to community: Making music in neurological rehabilitation. In M. Pavlicevic & G. Ansdell (eds.), *Community music therapy* (pp. 48–62). London: Jessica Kingsley.

Zharinova-Sanderson, O. (2004). Promoting integration and socio-cultural change: Community music therapy with traumatized refugees in Berlin. In M. Pavlicevic & G. Ansdell (eds.), *Community music therapy* (pp. 233–248). London: Jessica Kingsley.

CHAPTER 11

COMMUNITY MUSIC AND SOCIAL JUSTICE: RECLAIMING LOVE

MARISSA SILVERMAN

> To think out in every implication the ethic of love for all
> creation—this is the difficult task which confronts our age.
>
> —Albert Schweitzer, "Reverence for Life"

The topic of values is central to all forms of school music and community music (CM) (Bowman, 2009; Koopman, 2007; Higgins, 2006, 2007). But are the values of community music distinctive? If so, why? Asked another way, is CM in a better position than school music to achieve some values rather than others? If so, what values? And if certain values are omitted, who suffers?

This chapter reflects on the values of community music in the context of social justice. I begin with a brief overview of what, to me, community music is. I follow this with a discussion of social justice, with special attention to a neglected aspect of this concept: love. The remainder of the chapter examines the social justice values of community music as practiced in one urban community.

COMMUNITY MUSIC

As noted in the other chapters in this part of the volume, there is no national or global consensus on the meaning of community music. Some writers define community music quite simply—as any type of "informal" music teaching and learning that occurs outside school walls, and/or partnerships between various types of school music instruction and professional or amateur music groups in community settings (e.g., symphony orchestras, community choirs). But community music scholars and practitioners often find these notions inadequate. For example, the editors of the *International Journal of Community Music* argue that community music has many meanings and forms, depending on a range of variables, including:

> (a) the people involved (e.g., "community music workers" and/or musicians, clients, or students); (b) the communities and institutions involved; (c) the aims, purposes, or needs that a Community Music program intends to achieve; (d) the relationships between a given Community Music program and its geographical, social, economic, religious, cultural, and/or historic circumstances; and (e) the financial support a Community Music program receives, or not. (Elliott, Higgins, & Veblen, 2008, pp. 3–4)

In this view, community music schools, projects, and facilities are situated in, and often responsive to, local needs and values. Moreover, community music schools, projects, and facilities are often "fluid, porous, negotiated affairs. . . . They are what they are by virtue of people's identification with others ('we') whose values, interests and actions are presumed similar enough to our own to sustain an ongoing sense of belonging" (Bowman, 2009, p. 110).

Three examples exemplify the above. First, the Happy Wanderers, a small choir of senior citizens in Victoria, Australia, performs primarily for residents in managed care facilities (Southcott, 2009). The choir, which maintains a very busy performance schedule, is motivated by a collective desire to enhance the well-being of its members, their families and friends, and their local community. The program Bambini al Centro (Children in the Center in Rome, Italy) is a recreational space that provides group-music activities for children, aged 0–12 months, and their families. These activities include, but are not limited to, early childhood music, music ensembles with Orff instruments, voice and percussion ensembles, and musical theatre productions (Iadeluca & Sangiorgio, 2008). The East Hill Singers, located in Lansing, Kansas, includes prison inmates, volunteer singers from the Kansas City Lyric Opera Chorus, and the Rainbow Mennonite Church choir (Cohen, 2008).

What do these community music programs have in common? Most obviously, as Koopman (2007) points out, they incorporate "collaborative music-making, community development and personal growth" (p. 153). In addition, however, Higgins (2006) maintains that community music, properly conceived and practiced, provides fellowship, hospitality, and a welcoming environment for "the Other." He argues that community music emphasizes empowerment and affords music access for all people toward enhanced citizenship. For example, Southcott notes that the Happy Wanderers choir contributes to its community and, in the process, it "receive[s] far more in return" (2009, p. 149). Southcott emphasizes that the group's original intention was to help others, but in the process of reaching out to others the members experience a renewed sense of purpose and meaning, communal bonding with each other and each others' families, and a sense of personal growth and self-esteem.

In relation to values, then, many community music programs emphasize more than collaborative music-making. They view music as a praxis for social "goods": community involvement, social interaction and bonding, friendship, social capital, happiness, and health and wellness. But what about social justice? Arthur Zajonc (2006) answers this way: "We are well-practiced at educating the mind for critical reasoning. . . . But is this sufficient? Do not the issues of social justice, the environment, and peace education all demand greater attention and a more central place in our universities and colleges?" (p. 1).

SOCIAL JUSTICE

Conceived as a form of research and thoughtful inquiry, social justice serves to uncover injustices, imbalances, and untruths in order to support and promote a more equitable social order. According to Ayers (2006), several questions serve as guidelines for social justice research and action:

> What are the issues that marginalized or disadvantaged people speak of with
> excitement, anger, fear, or hope?
> How can I enter a dialogue in which I will learn from a specific community
> itself about problems and obstacles they face?
> What endogenous experiences do people already have that can point the way
> toward solutions?
> What is missing from the "official story" that will make the problems of the
> oppressed more understandable?
> What current or proposed policies serve the privileged and the powerful, and
> how are they made to appear inevitable?
> How can the public space for discussion, problem posing, and problem
> solving be explained? (p. 88)

For more than a decade, discussions of social justice, as both a concept and a practice, have blossomed in music, music education, and community music (e.g., Bowman, 2000, 2007; Bradley, 2006, 2007; Elliott, 2007; Elliott & Veblen, 2006; Gould, 2004, 2005, 2007; Koza, 1994; Lamb, 1996; Morton, 1994; O'Toole, 2002, 2005). However, some of these discussions lack important foundational considerations. How so? For one thing, "social justice" is an extraordinarily complex concept because "social" and "justice" have no universally agreed-on meanings. Instead, social justice is context dependent, discipline dependent, and historically dependent. Thus, if we want to conceptualize and operationalize the nature and values of social justice, we need to think in multidimensional human terms. For example, one crucial dimension of social justice that is frequently overlooked in the theory and practice of music education is *love*.

bell hooks[1] (2000) argues that there can be no social justice without love, and no love without justice. What this means, in part, is that we should not avoid seeing that which is difficult, or that which has no easy solution. Freire also saw love as a vital force in the fight for social justice. Like hooks, Freire (1970) asks us to take notice of those around us, for "in the absence of a profound love for the world and for people. . . . No matter where the oppressed are found, the act of love is commitment to their cause—the cause of liberation" (p. 89). hooks writes: "Until we live in a culture that not only respects but also upholds basic civil rights for children, most children will not know love" (p. 19–20). She states: "all great movements for social justice in our society have strongly emphasized a love ethic" (p. xviii–xix). As Martin Luther King Jr. (1968) stated: "Love that does not satisfy justice is no love at all. . . . Love at its best is justice concretized" (p. 95). But what is meant by "love"? What is the connection between love, education, and community music?

Love and Social Justice

There are many kinds of love. Love can be passionate, tender, affectionate, benevolent, warm, friendly, full of devotion, and/or infatuation. There is the love between parent and child; between siblings; between lovers; the love of things; the love of pets; and so on. Experientially, then, most people know what love is, though many find it difficult to put into words. Given its conceptual elusiveness, and the common tendency to think in terms of romantic love, some psychological researchers (e.g., Gazzaniga & Heatherton, 2006) and laypeople are uncomfortable with the word itself, let alone the idea of linking education and love. Indeed, scholars and teachers may find this linkage "uncomfortable," embarrassing, odd, suspicious, abnormal, and/or unethical, if not downright dangerous. This is understandable. But why?

I would argue, as does hooks (2000), that the ethic of love is essential in any concept of care and, therefore in education and social justice. As Liston and Garrison (2004) argue, love is integral to teaching and learning (pp. 1–19). Martin (2004) makes the same point when she argues that in Western societies, love has been conceived wrongly, as an obstacle to educating children "for life in the public world" (p. 27). Hannah Arendt (1961) writes: "education is where we decide whether we love our children enough not to expel them from our world and leave them to their own devices, but to prepare them in advance for the task of renewing a common world" (p. 196). Indeed, and with equal emphasis, hooks (2000) emphasizes that we must learn to love, because with love we exist *for* others and *with* ourselves. In short, hooks conceives love as *action*, rather than pure feeling.

In my view, engaging in reciprocal teacher-teacher and teacher-student discourses for social justice that privilege love as action (rather than a private feeling) is essential to the future of music education. Music educators and community music facilitators must infuse artistic techniques and teaching-and-learning strategies with love, and support the intellectual and political ideals of social-constructivist practices and education for democratic engagement. In other words, if we love those around us, we more openly and willingly assume responsibility for, and accept accountability in, the human relationships in our professional spheres of action. And through love-as-action we enter these relationships fully, not as individuals filling roles, but as people caring for people.

hooks (2000) elaborates her themes in these words: "the heart of justice is truth telling, seeing ourselves and the world the way it is, rather than the way we want it to be" (p. 33). She exhorts us to focus on that which is difficult and engage that which has no easy solution. Unfortunately, says hooks, many people in our society consider affirmative love-as-action as an impossibility. Many educators are cynical about love. Many believe that love does not exist, nor can it be found. A number of factors contribute to this cynicism. hooks (2000) writes:

> One of the most important social myths we must debunk if we are to become
> a more loving culture is the one that teaches parents that abuse and neglect
> can coexist with love. Abuse and neglect negate love. Care and affirmation, the
> opposite of abuse and humiliation, are the foundation of love. (p. 22)

What is missing in our world? It is love-as-action. Some teachers and community music makers may be hesitant to embrace this action-ethic because it threatens their security. But as Rilke (1975) writes: "it is a high inducement to the individual to ripen, to become something in himself, to become world, to become world for himself for another's sake" (p. 31). According to hooks, one must make this a deliberate choice. She writes: "To practice the art of loving we have first to choose love—admit to ourselves that we want to know love and be loving even if we do not know what that means. The deeply cynical, who have lost all belief in love's power, have to step blindly out on faith" (2000, p. 155). She continues by reemphasizing love-as-action, love as a participatory emotion, and love as a social practice:

> Love is an action, a participatory emotion. Whether we are engaged in a process
> of self love or of loving others we must move beyond the realm of feeling to
> actualize love. This is why it is useful to see love as a practice. When we act, we
> need not feel inadequate or powerless . . . but we must choose to take the first
> step. (p. 165)

Is there hope for love-as-action in music schools and musical communities? I believe so. When we recognize the acute differences between (1) temptation and immediate gratifications and (2) the lasting effects of the politics of communalism, then we will find our place in and our connections to our local and global communities. For hooks, hope lies in the forming of communities. "Communities sustain life . . . there is no better place to learn the art of loving than in community" (2000, p. 129). Community, extended family, creative or political collaboration, friendship—these are our true capitals, and they are equal in importance to the love between couples and among members of a nuclear family. Martin (2004) agrees:

> The truth is that we can no longer assume—once again, perhaps we never could
> assume this to be true—that home is children's primary provider and teacher of
> love or that home all by itself is capable of blocking the inheritance of cultural
> liabilities that stunt the next generation's healthy development. (p. 31)

I want to propose now that the priorities I have sketched above are, or should be, central aims of music education and community music. Let me explain more of what I mean in relation to community music.

Community Music and Love

Community music scholars often overlook and/or avoid explicit discussions of the nature and value of love. The same holds for education generally and school music particularly. hooks (1994) asks educators of all kinds to transform their teaching into a form that deliberately strives for affective ways of knowing and learning. When school and community music educators ground their work on teacher-student mutuality and openness we can "teach in ways that transform consciousness, creating a climate of free expression that is the essence of a truly liberatory liberal arts education" (p. 44). Martin (2004) makes the point in different terms: "love is missing today from public discourse about education in general and schooling in particular" (p. 29). While Bowman (2009) and Higgins (2006, 2007) discuss the ethical implications of benevolence in community music, and while their discussions imply the values of love-as-action, much more needs to be said explicitly.

Why? For one thing, many community music programs exist because of an implicit ethic of love: community music programs are often guided by a fellowship ethic and a community service ethic aimed at providing a range of musical values to people of all ages. In addition, community music practitioners often focus deliberately on people who are socially and economically disenfranchised. Many community music programs have at their core a love that respects the self-empowerment of others. community music often encourages people to observe their social obligations, as well as uphold individual moral values. Because of this, the ideals of many community music programs align with Albert Schweitzer's "projects of love." That is, Schweitzerian projects establish a commitment to moral ideals of excellence (Martin, 2007, p. 18). Such commitments can be made to family, friends, work, philanthropy, or anything based on an ethic of care. Conceived as Schweitzerian projects, community music programs assume the "active, enthusiastic love of one's neighbor" (Schweitzer quoted in Barsam, 2008, p. 36). Such projects not only give meaning to "Our" lives; they give meaning to the lives of "the Other." In addition, and according to Schweitzer, such civic engagement motivates "active engagement in the world" (quoted in Martin, 2007, p. 26).

Love as Action in Community Music

In the Happy Wanderers, Bambini al Centro, and the East Hill Singers, the focus is on the musical-social actions and connections of performers and practitioners. A variation on this focus is found in many community music therapy (CoMT)

situations that use music to care for people with physical, psychological, neurological, emotional, behavioral, and social needs. One such program is found at the
Thirtieth Street Men's Shelter at New York City's Bellevue Hospital. Noah Shapiro has
been the activity therapies supervisor since the shelter's inception in 1987. Shapiro
works with a multidisciplinary arts team that treats mentally ill, homeless men. In
addition to music therapy, the men receive other kinds of therapy, including drama
therapy and dance therapy. According to Shapiro, the purpose of the program is
to resocialize the men and "to find them more stable, permanent housing" (p. 31).
Shapiro continues:

> These men are suffering from isolation because of their illness, their
> homelessness, and in many cases, because they are in a foreign country. At the
> present time, half of the program's population of 30 men was not born in the
> United States. Music with these men is a unique conduit for communication.
> (p. 31)

A number of the men in the shelter lack English fluency. Shapiro notes that although there are many different therapeutic strategies available at Bellevue, some
men do not benefit from strategies that use spoken language as a means of communication. Shapiro (2005) states: "As a music therapist, I find myself in the role of
'integration-facilitator,' helping to integrate the clients into the music therapy group
and into the community they are living in. At the same time I try to honor the individual cultures from which they came" (p. 31). Because of this, Shapiro has a strong
commitment to multicultural musics. For him, this is the best way to facilitate the
development of community and to develop the men's respect for diversity. As Stige
(2002) says, "music therapists need to be able to relate to a plurality of musics in
order to meet the individual needs of clients coming from different backgrounds
with different histories of music use" (p. 93). In Shapiro's therapy sessions the men
listen to, perform, and improvise Cantonese, Puerto Rican, Haitian, Javanese, and
other musics. Shapiro affirms Stige's perspective when he says that, "in this community, people from various countries and cultures are trying to live together is some
kind of 'harmony.' The group becomes a microcosm of the program, the program
is a microcosm of New York City, and, in this multicultural context, New York City
can be seen as a microcosm of the world" (p. 32). Harriett Powell (2005) puts this
a bit differently:

> Small group music therapy in this kind of setting facilitates meaningful
> communication and connection between people with different languages and
> cultural backgrounds, with different physical and mental difficulties—all can be
> enabled and empowered by being listened to and heard in musical terms (Proctor
> 2002, pp. 101–102), and connected in making music with others. (p. 174)

In any given music therapy session at the Thirtieth Street Men's Shelter there is
a revolving number of participants. While the unit consists of 30 men, those
participating in a session vary, depending on the men's needs and desires. They are
not forced to go to music therapy; they go because they want the musical-communal
interaction. The sessions are shaped around musical improvisation. The men sit in

a circle with a number of percussion and string instruments in the center. When the men walk into a session, they are free to choose whatever instrument appeals to them on that given day. They sit down and, as they wait for the session to begin, they play their chosen instruments, reacquainting themselves with musical materials. As Mercedes Pavlicevic (1997) writes: "music therapy improvisation appeals not only to the symptoms but to the whole person, including those aspects that are not 'ill,' and including those aspects of the client that have only an obtuse relationship to 'the illness'" (p. 93).

On the occasion of my visit, the men began by explaining to me the parameters of the music therapy session. Robert,[2] a man who was manic, highly irritable, and often sleepy (partially due to his medications), explained what went on in the sessions. He said: "We sing, we play instruments. We get to know each other better through our singing and our music making." This led to an introductory activity. We went around in a circle and introduced ourselves musically—by improvising on our chosen instruments, expressing our thoughts and feelings in the moment. Karl, a man with violent tendencies and a form of mental retardation, asked an intern (a New York University music therapy student) if she could explain the music she made. The intern replied: "That's my music. That's how I feel." In response, Tyrrell, a paranoid schizophrenic who tends to shy away from the group, asked: "What is music, anyway?" Shapiro seized the opportunity to explore the question with the group. Juan, a Hispanic man who never allowed his hands to stray from the head of his beloved conga drum, said that "music is music when there's a beat." As he said this, his fingers produced light Latin-influenced rhythms. After a little back and forth on this point, Robert asked: "What's the difference between music and noise?" This prompted further discussions.

This kind of communal public space, which encourages collective judgments and creates open networks of self-reflection and critical communication, emulates the best aspects of civil society. In other words, community music as love-in-action allows for this kind of communication, even when people disagree. Mark, a tense and depressed man with a defiant and antisocial demeanor, became impatient with the dialogue. Mark said: "There's too much talking! Not enough music!" And so went the give and take of love—love-as-action naturally moves through phases of conflict, but conflict that is both constructive and negotiated.

Shapiro shifted the men's attention back to music making. Shapiro asked the men to select musical partners. Mark chose the intern (according to Shapiro, he always chooses her) and myself. Mark also chose our instruments for us and signaled us to begin our improvisations. After a few moments, Mark leaned into Shapiro and said: "These notes are out of order and are messing me up." Shapiro quickly rectified the situation, and we went on with our improvising. When our musical interplay came to a close, another conversation ensued. Robert remarked on the fact that this was the first time anyone chose three similar instruments to play (Mark directed the intern and me to play mallet percussion). Robert found this interesting and the sounds soothing. Mark said he enjoyed playing with us.

When I first entered this group situation I didn't anticipate that Mark would have chosen a marimba and improvised such delicate melodic lines. Indeed, on first seeing him I was uncomfortable with his defiant and hardened appearance, and his first comment to me: "My name is 'Iron-Tech,' or you can call me 'Spider-Man.'" Hence my surprise and delight when his musical participation engaged, displayed, and expressed several positive, relaxed, and happier aspects of his selfhood. Shapiro remarked privately that Mark usually shed his depressed and antisocial tendencies during improvisations. In addition, Shapiro commented on Mark exhibiting "positive control" by choosing the instruments, choosing whom he wanted to play with, and controlling the duration of the music-making activity. According to Shapiro, Mark was asserting himself musically. Although there was freedom in musical expressions, it was controlled. Shapiro noted: "He's in a men's homeless shelter, he's been in prison, and he's mentally ill. Why can't he have something he can control?" For Mark, his music therapy seemed to be personally beneficial and uplifting. It "worked" for him and inside him. This was unlike the rest of his chaotic world.

The remainder of the therapy session unfolded in similar patterns. A trio of men improvised. Then a quintet played together. Within this quintet, Shapiro and Leon (a depressive, who is prone to self-injury) were not only playing similar African drums, they were mirroring, matching, and reflecting each other's improvised beat patterns; on top of these patterns, Robert played an Irish harp, Karl played a bass mallet instrument, and Reiss (a depressive and suicidal man) played the marimba. The group was impressed that these five people were able to work together seamlessly to make music. Karl noted, significantly, that "musical communication is challenging; the eye contact and body language is what kept us together to make beautiful music." At the end of the session the group engaged in vocal exercises, again through improvisation and mirroring, matching, and reflecting.

We said our farewells. As the group went off to their next session, Shapiro remarked that the session was "active, supportive, and expressive—even a little more than usual." Both the intern and Shapiro noted that this had probably been because a "stranger" was present. If so, then, these men, by creating personas in front of a non–group member, were learning real social skills. They were all musically acting and reacting in a positive and supportive manner. As we sat in a circle, we were all equal, all civilians, all members of a community working together, where everyone was musical.

CONCLUSION

The aims, strategies, and outcomes of the Thirtieth Street Men's Shelter program embody key characteristics of community music as an ideal and a practice. They also exemplify key characteristics of programs as/for social justice: care, trust, responsibility, and respect. Now view the Shelter program through the lens of love-as-action and hooks's words:

> most people who think they are not lovable have this perception because at
> some point in their lives they were socialized to see themselves as unlovable by
> forces outside their control. We are not born knowing how to love anyone, either
> ourselves or somebody else. However, we are born able to respond to care. As we
> grow we can give and receive attention, affection, and joy. Whether we learn how
> to love ourselves and others will depend on the presence of a loving environment.
> (2000, p. 53)

The following poem by Virginia Satir (2003, p. 123) aligns with all of the above:

> Making contact
> I believe
> The greatest gift
> I can conceive of having
> is
> to be seen by them,
> to be understood
> and
> touched by them.
> The greatest gift
> I can give
> is
> to see, hear, understand
> and to touch
> another person.
> When this is done
> I feel
> contact has been made.

If we take "love" and "lover" in their platonic, pedagogical, and active sense, then Toni Morrison (1970) makes a serious point in this regard: "Love is never any better than the lover. Wicked people love wickedly, violent people love violently, weak people love weakly, stupid people stupidly" (p. 163). It is up to the teacher and practitioner who loves to love rightly—to love ethically—and this is a learned action. Rilke (1975) writes:

> Young people must *learn* love. To take love seriously and to bear it and to learn it.
> For one human being to love another: that is perhaps the most difficult of all our
> tasks, the ultimate, the last test and proof, the work for which all other work is
> but preparation. For this reason, young people, who are beginners in everything,
> cannot yet know love: they have to learn it. (pp. 30–31)

To scholars past and present who advocate an ethic of love, living purposefully pivots on creating a life that means something beyond oneself. Contributing to a whole, no matter the task, is essential to social justice. Implicitly, or explicitly, community music facilitators tend to embrace this ethic. This is not to say that the majority of school music educators teach without an ethic of love. Not at all.

What I am suggesting is that because school administrators, school boards, and government policy-makers are so concerned with controlling and "measuring" the day-to-day actions of teachers and students, music educators may be more prone to experience their efforts as unrewarding, hopeless, empty, and without meaning. In contrast, and unfettered by the numbing constraints of contemporary schooling, community music practitioners tend to view and experience their work as fulfilling, rather than as "work" in the sense of a burdensome and negative obligation. As hooks (2000) writes: "When we work with love we renew the spirit; that renewal is an act of self-love, it nurtures our growth. It's not what you do but how you do it" (p. 65).

The educators and practitioners who *live for and in* the community music sites discussed in this chapter examine critically and empathetically their community's needs. Their efforts are rooted in, and operate in terms of, care. They consciously seek to be responsible and respectful. In turn, their students/patients tend to display and feel a willingness to learn with care. When we conceptualize and practice love-as-action, we infuse ourselves and the world with personal and interpersonal meaning. It is with an ethic of love that community music sites embody their civic engagement.

REFLECTIVE QUESTIONS

1. Does community music exemplify social justice? If so, how? If not, why not?
2. Can "love" be an action-ideal for music education, both in and out of community music settings? Explain.
3. What social values need to be brought into and explored in music education classrooms? Why?

KEY SOURCES

hooks, b. (2000). *All about love: New visions*. New York: William Morrow & Company.

Liston, D., & Garrison, J. (2004). Introduction: Love revived and examined. In D. Liston & Garrison, J. (eds.), *Teaching, learning, and loving: Reclaiming passion on educational practice* (pp. 1–19). New York: RoutledgeFalmer.

Martin, J. R. (2004). The love gap in the educational text. In D. Liston & J. Garrison (eds.), *Teaching, learning and loving: Reclaiming passion in educational practice* (pp. 21–34). New York: RoutledgeFalmer.

Rilke, R. M. (1975). *Rilke on love and other difficulties* (J. J. L. Mood, Trans.). New York: W. W. Norton & Company.

NOTES

1. Bell hooks is the pen name of the feminist scholar and social activist, Gloria
   Jean Watkins, who insists on using the uncapitalized version of her pen name.
2. All names are pseudonyms to provide anonymity.

REFERENCES

Arendt, H. (1961). *Between past and future*. London: Faber and Faber.

Ayers, W. (2006). Trudge toward freedom: Educational research in the public interest. In G.
Ladson-Billings & W. F. Tate (eds.), *Education research in the public interest: Social justice,
action, and policy* (pp. 81–97). New York: Teachers College Press.

Barsam, A. P. (2008). *Reverence for life: Albert Schweitzer's great contribution to ethical
thought*. Oxford: Oxford University Press.

Bowman, W. (2009). The community in music. *International Journal of Community Music*
2(2&3), 109–128.

Bowman, W. (2007). Who's asking? (Who's answering?) Theorizing social justice in music
education. *Action, Criticism, and Theory for Music Education*, 6(4), 1–20. http://act.
maydaygroup.org/articles/BowmanEditorial6_4.pdf.

Bowman, W. (2000). Music as ethical encounter (Charles Leonard Lecture, University of
Illinois). *Bulletin of the Council for Research in Music Education*, 151(Winter), 11–20.

Bradley, D. (2007). The sounds of silence: Talking race in music education. *Action, Criticism,
and Theory for Music Education*, 6(4), 132–162, http://act.maydaygroup.org/articles/
Bradley6_4.pdf.

Bradley, D. (2006). Music education, multiculturalism, and anti-racism—Can we talk?
Action, Criticism, and Theory for Music Education, 5(2), http://act.maydaygroup.org/ar-
ticles/Bradley5_2.pdf.

Cohen, M. L. (2008). Conductors' perspectives of Kansas prison choirs. *International Journal
of Community Music*, 1(3): 319–333.

Elliott, D. J. (2007). "Socializing" music education. *Action, Criticism, and Theory for Music
Education*, 6(4), 60–95.

Elliott, D. J., Higgins, L., & Veblen, K. (2008). Editorial. *International Journal of Community
Music* 1(1), 3–4.

Elliott, D. J., & Veblen, K. (2006). Canadian music schools: Toward a somewhat radical
mission. *Ecclectica* 5(2).

Freire, P. (1970). *Pedagogy of the oppressed*. New York. Seaburg Press.

Gazzaniga, M. S., & Heatherton, T. F. (2006). *Psychological science* (2nd ed.). New York;
London: W. W. Norton & Company.

Gould, E. (2007). Legible bodies in music education: Becoming-matter. *Action, Criticism,
and Theory for Music Education*, 6(4), 201–223, http://act.maydaygroup.org/articles/
Gould6_4.pdf.

Gould, E. (2005). Desperately seeking Marsha: Music and lesbian imagination. *Action,
Criticism, and Theory for Music*, 4(3), http://act.maydaygroup.org/articles/Gould4_3.pdf.

Gould, E. (2004). Feminist theory in music education research: Grrl-illa games as nomadic
practice (or how music education fell from grace). *Music Education Research*, 6(1), 67–80.

Higgins, L. 2007. Acts of hospitality: The community in community music. *Music Education Research, 9*(2), 281–292.

Higgins, L. (2006). The community in community music: Hospitality—friendship. In D. Coffman & L. Higgins (eds.), *Creating partnerships, making links, and promoting change.* Singapore: ISME Commission for Community Music Activity Seminar.

hooks, b. (2000). *All about love: New visions.* New York: William Morrow & Company.

hooks, b. (1994). *Teaching to transgress.* New York: Routledge.

Iadeluca, V., & Sangiorgio, A. (2008). Bambini at centro: Music as a means to promote wellbeing. *International Journal of Community Music, 1*(3), 311–318.

King, M. L. (1968). *Where do we go from here: Chaos or community?* Boston: Beacon Press.

Koopman, C. (2007). Community music as music education: On the educational potential of community music. *International Journal of Music Education, 25*(3), 151–163.

Koza, J. E. (1994). Aesthetic music education revisited: Discourses of exclusion of oppression. *Philosophy of Music Education Review, 2*(2), 75–91.

Lamb, R. (1996). Discords Feminist Pedagogy in music education. *Theory into Practice, 35*(2), 124–131.

Liston, D., & Garrison, J. (2004). Introduction: Love revived and examined. In D. Liston & J. Garrison (eds.), *Teaching, learning, and loving: Reclaiming passion on educational practice* (pp. 1–19). New York: RoutledgeFalmer.

Martin, J. R. (2004). The love gap in the educational text. In D. Liston & J. Garrison (eds.), *Teaching, learning and loving: Reclaiming passion in educational practice* (pp. 21–34). New York: RoutledgeFalmer.

Martin, M. W. (2007). *Albert Schweitzer's reverence for life: Ethical idealism and selfrealization.* Aldershot, UK: Ashgate.

Morrison, T. (1970). *The bluest eye.* New York: Holt, Rinehart and Winston.

Morton, C. (1994). Feminist theory and the displaced music curriculum: Beyond the "Add and Stir" projects. *Philosophy of Music Education Review, 2*(2), 106.

O'Toole, P. (2005). Why don't I feel included in these musics, these matters. In D. J. Elliott (ed.), *Praxial music education: Reflections and dialogues* (pp. 297–307). New York: Oxford University Press.

O'Toole, P. (2002). Threatening behaviors: Transgressive acts in music education. *Philosophy of Music Education Review, 10*(1), 3–17.

Pavlicevic, M. (1997). *Music therapy in context: Music, meaning, and relationship.* London: Jessica Kingsley.

Powell, H. (2005). A *Dream Wedding*: From community music to music therapy with a community. In M. Pavlicevic & G. Ansdell (eds.), *Community music therapy* (pp. 167–185). London: Jessica Kingsley Publishers.

Rilke, R. M. (1975). *Rilke on love and other difficulties* (J. J. L. Mood, Trans.). New York: W.W. Norton & Company.

Satir, V. (2003). Making contact. In S. Intrator & M. Scribner (eds.), *Teaching with fire: Poetry that sustains the courage to teach.* San Francisco: Jossey-Bass.

Shapiro, N. (2005). Sounds in the world: Multicultural influences in music therapy in clinical practice and training. *Music Therapy Perspectives, 23,* 30–35.

Southcott, J. E. (2009). "And as I go, I love to sing": The happy wanderers, music and positive aging. *The International Journal of Community Music, 2*(2&3), 143–156.

Stige, B. (2002). Culture-centered music therapy. Gilsum, NH: Barcelona.

Zajonc, A. (2006). Cognitive-affective connections in teaching and learning: The relationship between love and knowledge. *Journal of Cognitive Affective Learning, 3*(1), 1–9.

CHAPTER 12

SONIC HOSPITALITY: MIGRATION, COMMUNITY, AND MUSIC

HELEN PHELAN

Migration has always been a characteristic of human social, cultural, and economic development, but never so much as at the turn of the twenty-first century. From the earliest migrations of *Homo erectus*, mobility has been a defining aspect of our human origins and evolution. Unique to our time, however, is the scope, impact, and nature of this movement. In *The Age of Migration*, Castles and Miller (2009) note that

> while movements of people across borders have shaped states and societies since time immemorial, what is distinctive in recent years is their global scope, their centrality to domestic and international politics and their enormous economic and social consequences. (p. 3)

From the 1980s to the present time, the number of international migrants has doubled to an estimated 200 million people. Before 1990, the majority of international migrants lived in the developing world. Today, most live in the developed world, and the proportion of migrants in developed countries is rising (Koser, 2007). Approximately 3% of the world's population are migrants (Castles & Miller, 2009). Many of these are forcibly displaced people. According to *Global Trends: Forced Displacement in 2015*, a report of the United Nations Refugee Agency, there are more than 65 million people currently displaced across the world. This is the largest number in recorded history. Approximately 1% of the global population is an asylum seeker, a refugee, or a forcibly displaced migrant (June, 2016).

This unprecedented level of human movement has important repercussions for the ways we think about constructs such as "community" and "music."

Understandings of community, for example, can become paradoxically conflicted in the face of migration: they become both more fluid, dynamic, and transient, as well as more inflexible, dogmatic, and nostalgic (Vergalli, 2006). John Blacking's (1973) famous definition of music as "humanly organised sound" that is "a product of the behaviour of human groups" (p. 10) also becomes more complex as those same human groups become less permanent and more diverse, and as humans move across and between various sound communities or networks. Sound networks are as likely to be virtual as actual (Veblen & Waldron in McPherson & Welch, 2012). Ethnomusicologist Timothy Rice (2003) notes that, in this age of mobility, there is a new awareness of "routes rather than roots" in our understandings of music (p. 153):

> If we now understand our world as not so simple, but rather as a complex
> of unbounded, interacting cultures and of consisting crucially of the rapid
> movement of people, ideas, images and music over vast distances, then what
> sorts of questions arise? . . . in what way does musical experience change
> through time? . . . what happens to musical experience as mediated musical
> sound shuttles through space? (pp. 151–152)

This chapter explores the phenomenon of human migration and its impact on the formation, negotiation, and contestation of community and music. It will explore migration patterns in more detail with reference to one particular country, the Republic of Ireland. Ireland provides an interesting example of a dramatic change in migration patterns, which resulted in it becoming one of the most globalized countries in the world by the end of the twentieth century (Kuhling & Keohane, 2007). Limerick, located in the southwest of Ireland, is the third largest city in the Republic and the site of my own work in community music (CM) with migrant communities, and each section of this chapter will conclude with a brief exploration of a different community-based project. The first section will provide a context for contemporary migration through a survey of migration patterns over the last three decades. In addition, it offers an example of Comhcheol, a CM initiative developed by the University of Limerick to address issues of integration in the face of unprecedented immigration.

The second section explores the impact of migration on community and introduces the concept of sonic hospitality. Through an engagement with a Derridian approach to hospitality, it will suggest that constructs of "community" are increasingly contested in the face of migration. This section explores the proposal that music can act as an agent of sonic hospitality. World Carnival, a second CM initiative, based at the most multicultural primary school in Limerick, will be explored as an example of sonic hospitality.

The final section will examine the connection between migration and knowledge transfer, with particular reference to tacit, embodied knowledge and the implications of this for teaching and learning in a multicultural context. An exploration of new ritual communities in Limerick city will propose ways the body acts as a carrier and transmitter of embodied, musical knowledge.

A Brief Survey of Recent Migration Patterns

Since the eighteenth century, a number of significant migration waves have both been a product of and resulted in significant economic, social, and cultural change (Cohen, 1995).

During the eighteenth and nineteenth centuries, the largest wave of migration involved forced labor and indentured servitude. It is estimated that approximately 15 million people were forced through slavery from West Africa to the Americas, while indentured labor from Asia (primarily India, China, and Japan) continued to feed the labor needs of New World plantations after the collapse of slavery. European colonization also led to several waves of migration. Because Britain, France, Spain, Portugal, and the Netherlands promoted voluntary migration from Europe to the colonies, soldiers, farmers, entrepreneurs, missionaries, and political administrators settled in Africa, Asia, and the Americas. The colonial powers also viewed the colonies as places of settlement for forced migrants such as criminals, orphans, and political dissidents.

Cohen (1995) correlates the next important wave of migration with the emergence of the United States as a major industrial power in the latter part of the nineteenth century. During this period, migrants from Italy, Spain, eastern Europe, and post-Famine Ireland came to the United States to escape poverty and persecution. Since this time, the United States has been viewed as one of the most significant immigration countries, with almost 20% of the world's migrants living there today.

The post–World War II boom years brought about the next significant wave of global migration, including, for example, the Turkish *Gastarbeiter* in Germany, the North African *pieds noirs* in France, and the growing number of *alambristas* crossing the Mexican/U.S. border. Decolonization also led to significant migration of, for example, Hindus and Muslims after the partition of India, and of Jews and Palestinians after the establishment of Israel. These economic boom years, characterized by a shortage of labor to feed growing industrial development, continued in Europe until the post–Cold War period and in the United States until the 1990s and has now shifted to the growing Asian economies of India and China.

Contemporary migration continues to follow the demands of the economy but is also unique in a number of ways. Castles and Miller (2009) suggest six defining characteristics of contemporary migration:

- *The globalization of migration:* This involves both the tendency for more countries to be involved in migration movements at the same time, as well as for migration to any one country to be increasingly diverse.
- *The acceleration of migration:* While migration numbers doubled from 100 to 200 million between the 1980s and 2005, 25 million of these people migrated in the five-year period between 2000 and 2005.

- *The differentiation of migration:* Most countries are experiencing several forms of migration at the same time, including economic migrants (both legal and irregular), refugees and asylum seekers, highly skilled migrants, nonpermanent and permanent migrants, and so on.
- *The feminization of migration:* In the modern period, economic migrants and refugees were predominantly male. Since the 1960s, due to the changing nature of employment opportunities, particularly in the service and health care sectors, a growing number of women have been migrating. In Ireland, many pregnant women came to Ireland as asylum seekers, hoping to gain citizenship rights through their Irish-born child, before changes in citizenship laws in 2004 (Phelan, 2009). The sex industry also accounts for growing levels of female trafficking.
- *The politicization of migration:* The relationship between migration and security has become more acute since 9/11, and there is a growing awareness of the necessity of some level of global governance in monitoring human movement.
- *The proliferation of migration transition:* Migration patterns are less stable, and there are a growing number of "circular migrants" who move back and forth between their countries of origin and their new host countries.

All these characteristics make migration one of the more pressing issues of our contemporary world, whether we are ourselves migrants, or living in a country that is experiencing the "drain" or "gain" of peoples through migration. Our sense of identity, community, and belonging are all threatened, reinforced, or reimagined in the face of migration (Kurien, 2002). Our ability to negotiate identity, community, and belonging through cultural practices such as music is also inevitably influenced (Turino, 1993; Diehl, 2002).

CONTEMPORARY IRELAND AND MIGRATION

Ireland provides an interesting example of a country where migration has had a profound impact in recent history, changing that country from one characterized by consistent emigration to one of the most multicultural countries in the world at the turn of the twenty-first century. From the 1990s to the early years of the twenty-first century, Ireland was known as the Celtic Tiger, a title borrowed from the "Tiger" economies of Asia, and used to indicate the sudden and dramatic prosperity of the country during this period. Before this period of economic prosperity, Ireland had the unique distinction of being a third world, colonized country in first world western Europe. This had a significant impact on patterns of migration (O'Sullivan, 1997). From the Great Famine of the mid-nineteenth century until the end of the twentieth century, the level of emigration from Ireland was consistently higher than in any other western European country during the same period, making Ireland the only country in western Europe to experience a decline in population in the second part of the nineteenth century (Tovey & Share, 2003). With entrance to the European Union in 1973, this trend halted briefly, only to return with the economic setbacks of the 1980s. The turning point came in the 1990s. Major investments in education over the previous 30 years, as well as a policy of social partnership, foreign investment, and low inflation led to unprecedented employment opportunities and economic prosperity.

Until this time, immigration into Ireland was relatively small. The economic changes of the 1990s resulted in the first significant flow of immigration, consisting primarily of migrant workers in the burgeoning economy and asylum seekers hoping to be granted refugee status (Cullen, 2000). For the first time, the profile of migrants expanded beyond those coming from the Irish diaspora or the European Union to include significant numbers from eastern Europe (with a majority from Poland) and Africa (with a majority from Nigeria). In the mid-1990s, net migration into Ireland overtook emigration for only the second time since the mid-nineteenth century (Watt, 2002), and in 2004, the population exceeded four million for the first time since 1871. While economic migrants came primarily from those eastern European countries that were incorporated into the European Union in 2004, the top five countries of origin for asylum seekers were Nigeria, Somalia, Romania, Afghanistan, and Sudan (Kuhling & Keohane, 2007).

In 2000, I established Sanctuary, an access program for new migrants at the Irish World Academy of Music and Dance, University of Limerick, in collaboration with Doras Luimní (The Door of Limerick), the support group for new migrants in Limerick. Among other things, this program developed and supported several CM initiatives. DeNora (2002) reminds us that "to divorce fieldwork from theory impoverishes socio-musical study" (p. 4). With this in mind, I will attempt to ground the theoretical explorations of this chapter with examples from my own work with Sanctuary over the last decade (Phelan, 2006, 2007, 2009, 2017; Phelan & Kuol, 2005).

Comhcheol: A Women's Community Choir

One of the first community-based initiatives of Sanctuary was Comhcheol (Gaelic: "harmony"), a women's choir. It developed out of recognition of the particular obstacles that face women in accessing higher education. Child care was one of the most significant. Many women, particularly those in the asylum process, were single parents, having come to Ireland alone or in advance of a spouse. The Irish World Academy coordinated Nomad, a second access program for the traveler community in Ireland, which conducted a weekly women's group at the university.

Comhcheol brought together women from the traveler community and from new migrant communities in Ireland to form a community choir. The choir met at the university once a week. Travel was provided for anyone who wished to join, and all children were welcome. Repertoire consisted of song exchanges, supported by a number of musical facilitators, including myself; the Nomad facilitator; and members of the Irish Chamber Orchestra. The initiative lasted one year and culminated in a performance at a Festival of Community Music in Limerick. Subsequently, members of the group went on to develop other community-based ensembles.

Issues around discrimination and integration emerged quickly within the group. In a film documentary of the project, one of the women from the traveler community reflected on the experience of discrimination, shared by both women from traveler and migrant backgrounds: "There are a lot of discrimination against travelers as well and there are a lot of discrimination against the refugee people, like, which it's wrong, between the both sides, it's wrong" (Comhcheol, 2001).

Igbo, Yoruba, and Romanian songs mixed with songs in Cant, the traditional language of the travelers, as well as songs from *Sister Act* and Irish ballads. Repertoire provided the currency of exchange, with culture bearers from diverse communities offering their expertise and knowledge to the group. The public performance at the Community Music Festival offered most of the women from new migrant communities a first opportunity to represent themselves in the public domain since coming to Ireland. Joe McGlynn, a founding member of Doras Luimní, reflected on the particular way music brought people together, acting as an agent of support in the face of isolation: "I think there will be a lot more of this kind of bringing together of these minority groups and again highlighting the situations in the alienation sometimes of minority groups in Limerick and in Ireland" (Comhcheol, 2001). The potential of music to act as an agent of "bringing together," as an agent of community building and hospitality, particularly in the face of migration, is the topic of the next section.

COMMUNITY, MUSIC, AND SONIC HOSPITALITY

As the movement of people around the globe accelerates; as receiving countries are host to a greater diversity of peoples and cultures; as migrants embody a wider spectrum of cultural and social roles (legal, irregular, affluent, impoverished, educated, unskilled), the construct of "community" becomes both contested and championed. This section explores changing understandings of community and suggests that sound may act as a form of sonic hospitality, allowing communication and meaning to emerge through musical encounters across complex and multifaceted communities of people.

COMMUNITY AND HOSPITALITY

Olwig and Hastrup (1996) note that "the loss of place as a dominant metaphor for culture" is accepted by anthropologists in their engagement with the fragmented, dislocated, and destabilized aspects of postmodern culture (p. 7). Similarly, the construct of "community" is questioned as an adequate term for the social and cultural networks that characterize so much of contemporary life. Higgins describes it as both powerful and problematic (Higgins in McPherson & Welch, 2012). Bauman (1996) argues that our attachment to terms such as "community" or "nation" can have more to do with the emotion they evoke than their existence in reality: this is why they are so often utilized in public rhetoric: "In Northern Ireland, the 'Catholic community' and the 'Protestant community' are exhorted to make peace for the sake of the 'community'" (p. 14). While such rhetoric would seem to throw into relief the lack of community, it simultaneously reaffirms the desirability of the collective. Similarly, Anderson (2006) notes that communities (like nations) are something we often imagine into existence out of a desire for a shared identity as much as from the actuality of shared experience. Amit and Rapport (2002) argue that migration simultaneously contributes to the disintegration of community, the nostalgia for community, and the reimagining of community as less rooted in any one place, ethnicity, or culture and more likely to be built out of intersecting, transient, and overlapping social, cultural, and personal networks:

> Our personal networks are often cumulatively developed over the course of multiple opportunities for consociation, in the process transforming collective experiences into personal intimacies. It is this process that probably most ensures some sense of personal continuity in circumstances of spatial and social mobility, even though it is the least institutionalized and hence structurally the least enduring. Indeed one has to wonder whether what anthropologists have identified as transnational fields or communities are not more often instances of personal networks of family and friendship? Are people forming transnational communities or transnational personal networks? (p. 64)

Poststructuralist writers have also interrogated the concept of community. Caputo (1997) notes that Derrida highlights the paradoxical nature of community, which on the one hand emphasizes aspects of sameness within a group of people but on the other often forms that identity with reference to their difference from or uniqueness among others. Belonging, in this sense of community, is often defined against nonbelonging. Community formation depends as much on who is kept out as who was let in:

> Derrida's use of the word "guard" converges with the meaning of "community," which means of course a military formation, the wall of protection that the same builds against the other, the way a "people" (the "same") builds a common fortification (*com, munire*) around itself against the other. (Caputo, 1997, p. 272)

Derrida is drawn to the concept of hospitality as an approach that attempts to integrate both the insider and the outsider. As with many concepts, his engagement with the construct of hospitality is as a dual-stranded helix, incorporating both conditional and unconditional dimensions. The conditional involves that which is possible, bounded in time and space and therefore relative, and located within changeable sociopolitical frames. The unconditional is impossible, beyond temporal or spatial limits, and absolute. These are not opposites, but paradoxical and necessary sides of the same coin. The conditional allows for the possibility of the impossible unconditional, and only in this way can the conditional be exercised to maximum effect. An example of this can be found in his discourse on forgiveness (Derrida, with Dufourmantelle, 2001). Invoking the same paradoxical understanding he suggests that

> it is necessary, it seems to me, to begin from the fact that, yes, there is the unforgivable. Is this not, in truth, the only thing to forgive? . . . That is to say that forgiveness must announce itself as impossibility itself. It can only be possible in doing the impossible. (pp. 32–33)

Similarly, he is drawn to the double meaning of *hospes:* both host and stranger. He (Derrida, with Dufourmantelle, 2000) suggests that conditional hospitality is relative, political, and law-based. It involves a host/patron/patriarch, as well as a guest/stranger to whom an invitation is issued. The invitation is issued in the language and the culture of the host, and it is this that first reveals the intrinsic inequality of the relationship. The foreigner must

> ask for hospitality in a language which by definition is not his own, the one imposed on him by the master of the house, the host, the king, the lord, the authorities, the nation, the State, the father etc. This personage imposes on him translation into their own language and that's the first act of violence. (p. 15)

The necessity of language is imposed by the conditional invitation, through which the terms and conditions of hospitality are extended. One must understand the question in order to provide an adequate answer; an answer that indicates one's status as a guest and not a parasite. The first aspect of this question is the ability to provide one's own *identity:* "to receive him, you begin by asking his name" (Derrida, with Dufourmantelle, 2000, p. 27). The ability to identify the stranger is inextricably linked with the ability of the host society to define its own identity. For example, the host society may be made up of "citizens," and the stranger's identity as an "economic migrant" or "asylum seeker" is formed in contrast to the identity of the host community. Thus migration laws begin with documentation: accountability of the migrant as both individual and type (name, label). Among the first questions asked of any migrant is What is your name? The most frequently asked question of all foreigners is Where do you come from?

These are forms of hospitality. They reveal interest and curiosity. But do they also embed a desire to categorize and, perhaps, ghettoize? By forcing the other to define herself according to the questions of the host, does this ultimately reinforce the intrinsic power of the host, by allowing herself to be defined differently/better? "Does hospitality consist in interrogating the new arrival?" (Derrida, 2000, p. 27). This conditional form of hospitality includes aspects of welcome, but also aspects of interrogation and transgression (it is here that the dimension of hostility/violence is most apparent). Offering conditional hospitality may involve necessary interrogation. Accepting it can be a transgressive act; a breaching of protective barriers that may involve illegal or violent acts.

Conditional forms of hospitality are necessary, if limited. Without them, "*the* unconditional Law of hospitality would be in danger of remaining a pious and irresponsible desire, without form and without potency" (Derrida, with Dufourmantelle, 2001, pp. 22–23). But for conditional hospitality to operate at its maximum potential, it must allow for the unconditional, the impossible, the pursuit of hospitality beyond limits, beyond interrogation, transgression, violence, and inequality.

What is the medium of this unconditional dimension of hospitality? Questioning claims from Levinas regarding language and hospitality, Derrida (2000) notes that "we have come to wonder whether absolute, hyperbolical, unconditional hospitality doesn't consist in suspending language" (p. 135). If this dimension of unconditional hospitality resides somewhere beyond the interrogative power of language, could it imply a pursuit of sound beyond the limits of language?

Music as Sonic Hospitality

Anne Dufourmantelle (Derrida, with Dufourmantelle, 2000) describes a Derridean lecture: "the first impression you draw from listening to the seminar is of hearing a musical score being played that makes the very movement of thinking audible" (p. 22). Can music act as a kind of "audible" thinking; a way to suspend language and move from the law-based to the "lawless" liberation of absolute hospitality? Is it possible to propose that music has the potential to act as an agent of "sonic" hospitality—one that does not reject language, but that immerses it in the wider sonic pool of silence and song? At the point at which language is suspended, silence may occur. Derrida (2000) notes that "keeping silent is already a modality of possible speaking" (p. 135). Kristeva (1991) suggests that "between two languages, your realm is silence" (p. 15). But what emerges after silence? Kristeva relates the story of a famous Russian linguist who claimed to speak Russian in 15 different languages: "As for me I had the feeling that he rejected speech and his slack silence led him, at times, to sing" (pp. 15–16).

Higgins (2007) draws on this interpretation of hospitality in his description of the CM workshop. He describes the entrance of a new arrival to a workshop in terms of conditional hospitality: "a new arrival does not simply cross a threshold to enter a community: s/he is always also a direct challenge to the community at hand" (p. 83). But he also describes the unconditional nature of the aspired-for space: "the unconditional welcome prevents the closure characteristic of a determinate community" (p. 84). Significantly, the medium of this unconditional welcome is music: "creative music-making experiences are movements towards rapport with 'the other,' instances of encounters with the unexpected and the unpredictable. The creative music-making journey invites an experience of the unforeseeable, a venture towards the unconditional" (pp. 86–87).

World Carnival

Another Sanctuary initiative, World Carnival, emerged through the vision of Pat Lyons, principal of Maria King Presentation Primary School, the most multicultural school in Limerick, with over 25 different nationalities. Most of these children are first generation migrants or children born of recent migrants to Ireland. While the school has several projects to promote language skills, literacy, integration, and intercultural awareness, Lyons believed that music had a unique role to play in creating a sense of belonging and hospitality at the school. The World Carnival project is facilitated by Kathleen Turner, who has a master's in CM and is education officer for the Irish Chamber Orchestra, an artist-in-residence ensemble at the University of Limerick. Kathleen meets with students and teachers every week. In the first year of the program, she was accompanied by a student musician from Singapore who had a background in music education and Asian children's songs and a student percussionist from the United States who had a specialist interest in salsa. In the second year, musicians from the Irish Chamber Orchestra joined the program. In the coming year, the program will expand to include contributions from parents of children who are themselves musicians and culture bearers. As principal of the school, Lyons is convinced that this music program has created a visible change in his students: "Absolutely. You can see it, they are enjoying themselves so much and are so full of enthusiasm—their confidence has improved noticeably" (in Owens, 2010, p. 8). Turner notes the importance of connecting the musical activity with the wider community and of extending the sense of welcome and hospitality created in the school through the music program to include parents, extended families, neighbors, teachers, and friends: "Working with the kids has been fantastic. They love music and it is great for them to have their community come along to support their performance" (Commane, 2010, p. 24).

Research on the relationship between music and social inclusion/exclusion (Welch et al., 2009; Odena, 2007; Almau, 2005) points toward a correlation between musical development and social inclusion. The ability of music-making activities, such as World Carnival, to promote a sense of communal identity, while also celebrating diversity, is key to their function as a medium for sonic hospitality.

Music, Migration, and Knowledge Transfer

In this concluding section, I would like to explore the unique role played by migration in knowledge transfer and the possible consequences of this insight for hospitality in our teaching and learning practices.

In his discourse on knowledge, Polanyi (1958, 1966) distinguishes between explicit and tacit forms. Explicit knowledge is that which can be transmitted in formal, structured modes (through systems that are capable of transcending human transfer, such as literacy and numeracy) while tacit knowledge is person and context specific. It includes the "touch and feel" dimension of human knowledge, the embodied, the "know-how" we possess but cannot always articulate verbally. It is dependent on human-to-human contact for transmission: "tacit knowledge sticks to the individual and is difficult to transfer other than via personal contact. Tacit knowledge usually is shared through highly interactive conversation, storytelling, observation and/or some form of shared experience" (Williams & Baláž, 2008, p. 57).

Knowledge transfer is a critical aspect of the knowledge-based economy. Williams and Baláž (2008) argue that this positions the migrant as a key player, particularly in areas where tacit knowledge is important: "human mobility is a highly effective, and distinctive channel for knowledge transfer. Moreover, for some forms of tacit knowledge, it may be the only means of transfer" (p. 3).

As musicians, our medium is one that is highly dependent on tacit knowledge (Elliott, 1995; Schatzki et al., 2001; Bannerman, Sofaer, & Watt, 2006). There is a recognition among music educators, in both formal and informal contexts, that a key aspect of multicultural education involves the inclusion of tacit forms of knowledge. O'Flynn (2005) argues that multicultural education has too often focussed on repertoire (a "world music" approach, which includes a selection of repertoire from around the world) without adequately recognizing that the transmission of this repertoire must also involve embracing other "world" models of musicality and pedagogy. This will almost always necessitate an engagement with performers/pedagogues from other musical practices. Shehan Campbell (2002) notes that "a growing recognition of the value of culture-bearers has led teachers to invite musicians from the community into school classrooms" (p. 30). Likewise, with reference to the teaching and learning of Irish traditional and Balinese music, Downey (2009) and Dunbar-Hall (2009) argue for an "ethnopedagogical" approach, which recognizes that teaching different musical traditions involves a holistic embrace of music's cultural context (including contexts of transmission) and not just its cultural outputs (repertoire). The same point is made by Elliott (1990) when he argues against an understanding of culture as product oriented, proposing instead that we think of culture not as something we have, but as something we do—as "an *interplay* among a group's beliefs, informed actions (or action systems) and the outcomes of those informed actions" (p. 149). Walker (1996) and Vaugeois (2007) argue that in a postcolonial context, not doing so is simply another act of colonization, whereby repertoires are appropriated as commodities, rather than engaged in as shared experiences within the context of sonic hospitality.

As the "world" is increasingly present in all its diversity in a greater number of villages, towns, and cities across the globe, migrants are uniquely positioned to act as knowledge brokers: "migrants frequently develop a consciousness of their transcultural position, which is reflected not only in their artistic and cultural work, but also in social and political action" (Castles & Miller, 2009, p. 311).

The transmission of tacitly "embedded" knowledge is of course not unique to migrants. Indeed, one could argue that it is a prerequisite of all teaching and learning within musical traditions. But in a world characterized by increased diversity and mobility, migrants occupy a unique position as cultural brokers and mediation figures. Human mobility expands our access to the kinds of things we can't learn solely through reading books or interfacing with new technologies—the kinds of knowledge we literally carry around with us in our bodies.

A Ritual Example of Embodied Knowledge and Sonic Hospitality

Because my background is that of a ritual scholar, my work with Doras Luimní immediately drew me to encounters with many of the new ritual communities being formed in Limerick as a result of the influx of refugee and asylum seekers, and my fieldwork for a number of years revolved around the chant and song traditions of, among others, the emergent Russian Orthodox and Nigerian Pentecostal communities there (Phelan, 2006). Most asylum seekers are unable to bring a great number of artifacts from their countries of origin, as their journeys often happen in haste, in secret, or illegally. As a result, many of these ritual communities arrived with none of the clothing, books, or ritual artifacts that would have been intrinsic to their ritual practice at home. They celebrated their rituals in borrowed spaces. All they carried from their ritual practices were those things that they could carry in their bodies: their chants, songs, prayers and gestures. I began to wonder how much of the ritual burden could be carried solely by the body? How much of the "missing" external space could it recreate or reimagine for its participants? In particular, I was interested in the ability of sound to create or recreate a sense of space or place.

The conceptualization of space and its relationship to sound and performativity is the preoccupation of much recent scholarship (Boyd & Williams, 1989; Brown, 2003; Solomon, 2000; Stokes, 1994; Thrift, 1996). This relationship comes under a particular kind of cultural stress when ritual sound is forced to "re-sound" in the "wrong" ritual space.

In the case of the ritual communities I studied, there was a "rupture" between sound and space. Chants and songs were forced to carry much of the ritual burden, given the absence of so many other aspects of the ritual performance—most critically, the ritual space itself. The ability of sound to do this—to "represent" cross-sensory reality—is well documented. Solomon (2000) notes that

> recent research in ethnomusicology and popular music has drawn attention to
> the close relationships between music, place and identity. . . . Among the insights
> generated by this new scholarship is the idea that musical performance serves as a
> practice for place-making. (p. 257)

One of the most interesting ways music can do this lies in its ability to suggest sounds and images that are not explicit in its performance. Kubik (2000) drew on his experience in Uganda to illustrate how musicians can create acoustic illusions by playing auditory tricks. Through compositions of extreme complexity, they were able to create an illusion for the listeners, who seemed to hear certain sounds that were not actually being played. Similarly, sound can create visual and physical "presences" that are also not present, but are reimagined through sound.

In this sense, one could argue the paradox of sound being at once one of the most incarnate (embodied) and transcendent of the human sense experiences. The human body finds it less easy to generate, from within itself, that which it sees, touches, tastes, and smells. But the extraordinary connection between vocal production (controlled by the ability to breathe and therefore intimately linked with our very survival) and auditory perception allows us to be creative agents in both the production and reception of sound in a way that is unique among our sensory possibilities.

From this perspective, humanly embodied sound becomes a source not just of musical knowledge but of musical hospitality, in its ability to "invite" and evoke "missing" cultural landscapes. The movement of embodied sound carries with it a powerful ability to conjure up its place of origin and, equally, to re-produce and reimagine that place of origin when one finds oneself in landscapes and culture-scapes far removed from where it emerged.

CONCLUSIONS

Contemporary experiences of migration challenge us to take on new ways of understanding community, which go beyond social, cultural, or ethnic commonality, to embrace the difficulty of difference—both our own and others'. It is community beyond commonality; community predicated on transience, fragmentation, and rupture, but also on affinity, empathy, and invitation. Derrida (2000) puts it another way:

> Let us say yes *to who or what turns up,* before any determination, before any anticipation, before any *identification,* whether or not it has to do with a foreigner, an immigrant, an invited guest or an unexpected visitor, whether or not the new arrival is a citizen of another country, a human, animal or divine creature, a living or dead thing, male or female. (p. 77)

This approach, which "resists any interpretation of community that privileges 'gathering' over 'dislocation'" (Higgins, 2007, p. 87), has important implications for how we think about teaching and learning music. As Bowman (2005) suggests, music educators need to think less in terms of content and product, and more in terms of process and reflexivity, so that students learn to "cope creatively with a changing world" (p. 25).

This chapter proposes that music has the potential to act as an agent of sonic hospitality in a number of significant and unique ways. While it does not bypass language, its embrace of sound goes beyond the "conditional" limits of language. The ability of the human body to both generate and perceive sound renders it particularly mobile. The migrating human body is capable of transferring and brokering a great deal of cultural information through the sounds it embodies. It is therefore a very successful agent of knowledge transfer, particularly in the transfer of tacit knowledge, so central to our understanding and expression of music. These characteristics underscore the potential of music to engage with new constructs of community, and the potential of music education to open a door that "leads into a space of hospitality and possibility" (McCarthy, 2009, p. 3).

REFLECTIVE QUESTIONS

1. In what ways can migration affect community?
2. How does migration affect music-making?
3. What is the relationship between migration and musical identity formation?
4. What is the relationship between conceptions of community and hospitality?
5. How can sonic hospitality provide a foundation for community music activities?

KEY SOURCES

Brown, G. (2003). Theorizing ritual as performance: Explorations of ritual indeterminacy. *Journal of Ritual Studies, 17*(1), 3–18.

Phelan, H. (2006). Borrowed space, embodied sound: The sonic potential of new ritual communities in Ireland. *Journal of Ritual Studies, 20*(2), 19–32.

Phelan, H. (2007). Let us say yes: Music, the stranger and hospitality. *Public voices, 9*(1), 113–124.

Phelan, H. (2017). *Singing the Rite to Belong: Music, Ritual and the New Irish.* Oxford and New York: Oxford University Press.

Stokes, M. (ed.). (1994). *Ethnicity, identity and music: The musical construction of place.* Oxford: Berg.

REFERENCES

Almau, A. (2005) Music is why we come to school. *Improving schools 8*(2), 193–197.

Amit, V., & Rapport, N. (2002). *The trouble with community: Anthropological reflections on movement, identity and collectivity.* London: Pluto Press.

Anderson, B. (2006). *Imagined communities* (rev. ed.). New York: Verso.

Bannerman, C., Sofaer, J., & Watt, J. (eds.). (2006). *Navigating the unknown: The creative process in contemporary performing arts.* London: University of Middlesex Press.

Bauman, G. (1996). *Contesting culture: Discourses of identity in multi-ethnic London.* Cambridge: Cambridge University Press.

Blacking, J. (1973). *How musical is man?* Seattle & London: University of Washington Press.

Bowman, W. (2005). After the silence of aesthetic enchantment: Race, music and music education. *Action, Criticism and Theory for Music Education, 4*(3). http://act.maydaygroup.org/articles/Bowman4_3.pdf [accessed November 23, 2017].

Boyd, J., & Williams, R. (1989). Ritual spaces: An application of aesthetic theory to Zoroastrian ritual. *Journal of Ritual Studies, 3*(1), 1–44.

Brown, G. (2003). Theorizing ritual as performance: Explorations of ritual indeterminacy. *Journal of Ritual Studies, 17*(1), 3–18.

Caputo, J. (1997). *The prayers and tears of Jacques Derrida: Religion without religion.* Bloomington & Indianapolis: Indiana University Press.

Castles, S., & Miller, M. (2009). *The age of migration: International population movements in the modern world* (4th ed.). Basingstoke, UK, and New York: Palgrave Macmillan.

Cohen, R. (1995) *The Cambridge survey of world migration.* Cambridge: Cambridge University Press.

Comhcheol: In Harmony. (2001). [Film documentary]. Limerick: S.M.V.I. Productions.

Commane, R. (2010, March 27). Twenty-five nations join song at Presentation Primary. *Limerick Post*, 24.

Cullen, P. (2000). *Refugees and asylum seekers in Ireland.* Cork: Cork University Press.

DeNora, T. (2002). The everyday as extraordinary: Response from Tia DeNora. *Action, Criticism and Theory for Music Education, 1*(2). http://act.maydaygroup.org/articles/DeNoraResponse1_2.pdf [accessed November 23, 2017].

Derrida, J., with Dufourmantelle, A. (2000). *Of hospitality* (trans. R. Bowly). Stanford: Stanford University Press.

Derrida, J., with Dufourmantelle, A. (2001). *On cosmopolitanism and forgiveness* (M. Dooley & M. Hughes, Trans. with a preface by S. Critchley & R. Kearney). London & New York: Routledge.

Diehl, K. (2002). *Echoes of dharamsala: Music in the life of a Tibetan refugee community.* Berkeley, Los Angeles, & London: University of California Press.

Downey, J. (2009). Informal learning in music in the Irish secondary school context. *Action, Criticism and Theory for Music Education, 8*(2), 46–59. http://act.maydaygroup.org/articles/Downey8_2.pdf [accessed November 23, 2017].

Dunbar-Hall, P. (2009). Ethnopedagogy: Culturally contextualised learning and teaching as an agent of change. *Action, Criticism and Theory for Music Education, 8*(2), 60–78. http://act.maydaygroup.org/articles/Dunbar-Hall8_2.pdf [accessed November 23, 2017].

Elliott, D. (1990). Music as culture: Toward a multicultural concept of arts education. *Journal of Aesthetic Education, 24*(1), 147–166.

Elliott, D. (1995). *Music matters: A new philosophy of music education.* Oxford: Oxford University Press.

Higgins, L. (2007). The impossible future. *Action, Criticism and Theory for Music Education, 6*(3). See http://act.maydaygroup.org/articles/Higgins6_3.pdf [accessed November 23, 2017].

Higgins, L. (2012). The Community in Community Music. In G. McPherson & G. F. Welch (Eds.), *The Oxford Handbook of Music Education* (Vol. 2, pp. 104–119). New York: Oxford University Press.

Koser, K. (2007). *International migration: A very short introduction.* Oxford: Oxford University Press.

Kristeva, J. (1991). *Strangers to ourselves* (trans. L. Roudiez). New York: Columbia University Press.

Kubik, G. (2000). Interconnectedness in ethnomusicological research. *Ethnomusicology*, 44(1), 1–14.

Kuhling, C., & Keohane, K. (2007). *Cosmopolitan Ireland: Globalisation and quality of life*. London, Dublin, & Ann Arbor, MI: Pluto Press.

Kurien, P. (2002). *Kaleidoscopic ethnicity: International migration and the reconstruction of community identities in India*. New Brunswick, NJ: Rutgers University Press.

McCarthy, M. (March, 2009). Music education and narratives of social cohesion: From national melting pot to global community. Keynote address to 6th International Symposium on the Sociology of Music Education, Mary Immaculate College, Limerick.

Odena, O. (2007). *Music as a way to address social inclusion and respect for diversity in early childhood*. Belfast: National Foundation for Educational Research & Queen's University.

Olwig, K. F., & Hastrup, K. (eds.) (1996). *Sitting culture*. London: Routledge.

O'Flynn, J. (2005). Re-appraising ideas of musicality in intercultural contexts of music education. *International journal of music education*, 23(3), 191–203.

O'Sullivan, P. (1997) (ed.). *Patterns of migration*. The Irish world wide series. Leicester: Leicester University Press.

Owens, A. (2010, March 23). ICO helps children to find their voices. *Limerick Chronicle*, 8.

Phelan, H. (2006). Borrowed space, embodied sound: The sonic potential of new ritual communities in Ireland. *Journal of Ritual Studies*, 20(2), 19–32.

Phelan, H. (2007). Let us say yes: Music, the stranger and hospitality. *Public voices*, 9(1), 113–124.

Phelan, H. (2009). Religion, music and the site of ritual: Baptismal rites and the Irish citizenship referendum. *International journal of community music*, 2(1), 25–38.

Phelan, H. (2017). *Singing the Rite to Belong: Music, Ritual and the New Irish*. Oxford and New York: Oxford University Press.

Phelan, H., & Kuol, N. (2005). *Integration and service provision: Survey of persons with refugee and leave to remain status in Limerick city*. Limerick: Limerick City Development Board.

Polanyi, M. (1958). *Personal knowledge*. London: Routledge and Keegan Paul.

Polanyi, M. (1966). *The tacit dimension*. London: Routledge and Keegan Paul.

Rice, T. (2003). Time, place and metaphor in musical experience and ethnography. *Ethnomusicology*, 47(2), 151–179.

Schatzki, T., Knorr Cetina, K., & Von Savigny, E. (eds.) (2001). *The practice turn in contemporary research*. London & New York: Routledge.

Shehan Campbell, P. (2002). Music education in a time of cultural transformation. *Music Educators Journal*, 89(1), 27–32.

Solomon, T. (2000). Dueling landscapes: Singing places and identities in highland Bolivia. *Ethnomusicology*, 44(2), 257–280.

Stokes, M. (ed.) (1994). *Ethnicity, identity and music: The musical construction of place*. Oxford: Berg.

Thrift, N. (1996). *Spatial formations*. London: Sage Publications.

Tovey, H., & Share, P. (2003). *A sociology of Ireland*. Dublin: Gill and Macmillan.

Turino, T. (1993). *Moving away from silence: Music of the Peruvian Altiplano and the experiment of urban migration*. Chicago: University of Chicago Press.

UNHCR. (2016) Global Trends Forced Displacement in 2015, A Report of the UNHCR, the UN Refugee Agency [Online] available: http://bit.ly/28DBbNH

Vaugeois, L. (2007). Social justice and music education: Claiming the space of music education as a site of postcolonial contestation. *Action, Criticism and Theory for Music Education*, 6(4), 163–200. http://act.maydaygroup.org/articles/Vaugeois6_4.pdf [accessed November 23, 2017].

Veblen, K. K., & Waldron, J. L. (2012). Fast forward: Emerging trends in community music. In McPherson, G., Welch, G. (Eds.), *The Oxford handbook of music education* (Vol. 2, pp. 203–219). New York, NY: Oxford University Press.

Vergalli, S. (2006). The role of community in migration dynamics. FEEM Working Paper No. 4. Available at SSRN: http://ssrn.com/abstract=876428 [accessed November 23, 2017].

Walker, R. (1996). Music education freed from colonialism: A new praxis. *International Journal of Music Education*, 27(1), 2–15.

Watt, P. (2002). Introduction and overview in *Migration policy in Ireland: Reform and harmonisation*. National Consultative Committee on Racism and Interculturalism Report. https://www.pobal.ie/Publications/Documents/Migration%20Policy%20in%20Ireland%20-%20NCCRI%20-%202002.pdf

Welch, G. F., Himonides, E., Saunders, J., Papageorgi, I., Vraka, M., & Preti, C. (2009). *Singing and social inclusion: Evidence from the UK's national singing programme*. Report to Youth Music. London: Institute of Education.

Williams, A., & Baláž, V. (2008) *International migration and knowledge*. New York: Routledge.

CHAPTER 13

AT-RISK YOUTH: MUSIC-MAKING AS A MEANS TO PROMOTE POSITIVE RELATIONSHIPS

MARY L. COHEN, LAYA H. SILBER,
ANDREA SANGIORGIO, AND
VALENTINA IADELUCA

The purpose of this chapter is to investigate research and instances of music programs involving youth in challenging situations and examine implications for music education and community music practices[1]. The international perspectives examined by the broad authorship and the programs happening in multiple countries indicate that effectively facilitated music-making can be a positive and helpful tool for youth populations in different cultural contexts. We define key terms, examine theoretical frameworks related to teaching at-risk youth, and describe practical applications of these frameworks. We discuss philosophies of interactions with deviant behavior, particularly comparing controlling modes imposed from the outside to systems of cooperation. A range of such philosophies exists, and we argue that cooperative systems are effective for at-risk youth, particularly with respect to facilitating music-making. We conclude with implications for music education, suggestions for advocacy considerations, reflective questions, and a list of additional sources.

DEFINITIONS

For the purposes of this chapter, the term "youth" is understood as a combination of both "adolescence" and "childhood." Christenson and Roberts (1998) define adolescence as "beginning with entry into puberty—a biological definition—and ending with the adoption of adult roles—a social definition" (p. 13). Reber and Reber (2001) define childhood as, "usually, the period between infancy and adolescence" (p. 116). With respect to the phrase, "youth in challenging situations," McWhirter et al. (2007) suggest that a particular behavior, deficiency, or attitude marks potential problem behavior. For instance, an adolescent who smokes might begin drinking alcohol. One who drinks alcohol is at risk for illicit drug use. Aggression, low achievement, and conduct disorders in elementary school mark potential antisocial and delinquent behavior in adolescence. So the idea of challenging situations does not only indicate a current situation but also situations in which future problems may result without adequate intervention.

According to McWhirter et al. (2007), at-risk factors occur along a continuum: (1) minimal risk; (2) remote risk; (3) high risk; (4) imminent risk; and (5) at-risk activity. As at-risk factors accumulate in a child's life, consistent moderating factors or structured interventions must occur to avoid negative outcomes. The ability of a youth to navigate physical and social stresses affects his ability to function. Such responses to one's environment are known as an individual's resiliency.

Michael Ungar (2008) defines "resilience" as the capacity of "individuals to navigate their way to resources that sustain well-being, individuals' physical and social ecologies to provide these resources, and individuals and their families and communities to negotiate culturally meaningful ways for resources to be shared" (pp. 22–23). Ungar's broad definition encompasses three aspects of resiliency:

- How individuals work through their stresses
- How they deal with environmental influences
- The extent to which an individual's social networks embrace a culturally sensitive support system

With respect to the first two aspects of resiliency, when youth navigate personal and environmental stresses with deviant behavior, laws and other forms of social control are employed in an attempt to regulate such behavior. Although systems of social control applied from a top-down approach may on first glance appear easier, less costly, and efficient in the short run, they may result in rebellious responses and drive youth toward more deviant behavior. A youth's sense of responsibility may be thwarted because she may react in self-protective ways that are socially destructive rather than seek to understand how deviant behavior has harmed others. Such self-protective and destructive behaviors may be the result of suppressed feelings of anger or depression, particularly if the youth has experienced a childhood trauma.

The third aspect of resilience, one's social support system, is a primary moderating factor for youth at any point along the continuum of potential risk. An individual may have multiple support systems, such as peers, teachers, family, and the broader community. Sometimes youths embrace one of these support systems at the expense of another, such as gang behavior that harms the broader community. Clearly, in this example relationship-building may result in problem behavior. The process of navigating through social interactions is known as socialization.

Gerald Handel (2006) defines socialization as "the process of gaining the capacities for social interaction that enable the person to function in society" (p. 1). He suggests two aspects of this process: (1) the development of an individual's self, human sentiments, and acquisition of language, and (2) the socialization agents, such as parents, designated surrogates, schools, and peer groups that enable successful functioning (p. 16). Social class, neighborhood type, and ethnic groups influence these agents. In other words, socialization involves interaction between one's social experiences and one's individual attributes. These two parts interact in complex ways.

Hans Peter Dreitzel (1973) argues that adults' and children's behaviors are mutually dependent variables. Successful teachers of at-risk youth, therefore, must be aware of their role as socialization agents and ideally understand other variables in their students' social influences that may be pushing them along the continuum toward at-risk activities.

With respect to individual attributes, Handel (2006) indicates that empathy is perhaps the most basic sentiment that one develops through socialization, requiring someone to imagine oneself in another's place in differentiated and complex ways (p. 13). A sense of empathy is necessary for youth to cooperate with others and navigate successfully through all types of social interactions.

THEORETICAL FOUNDATIONS

Noddings: Ethics of Care

Noddings's (1984) ethics of care provides a pedagogical foundation for music teachers and community musicians who want to create positive relationships with and among learners, thereby establishing a system of cooperation. Noddings suggests that human encounters and affective responses are basic to people's lives. Three aspects of Noddings's relational ethics theory inform community music and music education pedagogy. First, she emphasizes that the carer needs to understand the other person's reality, no matter how difficult that may be. In a group setting, acquiring such "engrossment" for multiple people may be challenging. She suggests that varying degrees of intensity and levels of engrossment may occur in various situations, including teaching contexts (pp. 16–17).

Second, Noddings suggests that this process of engrossment must be balanced with "motivational displacement," where the carer's behavior is determined by the needs of the person being cared for. In a music education or community music context, the teacher ideally creates an atmosphere where each learner cares for the broader musical goals of the group and in turn notices others' needs in the processes of group music-making. In addition to these group dynamics, music educators have a duty to understand the learners' needs, including musical background and preferences, cognitive and affective abilities, and where they are along the at-risk continuum.

Third, Noddings (1984) describes aesthetical caring, natural caring, and ethical caring (pp. 21–23, 81–83). Aesthetical caring is the care of ideas or things. Problems may occur with respect to building positive human relationships in a music education/community music setting if the teacher or leader cares more for the sonic aspects of music-making than for the people performing. Examples of natural caring are "I want" behaviors, such as hugging a friend who needs love. "I must" deeds, such as visiting a sick relative in the hospital or hugging an acquaintance even if one prefers to avoid dealing with that person's painful situation, are examples of ethical caring. Ethical caring is difficult to learn and practice. Music educators who model this behavior and facilitate music-making experiences that encourage ethical caring help youth develop social bonds and aptitude for functional socialization.

Noddings (1995) explains four benefits of incorporating care into instruction: (1) it expands children's cultural literacy, (2) it helps children perceive transfers across standard school subjects, (3) it addresses existential questions, such as how one should live and the meaning of life, and (4) it helps children connect with one another and demonstrate respect for all human talent. When teachers demonstrate care for their students, the relationships built into the learning processes tend to be more personal and important. Music teachers' opportunities to establish caring relationships are particularly distinctive because facilitating music-making affects children's musical growth and identity formation. The relationships between identity formation and musical growth are unique to each particular learning environment.

Communities of Practice

The notion of communities of practice helps us consider group dynamics within the learning process. Lave and Wenger (1991) first coined the term "communities of practice" (COP). They described these communities as apprenticeship-based through a process called "legitimate peripheral participation" (LPP). The idea behind LPP is that a newcomer to a community learns from a seasoned member until the newcomer gradually moves into full participation in the community. Characteristics of COP include informal growth around a need, a common purpose and goal, group development and change as a natural outcome of group processes, relationships that allow trust and identity to flourish, and internal motivation among members (Hindreth & Kimble, 2008).

According to Wenger (1998), "*Practice is about meaning as an experience of everyday life*" (p. 52, italics in original). "Practice," for Wenger, involves a duality of participation and reification. Participation refers to the process of taking part in the social experience of living, while reification is the process of giving form to an experience. These two dimensions interplay in life situations in complex ways. Wenger illustrates this interplay by describing how a mountain and a river shape each other (p. 71). They have their own existence while they simultaneously transform each other. We suggest that COP with youth who are along an at-risk continuum ought to be established from an attitude of care.

Music educators have connected the notion of COP to aspects of teaching musical ensembles in schools. Countrymen (2009) interviewed 30 Canadians one to six years after completing high school about their experiences in school music programs. One theme that emerged most strongly from her data analysis was the enormous importance of community as an overarching concept for music-making. She indicates that particular ways of facilitating music-making in schools foster growth of COP, such as encouraging "individual musical creativity within the group," "independent musical decision-making," and "musical leadership."

Froehlich (2009) shares suggestions for building COP in music settings. She acknowledges both connectedness within community relationships and the process-oriented aspects of such interactions. Similar to Countrymen's suggestions, collegiality is preferred over hierarchical relationships:

> As each of us examines our own place and role in the scripts called school music and community, we may become aware of and begin to understand our own experiences and practices for what they are: the product of specific socialization processes that enable us to connect more easily to one group than to another. Awareness of those processes as well as an understanding of their impact on our own biographies may lead to getting to know "the others" and empower us to effect changes in the way we inter-react with those unlike us. (p. 101)

Froehlich's suggestions point toward a need for teachers and students to be mindful about our roles as socialization agents and to be particularly attentive to our interactions with people who have different life contexts from ours. Countrymen and Froehlich both emphasize facilitation over direction and cooperation rather than competition as important aspects of music education.

Positive Youth Development

Researchers have examined a strength-based approach to working with youth in challenging situations known as Positive Youth Development. Catalano et al. (2004, pp. 102–108)) reported that in the 15 most common outcomes, Positive Youth Development programs did the following:

- Increased positive bonding with others
- Increased resilience

- Increased social competencies
- Increased cognitive competencies
- Increased emotional competencies
- Increased behavioral competencies
- Increased moral competencies
- Increased self-determination
- Increased spirituality
- Increased feelings of self-efficacy
- Supported more clear and positive identity
- Encouraged beliefs in the future
- Provided recognition for positive behavior
- Provided opportunities for prosocial involvement
- Supported adoption of prosocial norms

Susan O'Neill (2006) suggests that the main premise of positive youth development is that "*all* young people have the *potential* and *capacity* for healthy growth and development" (p. 263). Furthermore, she indicates that in order to develop a young person's sense of self, motivation, self-responsibility, and interest in relation to their musical development, all individuals within a community must collaboratively engage with each other. One possible motivation for such work is rooted in a concept of "generativity," defined as "a concern for establishing and guiding the next generation" (p. 461), a common interest for music educators.

Shirley Brice Heath and Elizabeth Soep (1998) completed a 10-year study of places where positive youth development occurs outside a school setting. They began looking at three categories of programs: (1) athletic-academic, (2) community service, and (3) arts-based. Seven years into the study, they came up with some surprising data. They learned that notable characteristics of motivation, critical analysis, persistence, and planning were evident in the youth participating in arts-based programs—drama, music, dance, visual arts, and writing. They reported that the arts "intensified the characteristics of effective learning environments." When compared with other out-of-school activities, the arts involved greater risk, individual identity, responsibility for consequences, setting rules, changing rules, and imaginative planning. These complex learning processes helped the youth develop vital life skills.

KEY PRINCIPLES AND APPROACHES

"Music" as Lived Experience Rooted in Caring Relationships

We consider the nature of "music" as a lived experience or as an encounter with other people, thereby emphasizing group relevancy as a central factor in facilitating musical activities. In order to empower each person, we suggest a variety of expressive communication forms used in conjunction with music-making, such as movement, dance, speech, narration, poetry, theatre, drama, visual images, and technology.

When the focus is on building primary, meaningful experiences within the group, the activation of the resources, imagination, and motivation of the group members becomes the starting point. As rapport develops among all participants, the particular musical styles and ways youth choose to express themselves become apparent. The ultimate goal is to foster social learning, to create trust, respect, sensitivity, responsibility, cooperation, and teamwork. Such meaningful interactions are based on caring relationships between the facilitator-teacher and members and among the group members (Noddings, 1984).

Organizing Learning Processes: The Child at the Center

Ideally, learning processes with youth in challenging situations reflect a holistic concept of music-making. The ultimate aim is to contribute to the formation of identity and personality through:

- Sensory stimulation (sharpening auditory, visual, tactile, kinesthetic perception as the base for every further conceptualization)
- Cognitive activation (developing new skills and new nets of mental representations)
- Emotional involvement (promoting subjectively meaningful learning that is deeply rooted in each student's needs for growth and self-fulfillment)
- Social involvement (promoting cooperation and team work)

Music-making, considered as a human experience, encourages an "indissoluble unit of body, spirit, and mind" (Sangiorgio, 2010, p. 4), with the musical learning processes supporting the holistic aspects of our humanity.

Organizing Learning Processes: The Central Quality of Group Interaction

Forms of social interaction are manifold and foster interactions among individuals such as imitation or problem solving. These activities may occur with partners, small groups, or a large group. Musical or movement imitation validates an individual's creative expression. Problem-solving processes integrate decision-making and cooperation. In these contexts, learning happens within the group and especially through the group. A balance between each person's contribution and structured action supports important psychological processes ranging from individualization to socialization. Ideally, the activities help the learner develop individual personality attributes, acquire psychosocial skills, and cultivate virtues such as empathy, respect, responsibility, and perseverance.

Elaine Goodman (2002) describes the primary characteristics of ensemble dynamics as an ideal intimate interactive framework. She states that performing in time with other people involves anticipation and reaction, constant feedback, aural and visual signals, eye contact, gestures, and body movements. In this dynamic interdependent process, players accommodate one another by exchanging roles based on trust and respect for individual boundaries. While players predict and respond to signals and cues by fellow musicians, they also contribute by giving out their own signals. In this way musicians share their own identities while blending with the group.

PURPOSES, GOALS, AND FUNCTIONS OF MUSICAL ACTIVITIES FOR YOUTH IN CHALLENGING SITUATIONS

Among the purposes, goals, and functions of musical activities for this population are the following:

- To learn and practice performing and inventing different genres of musical styles: the development of participants' broader cognitive views, artistic sensitiveness, aesthetic taste, and skill development are principal aims of music education in conjunction with overall growth of each individual.
- To develop integrated body awareness: the practice of music-making nurtures a "musical body," an awareness of the relationships between voice and melody, movement and rhythm. In addition, one gains an awareness of how one's body interacts with other bodies through glance, contact, and synchrony—not an object-body (in German, *Körper*) but a subject-body (*Leib*).
- To foster the growth of musical thought in its various forms and expressions: participants develop a musical intelligence that is lively, bright, keen, dynamic, communicative, creative, open, well rooted in perception and oral skills, motivated toward further cognitive growth, and integrated smoothly with other intelligences.
- To promote the expression of emotions: music-making and dance are a powerful means to manifest inner feelings.
- To promote communication, socialization, and integration: participation helps the child to get along well with others and foster synergy and cooperation among group members (Sangiorgio, 2010).

Musical learning and psychosocial learning proceed in conjunction with each other.

Characteristics and Attributes of an Effective Leader

An effective leader has excellent musical training and knowledge of many different musical genres and styles and is open to facilitating a wide variety of musical ideas. The leader or "active anthropologist" (Sangiorgio, 2010, p. 10) should be able to observe the culture of the group, connect with group members both at a human and at a musical level, and understand their ideas, perspectives, and identities. The role of this leader is that of facilitator, creator of a group culture, carrier of conceptions and values, and initiator of a social, cultural, and human experience through music-making.

From a psycho-pedagogical point of view the relevant personality traits and skills of an effective leader may be synthetically (and not exhaustively) enunciated as follows. The effective leader:

- Is competent in her subject
- Has a strong inclination toward learning
- Is creative, constructive, and emotionally ready to experiment
- Takes risks
- Is communicative at different levels, using different media and adapting her message to the recipients
- Has good management and leadership skills
- Is motivated, is motivating, and easily generates enthusiasm
- Knows how to develop an atmosphere of trust within the group
- Is empathetic
- Has an open and functional teaching style
- Is able to encourage learner growth
- Is in contact with himself and his own emotions
- Is aware of the psychodynamic aspects of group learning and teaching

Benefits of Music Programs for Youth

Effectively facilitated music-making addresses a variety of issues related to delinquency and potential at-risk behaviors:

- Music-making allows the individual to communicate emotion within a psychologically safe environment if facilitated effectively (Silber, 2005).
- Music-making of any kind requires think-first anger management techniques (Silber, 2005; Portowitz et al., 2009).
- Musical interactions and experiences are simulations of life experiences and springboards for discussions on social interaction.

"Relationships . . . Change People": Practical Applications of Theoretical Foundations

Robert F. Kronick (1997) indicates that massive overhauls are needed for programs for youth in challenging situations and that "relationships, not programs, change people" (p. 22). We argue that such musical programs must be rooted in meaningful social relationships that foster a sense of care, empathy, culturally sensitive support systems, and collegiality in order to promote positive human relationships. A great number of these types of programs exist. This section describes a few promising programs in the United States, Europe, Israel, and South America.

United States Programs

In 1992, John Hornsby, who has written songs for his brother, Bruce Hornsby, and other well-known musicians, such as Huey Lewis and Willie Nelson, joined with other musicians from Charlottesville, Virginia to create an after-school music center. They thought this type of center would help students get out of trouble. Music Resource Center (MRC) opened its doors on June 17, 1995, after three years of researching young people's interest and planning for its organization.

The mission of the MRC is "to educate and inspire young people and through music equip them with life skills for the future" (http://musicresourcecenter. org/). They emphasize patience, acceptance of others, respect, organization, and self-responsibility.

MRC's original home was the practice space of the Dave Matthews Band. The Dave Matthews Band has performed benefit concerts for MRC, and they participated in the March 2004 ribbon-cutting ceremony at a new location for MRC. MRC's structured "Fun to Fame" program has three tracks: Fun Track (beginner), Fame Track 2 (intermediate), and Fame Track 3 (advanced). Members start out on the Fun Track and advance through this system by earning points for daily activities such as songwriting, music and dance lessons, performance, and recording. The members must be currently enrolled in school and be between the ages of seventh and twelfth grade. They pay an annual fee on a sliding scale, between $10 and $200. Annual cost for each student to participate is approximately $350. MRC is open during the school year on weekdays from 2:30 to 7:00 p.m. and on Saturdays from noon to 5:00 p.m. In the summer months, the weekday hours are 1:00 to 7:00 p.m.

This center has used positive youth development as a grounding philosophy. They provide music and life skills mentoring in a safe and supportive context. Davis (2007) reported that the members have freedom within structured rules and close adult supervision. At times, the adult staff uses humor to keep members in line; for example, when one youth was abusing his computer privilege and left his MySpace page open on an MRC computer, a staff member altered his MySpace picture in a funny way.

MRC offers members a place to socialize, develop musical and dance skills, explore songwriting and performing, and record original compositions. Davis noted that MRC meets criteria established for successful youth programs (McLaughlin, 1993; Halpern, 2003) because MRC connects to youths' lives while flexibly responding to their needs and perspectives and allowing freedom for enthusiasm and creative processes. In Davis's focused interview groups, both members and staff described their connection to MRC as a "second home" (2007, p. 133). Members benefited through positive bonding with others, behavioral and social competencies, self-determination, beliefs in the future, and positive identity (p. 134).

In 2007 Karen D'Agostino began a similar program in Cincinnati. D'Agostino realized a need for an after-school center for urban youth in Cincinnati. She recalled that the Dave Matthews Band performed a fundraiser for a program in Charlottesville, so she decided to contact the MRC. The Charlottesville program adopted the Cincinnati project as their first "sister" program, and the Cincinnati MRC uses the same philosophy, program, and name as the original MRC. A third program opened and then reopened in Duluth, Minnesota. The organizers of MRC hope many communities across the United States will adopt the MRC model and provide music centers for youths in other urban areas.

In East Boston, Madeline Steczynski and Bob Grove cofounded Zumix, a nonprofit organization aimed to provide top-quality cultural programming as an alternative way for young people to deal with anger, fear, and frustration, as well as building acceptance and cultural understanding. Concerned that Boston experienced one of its highest homicide rates in 1991 and that a large percentage of these crimes were youth opposing other youth, Steczynski and Grove wanted to use music as a means to lessen violent behavior. They drove a van they named "Music Mobile," full of instruments, into areas of East Boston where gangs loitered, but youth did not join them as they had hoped. They learned the name "Music Mobile" was already used by Ruth Pelham, who had begun a program in Albany, New York, in 1977.[2]

Restructuring, they invited youth to their apartment and facilitated hip-hop songwriting, the style most familiar to them. The participants decided to name the new organization Zumix, an anagram of "muzix." Zumix's first official program was a songwriting class in the East Boston Community Center. Their philosophy is that all youth are empowered individuals who are searching for the right tools to express themselves. The teaching approach is participant-driven, as the facilitators stress mutual respect, dialogue, and openness as fundamental values. Musical activities included songwriting, music technology, Zumix Radio 94.9 FM, hip-hop beat making, music theory, and popular and folk music ensembles including African drumming, Las Mariposas, and rock ensembles. According to Morin (2008) the staff members avoid categorizing teaching methods and prefer an open, flexible approach to facilitating music with youth based on mutual respect.

Total Learning (TL), based in Norwalk, Connecticut, was developed by Dr. Sue Snyder. It is a "multi-sensory, multi-modal, arts-infused, hands-on, brains-on approach to curriculum delivery" (http://totallearninginstitute.com). The program targets youth from birth through age nine, and is replicable and sustainable with the goal of implementation in other locations. This approach has been employed in schools, which makes it different from the other programs described in this chapter. They have trained teachers to incorporate music, movement, theatre, and visual arts to build arts skills and use those skills to deliver the entire curriculum. In the Bridgeport, Connecticut, Total Learning Initiative, the teachers reported that students demonstrated more self-control and were engaged in the learning process during TL classes. Cohen and Frank (2009, 2008) report significantly greater gains in Developmental Reading Assessments for TL first graders, kindergarteners, and English Language Learners when compared with children who did not participate in the program, and that children who participate in TL have significant increases in reading skills (word recognition, decoding of written text) and develop a passion for reading; and that parents learn new, positive ways to interact with their children. Social development is an intentional and explicit part of TL. Music and movement activities build independence and group cohesiveness. Observers of TL classes describe a caring and family-like atmosphere in the classrooms.

Started in 1990, the Storycatchers Theatre in Chicago, formerly Music Theatre Workshop, prepares young people to make positive life choices through writing, producing, and performing original musical theatre based on personal stories. Their Fabulous Females program is based at the Illinois Youth Center, a locked state residence for convicted girls. Their Firewriters program modeled after Fabulous Females is for boys incarcerated at the Illinois Youth Center–Chicago. Many times, these youth have dealt with traumatic physical and mental abuse. With the guidance of the founder and artistic director, Meade Palidofsky, the Storycatchers' artists choose a central theme and combine the youths' stories into a musical with a few main characters. This collaborative work helps the youth work through their differences in a structured environment. They make more eye contact, fidget less, and engage in fewer self-destructive behaviors. Through writing and performing their stories, they learn to perceive their past trauma in different ways and begin to believe in their capacity to move on with their lives (Palidofsky, 2010). Changing Voices is an employment program for groups of up to 12 recently released youth. They develop and perform a musical that explores the difficulties they deal with upon reentry.

European Programs

A Portuguese program called BébéBábá teaches mothers how to interact with their babies, using music to assist in building positive parent-child relationships. A special project of this program took place in Estabelecimento Prisional Especial de

Santa Cruz do Bispo. Incarcerated mothers in Portugal have their children with them until age three or four. Rodrigues et al. (2010) report a strong bonding between children, mothers, and the communities through participation in this program. The musical guidance helps mothers interact with their children and rebuild lost daughterhood.

Sing Up, the United Kingdom's national singing program for youth, was launched in October 2007. The government invested over 40 million pounds over four years to work toward a singing school in every English school. The introduction to the Second Report of the Music Manifesto group states that singing "is a powerful community activity binding individuals and community together" (Welch et al., 2009, p. 4). Although this program is not designed specifically as an intervention for at-risk youth, it does function as a preventative measure. Supporters of the project argue that singing improves confidence, learning, health, and social development. It has the power to change lives and build stronger communities (Music Manifesto Report, 2006).

An example of music-making as a means to build socialization is the Marokko Project, near Frankfort, Germany (Widmer & Widmer, 2001). In Rüsselsheim, Germany, problems of prejudice and violence against a community of Moroccans (and other nationalities) had developed. Such prejudice may have developed because labor migration took jobs away from German citizens. Because of the stresses between these cultures, many adolescents resisted authority through violent behavior. The Marokko Project used music and theater with Moroccan adolescents to help integrate them into German society by better acquiring a sense of their identity (in contrast with their parents' identity and their German peers). Outcomes included a short publication, with photos, family stories, texts, and music. Performance themes related to homelessness and separation. The second phase included a 10-day trip to Morocco, visiting cities, relatives, friends, youth centers, and the emigration ministry. The intention of the trip was to give the youngsters a deeper insight into the life of Morocco as a land suffering from problems of migration.

A significant experience in Italy is represented by the project Bambini al Centro, literally "Children in the Centre" (Iadeluca & Sangiorgio, 2008), a complex system of recreational-musical services that from 1999 to 2010 aimed at promoting the well-being and the quality of spare time of at-risk children 0–12 and at supporting their parents in practical, educational, emotional, and relational aspects. The main characteristic of the Centre was the experience with and through group music making as a means of enhancing meaningful interpersonal encounters among children and adults, as well as the children themselves.

Israeli Programs

At-risk populations in Israel include (1) children of immigrant parents, particularly from Ethiopia and the former Soviet Union, who suffer from cultural clashes and discord within the family, (2) Jewish and Arab populations suffering from poverty and domestic violence, and (3) middle- and upper-class delinquent youth (Shoham et al., 2004; Addad & Wolf, 2002). Music programs for at-risk youth are primarily funded by municipal welfare departments, the Advancement for At-Risk Youth Department of the Ministry of Education, nonprofit organizations, and private donors.

Programs typically take place in four country-wide villages for physically, emotionally, or sexually abused youth between 12 and 17 years of age, in after-school treatment centers, in community and child-care centers, and occasionally in conservatories, such as the Dunie Weizman Conservatory of Music in Haifa. Haifa and Jaffa, two integrated Arab-Jewish cities with the highest concentration of at-risk youth in Israel, are the primary centers of music activity for at-risk youth.

The Push program in Haifa, founded by Momi Almog, operates as a "musical laboratory," located in a two-room state-of-the-art music studio in the Haifa municipal building. At-risk youth participate in weekly individual music lessons and therapy, ensemble playing, and group discussions. For example, the youth learn how to build phrases and balance sounds, which then serve as springboards for discussion on how to create an ensemble, accommodate one another, and understand principles of teamwork.

Youths in the Push program also participate in the "Violence Prevention Cultural Exchange Program" in conjunction with the Berlin-based "Roter Baum Berlin." Participants travel to one another's countries, participate in exchange programs of music and instrumental study, share musical performances, and engage in discussions related to violence.

The Israeli "Musical Minds Jaffa," founded and directed by Adena Portowitz of the Yehuda Amir Institute for Social Integration in the Schools, Bar-Ilan University, provides at-risk youth with quality music education while promoting cognitive, social, and emotional skills. The pedagogical approach is modeled after Mediated Learning Experiences (MLE), where children learn to think in a broader and more flexible way (Feuerstein et al., 2006; Klein, 1996). Specially trained MLE teachers instruct at-risk children from first to sixth grade to play instruments, organize them in ensemble performance groups, and teach listening skills. At the same time, the children learn to identify patterns, develop holistic perceptions, relate simultaneously to multiple sources, and practice self-regulation. Results of a two-year study of the effectiveness of mediated learning with at-risk youngsters indicated significant advantages in targeted cognitive skills among those who participated in the music program (Portowitz et al., 2009).

El Sistema Programs: Transforming the Whole Child

Dr. Jose Antonio Abreu began the original El Sistema program in Venezuela in 1975. The Venezuelan government funds this program, in which, Lakshmanan (2005) reports, over 400,000 children, mostly from poor socioeconomic backgrounds, have participated. Hollinger (2006) interviewed Abreu, who stated he was most proud of El Sistema's social results: "the possibility of transformed life for very poor children and youngsters" (p. 127). He indicated that the social and musical goals have equal value and that the social goals are reached through artistic means. Abreu conveyed that the program transforms the whole child, improving children's minds, aspirations, and ideas. Children in the program remarked: "It is like a family here"; "It changes our hearts"; "Playing music changes our souls" (p. 119). In the summer of 2008, Scotland started an El Sistema program that officially partners with the Venezuelan program. Their goals are to foster confidence, teamwork, pride, and aspiration in children and the wider community through music-making. Other countries have adopted a similar model.[3]

IMPLICATIONS FOR MUSIC EDUCATION

Youth in challenging situations are a very demanding target group and require well-grounded leadership. It is vital to consider appropriate theoretical frameworks that promote leadership based on caring when training future music facilitators. Noddings's (1984) ethics of care provides a fitting theoretical foundation. The Austrian/German model for training teachers attributes great importance to the psycho-pedagogical training and developing their abilities to be interactive, communicative, kindhearted, and charismatic—in short, building good leaders. Teachers need to be aware of the intricacies within the social, affective, and cognitive learning processes. If teachers are facilitating musical learning activities in a school setting, they also need to be aware of the social control mechanisms that are inherent in school contexts. The ability to coordinate a system of cooperation within group musical activities is vital for teaching at-risk youth. Such a system provides empowerment, enhanced sense of self, and intrinsic motivation for promoting positive relationships.

FUTURE ADVOCACY

When we discuss youth and the specific challenges they face, we must take into consideration the complexity of creating long-lasting meaningful educational experiences that will help them deal with their life stresses. Musical programs provide opportunities to build positive relationships, group responsibility, aesthetic sensitivity, and individual attributes such as empathy, respect, and perseverance.

REFLECTIVE QUESTIONS

1. Considering the concept that "relationships, not programs, change people," how should teacher training programs include the growth of the teacher/facilitator to learn how to interact positively with others?
2. In what ways do our teaching practices and performance traditions in school systems help or hinder students who are along the at-risk continuum? How do power structures inherent in schools and communities affect the process of music-making for youth in challenging situations?
3. In what ways do our rehearsal and performance traditions help or hinder social relationships among the participants?
4. In what ways do musical skills learned in community or school programs stimulate or deemphasize independent creativity?
5. In what ways do our programs stimulate or deemphasize ongoing social interaction?
6. For the leader: Which parts of you and which emotions emerge when you face weak or problematic sides of your at-risk learners? How "centered" are you? How "at-risk" are you?
7. How can public resources coordinate effectively in order to create a system of integrated social services for youth that includes music, art, and other media?

KEY SOURCES

Brice Heath, S., & Soep, E. (1998). Youth development and the arts in nonschool hours. *GIA Newsletter*, 9(1). Retrieved June 1, 2010, http://www.giarts.org/article/youth-development-and-arts-nonschool-hours.

Hartogh, T., & Wickel, H. H. (eds.) (2004). *Handbuch Musik in der Sozialen Arbeit*, Juventa Verlag: Weinheim und München.

Taylor, J. A., Barry, N. H., Walls, K. C. (1997). *Music and students at risk: Creative solutions for a national dilemma*. Reston, VA: Music Educators National Conference.

NOTES

1. Subsequent to the publication of our original chapter in 2012 and its title *At-Risk Youth: Music-Making as a Means to Promote Positive Relationships*, we have reflected on the title and believe that the label "at risk" might be misunderstood due to its potentially negative connotation. Consequently, we believe that an alternative title is more appropriate, i.e., *Music-Making as a Means to Promote*

Positive Relationships for Youth in Challenging Situations. Whilst we recognise the publishing difficulties in changing the title such that the links to the original chapter would be lost, nevertheless we have revised the content of this updated chapter to take account of our new conceptualisation.

2. According to Morin (2004) Pelham threatened a lawsuit because the name was already copyrighted. Music Mobile's mission is "to promote cooperation, empowerment, tolerance, civic responsibility, community pride, and self-esteem by developing and presenting innovative music and creative arts programs, and creating and disseminating educational resource materials" (http://www.musicmobile.org/about/mission.htm).

3. According to George Anderson, Sistema Scotland's communication advisor, other countries are beginning Sistema-type programs, including the United States, in New York and Boston; Canada, in New Brunswick; Portugal, in Lisbon; and in Finland. El Sistema USA trains leaders who want to teach or initiate an El Sistema program. Possible observation and internship sites are the Community Music School of Boston, Project STEP, Artists for Humanity, Raw Art Works, and the Theater Offensive, among others. El Sistema programs also exist in other South American countries, the Caribbean, Spain, Egypt, Kenya, and South Africa (Hollinger, 2006).

REFERENCES

Addad, M., & Wolf, Y. (2002). Crime and social deviance: Theory and practice. Ramat Gan: Bar-llan University Press.

Brice Heath, S., & Soep, E. (1998). Youth development and the arts in nonschool hours. *GIA Newsletter*, 9(1). Retrieved June 1, 2010, http://www.giarts.org/article/youthdevelopment-and-arts-nonschool-hours.

Catalano, R. F., Berglund, M. L., Ryan, J. A. M., & Hawkins, J. D. (2004). Positive youth development in the United States: Research findings on evaluations of positive youth development programs. *Annals of the American Academy of Political and Social Science*, 591, 98–124.

Christenson, P. G., & Roberts, D. F. (1998). *It's not only rock and roll: Popular music in the lives of adolescents*. Cresskill, NY: Hampton Press, Inc.

Cohen, M., & Frank, M. (2008). Evaluation report: The effect of Total Learning on kindergarteners' and preschoolers' academic performance and school readiness in Bridgeport, Connecticut. http://totallearninginstitute.com/pdf/TLSummative07_08.pdf [accessed November 23, 2017].

Cohen, M., & Frank, M. (2009). 2009 evaluation of the educational impact of Total Learning on public school kindergarten and first grade students in Bridgeport, Connecticut. Retrieved January 13, 2010.

Countrymen, J. (2009). High school music programs as potential sites for communities of practice—A Canadian study. *Music Education Research*, 11(1), 93–109.

Countrymen, J. (2009). High school music programmes as potential sites for communities of practice—a Canadian study. *Music Education Research*, 11(1), 93–109. doi: 10.1080/1461300802699168

Davis, M. (2007). *A study of a youth music center: Out of school time programs, music and positive youth development*. Doctoral diss., University of Virginia. Available from ProQuest Dissertations and Thesis Database (UMI No. 3239980).

Dreitzel, H. P. (1973). *Childhood and socialization*. New York: Macmillan Publishing Co., Inc.

Feuerstein, R., Feuerstein, R. S., Falik, L., & Rand, Y. (2006). *Creating and enhancing cognitive modifiability: The Feuerstein instruments enrichment program*. Jerusalem: ICELP Publications.

Froehlich, H. (2009). Music education and community: Reflections on "Webs of Interaction" in school music. *Action, Criticism, and Theory for Music Education, 8*(1), 85–107.

Goodman, E. (2002). Ensemble performance. In J. Rink (ed.), *Musical performance: A guide to understanding* (pp. 153–167). Cambridge: Cambridge University Press.

Halpern, R. (2003). Making play work: The promise of after-school programs for low-income children. New York: Teacher's College Press.

Handel, G. (2006). *Childhood socialization*. Piscataway, NJ: Aldine Transaction.

Hindreth, P., & Kimble, K. (2008). Introduction and overview. In C. Kimble, P. Hildreth, & I. Bourdon (eds.), *Communities of practice: Creating learning environments for educators* (pp. vi–xix). Charlotte, NC: Information Age Publishing, Inc.

Hollinger, D. M. (2006). Instrument of social reform: A case study of the Venezuelan system of youth orchestras. Doctoral diss., Arizona State University. Available from ProQuest Dissertation and Thesis Database. (UMI No. 3241291).

Iadeluca, V., & Sangiorgio, A. (2008). Bambini al Centro: Music as a means to promote well-being. Birth and configuration of an experience. *International Journal of Community Music, 1*(3), 311–318.

Klein, P. S. (1996). *Early intervention. Cross-cultural experiences with a meditational approach*. New York: Garland.

Kronick, R. F. (1997). At-risk youth: The state of the art. In R. F. Kronick (ed.), *At-risk youth: Theory, practice, reform* (pp. 3–37). New York & London: Garland Publishing, Inc.

Lakshmanan, I. (2005, June 22). For Venezuela's poor music opens doors: Classical program transforms lives. *Boston Globe*.

Lave, J., & Wenger, E. (1991). *Communities of practice: Learning, meaning and identity*. Cambridge: Cambridge University Press.

McLaughlin, M. W. (1993). Embedded identities: Enabling balance in urban contexts. In S. B. Heath & M. W. McLaughlin (eds.), *Identity and inner city youth: Beyond ethnicity and gender* (pp. 36–68). New York: Teacher's College Press.

McWhirter, J. J., McWhirter, B. T., McWhirter, A. M., & McWhirter, E. H. (2007). *At-risk youth: A comprehensive response for counselors, teachers, psychologists, and human service professionals* (4th ed.). London: Brooks/Cole Publishing Company.

Morin, M. M. (2008). *Facilitating praxial music education at the East Boston Youth Center, Zumix*. Master's thesis, Tufts University. Available from ProQuest Dissertations and Thesis Database (UMI No. 1456633).

Music Manifesto Report. (2006). *Making every child's music matter: Music Manifesto Report No. 2: A consultation for action*. London: Crown Copyright. Retrieved June 2, 2010, http://www.musicmanifesto.co.uk/assets/x/50226.

Noddings, N. (1984). *Caring: A feminine approach to ethics and moral education*. Berkley: University of California Press.

Noddings, N. (1995). Teaching themes of care. *Phi Delta Kappan, 76*(9), 675–679.

O'Neill, S. (2006). Positive youth musical engagement. In G. McPherson (ed.), *The child as musician: Handbook of musical development* (pp. 461–474). Oxford: Oxford University Press.

Palidofsky, M. (2010). If I cry for you . . . Turning unspoken trauma into song and musical theatre. *International Journal of Community Music, 3*(1), 121–128.

Portowitz, A., Lichtenstein, O., Egorova, L., & Brand, E. (2009). Underlying mechanisms linking music education and cognitive modifiability. *Research Studies in Music Education, 31*(2), 107–128.

Reber, A. S., & Reber, E. S. (2001). *The Penguin dictionary of psychology* (3rd ed.). London & New York: Penguin Books.

Rodrigues, H., Leite, A., Faria, C., Monteiro, I., & Rodrigues, P. M. (2010). Music for mothers and babies living in a prison: A report on a special production of BébéBábá. *International Journal of Community Music, 3*(1), 77–90.

Sangiorgio, A. (2010). *Orff-Schulwerk as anthropology of music.* In Orff-Schulwerk Egitim ve Danismanlik Merkezi Türkiye (ed.), *"Orffinfo" 16.* http://emp.hmtm.de/files/Sangiorgio_2010_Orff-Schulwerk_as_Anthropology_of_Music.pdf [accessed November 23, 2017].

Shoham, G., Addad, M., & Rahav, G. (2004). *Criminology.* Tel Aviv: Schocken.

Silber, L. (2005). Bars behind bars: The impact of a women's prison choir on social harmony. *Music Education Research, 7*(2), 251–271.

Ungar, M. (2008). Putting resiliency theory into action: Five principles. In L. Liebenberg & M. Ungar (eds.), *Resilience in action* (pp. 17–36). Toronto: University of Toronto Press.

Welch, G. F., Himonides, E., Papageorgi, I., Saunders, J., Rinta, T., Stewart, C., Preti, F. & Lani, C. (2009). The National Singing Programme for primary schools in England: An initial baseline study. *Music Education Research, 11*(1), 1–22.

Wenger, E. (1998). *Communities of practice: learning, meaning, and identity.* Cambridge: Cambridge University Press.

Widmer, M., & Widmer, M. (2001). Elementares Musiktheater als integrative und integrierende Spielform der Musik- und Bewegungserziehung. In S. Salmon & K. Schumacher (eds.), *Symposion Musikalische Lebenshilfe. Die Bedeutung des Orff-Schulwerks für Musiktherapie, Sozial- und Integrationspädagogik* (pp. 193–208). Hamburg: Books on Demand.

CHAPTER 14

FAST FORWARD: EMERGING TRENDS IN COMMUNITY MUSIC

KARI K. VEBLEN AND JANICE L. WALDRON

This is a chapter about the unknowable but imaginable future of Community Music (CM). At the present time, Community Music is an umbrella term for a variety of practices and forms found internationally as well as an emerging field in music education grounded in research. At the most basic level, CM currently consists of informal music teaching-learning processes and amateur music-making carried out in noninstitutional situations. However, CM may also take the form of partnerships between informal and formal music teaching/learning contexts.

Community Music programs are shaped by five aspects: (1) the kinds of music and active music-making; (2) the participants; (3) the intentions and aspirations of those involved; (4) the teaching/learning practices; and (5) interplay between informal and formal social/educational/cultural contexts.

The impetus for this chapter comes from our conviction that music is and should be for all and that music education as a discipline has changed, is changing, and will change. Areas of informal music teaching and learning processes and contexts will be part of these changes, as will diverse groups of learning musicians. By examining emerging research in CM, as well as related literature from education, ethnomusicology, sociology, and media and communication studies, we attempt an interdisciplinary perspective. Issues explored include forces influencing CM, such as demographics, notions of *communitas*, international trends, and new networks for collaboration.

Predicting the future may be impossible. However, by synthesizing patterns, current trends, structures, and systems, it is feasible to uncover power relationships and underlying assumptions. Through these it is possible to consider what could be—the probable, the possible, and desirable as people create, teach, learn and connect through music.

Evolving Understandings of *Communitas*

Concepts of community embrace both ideals and realities. Most people in the field of CM inevitably grapple with many challenging details surrounding the meaning of community, whether these details concern community as geographically situated, culturally based, artistically concerned, re-created, virtual, imagined, or otherwise. Indeed, many contemporary music scholars are heavily involved in documenting how musical cultures embody (mirror, reflect, and shape) social cultures, and vice versa.

Impetus for and threaded through many CM programs and projects are notions of belonging to a group, sometimes termed *communitas*. *Communitas* may be described as a moment "in and out of time" where everyone becomes absorbed in shared experiences (often in connection with rituals) and intense feelings of acceptance transcending the routine and day-to-day. There are more particular nuances to the term in social sciences and anthropology. For example, in communitas, people stand together outside society, and society is strengthened by this. The concept is in many ways the opposite of Marx's alienation or Durkheim's anomie, and is closely related to the latter's ideas about the sacred (vs. the profane)."[1] This suspension of time and intensification of belonging are recurring elements in music-making; musicians may refer to being "in the groove," "jamming," being "in sync," "flow," or being "in harmony."

Cunningham (2008) explores facilitation through drumming circles. One of Cunningham's collaborators described communitas through the absorbing experience of a drumming context:

> It is a feeling of togetherness without words, a conversation through the
> instruments. I have experiences this many times at the large circles at the Seattle
> Rhythm Festival where there are about 300 to 500 people all playing what
> they want or can, from their own spirit. I have also experienced it many times
> facilitating people in schools, elder care facilities and corporate events. (p. 82)

Community Music and ethnomusicological research is replete with examples of communitas found in informal settings such as festivals (Karlsen, 2007; Gardner, 2004; Snell, 2005), workshops (Cope, 2002), and transnational cultural gatherings (Lavengood, 2008), or more formal settings such as hospitals and institutions (Grocke, Bloch, & Castle, 2009) or prisons (Graham, 2001; Cohen, 2008). Themes of communitas thread throughout participant experiences in choirs (Hayes, 2009;

Kennedy, 2009; Southcote, 2009), instrumental ensembles (Dabback, 2008; Ruggeri, 2003), sacred music-making (Kapchan, 2009; Phelan, 2007; Hirabayashi, 2009), and intergenerational assemblages (Russell, 2002; Alfano, 2009).

Clearly the notions embodied in communitas—belonging to a group—compel many people to seek out opportunities to merge in music-making with others. In addition, CM practices hinge on the reality of learning in social contexts and construction of meaning dependent on group consensus. Identity is formed in connection with others; in such communities of practice,[2] humans learn through "an evolving, continuously renewed set of relations" (Lave & Wenger, 1991, p. 49). In CM subgroups, musicians share information and experiences.

Another essential aspect of CM is the recognition of music's use in human and social enterprises. Music cannot be disembodied from context in CM activities. Music teaching and learning is an important component, but only in part. In addition to music-making, social activities (such as healing, community building, self-expression, networking, consciousness raising, celebration of cultural heritage, and so forth) may be as important or more important than the music itself.

FUTURECAST: SOCIAL NETWORKS FACE-TO-FACE (F2F)

Many forces will contribute to expansion and change in existing social networks, including those forged through CM. Lives are increasingly interconnected, and we see each other's faces and circumstance more clearly than ever before. Over the next hundred years, monumental change will be wrought by forces such as shifts in demographics, aging populations, expansion and contraction of the marketplace, environmental and resource challenges, and globalization. In addition, these influences will weave into the continual patterns of war, peace, and negotiation begun in the past and always unfolding.

According to Shackman, Wang, and Liu 2010), world population growth has been decelerating since 1970, at a slower rate of decline in developed countries compared to developing ones. Infant mortality rates and fertility have declined while there have been changes in age distribution. According to Harper (2008) at the Oxford Institute of Aging, "by 2050, there will be 2 billion older people globally, 500 million of them aged over 80" (p. 1). At the same time that population growth has decelerated, in some countries both literacy rates and life spans have increased; it is likely in these parts of the world that the aging populations will seek out opportunities for learning. In some parts of the world, this process has already begun. While lifelong learning in North America continues to be largely market driven, there are social programs and community outreach efforts that are less cap-italistically driven and more structured for the common good.

And in China there are currently over 20,000 "universities for old people"; funded by the state, the missions of these universities is to "enable an older cit-izen to carry out her 'sacred duty' to society by avoiding boredom and depression" (Manheimer, 2005, p. 216).

Demographic studies, such as Inglehart, Foa, Peterson, and Welzel's (2008) survey of global happiness, conclude that indices of happiness rose in 45 of the 52 countries where time-series evidence was available. Factors that influence happiness include democratization, social tolerance, and economic sufficiency.[3] Other factors that will profoundly influence people's lives include the interactions of globalization with localization, immigration, shifting affluences, and increasing opportunities to choose where and how one lives.

As demographics shape societal structures, ways people learn and connect through music will adapt. Likewise, the field of music education likely will alter to include the entire life range of an individual. As further understanding of music's influence on mind and body is documented, musical education with the very young—the fetus even—throughout each phase of lifelong learning may come to be increasingly championed.

In future times, what seem at first to be cutting-edge changes will become com-monplace, as older structures (like museums, libraries, orchestras, and churches) adapt and change.[4] Community Music will become increasingly a part of such repurposing as either designated permanent programs or series of initiatives. For example, museums such as the National Museum of Australia, Canberra, and the National Museum of Iceland have regular docent tours, events for children, school outreach, hands-on displays, new exhibits, and lectures; the Smithsonian in Washington, D.C., and the Royal Ontario Museum in Toronto offer photog-raphy tours and study expeditions to natural sites such as the Galapagos Islands and culture-rich destinations such as Florence and Kyoto. Likewise, libraries routinely provide story hours, senior classes, and workshops for the community. It is thus not a far stretch to imagine these institutions encompassing musical partnerships, ongoing participatory activities such as in-house gamelan, folk ensemble, or early childhood musical exploration rooms, interactive composition/improvisation sculptures, music-making installations or music-oriented outings.

Many orchestras partner with schools and offer community outreach. Imagine the full exposition of these activities as the orchestra of the future embraces the community and school with interaction and teaching as the heart of its mission. Future orchestras may encompass a wide range of musical and artistic genres as a bank of musicians, dancers, and others work with each other and community members on specific projects.

The structures and ways CM is expressed depend on socioeconomic frameworks; they are thus geographically diverse. While CM programs in some places are less developed and sparsely documented, other regions have a fruitful history of funding and professionalism. At the present time, regional and national networks for CM are developing rapidly. It seems very likely that as networks expand, lobbying and advocacy efforts will catalyze new funding streams for projects.

Current development of training programs for CM workers[5] seems likely to continue. Furthermore, in the century to come, it may well be that the roles of CM worker, music educator, and music therapist begin to merge in significant ways. It is common now for music teachers in a school setting to also work with church-based or community groups, to play with various ensembles in various genres, and to take on a variety of roles in a natural extension of individual interests, enthusiasms, and in fulfillment of needs. Community Music will be a respected, fully licensed profession. Responsive to the many needs of a changing world, musician-educator-workers will facilitate music-making in multiple situations with all kinds of people. In a perfect world,[6] everyone will have the right to make music, and everyone will have access to individualized and group musical experiences.

FUTURECAST: SOCIAL NETWORKS AND COMPUTER-MEDIATED COMMUNICATION (CMC)

One of the most radical developments in CM goes far beyond physical structures or networks. The next renaissance of CM—which is already under way—surfaces in modes and mediums through which people learn and connect musically. Media researchers contend that each emergent technology facilitates new ways to structure, perceive, and interpret human interactions (Edgerton in Atay, 2009, p. 93). The development of the internet, with its easy support of life online, offers a particular case in point. Over the past decade, online communities have emerged in relation to a plethora of human interests and activities, including musical genres and practices. As reflections of their offline counterparts, online communities offer an entry point into musical cultures and practices that would have been difficult or impossible to identify or pursue before the development of the internet. As a rule, online music communities do not specify music learning as their raison d'être; however, music learning weaves through the fabric of many virtual music groups.

Music education researchers have only begun to focus on music learning in online communities (Salavuo, 2006; Salavuo & Hakkinen, 2005; Waldron & Veblen, 2008, Waldron, 2011) and composition (Beckstead, 1998; Hugill, 2001). With a few exceptions (Salavuo, 2008; Waldron, 2009), they have overlooked cultural issues associated with meaning and identity. Conversely, researchers in media-communication studies, anthropology, sociology, and ethnomusicology have a history of examining online music communities and ways in which the medium of cyberspace shapes music transmission, culture, discourse, identity, gender, and social capital in community rather than issues surrounding music learning.[7]

Regardless of the research lens of the above studies, internet music communities can generally be categorized by the primary reasons for the online community's original formation; for example, some websites are primarily devoted to music fandom, while others are dedicated to swapping and collecting audio recordings of various types of music.

As stated earlier, the content and focus of each online music community is a reflection of its offline counterpart; thus the primary interests of members and how the community operates in both spheres are similar from a cultural and sociological perspective. Boundaries between the two communities can be and are often blurred. According to Atay (2009), this is a common occurrence in communities that exist in both virtual and physical space because "our offline associations [in communities are] a reflection [of] our online interactions" and vice versa" (p. 143). However, Atay also argues that one can be examined independently of the other, provided the researcher understands how the community under exploration is linked contextually to its online or offline counterpart.

The ways online and offline communities operate differently in their respective spaces is due to the nature of face-to-face (F2F) communication and computer-mediated communication (CMC). One hallmark of the latter is that it enables people to communicate asynchronously, defined as "any form of communication in which the parties to the interaction need not be present simultaneously" (Hine, 2000, p. 157).

Hugill (2001) discusses how some new technologies may facilitate online communities to function in ways that differ from their offline community counterparts. Writing before the arrival of Web 2.0, Hugill contended that "there are numerous types of sites involving music or sound: resources; information and support; education; composition; commercial; broadcasting; audio handling; wired spaces and performers; e-operas, e-symphonies and e-instruments; and many more" (p. 1). With internet use booming, and new technologies and support systems like YouTube and Web 2.0 enabling hyperconnectivity (an amped-up version of interconnectivity)[8] among users, the content and possible functions of online music communities has grown exponentially since Hugill's research. However, his categories still remain relevant. What has changed is how hyperconnectivity has had a snowball effect as online music communities constantly reinvent themselves, in terms of technological content, perspectives, and larger philosophical questions, and members adapt evolving technology for specific niches and needs in their respective communities. The next section will explore how CMC promotes online music communities.

A Conspectus of Research on Internet Music Communities

Research on online music communities can be classified into studies that focus primarily on:

1. Music learning in online community (Salavuo, 2006, 2008; Waldron & Veblen, 2008; Waldron, 2009, 2011)
2. Traditional composition and online electronic music composition (Beckstead, 1998; Hugill, 2001, Silvers, 2007)
3. Music trading, as in the digital, taper, and mod music online communities (Lysloff, 2003; Nieckarz, 2005)
4. Discussions about bands or music genres (Andrus 2006, Bryant, 1995; Dyck, 2008; Scully, 2005)
5. The redistribution of power relationships in offline music communities through the corresponding online one (Hughes & Lang, 2003)
6. Gender issues in online music communities (Derecho, 2008; Farrugia, 2004; Stokes, 2004)

Although the studies cited above survey different aspects of many online music communities, researchers independently observed that the desire to belong, socially and culturally, compelled participants. In each case, members of respective web enclaves freely contributed and shared information with one another.

Music Education Research: Music Learning and Online Community

Music education studies have explored online music communities whose primary function is to facilitate music learning centered on a particular genre.[9] In his investigation of social media, Salavuo (2008) sought to discover the influences of social media on pedagogical change in music learning. He concluded that communities of practice supported by social media provided new opportunities for music learning, and this included learning in online music communities. Salavuo (2006) presents findings from a study that he and Hakkinen conducted in 2005 to find why members participated in the Finnish-based fusion music site milkseri.net. Motives ranged (in the following order) from musical, social, knowledge, and learning related to fame/wealth. Salavuo and Hakkinen discovered that fusion music participants connected in order to interact with each other for 16 reasons, including (1) uploading their own music and expecting feedback; (2) listening to music contributed by peers and providing feedback; (3) discussing, asking questions, providing answers, and engaging in arguments; (4) recommending music; and (5) connecting together to engage in joint projects (2005, p. 126).

Waldron and Veblen (2008) examined music teaching and learning in the Irish traditional virtual music community (IrTrad) by surveying multiple online sites involving members of the IrTrad community for online music learning. Sites included websites, blogs, forums, chat sites, links to different types of written notation, and YouTube videos. Waldron (2009, 2011)) conducted a cyber ethnography of music teaching and learning practices that characterized the Old Time (OT) music online community as a community of practice.

Although participants in all of the above studies valued the social connections made in online community, musical reasons superseded social motivations for why members belonged to each of the respective online groups.

Music Education Research: Composing on the Internet

Other studies by music education researchers have focused on online communities formed around music composition, sharing music compositions, and collaborative online composition. Hugill (2001), in his discussion of online music creation, mentions several examples of sites where one can compose, record, remix, explore, or jam online, such as Shockwave, the Rocket Network, Jsyn, and Electronic Music Interactive.

Beckstead (1998) examined the Composers in Electronic Residence (CIER) program, which linked professional composers with high school music students through online musical and textual exchanges. Students used a variety of technological and telecommunications tools to compose original works under the mentorship of the professional composers in the program, and Beckstead credited the creation of a CIER community to the ongoing discourse between both student and professional composers for duration of the project and afterward (p. iii).

In his musicological case study of a Brazilian virtual community of electronic musicians, Silvers (2007) contended that, in addition to changing the ways in which communities are constructed, technologically mediated listening via the internet has changed the way music is heard and perceived. Members of this Brazilian community exchanged musical ideas and compositions, creating a live cyber-feedback loop that shaped "musical creation as well as a sense of place and community" (p. 5).

Online Music Trading Communities

Researchers outside music education have examined online communities formed around collecting and trading archival sound materials on tapes, CDs, digital audio tape recorders (DATs), and laptop computers that feature a specific artist, genre, or musical group of interest. Such recordings—referred to as "bootlegs"—are, by definition, a violation of copyright laws and are technically illegal. Often, however, the recordings of the artist in question are authorized by the artist and thus violate no laws (Nieckarz, 2005). Nieckarz conducted his cyber ethnography of the taper community to determine the emergence of social dynamics on the internet. Once a concert is recorded, tapers—as they are referred to—copy and circulate recordings to members via direct downloads from websites and person-to-person file transfers through a file transfer protocol (FTP). Numerous websites are now devoted to collecting and trading of sound recordings that exist in conjunction with an online community formed around a specific artist(s), and these websites function as a conduit for the group in question. Nieckarz (2005) concluded that, when viewed through the lens of sociological theory, online communities—like the taper community—are not only possible, but do indeed exist on the internet, thus giving further credence to the idea of disembedded community.

In his ethnographic exploration of an online community of electronic music composers of the mod scene—which refers to digital music modules created and exchanged by composers in this online group—Lysloff (2003), like Nieckarz, investigated the ways in which locality and community are established in a virtual medium (pp. 234–235). He concluded that not only does the internet provide un-limited opportunities for growing and maintaining social networks but also—and more significant, from a musical perspective—the web provides for "innovative new uses of current technology, and for collective and collaborative artistic crea-tivity" (p. 258).

In his sociological study of the contemporary indie music scene, Elliott (2004) argued that the rise of the digital music collecting in the past decade has resulted in an "increasingly intimate and socially-constituted form of music collecting and consumption" (p. ii). Using the indie music scene as an example, he suggested that, through the use of "portable audio devices, online download infrastructures, and social networking software," music collectors are now linked together in online so-cial communities that promote connoisseurship, which, Elliott contends, is a major contributing factor in the canonization of indie music (p. ii).

Music Genres in Online Community

Researchers from diverse fields including theology, ethnomusicology, and media studies have examined online music communities devoted to a particular band or music genre. Bryant's (1995) seminal study explored the virtual folk music com-munity of singer-songwriters as a "microcosm of the larger musical subculture of singer-songwriters" (p. ii). She concluded that, although the cultural system of the online bulletin boards appeared to be democratic, it was in fact delineated by a two-tiered power structure; that of the list owner and the other subscribers to the list, all of who were subservient to him or her. Finally, "this virtual community, as a ritual enactment site, reflects a search for community in contemporary society" (p. ii).

Exploring the revival of the folk music scene, Scully (2005) sought to discover the representation of identity and meaning in contemporary folk music culture;

how do members of multiple online folk communities adapt and shape internet use to fit their online communities? Because folk music is a broad, inclusive term, online music communities that fall under its aegis have exploded, resulting in revivalists of a number of diverse folk subgenres—such as Appalachian fiddle fans and singer-songwriters—conversing and debating with one another through listservs and bulletin boards. This has resulted in new levels of knowledge and empathy among participants in various folk music subgenres.

Andrus (2006) explored the connection between the bluegrass music community and evangelicalism, including online discussion groups. She concluded that bluegrass music represented an alternate model of spirituality in American popular music culture.

In the practice of music blogging, participants upload their own recordings onto personal weblogs. Dyck (2008) studied the origins and technological foundations of the Indian music blogging community. Members of that community produce and record albums, then upload their recordings to websites for free access to all. Dyck concluded that, although the Indian blogging community is a virtual phenomenon, it is grounded in embodied experience and offers a significant dynamic in facilitating discourse among the global South Asian community.

Music, Power Relationships, and the Web

According to Hughes and Lang (2003), the internet "enables the development of widely dispersed, interactive audiences for musical products and services, and therefore the emergence of highly fragmented and highly specific niche markets for any conceivable form of music" (p. 180). As a result, there has been a shift in power networks—represented by large music industry corporations on one end and digital virtual community networks on the other—as music increasingly moves from being an analog to a digital entity. Through CMC and hyperconnectivity, these new virtual music communities consist of both artists and connoisseurs who have morphed into self-organizing groups centered around specific musics and interests. This redistribution of power through technological means has revolutionized the way music is disseminated, recorded, and purchased by consumers.

Music and Gender in Online Music Communities

Researchers in feminist and media studies have examined how the development of online music communities is interconnected with issues of gender. Derecho (2008) examined "remix" culture as a case study of the representation of race, gender, class, and sex within the context of the U.S. "culture wars" of the 1980s and 1990s. She defines current "remix" culture as "mash-up videos and movie parodies" authored primarily by white teenage males and distributed on the web through YouTube.

Although pioneered by African-American men and white American women through virtual communities like Usenet in the early 1990s, Derecho argued, "remix" culture has now been co-opted by privileged, white, young males, and that this is a prime example how communities of the Other continue to be marginalized by the media.

In her cyber ethnographic exploration of sexuality, identity, and the romantic relationships of black adolescent girls, Stokes (2004) investigated an online community she called NevaEvaLand. She chose this website because it was an example of an emerging context in which black adolescent girls could discuss their sexual development, including the influence of hip-hop music and culture on the gender ideologies prominent in *hip-hop* culture on the web.

Farrugia (2004) examined the process through which women become DJs in the predominantly male culture of electronic/dance music (E/DM). She discovered that the hegemonic representation of women in that culture led women to create their own communities of practice in E/DM, facilitated primarily through the internet, both for knowledge acquisition and access to a supportive community. She concluded that the online community of women E/DM DJs contributed to building an offline and face-to-face network, and, as a result, the online and offline community of women E/DM DJs is now inextricably intertwined.

CONNECTIVITY SCHEMAS

Social networks, including those formed through CM, may go through a progression ranging from (1) face-to-face encounters to (2) friends-of-friends (or acquaintances) who expand social spheres to (3) a hypothetical six degrees of separation as shown by Milgram, and to (4) the most elaborate as facilitated through virtual mediums (Travers & Milgram, 1969; Boyd & Ellison, 2007; Liu, 2007; Christakis & Fowler, 2009).

Although cyberspace enhances the ease and speed of reaching out to many people, it may be that this "more" is actually less. For example, if a passing acquaintance, working colleague, and former classmate have equal access to a dialogue shared between dear friends, the dialogue may become shallow and limited.[10] However, in the case of those who share a musical passion, this may not matter.[11]

Boyd and Ellison comment:
Although exceptions exist, the available research suggests that most SNSs (Social Network Sites) primarily support pre-existing social relations. Ellison, Steinfield, and Lampe (2007) suggest that Facebook is used to maintain existing offline relationships or solidify offline connections, as opposed to meeting new people. . . . Research in this vein has investigated how online interactions interface with offline ones. For instance, Lampe, Ellison, and Steinfield (2006) found that Facebook users engage in searching for people with whom they have an offline connection more than they "browse" for complete strangers to meet. Likewise,

Pew research found that 91% of U.S. teens who use SNSs do so to connect with
friends (Boyd & Ellison, 2007, p. 2)

In our linearly oriented society, temporal references are embodied: the past is behind us; we stand in the present, and the future spreads before us. In other cultures
and at other times, people believed that the past and future were more fluid and
porous, not constrained to a particular direction or location, and that both past
and future overlapped. It would seem that we are on the cusp of a broader and less
linear concept of past, present, and future in which more fluid and porous ways of
knowing may prevail.

At the same time, it would appear that individuals have come full circle as far
as musicing and music learning in communities are concerned. At one time people
learned music and other things directly face-to-face in their smaller province or
village units. Although educational possibilities increased with literacy and mobility, some of the benefits of local social bonds may have simultaneously weakened.
Technology reenables learning in small groups, learning with friends, and lifelong
learning, but with more choice in who, where, and what is learned. Learners are
no longer rooted geographically, and there are multiple entry points. The learner
chooses the entry point to take control of the journey; perhaps the seeker is not even
aware of what he or she wants discover. There is a power to pick and choose and not
in a linear way. The internet allows access to everyone regardless of location, cultural
background, and chains of received individuality (gender, race, challenges etc.).[12]

Conclusion

In the future, music education may look very different. It may happen in many more
places than schools, facilitated by teacher-musicians who have both similar and very
different expertise compared to what is the norm today. As music education softens
to embrace more of the world, the roles of CM worker, music teacher, and music
therapist—already in flux and already with overlapping mandates—may blend and
blur more. As music education grows to include a wider range of learners with the
changing face of students, from school-aged to all ages, the kinds of music taught and
learned will change and change continually. Most important, more of the potential
and power of this medium for human expression and interaction will be realized.

Reflective Questions

1. Why should music educators at all levels consider emerging trends in CM?
   What are the implications for teacher education?

2. How does belonging to an online music community facilitate informal music learning as praxis for participants?

3. What online resources and technologies—for example, YouTube videos—do participants use to engage and promote participatory informal learning in online community? Which resources and technologies are applicable and most useful for your teaching context and why?

4. What other emerging trends in CM might be envisioned?

KEY SOURCES

Turino, T. T. (2008). *Music as social life: The politics of participation*. Chicago: University of Chicago Press.

Veblen, K. K., Messenger, S. J, Silverman, M., & Elliott, D. J. (eds.). (in press). *Community music today*. Landham, MD: Rowman and Littlefield Publishers.

Waldron, J. (2011). Locating narratives in postmodern spaces: A cyber ethnographic field study of informal music learning in online community. *Action, Criticism, and Theory in Music Education*, 10(2), 31–60.

WEBSITES

Electronic Music Interactive: http://pages.uoregon.edu/emi/index.php.

Jsyn: http://www.softsynth.com/jsyn.

Rocket Network: http://rocketnetwork.com.

Shockwave: https://www.shockwave-sound.com.

NOTES

1. Definition of *communitas* from Anthrobase.com Dictionary, available at http://www.anthrobase.com/Browse/Thm/C/communitas.htm.

2. As Wenger and Lave term them (Lave & Wenger, 1991; Wenger, 1998).

3. Until recently it has been widely held that neither societies nor individuals can sustain increasing happiness. However, through their examination of data from the World Values Survey and European Values Study of 1981–2007, Inglehart, Foa, Peterson, and Welzel (2008) write: "Happiness reflects not only people's objective experiences, but also how they evaluate these experiences in light of their values and religious and ideological beliefs. . . . We suggest that all minutes are not equally important: They are weighted by one's values and worldview. In this value-laden process, one minute when your child comes running to greet you with a smile and a hug may be worth a hundred minutes of cleaning up after them. . . . Happiness is an immediately accessible feeling, not something that requires elaborate cognitive processing" (p. 279).

4. See chapters in Part 2 of this volume for specific examples of current programs.

5. There are significant differences in the names assigned to CM specialists around the world. While CM "worker" is a common in the UK and Europe, other localities use the terms "CM facilitator," "Community Musician," "CM educator," "CM trainer," or "tradition bearer." As some of these names suggest, the CM worker's role is typically multidimensional, or "elastic." Accordingly, and in addition to his duties as a "teacher," the CM worker usually takes on many other roles—prompter, mentor, facilitator, catalyst, coach, director—one or more of which may require him to draw on his expertise as a music educator, entrepreneur, fundraiser, therapist, social worker, performer, composer, arranger, music technology expert, ethnomusicologist, dancer, poet, visual artist, storyteller, and more.

6. Here we visualize the best case scenario. This assumes that over the next hundred years humans will work out solutions to environmental challenges; likewise, that increasing educational and economic stability will prevail over ignorance, poverty, and oppression.

7. See Nugyen, 2007; Derecho, 2008; Farrugia, 2004; Font, 2007; Kibby, 2000; Lizie, 2000; Lysloff, 2003; Scully, 2005; Silvers, 2007; Stokes, 2004; Williams, 2006.

8. Coined by Wellman et. al (2006), the term *hyperconnectivity* refers to the use of a variety of communication modes such as face-to-face, telephone and email. The primary tenet behind hyperconnectivity is that everything that can connect will communicate through the network; consequently, the diversity, complexity and integration of new devices and applications will shape and define the communication. *Interconnectivity*, as a foundational basis of cyber culture, is understood as in this statement: "every computer, every device, every machine, *must* have an Internet address" (Huitema in Levy & Bononno, 2001, p. 107). Without interconnectivity, there could be no online community. Interconnectivity is closely related with the idea of interactivity, which refers to the amount of active participation required on the part of those who benefit from information transactions. This ranges, depending on the amount of involvement required on the part of the participant (p. 107).

9. Genres found online include fusion, autoharp, Irish traditional music, Old Time music, rock-and-roll, classical, and jazz.

10. Boyd and Ellison (2007) describe the rise and fall of the early social network site Friendster in 2002. Based on the premise that friends of friends could link together organically to share common interests, the site became unwieldy when it grew out of control and faced both technical and social difficulties.

11. More research is needed on the connections or disconnections of real-time and personal links with internet connects in music learning situations.

12. Although global access is an unrealized dream thus far, due to economics.

REFERENCES

Alfano, C. J. (2009). Seniors' participation in an intergenerational music learning program. Unpublished doctoral diss., McGill University, Montreal.

Andrus, E. H. (2006). High lonesome gospel: The role of evangelicalism in shaping an American music culture. Unpublished doctoral diss., University of California, Santa Barbara. UMI 3233000.

Atay, A. (2009). Identities in motion: Cyberspace and diasporic queer male bodies in the context of globalization. Unpublished doctoral diss., University of Illinois. UMI 3372507.

Beckstead, D. J. (1998). Composers in electronic residence: Music, technology and textual presence. Unpublished diss., Simon Fraser University. National Library of Canada 0–612-37682–6.

Boyd, D. M., & Ellison, N. B. (2007). Social network sites: Definition, history and scholarship. *Journal of Computer-Mediated Communication*, 13(1), pp. 1–11. http://jcmc.indiana.edu/vol13/issue1/boyd.ellison.html.

Bryant, W. (1995). Virtual music communities: The Folk-Music Internet discussion group as a cultural system. Unpublished doctoral diss., University of California, Los Angeles, AAT 9529095, UMI 9529095.

Christakis, N. A., & Fowler, J. H. (2009). *Connected: The surprising power of our social networks and how they shape our lives.* New York: Little, Brown & Company.

Cohen, M. L. (2008). Conductors' perspectives of Kansas prison choirs. *International Journal of Community Music, 1*(3), 319–333.

Cope, P. (2002). Informal learning of musical instruments: The important of social context. *Music Education Research, 4*, 93–104.

Cunningham, A. (2008). Drumming toward communitas: The study of facilitated recreational music making and the Arthurian method. Unpublished master's thesis, Brock University. ISBN: 978–0-494-46552-3.

Dabback, W. M. (2008). Identity formation through participation in the Rochester New Horizons Band programme. *International Journal of Community Music 1*(2), 267–286.

Derecho, A. T. (2008). Illegitimate media: Race, gender and censorship in digital remix culture. Unpublished diss., Northwestern University. UMI 3303803.

Dyck, J. (2008). Blogging music: Indian musicians and online musical spaces. Unpublished master's thesis, University of Alberta. ISBN: 978–0-494-45728-3.

Elliott, L. (2004). Goa trance and the practice of community in the age of the internet. *Television & New Media, 5*(3), 272–288.

Ellison, N. B., Steinfield, C., & Lampe, C. (2007). The benefits of Facebook "friends": Social capital and college students' use of online social network sites. *Journal of Computer-Mediated Communication, 12*, 1143–1168. doi:10.1111/j.1083-6101.2007.00367.x

Farrugia, R. L. (2004). Spinsters: Women, new media technologies and electronic/dance music. Unpublished doctoral diss., University of Iowa. UMI 3138708.

Font, D. (2007). Alan Lomax's iPod? Smithsonian global sound and applied ethnomusicology on the internet. Unpublished master's thesis. University of Maryland, College Park. UMI 1443450.

Gardner, R. O. (2004). The portable community: Mobility and modernization in bluegrass festival life. *Symbolic Interaction. 27*(2), 155–178.

Gavlak, D., & Jamjoum, L. (2009). Rebuilding lives, healing minds. *Bulletin of the World Health Organization 87*, 408–409. doi:10.2471/BLT.09.010609.

Graham, L. E. (2001). Musik macht frei: Choral music composed and performed in the Nazi concentration camps, 1938–1944. Unpublished diss., University of Southern California. AAT 3065789.

Grocke, D., Bloch, S. & Castle, D. (2009). The effect of group music therapy on quality of life for participants living with a severe and enduring mental illness. *Journal of Music Therapy, 46*(2), 90–104.

Harper, S. (2008). Generations and life course: The impact of demographic challenges on education 2010–2050. http://www.ageing.ox.ac.uk/ [accessed November 23, 2017].

Hine, C. (2000). *Virtual Ethnography.* Thousand Oaks, CA: Sage.

Hayes, C. J. (2009). Building bridges through song: A qualitative study of educational outreach by the New York City Ambassador Chorus. Unpublished doctoral diss., AAT 3346264.

Hirabayashi, E. (2009). Identity, roles and practice in ritual music. *International Journal of Community Music*, 2(1), 35–55.

Hughes, J. & Lang, K. R. (2003). If I had a song: The culture of digital community networks and its impact on the music industry. *The International Journal on Media Management*, 5(3), 180–189.

Hugill, A. (2001). Some issues in the creation of music online. Paper presented at Conference Music Without Walls? Music Without Instruments? De Montfort University. Retrieved March 30, 2012, from www.mti.dmu.ac.uk/events-conferences/0106nowalls/papers/Hugill.PDF

Inglehart, R., Foa, R., Peterson, C., & Welzel, C. (2008). Development, freedom, and rising happiness: A global perspective (1981–2007). *Perspectives on Psychological Science*, 3(4), 264–285.

Kapchan, D. (2009). Singing community/remembering in common: Sufi liturgy and North African identity in southern France. *International Journal of Community Music*, 2(1), 9–23.

Karlsen, S. (2007). The music festival as an arena for learning: Festspel I Pite Älvdal and matters of identity. Doctoral diss., Luleå University of Technology. ISSN: 1402–1522.

Kennedy, M. C. (2009). The gettin' higher choir: Exploring culture, teaching and learning in a community choir. *International Journal of Community Music*, 2, 183–200.

Kibby, M. D. (2000). Home on the page: A virtual place of music community. *Popular Music*, 19(1), 91–100.

Lampe, C., Ellison, N., & Steinfield, C. (2006). A Face(book) in the Crowd: Social Searching vs. Social Browsing. *In Proceedings of the 2006 20th Anniversary Conference on Computer-Supported Cooperative Work (CSCW 2006)*. 167–170. New York, NE: ACM Press.

Lave, J., & Wenger, E. (1991). *Situated learning: Legitimate peripheral participation*. Cambridge: Cambridge University Press.

Lavengood, K. E. (2008). Transnational communities through global tourism: Experiencing Celtic culture through music practice on Cape Breton Island, Nova Scotia. Unpublished doctoral diss., Indiana University. UMI 3319835.

Levy, P. L., & Bononno, R. (2001). *Cyberculture*. Minneapolis: University of Minnesota Press.

Liu, H. (2007). Social network profiles as taste performances. *Journal of Computer-Mediated Communication*, 13(1), 1–12. http://jcmc.indiana.edu/vol13/issue1/liu.html.

Lizie, A. (2000) Community and identity in cyberspace: Popular music and the international flow of information. Unpublished doctoral diss., Temple University. UMI: 9990333.

Lysloff, R. T. (2003). Musical community on the internet: An on-line ethnography. *Cultural Anthropology*, 18(2), 233–263.

Manheimer, R. J. (2005). The older learner's journey to an ageless society: Lifelong learning on the brink of a crisis. *Journal of Transformational Education*, 3(3), 198–220.

Nguyen, A. (2007). Cybercultures from the East: Japanese rock music fans in North America. Unpublished master's thesis, Carleton University, Ottawa. ISBN: 978-0-494-26963-3.

Nieckarz, P. P. (2005). Community in cyber space?: The role of the internet in facilitating and maintaining a community of live music collecting and trading. *City & Community*, 4(4), 403–423.

Phelan, H. (2007). Let us say yes . . . music, the stranger and hospitality. *Public Voices* 9(1), 113–124.

Putnam, R. D. (2000). *Bowling alone: The collapse and revival of American community*. New York: Simon and Schuster.

Ruggeri, S. M. (2003). Passionate devotion: A study of aesthetic learning among amateurs, in four movements. Unpublished doctoral diss., Pennsylvania State University. UMI 3106317.

Russell, J. (2002). Sites of learning: Communities of musical practice in the Fiji Islands. Focus Areas Report. Bergen, Norway: International Society of Music Education.

Salavuo, M. (2008). Social media as an opportunity for pedagogical change in music education. *Journal of Music, Education, and Technology* 1(2), 121–136.

Salavuo, M. (2006). Open and informal online communities as forums of collaborative musical activities and learning. *British Journal of Music Education* 23(3), 253–271.

Salavuo, M. & Hakkinen, P. (2005). Informal online communities as music learning environments. Case: milkseri.net. *Musiikki* 1(2), 112–138.

Scully, F. S. (2005). American folk music revivalism, 1965–2005. Unpublished doctoral diss., University of Texas, Austin. UMI 3287336.

Shackman, G., Wang, X., & Liu, Y. (2010). Brief review of world demographic trends. http://gsociology.icaap.org/report/demsum.html [accessed November 23, 2017].

Silvers, M. B. (2007). Musical creation, reception, and consumption in a virtual place. Unpublished master's thesis. University of Arizona. UMI 1449313.

Snell, K. (2005). Music education through popular music festivals: A study of the OM music festival in Ontario, Canada. *Action, Criticism and Theory for Music Education*, 4(2), 1–36. http://act.maydaygroup.org [accessed November 23, 2017].

Southcote, J. (2009) "And as I go, I love to sing"; The Happy Wanderers, music and positive aging. *International Journal of Community Music*, 2, 143–156.

Stokes, C. E. (2004). Representin' in cyberspace: Sexuality, hip hop, and self-definition in home pages constructed by black adolescent girls in the HIV/AIDS era. Unpublished doctoral diss., University of Michigan. UMI 3150100.

Travers, J., & Milgram, S. (1969). An experimental study in the small world problem. *Sociometry*, 35(4), 425–443.

Turner, V. (1974). *Dramas, fields, and metaphors: Symbolic action in human society*. Ithaca, NY: Cornell University Press.

Waldron, J. (2011). Locating narratives in postmodern spaces: A cyber ethnographic field study of informal music learning in online community. *Action, Criticism, and Theory for Music Education*, 10.

Waldron, J. (2009). Exploring one virtual music "Community of Practice": Informal music learning on the internet. *Journal of Music, Education, and Technology*, 4(2–3), 189–200.

Waldron, J., & Veblen, K. K. (2008). The medium is the message: Cyberspace, community and music learning. *Journal of Music, Technology and Education*, 1(3). 99–111.

Wellman, B., Quan-Haase, A., Witte, J., &. Hampton, K. (2001). Does the Internet increase, decrease, or supplement social capital? Social networks, participation, and community commitment. *American Behavioral Scientist*, 45(3), 436–455.

Wenger, E. (1998). *Communities of practice: Learning, meaning, and doing*. New York: Cambridge University Press.

Williams, J. P. (2006). Authentic identities, straightedge subculture, music, and the Internet. *Journal of Contemporary Ethnography*, 35(2), 173–200.

PART 3

ADULT LEARNING IN A LIFESPAN CONTEXT

Part Editors
DAVID E. MYERS AND CHELCY L. BOWLES

CHAPTER 15

COMMENTARY: ADULT LEARNING IN A LIFESPAN CONTEXT

DAVID E. MYERS

The words of James Taylor's 1977 hit song aligned well with growing interests at the time in adult learning: "The secret of life is enjoying the passage of time. . . . It's a lovely ride." Across cultures and societies, music participation is considered an important element of making the life course a lovely ride. This fact has long been acknowledged by the music education profession, yet only in the last two and a half decades have serious research and pedagogical attention been devoted to fulfilling the music *learning* needs and interests of adults. Providing opportunities for lifelong music learning is now a recognized important dimension of the work of professional music educators.

The standard goal of formal school programs growing out of the industrial era was to *prepare* students with sufficient knowledge and skill to become successful, productive, and satisfied adults. For music educators, that generally meant equipping students to make informed choices regarding the types and levels of music engagement they would pursue through adulthood. Outside of professional preparation, adults' music activities were of interest largely as manifestations of the success of school programs and as indicators of musical life in communities.

Though music educators worked with adults in private lessons, church choirs, and community ensembles, there was little, if any, interest in understanding adults as continuing music learners. Just as educators came to consider children's developmental learning needs after many years of emphasizing technical aspects of the *subject* of music, teaching adults was either an extension of activities used with children, or conducting community ensembles. In Western culture, music education was a way to advance a more literate and culturally aware society, preparing children for adult activities such as listening to classical music by purchasing recordings, accessing radio and television music programs, and attending concerts.

Learning through adulthood gained increasing professional attention in the latter half of the twentieth century, as greater numbers of adults began participating in education services. Between 1978 and 1981, participation in adult education programs in the United States increased by 17% (U.S. Department of Education, NCES, 1983). Reasons for this trend included: (1) a demographic shift toward a greater percentage of adults in society; (2) an increase in availability of programs; (3) a need for professional updating relating to rapid change; and (4) pursuit of personal interests, such as financial management, health, sports, cooking, and the arts. In 1981, the National Research Center of the Arts, Inc., noting a rise in arts participation, concluded that "the arts are now earning a special place in the lives and consciousness of the majority of the people in [the United States]" (pp. 6, 10). This report did not address arts *learning*; however, combined with the National Center for Education Statistics data, it did suggest a potential for growth in arts education among adults.

Expanding international interest in adult learning and education was reflected in a statement by UNESCO's General Conference in 1976:

> the term "life-long education and learning" . . . denotes an overall scheme
> aimed both at restructuring the existing education system and at developing
> the entire educational potential outside the education system; education and
> learning, far from being limited to the period of attendance at school, should
> extend throughout life, include all skills and branches of knowledge, use all
> possible means, and give the opportunity to all people for full development of
> the personality; the educational and learning processes in which children, young
> people and adults of all ages are involved in the course of their lives, in whatever
> form, should be considered as a whole. (Annex 1, p. 3)

K. Patricia Cross's seminal book *Adults as Learners* (1981) was intended "to preserve the concept of lifelong learning as involving learning on the part of people of all ages and from all walks of life using the multiple learning resources of society to learn whatever they wanted or needed to know" (p. xxii). Cross urged educators of adults to move away from a "consumer orientation," that is, basing experiences on simple surveys of what adults say they *want and like,* and toward increased sensitivity to the complex nature of learning through adulthood and the "physical/psychological/ sociocultural characteristics of older learners" (p. 247).

Building on an earlier call to provide "opportunity to move as far in depth or in breadth as each [person] can" (Choate, 1968, p. 115), the Music Educators National Conference (MENC) issued a 1974 position paper listing self-realization, human relations, enrichment of family life, sustaining and improving health, and improvement of occupational competence as objectives for adult and continuing music education. In 1981, MENC's national conference focused on the theme of lifelong music learning, giving tangible form to President Mary Hoffman's belief that "A personal commitment to music education implies having the ability to understand fully the way *students of all ages* learn music" (*Music Educators Journal*, 1978, pp. 100–101).

Though age is the most convenient and obvious indicator of one's stage in life, developmental researchers understand that age-related characteristics are far more complex than the number of years one has lived. Historically, the years of adulthood following formal education were commonly viewed, both in lay and scientific terms, as a lengthy period of relative stasis and decline as one moved through the stages of occupational endeavor, into retirement, and then into the final years of life. This decline mentality was equally applied to both the physical and mental trajectories of adulthood. Today, the work of developmental psychologists such as Erik Erikson, a vast array of research publications in a variety of disciplines, and books and articles in the popular press have essentially laid that perspective to rest. Though acknowledging the reality of change associated with increasing age, some of which inevitably involves lessened capacities, adulthood is nevertheless seen as a passage of time involving a complex of characteristics, traits, and influences that reflexively interact with the ways one pursues meaning and productivity across the life course. Mental agility in younger adulthood may facilitate rapid processing of new information, while the accumulated experience and wisdom of older adulthood may yield deeper processing and richer meaning making. Younger adults may focus on problem solving, while increasing maturity may be associated with a greater ability to foresee emerging problems. Active engagement in learning through adulthood may nurture confidence, self-efficacy, more self-initiated learning, and effective compensatory strategies for declines in memory, visual and auditory functioning, and physical capacity. And continued learning at later ages may encourage the growth of dendrites, support nutrition and physical conditioning, and encourage creativity and generativity.

In a compelling work, *The Third Chapter: Passion, Risk, and Adventure in the 25 Years after 50* (2009), Harvard professor Sarah Lawrence-Lightfoot tells the story of a decorated journalist, now retired, who at age 60 decided to study jazz piano. Placing himself in the vulnerable position of pursuing study that didn't feel like it came to him naturally, "Josh" nevertheless embraced this new challenge. Not only did he find that he was able to learn to play jazz, he also learned a lot about music learning itself: understanding the relationship between technique and creativity; the place of patterns and protocols; the intervals and symmetries of jazz; the elements of expectation and surprise; and, most important, that music is about "thinking with your body" (p. 184). Lawrence-Lightfoot observes that Josh independently spends long hours practicing, having discovered the joy of learning for learning's sake and achieving personal incremental goals through collaborative work with his mentor. Moreover, learning in this new field contrasts markedly with the kinds of verbally dependent learning that had marked his earlier career.

As the following chapters in this section make clear, adult music learning covers the entire life span after age 18, comprises diverse personal and professional motivations, and includes a wide cross-section of performing, creating, and listening experiences. It may be formal, non-formal, or informal; it may occur in explicitly educational venues or in a variety of individual, social, and community contexts; it may be self-directed or collaboratively pursued; it crosses cultural boundaries; and it may accommodate a broad range of learner interests, needs, and preferences.

A variety of factors points toward the need for continued serious attention to music education for adults. More music is more accessible to more people today than at any time in the world's history. Earphones, connected to devices holding downloaded music, are ubiquitous in airports and offices, and on jogging paths and hiking trails. A study (2009) by the National Endowment for the Arts (NEA) in the United States found that of those adults who went online at least once a day for any purpose, nearly 40 percent used the internet to view, listen to, download, or post artworks or performances. A subsequent NEA survey in 2012 showed that 71% of Americans surveyed reported using electronic media to watch or listen to art; and the *only demographic group to show increases in attending live arts activities between 2002 and 2012 was older adults.* (italics added) Many community music schools are seeing increased enrollments by adults; neighborhood and workplace performance groups and music lessons are growing; and creativity, which ought to be inherently associated with arts experience, is cited regularly as a chief requirement of today's leaders and executives in both profit and nonprofit sectors. Added to this, new findings in neuroscientific inquiry are pointing to the roles of learning and participatory music in enhancing positive brain plasticity across the lifespan (Myers, 2015).

Regrettably, the 2009 NEA report documented a steady decline since the 1980s in participation among adults attending concerts and musical events. The lowest 2008 attendance rates across all art forms, not just music, were in classical and jazz music, Latin or salsa music, and opera. Opera and jazz attendance rates fell below those of 1982, and classical music attendance dropped 29% from 1992, with the steepest decline occurring in the last six years. Attendance among adults between 45 and 54, traditionally a large component of the arts-attending public, showed the greatest declines among all age groups for most arts events; and those in the 18- to 24-year-old category declined in attendance at jazz and classical music events. Moreover, performing arts attendees increasingly represented ages older than the average U.S. adult.

In contrast to these discouraging attendance data, Ivey and Tepper (2006) have written in the *Chronicle of Higher Education* about a growing renaissance of *personal art making and creative practices* made possible by new technologies, the explosion of cultural choice, and the growth of a do-it-yourself ethos. In *Engaging Art: The Next Great Transformation of America's Cultural Life* (2008), Tepper and Gao contended that data on artistic practice, as opposed to attending events and observing artists, show less negative relationships with barriers of age, income, and education than attendance data. In other words, attendance data may not be offering a realistic picture of the extent to which people are endeavoring to engage with the creative practices involved in making music.

There is little question that adults, like children, are innately intrigued with music and seek to gain a better understanding of it. The challenge to the music education profession is to provide universally available, sustained opportunities to systematically nurture intuitive music interests through learning experiences that enrich understanding and build perceptions of music's value in personal and social contexts. As Christopher Small (1998) has suggested, music is an active representation of personal relationships, and it is our responsibility to assure access to the value of this particular kind of relational experience for as many people as possible.

As we come to understand the nature of adult music learning more fully, we must exercise circumspect judgment in planning experiences that are consistent with a growing body of knowledge in the wider arena of adult learning and adult education design. Stephen Brookfield (1986) has pointed out, for example, that adult learning, though often voluntary, may not necessarily be a joyous, self-directed experience. Anxieties and frustrations may arise, learners may have unrealistic goals for themselves, and, particularly in music, there may be ambivalence regarding a desire for musical independence in light of ensemble experiences that often place learners in teacher-dependent situations. In many ways, best practices for teaching adults are similar to those for teaching children. However, adjustments of these principles to accommodate physical and mental changes that occur through adulthood, the ability of adults to commit fully to classes or lessons given the obligations of career and family, and the collaborative kind of learning experience adults tend to prefer with their teachers are important aspects of implementing successful music education programs for adults. There are many other considerations as well, and music educators will do well to acquaint themselves more generally with the field of adult learning as they endeavor to provide worthy opportunities for adults.

Among the most important concerns music educators must address are broadening access, conceptualizing adult education within a lifelong learning context, and assuring high-quality teaching and learning. At present, structured adult programs, particularly in the Western world, tend to serve homogeneous populations of middle- and upper-class individuals with discretionary time and financial resources. A cardinal principle of the field is to assure the relevance of programming to the needs and characteristics of a diverse array of learners, including locations and times when they are able to participate, finding avenues of financial assistance, and recognizing sociocultural factors that may influence participation.

In its multiple reports on adult education over several decades, UNESCO has emphasized the importance of an overriding context of lifelong learning. For music educators, the goal must be to think in terms of a music learning society, where adult education is not peripheral to the priority of precollegiate music education but is seen as an integral piece of a composite music education vision for the good of society. Such thinking will open many possibilities for ways music education for adults and youth may be intersecting and complementary, including intergenerational programs, programs that engage with distinctive dimensions of particular communities, programs that honor music legacies and traditions, and adult music education as an assumed piece of a lifelong music education paradigm.

Finally, today's career-aspiring musicians must be educated toward the opportunities associated with initiatives to advance music learning among adults.

As they move into the profession with open minds and a sense of initiative for adult music education, they must be equipped to provide the highest possible level of instruction, combining the best principles of music learning and teaching with those of adult learning and teaching. Mindsets, attitudes, and commitments that view adult music education as an integral dimension of music educators' work will lead toward continually improving programs and access to a lifetime of music learning for all.

REFERENCES

Brookfield, S. (1986). *Understanding and facilitating adult learning.* San Francisco: Jossey-Bass.

Choate, R. (ed.) (1968). *Documentary report of the Tanglewood Symposium.* Washington, DC: Music Educators National Conference.

Cross, K. P. (1981). *Adults as learners.* San Francisco: Jossey-Bass.

Ivey, B., & Tepper, S. J. (2006). Cultural renaissance or cultural divide? *Chronicle of Higher Education, 52*(37), B6–B8. http://chronicle.com/weekly/v52/i37/37b00601.htm [accessed November 23, 2017].

Music Educators Journal. (1978). National candidates for president-elect, *64*(5), 100–101.

Music Educators National Conference. (1974). A program for adult and continuing education in music. *Music Educators Journal, 61*(3), 66–67.

Myers, D. E. (2015). *Music, creativity, and positive plasticity in lifespan developmental context.* Keynote address, International Conference on Music in Lifelong Learning and Suncoast Music Education Research Forum. Tampa, FL.

National Endowment for the Arts. (2009). *2008 Survey of public participation in the arts* (Research report #49). https://www.arts.gov/publications/2008-survey-public-participation-arts [accessed October 26, 2010].

National Research Center of the Arts, Inc. (1981). *Americans and the arts.* New York: American Council for the Arts.

Small, C. (1998). *Musicking: The meanings of performing and listening.* Middletown, CT: Wesleyan University Press.

Tepper, S., & Gao, Y. (2008). Engaging art: What counts? In S. Tepper & B. Ivey (eds.), *Engaging art: The next great transformation of America's cultural life* (pp. 17–48). New York: Taylor & Francis.

UNESCO. (1976). *Recommendation on the development of adult education.* Recommendation adopted at General Conference, Nairobi, Kenya, October-November, 1976. Paris: UNESCO. http://unesdoc.unesco.org/images/0011/001140/114038e.pdf [accessed November 23, 2017].

U.S. Department of Education, National Center for Education Statistics (NCES). (1983). *The condition of education: 1983.* Washington, DC: U.S. Department of Education, National Center for Education Statistics. (ERIC Document ED 233 476).

CHAPTER 16

ELDERS AND MUSIC: EMPOWERING LEARNING, VALUING LIFE EXPERIENCE, AND CONSIDERING THE NEEDS OF AGING ADULT LEARNERS

WILLIAM M. DABBACK

AND DAVID S. SMITH

Longer life expectancy and decreased birth rates together point to a profound demographic shift around the globe: an increase in the overall age of the human population. With the graying of the species—already well under way in the most industrialized nations, and looming on the horizon for less developed countries—come important and inevitable debates about public services and health funding. Not surprisingly, these changing demographics are influencing the landscape of education philosophy, policy, and practice. As people live both longer and healthier lives, they seek engagement in meaningful activities. Educational programs emerge to meet the needs and interests of older populations. This chapter identifies important threads in aging, music research, and music education practice as they pertain to older adult populations; sets forth guiding principles of music teaching and learning relevant to older adult learners; and offers examples of some existing programs and models from around the world.

Changing Views of Aging and Learning

Shifting demographics have led to altered societal perceptions of the elderly. Though birth dates offer a convenient means of categorizing people by age, this simplistic approach fails to consider the complex and interrelated factors that comprise the aging process and the characteristics of various age groups. Nor does it capture the diversity that is increasingly apparent in the three generations of individuals over age 60, a frequent chronological marker of older adulthood. Biological, social structural, and psychosocial markers are all important to consider, for they offer different lenses through which to view aging (see Kerchner & Abril, chapter 18).

All humans experience varying degrees of physical and mental decline through the aging process; and older adulthood is often associated with the culmination of such declines. To the extent that society's institutions utilize an efficient chronological age marker such as 55 or 65 to determine eligibility for entitlements and services, they tend to contribute to cultural identification of older adults. On a macro level, these institutions define who is elder. However, in psychosocial processes, individuals create meanings for themselves in relation to social contexts and self-perceptions. When all of the factors of aging are taken together, the essence of aging "is fundamentally a biopsychosocial process" involving a confluence of biological indications of advanced age, institutional and cultural identification, and the acceptance of oneself as an older person in interaction with these factors (Bengtson, Gans, Putney, & Silverstein, 2009, p. 8).

Issues of aging ultimately reduce to issues of life change. Individuals often have little control over inevitable biological changes and the larger social contexts that frame their experiences; however, personal engagement resides at the core of the psychosocial processes that result in personal meaning, interpretation of experiences, and identity development in later life. Recognizing these complexities of defining and characterizing aging, information presented in this chapter pertains in general to individuals aged 60 and over.

Global music practice often entails cross-age engagement in noninstitutionalized music activity (Merriam, 1964; see Veblen, chapter 17). However, music education as practiced in schools, particularly in Western contexts, has not tended to parallel or reflect this practice (see Kerchner & Abril, chapter 18). Though adult and older adult learning has not been entirely absent from professional music educators' concern, the profession generally has lagged behind the disciplines associated with adult education, psychosocial gerontological research, and therapeutic music approaches in addressing the interests and needs of elders. With the professionalization of music teacher training and certification for K–12 schools, music education practices tended to utilize music teaching as a "means toward short term goals that end upon secondary school graduation" rather than as engagement through life (Mantie & Tucker, 2008, p. 217). Music pedagogy in schools and teacher education programs thus may remain entrenched in approaches that privilege a focus on education as the transmission of knowledge and skills to children in preparation for adulthood. Although the last several decades of the twentieth century saw increased attention to older adults (Flowers & Murphy, 2001), the predominant child-centric paradigm in formal music education and its related research only infrequently included serious attention to those beyond the traditional years of schooling.

Historical evidence suggests that music education programs once had closer ties to their communities, and thus presumably to the cross-section of ages in communities. Materials published by the Music Educators National Conference in the early decades of the twentieth century promoted the development of community music activities and advocated appropriate scheduling and remuneration for school music teachers to support these activities. The same organization published a 1974 position paper that promoted adult and continuing music education as a pathway to self-realization, enriched human relations and family life, and better health. Myers (2008) points out that many adults credit school music programs as the impetus for their adult musical pursuits, yet he also cites multiple authors throughout the past century who cautioned that formal music education has potentially placed itself in danger of cultural irrelevancy through its singular focus on survival in schools and maintenance of that status quo.

In his seminal work, Myers (1986, 1992, 1995) rejected the long-held assumption that music learning potential diminishes as people age. Rather, aging can and should be conceived of "as a lifelong developmental process rather than a period of decline in later adulthood" (Myers, 1986, p. 26). Myers advocates that older adults may succeed in music learning activities when teachers and facilitators provide necessary support and strategies to match their learning needs. Moreover, older adults may compensate for age-related deficits such as slowed perceptual speed or hearing loss, either through autonomously implemented strategies related to life experience, or through direct training. Models of mental and physical decline no longer dominate program planning for older adults; rather, increasing numbers of practices base themselves on principles of lifelong learning and vital engagement.

LEARNING AND TEACHING PRINCIPLES
AND APPROACHES

Due to the biopsychosocial nature of aging, evidence-based principles and practices for older adult music education require an interdisciplinary approach. General education, sociology, and psychology provide substantive perspective to enhance the dialogue. Constructs taken from these fields can provide music education practitioners with varied lenses through which to view their work among older populations.

CORNERSTONES OF ADULT EDUCATION

Adult music education research and practice have drawn extensively from the literature on adult education. Two of the foremost authors in the field, Knowles (1950, 1970, 1973, 1980) and Brookfield (1986, 1995, 2005) have advanced and debated important adult learning principles. Four overlapping areas of research emerged over the last 50 years to form the cornerstones of adult education theory: experiential learning; learning to learn; self-directed learning; and critical reflection (Brookfield, 1995).

Adult education scholars agree that adults' reservoirs of experience can serve as valuable resources for learning, although instructors must remain aware of the cultural frameworks and actual richness of those experiences (Brookfield, 1986). Every older adult possesses a lifetime of musical memories, which can serve as bridges to unfamiliar skills and activities (Coffman & Levy, 1997; Ernst & Emmons, 1992). In addition, positive attitudes and a serious work ethic emerging from lifetimes of responsibility often characterize older adults' engagement, which facilitates learning (Ernst, 2001).

Instructors can play a key role as facilitators in the area of learning to learn. With no commonly agreed-on definition, this phrase has generally functioned as an umbrella term for attempts through which adults develop insights into their personal ways of learning, including their underlying assumptions, justifications, and reasoning (Brookfield, 1995). School systems in Hong Kong have embraced such processes and shifted arts teaching strategy to a more student-centered, facilitation model that emphasizes lifelong learning (Cheung, 2004). In more adult-inclusive contexts, community music models generally feature role flexibility determined by individual contexts and an emphasis on the learning process rather than predetermined outcomes (Veblen & Olsson, 2002; see Elliott, chapter 7).

Brookfield (1995) insists that self-directed learning capacities constitute a goal of adult education rather than an inherent characteristic of adulthood. Research with older adult musicians suggests that they often seek guidance and parameters from instructors (Coffman & Levy, 1997; Johnson, 1996; Kruse, 2009); however, as a whole, the literature reveals a spectrum of self-direction. While older adults may wish for hierarchical leadership in certain situations, this preference is often context-dependent (Coffman, 2009; Rohwer, 2012). Considerations include the size of an ensemble, the need for efficiency in rehearsal and instruction, and perceptions of autonomy in musical decision-making (Dabback, 2007).

The usefulness of experience, learning to learn, and self-directedness in adult learning depend on heightened awareness gained through critical reflection (Mezirow & Associates, 1991). The ability to engage with and critically examine existing beliefs and knowledge allows adults to reach deeper understandings and transformation through learning. Brookfield (2005) states that, because of the extent of their life experience and accumulation of comparative data, adults can participate in meaningful critical reflection and, therefore, in self-directed learning. He links the latter inextricably with praxis (1986), which, in Aristotelian terms, involves deliberation to determine right action for specific social situations. When learning exists as praxis, music participants reflect on experiences, determine actions based on those reflections, and make decisions according to context and situation, thereby exerting control of their learning environment and demonstrating significant capacities for self-directedness. Some older adults find satisfaction in this process in private practice and solitary performance, while many others value the social aspects of group music-making (Ernst, 2001).

Effective programs and instructors individualize experiences, utilize learners' resources, and facilitate musical reflection and decision-making. Many traditional, more authoritarian models of music instruction do not feature such approaches, raising questions not only for older adult music education, but for music instruction at all ages and levels. Instructors and participants in even the most hierarchical ensemble programs can and should create space and time for incorporating learner experience and decision-making. Leaders must balance group efficiency and performance against equally valid participant needs for autonomy.

Music Mastery

Music programs that focus on mastery can be found across the age spectrum. Regardless of the specific ages of participants, these programs are characterized by teaching new skills, imparting new knowledge, and/or developing latent skills or interests. An additional component of mastery involves the use of an instructional design that relates to the effective practice of participatory, sequential learning; each lesson or technique is challenging, yet achievable, and increases in difficulty over prior ones. Whether geared toward an older adult demographic, such as the programs of the New Horizons International Music Association, or an intergenerational membership like the New Jersey Intergenerational Orchestra, mastery-based music programs mirror their K–12 counterparts in many ways. Several examples are described below:

- The New Horizons International Music Association (http:// newhorizonsmusic.org/) grew out of a desire to provide a place for older adult beginners to learn how to play musical instruments. Central to the

New Horizons philosophy is a group instruction format emphasizing socialization, a need that may increase with the isolation of aging. More than 200 New Horizons ensembles, including bands, orchestras, and choirs, currently operate in the United States and abroad.

- The New Jersey Intergenerational Orchestra, begun in 1994, and the Florida Intergenerational Orchestra of America, organized in 2005, provide opportunities for musicians of varying ages and abilities to study and perform orchestral music; elders, adults, and students work side by side with more experienced players who mentor their fellow performers. Both ensembles have received national media attention, leading to performance opportunities at Lincoln Center in New York City, the United States Capitol in Washington, D.C., and the United Nations International Plan of Action on Aging in Madrid.

- Encore Creativity for Older Adults was founded in 2007 at the Levine School of Music in Washington, D.C., to provide "an excellent and accessible artistic environment for adults age 55 and over, regardless of experience or ability, who seek arts education and performance opportunities under a professional artist" (http://encorecreativity.org/). Participants learn proper breathing techniques, with a focus on improving their voices through correct tone production. The Encore program now comprises more than 20 ensembles in Maryland, Virginia, and the District of Columbia, and affiliate programs in six other states, totaling over 1,500 Encore singers nationwide.

- The Intergeneration Orchestra of Omaha was founded in 1985. To ensure the intergenerational membership, which has recently spanned 12 to 82 years, musicians must not only audition, but must be either age 50 or older, or age 25 and younger. This program provides young musicians the opportunity to learn from seasoned players, and it exposes older musicians to the "rejuvenating influences of youth." The group plays a repertoire of pops music, frequently arranged by the director. The Intergeneration Orchestra has been recognized by the National Endowment for the Arts as a Creativity and Aging best practice.

IDENTITY AND THE OLDER ADULT

Extant research with older adult populations strongly suggests that music engagement facilitates identity development, which is arguably a proper goal of all teaching and learning interactions. Music activities with others can facilitate self-concepts of healthy older adulthood by providing structure to daily, weekly, and monthly living. Gardner (1998) speculates that the role of music as a cognitive organizer may constitute the one way musical intelligence distinguishes itself from other intelligences and hypothesizes that music may function as an organizer of emotional life as people age.

Studies have also identified connections between music engagement, memory, and identity. Hays and Minichiello (2005) found that particular music choices evoked life experiences, events, and their associated emotions. Music served as a medium for older adults to express their inner selves and convey individuality through performing, composing, or listening. The researchers concluded: "participants used music as a symbol for defining their own sense of *self* and identity. Music is a symbolic representation of 'who' the participants are and how they would like to be perceived by others" (p. 439).

Music education research findings indicate that the social conventions of music activities and others' perceptions play crucial roles in individuals' identity formation (Kruse, 2009). Social identity depends on group identification. Flowers and Murphy (2001, p. 27) contend that older adults are "shaped by the musical culture of their childhood and youth, some 50 or more years ago." Though hierarchical ensemble models of instruction may not always feature best practice teaching and learning approaches, they offer a familiar musical identity to many older adults who were enculturated into identifying such programs as the training and performance grounds for musicians. By association, participation in such programs can confer a musician identity (Dabback, 2007).

Interactions with other people serve to reinforce identities. Relationships with those people who are closest to an individual affect identity perhaps most strongly. Spouses and children who support participants' music activities reinforce identity perceptions by their words of encouragement and actions in concert attendance and support (Rohwer, 2013). Some older adults cite private music teachers and directors as significant others who interact with them as musicians during rehearsals, thereby strengthening their self-images as musicians (Dabback, 2008).

More distant others can also contribute to identity formation and maintenance. Dabback (2008) found that performances by an ensemble of older adults in assisted-living or long-term care facilities confirmed ensemble members' self-perceptions as healthy older adults. Contact with residents in these facilities inevitably prompted reflection. Musicians delimited their identities against others of approximately the same age, but whose physical autonomy or intellectual abilities were diminished and who may have lacked a sense of purpose or membership in a dynamic community.

Capable elders who seek music activity do so in part to find purpose in their lives. Although individuals create their own meanings in relation to their social contexts, effective practitioners utilize approaches and provide contexts that best facilitate and reinforce healthy self-concepts and self-efficacy. Life experience, autonomy, and support systems all play roles in teaching and learning interactions. Facilitating identity requires that program leaders seek input from participants regarding the musical content of instruction. Memories provide continuity to lives and shape individuals' identities. Music offers connections with the past; and melodies from throughout a person's life connect to experiences, people, places, and things. Sensitivity to genres, styles, and even specific works acknowledges the life histories of participants and potentially provides a source of continuity for people dealing with age-related change.

Quality of Life and Arts Involvement

Though the primary focus of music education at early childhood and adolescent levels remains on the acquisition and development of musical skills and knowledge, music education for older adults is increasingly paired with quality-of-life benefits. Community arts groups are also focused on enhancing the quality-of-life for older adults. One online resource, for example, that draws attention to arts and aging service fields, and the benefits of arts participation, is Creativity Matters: Arts and Aging Toolkit (2010). The site enumerates program goals designed to enhance the quality of life, including the following:

- Older adults have a sense of control and feel empowered (i.e., mastery).
- Older adults are socially engaged.
- Older adults exercise their bodies and brains to ensure high physical and mental function.
- Older adults are healthy, with reduced risk factors for disease and disability.
- Older adults have a positive attitude and zest for life.
- Older adults express themselves creatively.

These goals are not mutually exclusive. Social components may exist alongside skill development and instructional design focused on mastery goals. However, depending on learner needs and readiness, the focus might shift from mastery to social engagement as learners increase their performance capabilities. Regardless of such nuances, which may vary by learner, there will be a significant impact of arts experience in both goal areas. Musical experiences by nature contribute to the need for social involvement and community, whether the primary focus at any given time is educational, recreational, or therapeutic.

The quality-of-life focus is appealing to many, especially as changes in functioning levels and social supports lead to alterations in longtime views and practices associated with programs for older adults. The following are examples of programs emphasizing quality-of-life benefits.

- The Institute of Music and Health includes intergenerational programming through its Community Outreach Music Programs; its grant-funded program, Sing Out! Reach Out! takes youth ages 6 to 18 to senior living facilities for singing and relationship building in the Poughkeepsie, New York, area.
- In Great Britain, Sound-it-Out Community Music was one of twelve agencies selected to receive government funding for a cross-cultural, intergenerational music project entitled Down Your Way, which focused on music and reminiscence.
- In Brisbane, Australia, the Hand-in-Hand program allows children to engage individually with nursing home residents to encourage their musical participation though singing, movement, conversation, and physical

contact, with the goal of effecting a positive change in level of physical activity, mental acuity, and emotional state; the program was created to focus on peer and intergenerational social engagement through music-making during and beyond the school years.

- In 2007, the City of Dublin ETB Adult Education Service established the Forever Young Chorus Finglas, inspired by America's Young @ Heart Group. While initially resistant to singing covers of rock, punk, and other modern pop songs, the older adult singers now embrace the challenge.
- The Happy Wanderers in Victoria, Australia, were formed by a group of older people to perform for residents in care facilities and sufferers of dementia; the choir is a way for participants to actively engage with their community, and both give and receive considerable positive benefits.

Researchers are investigating extramusical benefits of music participation with increased frequency. Cohen (2006) found that after two years of participation in choral programs at the Levine School of Music in Washington, D.C., seniors averaging 80 years in age reported better health and fewer falls, a slowed rate of increase in doctor visits, a significantly lower rate of increased medications, greater improvements in depression, loneliness, and morale, and increased social interaction. The Music Making and Wellness Project (Koga & Tims, 2001) investigated effects of older adult keyboard instruction on extramusical variables. Older adult participants who participated in 20 weeks of group keyboard instruction showed significant decreases in anxiety, depression, and loneliness—three factors critical in coping with stress, stimulating the immune system, and improving health. Participants also showed increased levels of human growth hormone, which is implicated in effects of aging as they relate to osteoporosis, diminished energy levels, wrinkling, reduced sexual function, loss of muscle mass, and aches and pains.

Bugos (2004) examined the impact of individualized piano instruction on executive functions in well-elderly participants between the ages of 60 and 85. Experimental group members evidenced significant improvements on cognitive assessments, particularly in temporal working memory, planning, concentration, and strategy maintenance. Another investigation on cognitive function was conducted by Moser (2003) using active community band members as participants. Participants demonstrated higher cognitive functioning compared to the normative age-group means on global cognition, psychomotor function, memory recall, and executive function, suggesting an untested link between the lifestyles of amateur instrumental musicians and healthy cognitive aging.

MUSIC THERAPY

The music therapy profession has focused on extramusical benefits of music since its founding. Beginning in the early 1970s, geriatrics, defined as the care of elderly patients and treatment of their medical problems, became the primary area of clinical practice with the elderly. However, it soon became common practice to address composite physical, mental, and psychosocial needs, and to consider the needs of older adults in community settings, rather than focusing only on the elderly in extended-care facilities (Palmer, 1985). This expanded view of music therapy with older adults continued to gain momentum into the twenty-first century, owing in part to model programs such as the San Diego State University Rhythm for Life Project (Reuer, Crowe, & Bernstein, 2007) and the Music Making and Wellness Project (Koga & Tims, 2001). Both projects investigated the effects of active music-making interventions on extramusical benefits and quality of life in well-elderly participants.

The focus of music therapy in wellness involves the specialized use of music to enhance quality of life, maximize well-being and potential, and increase self-awareness in individuals seeking music therapy services across a range of functioning levels. The music education profession, by contrast, tends to work with the older adult population around teaching and learning, as well as providing meaningful performance opportunities. The term "wellness" clearly applies in both contexts, despite the lack of a historical association with lifelong music learning. Both music educators and music therapists can point to wellness as an outcome of the music-making and music learning process.

Summary

An increased aging profile of the world's population raises many questions regarding the place of music in education and society, including new opportunities associated with this demographic shift. Previously prevalent decline models of aging are giving way to perceptions of older adulthood as a time of healthy, active living, and as a time when positive experience may compensate for both routine and pathological change in older adulthood. As declines occur, they are strongly individualized and highly variable; there is no consistent pattern of aging that fits every person. There is strong evidence that music participation and learning can offer meaningful engagement for elders and provide biological, social, and psychosocial benefits.

The field of adult education offers useful principles for music teaching and learning in many contexts. Older adults' memories and experiences can offer a potent resource for planning effective music experiences. In addition, memories and experiences offer learners the advantages associated with a lifetime of accumulated wisdom and the ability to compensate for deficits that may affect learning, such as slowed acquisition speed or difficulties in physical manipulation of instruments. Regardless of participants' ages, teachers assist learners to uncover preconceptions and existing knowledge and use them as points of departure for activities. This reflective process underlies the best of adult learning models. Instructional approaches necessarily vary depending on contexts and goals; however, fluidity in mentoring and colearning may provide scaffolding and freedom, and support learner autonomy in pursuit of self-directedness. Arguably, this is a prime objective not only of adult and older adult education but of learning across all age groups. As such, it is particularly relevant to intergenerational contexts.

If self-direction signifies a desired culmination of learning interactions, self-knowledge may represent the true goal of all education. Effective leaders in programs for older adults create environments in which participant autonomy also serves identity development. Aging brings many types of change, and active engagement in music can stave off some of its more debilitating effects. Program structure, connections with like-minded others, the use of music as a memory agent, and experienced psychosocial and biological benefits reinforce members' identities as healthy older adults.

Similarly, self-identification as musicians can provide direction and purpose in later life. The support elders receive from others plays an integral role in the maintenance of their positive identities. Teachers should prioritize learning environments in which individuals may investigate both music and their identities, along with providing the structural and social supports to reinforce those explorations.

The sheer volume of evidence regarding extramusical benefits for those who participate in music reflects music's importance in the lives and learning of people of all ages. Demographic change toward an older populace is outpacing responsive change within the music education profession. Few disagree with the philosophical principles of lifelong learning; however, as older generations become an increasing social and political force, practical implementation of those principles must become a priority if the field of music education is to be a vital and relevant component of society and its educational institutions. Though both research and practical models exist, their quantity and quality must increase to meet current and future urgencies in the social-cultural landscape of a global society.

REFLECTIVE QUESTIONS

1. In what ways have biological, sociological, and psychosocial factors shaped your own identity? How can you use this knowledge to inform teaching and learning interactions?

2. Do you believe life experience constitutes one of older adults' greatest resources? Why or why not? If so, how many ways can you list to utilize those experiences in music teaching and learning?

3. What are the most valuable aspects of intergenerational music-making? What do older adults gain? What do younger participants gain? Are there any drawbacks?

4. How do you think the music education profession can design programs and engage in advocacy efforts for older adults? What programs might you

develop or encourage in your community? What instructional principles would you use to guide programs for older adults or for intergenerational groups?

KEY SOURCES

Brookfield, S. (1986). *Understanding and facilitating adult learning.* San Francisco: Jossey-Bass.

Coffman, D. D. (2002). Adult education. In R. Colwell & C. Richardson (eds.), *The new handbook of research on music teaching and learning* (pp. 199–209). New York: Oxford University Press.

Dabback, W. M. (2007). Toward a model of adult music learning as a socially-embedded phenomenon. Unpublished doctoral diss., University of Rochester, Eastman School of Music, Rochester, NY.

Myers, D. E. (1986). *An investigation of the relationship between age and music learning in adults.* Unpublished doctoral diss., University of Michigan, Ann Arbor.

REFERENCES

Bengtson, V. L., Gans, D., Putney, N. M., & Silverstein, M. (2009). Theories about age and aging. In V. L. Bengston, D. Gans, N. M. Putney, & M. Silverstein (eds.), *Handbook of theories of aging* (2nd ed.) (pp. 3–24). New York: Springer.

Brookfield, S. (1986). *Understanding and facilitating adult learning.* San Francisco: Jossey-Bass.

Brookfield, S. (1995). Adult learning: An overview. In S. Tuinjman (ed.), *International encyclopedia of education.* (p. 179). Oxford: Pergamon Press.

Brookfield, S. (2005). *The power of critical theory: Liberating adult learning and teaching.* San Francisco: Jossey-Bass.

Bugos, J. A. (2004). The effects of individualized piano instruction on executive functions in older adults (ages 60–85). Available from ProQuest Dissertations & Theses database. (AAT 3160993).

Cheung, J. (2004). *Artists in schools: A case study of the arts-in-education program.* Paper presented at the UNESCO Regional Expert Symposium on Arts Education in Asia, Hong Kong.   http://www.unesco.org/fileadmin/multimedia/HQ/CLT/CLT/pdf/Arts_Edu_RegSess_Symp_Asia_Cheung.pdf

Coffman, D. D. (2009). Survey of New Horizons International Music Association musicians. *International Journal of Community Music, 1*(3), 375–390.

Coffman, D. D., & Levy, K. (1997). Senior adult bands: Music's new horizon. *Music Educators Journal, 84*(3), 17–22.

Cohen, G. (2006). Research on creativity and aging: The positive impacts of the arts on health and illness. *Generations, 30*(1), 7–15.

Creativity Matters: The Arts and Aging Toolkit. (2010). http://artsandaging.org/ [accessed November 23, 2017].

Dabback, W. M. (2007). Toward a model of adult music learning as a socially-embedded phenomenon. Unpublished doctoral diss., University of Rochester, Eastman School of Music, Rochester, NY.

Dabback, W. M. (2008). Identity formation through participation in the Rochester New Horizons Band programme. *International Journal of Community Music, 1*(2), 267–286.

Ernst, R. (2001). Music for life. *Music Educators Journal, 88*(1), 47–51.

Ernst, R., & Emmons, S. (1992). New horizons for senior adults. *Music Educators Journal, 79*(4), 30–34.

Flowers, P. J., & Murphy, J. W. (2001). Talking about music: Interviews with older adults about their music education preferences, activities, and reflections. *Update: Applications of Research in Music Education, 20*(1), 26–32.

Gardner, H. (1998). Is musical intelligence special? *Choral Journal, 38*(8), 23–34.

Hays, T., & Minichiello, V. (2005). The meaning of music in the lives of older people: A qualitative study. *Psychology of Music, 33*, 437–451.

Johnson, R. (1996). The adult student: Motivation and retention. *American Music Teacher, 46*(2), 16–19.

Knowles, M. (1950). *Informal adult education.* New York: Association Press.

Knowles, M. (1970). *The modern practice of adult education: Andragogy versus pedagogy.* Englewood Cliffs, NJ: Prentice Hall.

Knowles, M. (1973). *The adult learner. A neglected species.* Houston: Gulf Publishing.

Knowles, M. (1980). *The modern practice of adult education: From pedagogy to andragogy.* Chicago: Associated Press.

Koga, M., & Tims, F. (2001). The music making and wellness project. *American Music Teacher, 51*(2), 18–22.

Kruse, N. (2009). "An elusive bird": Perceptions of music learning among Canadian and American adults. *International Journal of Community Music, 2*(2 & 3), 215–225.

Mantie, R., & Tucker, L. (2008). Closing the gap: Does music-making have to stop upon graduation? *International Journal of Community Music, 1*(2), 217–227.

Merriam, A. (1964). *The anthropology of music.* Evanston, IL: Northwestern University Press.

Mezirow, J., & Associates. (1991). *Fostering critical reflection in adulthood: A guide to transformative and emancipatory learning.* San Francisco: Jossey-Bass.

Moser, S. (2003). Beyond the Mozart effect: Age-related cognitive functioning in instrumental music participants. Available from ProQuest Dissertations & Theses database. (AAT 3084208).

Myers, D. E. (1986). An investigation of the relationship between age and music learning in adults. Unpublished doctoral diss., University of Michigan, Ann Arbor.

Myers, D. E. (1992). Teaching learners of all ages. *Music Educators Journal, 79*(4), 23–26.

Myers, D. E. (1995). Lifelong learning: An emerging research agenda for music education. *Research Studies in Music Education, 4*(1), 21–27.

Myers, D. E. (2008). Freeing music education from schooling: Toward a lifespan perspective on music learning and teaching. *International Journal of Community Music, 1*(1), 49–61.

Palmer, M. (1985). Older adults are total people: Music therapy with the elderly. In N. Weisberg & R. Wilder (eds.), *Creative arts with older adults: A sourcebook* (pp. 103–112). New York: Human Sciences Press.

Reuer, B., Crowe, B., & Bernstein, B. (2007). *Group rhythm and drumming with older adults: Music therapy techniques and multi-media training guide.* Silver Spring, MD: American Music Therapy Association.

Rohwer, D. (2013). Making music as an adult: What do the spouses think? *Texas Music Education Research*, 40–46.

Rohwer, D. (2012). Going to the source: Pedagogical ideas from adult band members. *Journal of Band Research*, 48(1), 45–57.

Veblen, K., & Olsson, B. (2002). Community music: Towards an international perspective. In R. Colwell & C. Richardson (eds.), *The new handbook of research on music teaching and learning* (pp. 730–753). New York: Oxford University Press.

CHAPTER 17

ADULT MUSIC LEARNING IN FORMAL, NONFORMAL, AND INFORMAL CONTEXTS

KARI K. VEBLEN

As our understanding of lifelong music education emerges, it becomes increasingly evident that people learn in varied ways throughout their lives, at dissimilar rates, with varied purposes in mind. Fortunately, the myths of talent and genius—and the common notion that musical skills must be cultivated early or not at all—is beginning to give way to an understanding of the complex ways all humans, throughout their lives, may learn and manifest musically. As life spans extend and we have more discretion in the ways we spend our time and material resources, the potential for musical expression by mature adults expands. The nurturing of this potential is a remarkable opportunity for music professionals seeking to advance human well-being.

While structures and pedagogical methods used with younger people may also accommodate adults, it seems equally true that mature persons can effectively acquire knowledge through other means and in other venues in response to their own perceived needs. Research is emerging, and needed, to fully understand (1) ways pedagogy and andragogy in music are continuous, overlapping processes throughout the lifespan; (2) how these differ; and (3) how more mature learners respond to different methods and settings for instruction based on their developmental characteristics and learning preferences.

Music learning in adulthood is generally self-initiated and embedded within so-cial contexts. Current research exploring the importance of social context in learning music indicates that musically saturated environments are extremely significant for lifelong music learning. Studies of the diversity of music activities and learning in given localities (Blau, Keil, Keil, & Feld, 2002; Rodriguez-Suárez, 2005; Shansky, 2009) reveal the fabric of musical community (visible or implied) as a constant necessary for musical learning. A musically saturated environment and rich social setting may be fostered in churches, classical concert series, and festivals (Gardner, 2004; Karlsen, 2007; Snell, 2005), and online communities (Dillon, Adkins, Brown, & Hitche, 2008; Salavuo, 2006; Waldron & Veblen, 2008), and may also be intergen-erational (Kerlin, 2004). Research also reveals that for adults, interplay of personal identity formation and group dynamics is a key factor in sustaining musical partici-pation (Kruse, 2007; Pitts, 2009; Ransom, 2001; Reed, 2008; Dyer, 2016). Identity, per-forming, and learning interweave within what Wenger and Lave term "communities of practice" (Lave & Wenger, 1991; Wenger, 1998). In such groups, "learning is the engine of practice and practice is the history of that learning" (Wenger, 1998, p. 96).

Busch's 2005 dissertation about performing groups in community colleges details the interplay between family music and school music and their pivotal roles as individuals choose to be in performing ensembles. She describes the way

> learning in music can be thought of as a multi-phased process that changes
> emphasis from independent learning in informal settings during childhood to
> formalized learning during the school years followed later by non-formalized
> style that occurs in community-like settings; the learning process is one of
> continual input and output, which involves periods of exploration, trial and error,
> and constant and varied stimulation to continually engage the learner and allow
> for a gradual deepening of their musical understanding; accomplishing goals
> and others' motivation helps individuals succeed at making music, which in turn
> inspires their continued involvement. (Busch, 2005, pp. iii–iv)

The mode of learning is often defined by the context in which adults choose to learn, whether in formal contexts similar to those they might have experienced in school music settings, or in less structured and informal diverse social contexts. Discourses of formal, nonformal, and informal learning contexts and processes be-come increasingly useful and valued as the field of music education extends to pro-mote and incorporate lifetime music learning. This chapter examines definitions and perspectives on these processes as they relate to music learning in adulthood.

DEFINITIONS: FORMAL, NONFORMAL, AND INFORMAL

Varieties of music transmission may be grouped into formal, nonformal, and in-formal categories. The terms "formal" and "informal" are also vernacularly referred to as "school" and "community" musics. Szego (2002) cites Strauss (1984) as coining "intentional" and "incidental" learning processes as an alternative to formal/informal (p. 723). Incidental learning, according to Schugurensky (2000), refers to "learning experiences that occur when the learner did not have any previous intention of learning something out of that experience, but after the experience she or he becomes aware that some learning has taken place. Thus, it is unintentional but conscious" (p. 4). These labels imply a whole range of pedagogical and andragogical practices, and a variety of perspectives concerning them. Until recently, formal learning practices have dominated attention and research agendas in music education. However, the continuum of lifelong music learning necessitates an awareness of the manifold ways of learning.

Formal and informal music learning may be paired as polarized constructs, as Finnegan (1989) finds in the English town of Milton Keynes. She notes that the formal, sequential music method based on notated music is "self-evidently *the* form of music learning" to those participating in this system (p. 136). In contrast, Finnegan characterizes informal music learning as the "mode of self-taught ('on the job' learning), which functions without any necessary reliance on written music or acquaintance with the classical music canons" (p. 136). Green (2002) also conceives of formal and informal learning as "extremes existing at two ends of a single pole" (p. 6). She defines informal learning as "a variety of approaches to acquiring musical skills and knowledge outside formal educational settings" (p. 16). In Green's view, informal learning practices may be both conscious and unconscious.

Folkestad (2006) contrasts formal and informal spheres to distill four ways they may differ: (1) physical situation, (2) learning style, (3) ownership, and (4) intentionality. In accord with O'Flynn (2006), he points out that

> since what is learned and how it is learned are interconnected, it is not only the choice of content, such as rock music, that becomes an important part in the shaping of an identity (and therefore an important part of music teaching as well), but also, and to a larger extent, the ways in which the music is approached. In other words, the most important issue might not be the content as such, but the approach to music that the content mediates. (Folkestad, 2006, pp. 141–142)

Coffman (2002) links the terms "formal" and "informal" in relationship to adult music education, adding a third descriptor, "nonformal," following the work of Colletta (1996). Coffman considers nonformal practices to be similar to formal practices in that they are both systematic and deliberate. However, non-formal learning practices occur outside educational structures and are less regulated, hence more responsive to a specific social action. Informal practices, notes Coffman, can refer to learner-initiated learning or to incidental learning through social interaction (2002, p. 200).

Szego (2002) agrees that music transmission does not always come neatly compartmentalized. Nor, she suggests, are the terms "formal" and "informal" value free. Hewitt (2009) cautions that the genre of music and community of practice

Table 17.1 Formal, nonformal, and informal learning practices.

	Formal Learning	Nonformal learning	Informal learning
Physical context or situation	School, institution, classroom	Institution or other un-regulated setting	Unofficial, casual, unregulated setting
Learning style	Activity planned and sequenced by teacher or other who prepares and leads teaching activity	Process may be led by a director, leader or teacher, or may happen by group interaction	Process happens through interaction of participants, not sequenced beforehand
Ownership	Focus on teaching and how to teach Teacher plans and guides activities	Focus on learning Student usually controls learning or goes along with teacher or group choice, but has ultimate control	Focus on learning, how to learn (student perspective) Student chooses voluntarily and controls Learning takes place, intended or not
Intentionality	Focus on how to play (work, compose) Intentional	Focus on laying music Social aspects and personal benefits intertwined Intentional or incidental	Focus on playing music Incidental or accidental
Modes for transmission	Often has notational component	May use aural and/or notation components, tablature, or other systems	Variety – by ear, cyberspace – many uncharted processes

Note: Adapted by Veblen expanding upon Folkestad (2006, pp. 141–142) with research drawn from Coffman, 2009; Cope, 2005; Green, 2006; Jaffurs, 2006; Kors, 2005; Livingstone, 1999; Mans, 2009; Rogers, 2004; Smilde, 2009; Szego, 2002; Veblen, 2007; Veblen, 2008; Waldron & Veblen, 2009.

will tend to dictate aspects of the formal/informal, and so on. In reality, intentional and incidental music learning systems may be porous, fluid, and combined. For instance, according to Pecore (2000), Japanese traditional music formerly passed on through the *iemoto* system of master to disciple is now conveyed in group context through notation as well as oral means. Feintuch (1995) indicates that both modalities are combined in learning the Northumberland small pipes. Cope (2002) interviewed Scottish session players who also learned officially and unofficially.

Table 17.1 contrasts formal, nonformal, and informal practices in lifelong music learning, with the caveat that these stages intertwine, overlap, and/or may be on a continuum. The following three sections examine current research and practice in each of these forms of learning for the adult music student.

RANGES OF TRANSMISSION:
FORMAL PRACTICES

Formal instruction, whether found in schools or lifelong learning, is typically institu-tionalized, graded, and hierarchical. These formal structures do not alter when new participants join in. In the received model of formal learning, a teacher controls and guides materials, pacing, and interactions in a structured environment. Processes are highly intentional and explicit: the student is informed as to what to learn and how to learn it. Basic skills and concepts are systematically transferred; then more complex skills and concepts are introduced. The effectiveness and efficiency of the process hinges on the teacher's qualifications (Mak, n.d., p. 4).

However, as Rohwer (2005) points out, there is a lack of research into the specifics of formal adult musical instruction. Her study of 35 adult band directors indicated that while the same concepts were presented as might be found in the standard school model, the manner of actual presentation varied in response to working with older players. Rohwer suggests that directors of adult ensembles might augment received models for musical training with more "musical journey" models that recognize the adult student's need for relevance in musical material, social connections, and individual agency.

In his 2007 study of adult learning practices, Kruse compared North American adult instrumental ensembles in the United States and Canada, noting that what he identified as andragogy may simply be examples of good teaching. "[Andragogy's] precepts could potentially provide students with enriched contex-tual relevance, improved critical thinking, enhanced musicianship, and heightened self-directedness" (p. 181). Kruse identified successful strategies for adult formal in-struction such as organization and structure in rehearsal, accommodation of social elements, opportunities for critical thinking and reflection, decreased reliance on notation for novice players, and encouraging chamber ensembles.

Formal transmission may be situated in universities, colleges, or other institutions where adults may take classes in music theory, history, or other aca-demic areas, as well as performance ensembles and vocal and instrumental lessons and classes. Likewise, some intergenerational band programs take place in public school settings, with some differences in learning styles and accommodations for age-related abilities when adults and elementary students (Winston, 2007) or adults and adolescents (Alfano, 2009; Schilf, 2001) learn together. Community ensembles such as bands, orchestras, and choirs tend to fall into formal learning categories since they are most frequently—but not always—led by conductors. As well, there are many instances of formal instruction being adapted to community contexts with various types of nontraditional and ethnic ensembles.

There are potentially many case studies that bridge formal and nonformal practices. Some ensembles modify instructional strategies to their own situations, thus moving from more formal to nonformal instruction. One case in point is that of the University of Illinois Russian Folk Orchestra in Urbana, Illinois. Livingston (1993) notes that the Russian Folk Orchestra is small, drawn from students and community members, and previous music training is not a requirement. Livingston describes the transmission:

> In the Russian Orchestra, the uneven technical ability of the players requires that the conductor work more extensively with each section to ensure that the proper notes and rhythms are played. Many of the same techniques used by the symphony orchestra conductor in communicating his intentions, such as facial expression, posture and verbal commands, are used with this ensemble, although the conductors of the Russian Orchestra supplement them with techniques such as tapping out the beat on the music stand, body movement such as dancing, and having the orchestra members sing the problematic rhythm or phrase. Many of these techniques would most likely not be found in a rehearsal of highly trained Western classical musicians. (p. 124)

Subsequently, Livingston goes on to talk about hierarchy and codes, or behaviors, that are instilled, albeit imperfectly, in this ensemble.

Private lessons provide another illustration of formal instruction, placed within a school, music store, private home, or other community context. Piano is the most popular instrument of choice according to several studies (Bowles, 1991; Cooper, 2001) from which adult students derive numerous personal benefits (Bugos, 2004; Jutras, 2006). Private or group piano lessons aimed toward amateur musicians parallel the grander traditions of virtuosic studies with master performers. In both cases, emphasis is on tutorial teaching and apprenticeship. However, developing technology and keyboard labs allow modern variations on this theme (Williams, 2002, p. 534).

RANGES OF TRANSMISSION: NONFORMAL PRACTICES

Nonformal learning practices, consisting of systematic and deliberate but less regulated pursuits that occur outside of educational structures, are often chosen by adult students continuing their musical lives. These activities are chosen, designed, or created for a specific learning community (which may consist of one individual) and may sometimes be called self-directed or participatory education (Campbell & Burnaby, 2001; Rogers, 2004). Unlike formal practices, nonformal practices change, adjust, and accommodate new participants or players since the members own and control the group interactions. Mak describes the nonformal context for music learning:

> In a *non-formal learning context*, learning is related to, and often situated in, a real life (professional) context. Skills, knowledge and attitudes that are learned

have a high practical value and are often acquired on the working spot or directly applied in the working situation. The context in which the student has to act and to learn is complex and requires not only knowing *that* (facts, skills) but also knowing *how* (how to apply them).

> ... The focus here is more on learning by doing than learning from books or instructions. Performativity (utility) will be a major criterion in legitimating knowledge, which is experimental, practical and pragmatic. ... Implicit knowledge as a result of learning by doing is conditional for reflecting on these real life experiences and for making this kind of knowledge explicit. This making explicit is conditional for transferring this knowledge to other more or less similar instances. (Mak, n.d., p. 5)

Examples of nonformal learning contexts may be exemplified by ensembles such as Ruggeri's (2003) adult amateur chamber quartet, members of which had played with each other for at least four years. Ruggeri observed how the group processed and focused on the piece of music through repetition, without need for much talk or leadership. As the chamber quartet worked on a movement, timing, intonation, and rhythm steadily improved as the musicians watched and responded to each other (p. 125).

The workshop, usually a limited-time occasion, may traverse or intersect nonformal and informal transmission modes depending on the students and the instructor. Orchestra and university outreach programs may sponsor workshops, or they may be held at festivals, fiddle camps, and gatherings for aficionados of any musical genre. In many cases, workshops are not age-specific. Cope (2005) observes:

> the workshop is a well-established learning context for traditional musicians and may be related to the longer tradition of informal learning within a community. One characteristic of the workshops described is the mixture of ages—old and young learn together, although the reported perception of greater skill and learning capacity of young people was a source of some frustration to the adult learners. This mixture of ages does not seem to occur with popular musicians. (p. 137)

Adult learners often employ several learning modes using a range of oral, notational, conserving, and experiential approaches. Whereas in some nonformal music practices adults learn primarily by ear, feel, or heart, many adult ensembles employ notation and read from sheet music (recorder consorts, brass bands, choirs, orchestras, bell ringers, etc.). Some groups, such as mandolin pickers and harmony note singers, may employ various tablatures. Nonformal processes may move between orality and notation, as described in Averill's (2003) study of barbershop singers. In the early days of the Barbershop Harmony Society (legally known as Society for the Preservation and Encouragement of Barber Shop Quartet Singing in America, Inc.; SPEBSQSA), quartets typically found their way through the music by ear:

> The woodshed, the place where cords (read "chords") were "chopped" (rehearsed or extemporized), gave its name to the informal ear singing of barbershop harmony. In the early days of the Society, quartets typically worked their way through songs with each singer finding an acceptable harmony for each melodic note, an approach dubbed "catch-as-catch-can." Although there were hundreds of sheet music arrangements available for quartets ... most early members read

little if any music notation. Many Society members maintained an attachment
to the informal wood-shedding approach of the early revival and opposed the
introduction of sheet music. (p. 124)

Waldron's (2006) work with adult learners at the Goderich Celtic College reveals a
wealth of self-initiated strategies for learning. In this weeklong immersion, students
encounter music through teachers who often learn their music informally and in
ways that are not compatible with usual notation-based instruction. Some teachers
insist that students learn everything by ear, with allowances for tape recording.
Waldron describes one student who supplemented aural learning with visual cues.
The tunes were played too fast for her, so she chose to concentrate on one note when
learning a new piece, watching other player's fingers to help her come in on her note.
Dunbar-Hall (2006), in a case study of Australian gamelan players, notes diverse self-
teaching schemes as students tried to "get inside" unfamiliar Balinese music systems.
Blanton (2016) investigates the self-chosen learning curriculums of five fiddlers at
the Swannanoa Gathering in North Carolina as they experience fear, frustration, and
enjoyment that serve to connect them to this community of practice.

RANGES OF TRANSMISSION:
INFORMAL PRACTICES

Informal practices in music transmission comprise those extensive aspects of
knowledge and skill acquisition that are largely experiential. Much of the world's
music is not explicitly taught, just as many concepts, skills, and facts that humans
know are not the result of formal instruction. Such knowledge often comes about
through unsystematic, accidental, unpurposeful, and incidental exposure to what
is happening in a person's environment. And yet, as Schugurensky (2000) notes,
there may be self-direction, intentionality, and awareness to varying degrees within
the processes of informal learning. One category of informal processes, which
Schugurensky refers to as "socialization" (p. 3), could also be termed tacit learning
or enculturation. Mans (2009) comments from her vantage point as a music educator and ethnomusicologist:

> Enculturation in music, a term that refers to the immersion in the musical
> world of a society, is a slow process, beginning shortly after birth and continuing
> throughout a lifetime. . . . Enculturation in a musical world involves immersion
> in the intra-musical sound structures of the culture—the rhythms, tonal
> patterns and combinations, preferred timbres and performance modes—of
> that culture. . . . These sound structures are conceptualised in certain defined
> relationships to one another, configured as basic musical templates or archetypes
> that inform the way in which an individual listens and responds to music. Such
> internalised templates offer insight into the basic structures for musical genres
> within a culture. . . . Learning to know the musical templates of one's culture is a

largely unconscious, enculturated process of which one only becomes fully aware
when confronted with music that does not conform to the template. (p. 84)

Enculturation happens in all societies. Cohen, Bailey, and Nilsson (2002) have
explored the mechanisms by which adults allow or block new musical information.
In their Canadian-based study of the importance of music to seniors, they proposed
a cognitive framework based on the plasticity of acquisition of musical grammar
throughout one's life. Their research indicates that musical styles heard early in life
establish a musical grammar that encodes music in those styles but may not accommodate other styles that do not fit the grammar. In other words, the adult learners
are enculturated to music of both time and place.

Findsen (2006) points to the family, church, and workplace as focal points for
where learning may happen. Gathering opportunities such as these are likely sources
of early music enculturation. Genres transmitted through informal learning, such
as rock, jazz, Appalachian fiddling, and Bulgarian pipe playing, among others, may
be learned in families and communities as well as in formal settings. In some cases,
informal learning may occur within formal or nonformal agency contexts.

Though there is considerable research into informal transmission processes,
current understandings are frequently supported by specific cases, which are not
necessarily cross-cultural or universal. Evidence may be found in ethnomusicological sources and captured through video documentation. In some instances,
musicians are learning through multiple modes, using a variety of strategies. The
learning process itself may be unconscious to the learner who says with a shrug that
she is self-taught or learns by ear. Goertzen (1997) illustrated this in interviewing
Norwegian fiddlers:

> Young fiddler Ståle Paulsen described himself as initially "self-taught," while older
> Bjørn Odde said that "no one" taught him. In both cases, the verbal formulation
> reflects the fact that in the traditional way of learning fiddle, there are no formal
> lessons, but rather unsystematic observation and imitation, and rote learning of
> repertoire. Odde's way of saying this is particularly old-fashioned in its modesty.
> He did not have a teacher, but claimed no role for himself in the learning process
> either. (pp. 61–62)

Rice (1995) describes his tutelage under a master Bulgarian piper. His first disas-
trous attempts illuminate what Hopkins (2002) calls tactile cue systems (p. 99). He
first learned the basic tune and then tried to recreate the distinct style of his teacher
through adding the ornamentation. His teacher, Kostadin, gently noted that Rice
"completely lost the style, saying, 'You don't have gaida player's fingers'" (p. 269).
After trying to understand through repetition, seeking explanation, and slowing the
tape down, Rice had an epiphany. He needed to discard his mental constructs of
melody and ornamentation to concentrate kinesthetically on the feeling of the pipe.
Rice notes: "my ornaments and their variation flowed not from some desire to imitate Kostadin's variations, but from my newly acquired gaida player's fingers" (p. 271).

The synthesis of feeling, doing, and knowing in context, richly fusing visual,
aural, and kinesthetic modalities, combines mental and physical processes that are

not easily explained. Being self-taught, learning by ear, or learning by feel may also make use of a variety of media, such as recordings, videos, internet resources, computer programs, and notated music, and symbol systems, such as tablature, chord charts and shape note singing. Furthermore, informal learning easily accommodates a blend of experiential, aural, oral, notational, and conserving elements.

REFLECTIVE QUESTIONS

Most music teachers' attention has traditionally been devoted to childhood music learning and to the potential young students possess. Much less attention is focused on the potential and promise that music learning holds for enriching the lives and audiences of more mature persons. The following questions invite readers to consider how the multiple ways and contexts for learning discussed in this chapter may influence music education in the future.

1. University music faculties and music education departments have proceeded with the supposition that music education is for children in school settings. How do demographics and current research on formal/nonformal/informal music learning affect these assumptions? What are the implications for teacher education? Participation in music-making by adults would seem to bring benefits beyond purely musical ones. How important is this?

2. If adults learn music through multiple ways and contexts, as is documented in this chapter, how might music educators adapt new strategies and mediums to best engage lifelong learners?

3. One of the justifications for music education in the school is the vision of music for all, the conviction that everyone is entitled to a musical education. Does this pertain only to the young or can it be expanded to reach all ages and economic circumstances?

4. Is the area of adult teaching and learning in music best left to entrepreneurs, community music workers, and individuals, or is there a place for teaching of adults within the more traditional music education profession?

KEY SOURCES

Coffman, D. D. (2002). Adult education. In R. Colwell & C. Richardson (eds.), *The new handbook of research on music teaching and learning* (pp. 199–209). New York: Oxford University Press.

Folkestad, G. (2006). Formal and informal learning situations or practices vs. formal and informal ways of learning. *British Journal of Music Education*, 23(2), 135–145.

Lave, J., & Wenger, E. (1991). *Situated learning: Legitimate peripheral participation.* Cambridge: Cambridge University Press.

Szego, K. (2002). Music transmission and learning. In R. Colwell & C. Richardson (eds.), *The new handbook of research on music teaching and learning* (pp. 707–729). New York: Oxford University Press.

Veblen, K. K. (2008). The many ways of community music. *International Journal of Community Music*, 1(1) 5–21.

REFERENCES

Alfano, C. J. (2009). Seniors' participation in an intergenerational music learning program. Unpublished doctoral diss., McGill University.

Averill, G. (2003). *Four parts, no waiting: A social history of American barbershop harmony.* New York: Oxford University Press.

Blanton, C. J. (2016). Pathways to learning: The musical journeys of five adult fiddle players. Unpublished doctoral diss., Greensboro: University of North Carolina. ProQuest 10123697.

Blau, D., Keil, C., Keil, A., & Feld, S. (2002). *Bright Balkan morning: Romani lives and the power of music in Greek Macedonia.* Middletown, CT: Wesleyan University Press.

Bowles, C. L. (1991). Self-expressed adult music education interests and music experiences. *Journal of Research in Music Education*, 39, 191–205.

Bugos, J. A. (2004). The effects of individualized piano instruction on executive functions in older adults (ages 60–85). Unpublished doctoral diss., University of Florida, Gainesville.

Busch, M. R. (2005). Predictors of lifelong learning in music: A survey of individuals participating in performing ensembles at community colleges in Illinois. Unpublished doctoral diss., University of Illinois, Champaign-Urbana.

Campbell, P., & Burnaby, B. (eds.) (2001). *Participatory practices in adult education.* London: Erlbaum.

Coffman, D. D. (2002). Adult education. In R. Colwell & C. Richardson (eds.), *The new handbook of research on music teaching and learning* (pp. 199–209). New York: Oxford University Press.

Coffman, D. D. (2009). Learning from our elders: Survey of New Horizons International Music Association band and orchestra directors. *International Journal of Community Music*, 2(2&3), 227–240.

Cohen, A., Bailey, B., & Nilsson, T. (2002). The importance of music to seniors. *Psychomusicology*, 18, 89–102.

Colletta, N. J. (1996). Formal, nonformal and informal education. In A. C. Tuijinman (ed.), *International encyclopedia of adult education and training* (2nd ed.) (pp. 22–27). New York: Elsevier Science.

Cooper, T. (2001). Adults' perceptions of piano study: Achievement and experiences. *Journal of Research in Music Education*, 49(2), 156–168.

Cope, P. (2002). Informal learning of musical instruments: The important of social context. *Music Education Research*, 4, 93–104.

Cope, P. (2005). Adult learning in traditional music. *British Journal of Music Education*, 22(2), 125–140.

Dillon, S., Adkins, B., Brown, A., & Hitche, C. (2008). Communities of sound: Examining meaningful engagement with generative music making and virtual ensembles. *International Journal of Community Music*, *1*(3), 335–356.

Dunbar-Hall, P. (2006). An investigation of strategies developed by music learners in a cross-cultural setting. *Research Studies in Music Education*, *26*, 63–70.

Dyer, W. L. (2016). Development and maintenance of identity in aging community music participants. Unpublished doctoral diss., Boston: Boston University. ProQuest Number: 10135048.

Feintuch, B. (1995). Learning music in Northumberland: Experience in musical ethnography. *Journal of American Folklore*, *108*, 298–306.

Findsen, B. (2006). Social institutions as sites of learning for older adults: Differential opportunities. *Journal of Transformative Education*, *4*(1), 65–81.

Finnegan, R. (1989). *The hidden musicians: Music-making in an English town*. Cambridge: Cambridge University Press.

Folkestad, G. (2006). Formal and informal learning situations or practices vs. formal and informal ways of learning. *British Journal of Music Education*, *23*(2), 135–145.

Gardner, R. O. (2004). "Welcome home": Performing place, community, and identity in the new west bluegrass music revival. Unpublished doctoral diss., University of Colorado, Boulder.

Goertzen, C. (1997). *Fiddling for Norway: Revival and identity*. Chicago: University of Chicago Press.

Green, L. (2002). *How popular musicians learn: A way ahead for music education*. London: Ashgate.

Green, L. (2006). Popular music education in and for itself, and for "other" music: Current research in the classroom. *International Journal of Music Education*, *24*(2), 103–120.

Hewitt, A. (2009). Musical styles as communities of practice: Challenges for learning, teaching and assessment of music in higher education. *Arts and Humanities in Higher Education*, *8*(3), 329–337.

Hopkins, P. (2002). Ways of transmitting music. In T. Rice, J. Porter, & C. Goertzen (eds.), *Europe: The Garland encyclopedia of world music* (vol. 8) (pp. 90–111). New York: Garland.

Jaffurs, S. (2006). The intersection of informal and formal music learning practices. *International Journal of Community Music*. https://www.intellectbooks.co.uk/MediaManager/Archive/IJCM/Volume%20D/04%20Jaffurs.pdf

Jutras, P. J. (2006). The benefits of adult piano study as self-reported by selected adult piano students. *Journal of Research in Music Education*, *54*, 97–110.

Karlsen, S. (2007). The music festival as an arena for learning: Festspel I Pite Älvdal and matters of identity. Unpublished doctoral diss., Luleå University of Technology, Luleå.

Kerlin, J. (2004). The transmission of song among the New York Irish: Teaching, learning, and Irish sensibility. Unpublished doctoral diss., New York University, New York.

Kors, N. (2005). *Case studies of non-formal education: Research report*. Groningen: Lectorate. Retrieved from Lifelong Learning in Music website, www.lifelonglearninginmusic.com

Kruse, N. B. (2007). Andragogy and music: Canadian and American models of music learning among adults. Unpublished doctoral diss., Michigan State University, East Lansing.

Lave, J., & Wenger, E. (1991). *Situated learning: Legitimate peripheral participation*. Cambridge: Cambridge University Press.

Livingston, T. (1993). Rehearsals and academic music-making: The Russian folk orchestra and the university symphony. In T. Livingston et al. (eds.), *Community of music* (pp. 119–132). Champaign, IL: Elephant and Cat.

Livingstone, D. (1999). Exploring the icebergs of adult learning: Findings of the first Canadian survey of informal learning practices. *Canadian Journal of Studies in Adult Education*, 13, 49–72.

Mak, P. (n.d.). Learning music in formal, non-formal and informal contexts. Lectorate Lifelong Learning in Music (North Netherlands Conservatoire—Groningen and Royal Conservatoire—The Hague). http://www.emc-imc.org/fileadmin/EFMET/article_Mak.pdf [accessed November 23, 2017].

Mans, M. (2009). Informal learning and values. *Action, Criticism, and Theory for Music Education*, 8, 79–93. http://act.maydaygroup.org/articles/Mans8_2.pdf [accessed November 23, 2017].

O'Flynn, J. (2006). Vernacular music-making and education. *International Journal of Music Education*, 24(2), 140–147.

Pecore, J. T. (2000). Bridging contexts, transforming music: The case of the elementary school teacher Chihara Yoshio. *Ethnomusicology*, 44(1), 120–136.

Pitts, S. (2009). Roots and routes in adult musical participation: Investigating the impact of home and school on lifelong musical interest and involvement. *British Journal of Music Education*, 26(3), 241–256.

Ransom, J. L. (2001). An investigation of factors that influence adult participation in music ensembles based on various behavioral theories: A case study of the Norfolk Chorale. Unpublished doctoral diss., Shenandoah University, Winchester, VA.

Reed, S. M. (2008). Sentimental journey: The role of music in the meaning-making processes of older performing musicians. Unpublished doctoral diss., Pennsylvania State University, University Park.

Rice, T. (1995). Understanding and producing the variability of oral tradition: Learning from a Bulgarian bagpiper. *Journal of American Folklore*, 108, 266–276.

Rodriguez-Suárez, E. (2005). Transmission of traditional musics and music teaching and learning in the Canary Islands: A perspective. Unpublished doctoral diss., University of Toronto.

Rogers, A. (2004). Looking again at non-formal and informal education—towards a new paradigm. In *The Encyclopaedia of Informal Education*. http://infed.org/mobi/looking-again-at-non-formal-and-informal-education-towards-a-new-paradigm/.

Rohwer, D. (2005). Teaching the adult beginning instrumentalist: Ideas from practitioners. *International Journal of Music Education*, 23(1), 37–47.

Ruggeri, S. M. (2003). Passionate devotion: A study of aesthetic learning among amateurs, in four movements. Unpublished doctoral diss., Pennsylvania State University, University Park.

Salavuo, M. (2006). Open and informal online communities as forums of collaborative musical activities and learning. *British Journal of Music Education*, 23(3), 253–271.

Schilf, P. R. (2001). An analysis of interactions between teenagers and their parents in an intergenerational concert band. Unpublished doctoral diss., University of Iowa, Iowa City. UMI No. 3009633.

Schugurensky, D. (2000). The forms of informal learning: Towards a conceptualization of the field. Doctoral diss., University of Toronto. https://tspace.library.utoronto.ca/bitstream/1807/2733/2/19formsofinformal.pdf [accessed October 26, 2010].

Shansky, C. L. (2009). A history of two New Jersey community bands: The Franklin and Waldwick bands. Unpublished doctoral diss., Boston University.

Smilde, R. (2009). *Musicians as lifelong learners: Discovery through biography.* Delft: Eburon Delft.

Snell, K. (2005). Music education through popular music festivals: A study of the OM music festival in Ontario, Canada. *Action, Criticism and Theory for Music Education, 4*. http://act.maydaygroup.org/ [accessed November 23, 2017].

Strauss, C. (1984). Beyond "formal" versus "informal" education: Uses of psychological theory in anthropological research. *Ethos, 12*(3), 195–222.

Szego, K. (2002). Music transmission and learning. In R. Colwell & C. Richardson (eds.), *The new handbook of research on music teaching and learning* (pp. 707–729). New York: Oxford University Press.

Veblen, K. K. (2007). Community music and ways of learning. In D. Coffman & L. Higgins (eds.), *Proceedings of the 2006 International 1998 ISME Commission on Community Music Activity, Singapore, Malaysia* (pp. 20–35).

Veblen, K. K. (2008). The many ways of community music. *International Journal of Community Music, 1*(1) 5–21.

Waldron, J. L. (2006). Adult and student perceptions of music teaching and learning at the Goderich Celtic College, Goderich, Ontario: An ethnographic study. Unpublished doctoral diss., Michigan State University, East Lansing.

Waldron, J. L., & Veblen, K. K. (2008). The medium is the message: Cyberspace, community and music learning. *Journal of Music, Technology and Education, 1*(3), 99–111.

Waldron, J., & Veblen, K. K. (2009). Lifelong learning in Celtic community: An exploration of informal music learning and adult amateur musicians. *Council for Research in Music Education, 108*, 59–74.

Wenger, E. (1998). *Communities of practice: Learning, meaning, and identity*. Cambridge: Cambridge University Press.

Williams, K. (2002). Piano pedagogy. In K. Burns, (ed.), *Women and music in America since 1900* (pp. 534–537). Westport, CT: Greenwood Press.

Winston, S. D. (2007). A descriptive study of an intergenerational beginning instrumental music instruction program for elementary school girls and well elderly adults. Unpublished doctoral diss., Shenandoah University, Winchester, VA.

CHAPTER 18

....

MUSIC TEACHER EDUCATION: CROSSING GENERATIONAL BORDERS

....

JODY L. KERCHNER AND CARLOS R. ABRIL

Throughout the twentieth century, there have been professional discussions about making music education programs relevant to life outside schools and beyond the school years (Myers, 2006). Further, the music education profession continues to engage in social justice discussions that include the development of theoretical underpinnings and practical strategies for providing musical access to marginalized communities (see Silverman, chapter 11). Yet the music education profession continues to place its greatest emphasis on teaching children and adolescents in formal school settings. It follows that most music teacher education programs, working within the boundaries, guidelines, and regulations established by educational accrediting agencies, have been designed to prepare teachers to teach music only in PK–12 school settings. This perspective loses sight of the greater aims of education, something Myers (2008) calls the "lifetime continuum of learning" (p. 3).

The music education profession needs to consider seriously its role in educating wide range of people of a given society to make, learn, and engage in music throughout their lives. A challenge for music teacher education is to assist pre-service and in-service music educators to cross generational borders by preparing them to teach students beyond the traditional school years, in a variety of settings. In so doing, music teacher educators should consider (1) how they can prepare all music majors to engage with community adults through music; (2) how they can better prepare teachers to teach people of all ages in a diverse array of settings in and beyond schools; (3) how they might infuse a lifespan perspective in existing music education courses, from introductory courses for undergraduate students to advanced courses for graduate students; (4) how community music can become a specialized track in music education, at the undergraduate and/or graduate levels; and (5) how they may incorporate additional resources (e.g., personnel, materials, field experience locations) to realize the aforementioned possibilities. In this chapter, we consider adult characteristics and developmental theories as they relate to the understanding and importance of a life-span perspective in music teacher education programs, particularly in designing curricula that develop skills for creating opportunities to bring instructional and experiential access to adults in diverse settings and contexts.

BACKGROUND

Adults

Global population trends suggest that the number of adults will continue to rise in the decades to come. In a report from the National Institute on Aging and the World Health Organization (WHO), for the first time in recorded world history, the "number of people aged 65 or older will outnumber children under age 5. Driven by falling fertility rates and remarkable increases in life expectancy, population aging will continue, even accelerate" (2011, p.2). In fact, the global population of older adults is predicted to triple from the period of 2010 to 2050, at which time it will represent 16% of the population. These figures are even more dramatic in China and India—the two most populous countries in the world—where populations of older adults are predicted to reach 330 million and 227 million, respectively (2011). In the United States, the adult population (age 18 or over) represents 77% of the nation's population, or approximately 247 million people (U.S. Census Bureau, 2015).

In the past 30 years, society has moved from viewing aging adults as individuals in the declining phase of life—the "deficit model of aging"—to seeing adults as individuals who continue to contribute to society regardless of physical or cognitive challenges they might eventually face—the "asset model" (Boyer, 2007, p. 4). "Productive aging" is the term used in the field of aging for "celebrating older adults' capabilities, potential, and social and economic contributions"—adults continuing to live life to its fullest (p. 8). Minichiello (1992) suggested that giving people "more direct contact with older persons . . . would lead to more accurate and empathic understanding [of them]" (p. 408). This interaction could assist in breaking down stereotypes of adult learners, a population that comprises subgroups representing diverse aging processes, capabilities, challenges, and goals.

Adulthood

Along with age shifts in the global population and perceptions of adult capabilities, there are also changes in how society defines adulthood. During the post–World War II era, American society considered people who were in their late teens and early twenties to be adults. At this age, men completed school and found full-time work, while women were assumed to marry and raise children. This age group was also financially self-sufficient in supporting and caring for their families. However, in the twenty-first century, transition into adulthood, at least by this definition, has been delayed until people's twenties or early thirties. To accommodate this phenomenon, the terms "early adulthood" (Furstenberg et al., 2003) or "emerging adulthood" (Shanahan, Porfeli, & Mortimer, 2004) refer to the life phase that immediately follows adolescence and precedes the fullness of adulthood.

Emergent adults are characterized by taking longer to create their own families and careers, in part because young adults seek advanced collegiate degrees that require longer financial and time commitments prior to assuming traditional adult roles.

> Based on one-percent of the samples [from the] 1960 and 2000 American censuses, [there is a] large decline in the past 40 years of the percentage of young adults who have completed all of the major transitions (leaving home, finishing school, becoming financially independent, getting married and having a child). Using this strict definition of adulthood, only 46 percent of women and 31 percent of men age 30 in 2000 had attained adulthood, compared to 77 percent of women and 65 percent of men of the same age in 1960. (Furstenberg et al., 2003, p. 6)

Thus, former external signals of adulthood (family and financial freedom) might no longer sufficiently define adulthood. A model of adulthood that considers the nature of people's personal characteristics *and* social interactions, responsibilities, and roles might better serve the contemporary identification of adulthood. This model might regard the extent to which people demonstrate the ability and willingness to assume responsibilities, the willingness and ability to formulate their self-identities, and personal choices in becoming a spouse or a full-time employee at a particular job as markers of adulthood. "The model of 'emerging adulthood' suggests that individualistic and subjective indicators (such as a sense of autonomy, financial independence, self-control, and personal responsibility) better signal adulthood" (Furstenberg et al., 2003, p. 6).

THEORIES OF ADULT DEVELOPMENT

Theories in psychology shed light on the processes of psychosocial development during adulthood. These key theories point to the learning differences between adults and children/youth and, ultimately, the type of meaningful musical opportunities that adults might seek in order to maximize their need for fulfillment.

Erikson (1963) offered eight stages through which humans potentially pass in the development of their personalities (epigenetic principle). His work acknowledged human development throughout the adult years, rather than having development conclude during adolescence, as earlier developmental theories had suggested (i.e., Freud, Piaget). Erikson's stages relevant to adulthood occur immediately after adolescence and continue until the end of life itself. The sixth stage, early adulthood, typically occurs in people's twenties and is a time when they develop intimacy at one end of the continuum and isolation at the other. It is in this stage that people work on developing personal relationships with family, friends, and life partners. If they are successful, people find their niche within groups of people, but a lack of success might lead to their being distanced from other people and becoming loners.

Stage 7, middle adulthood, begins in people's late twenties, continues through their fifties, and can lead to either self-absorption or generativity (contributing to society and future generations). People in this stage find their work to be a primary focus, along with issues involving their family life. It is a time when people wish to transmit knowledge, values, and traditions to others—typically their children. Another important feature of this stage is community involvement—moving beyond self and toward serving family and community. If one cannot find new meaning at the end of this stage, people might experience midlife crises or life stagnation.

Finally, beyond the 50s, is stage 8, older adulthood, a time when people can develop the highest level of integrity or, conversely, consider their life in terms of despair. This is the age of wisdom, reflecting on life events, relationships, and legacies and finding meaning in life that might have been missing during those times when events actually occurred. People find themselves fulfilled and accepting death as a part of the life cycle, or they feel bitter, depressed, and regretful from a life that was perceived to lack personal meaning. Butler (1963) stated that adults engage in life reviews as

> a naturally occurring, universal mental process characterized by the progressive
> return to consciousness of past experience, and particularly, the resurgence of
> unresolved conflicts; simultaneously, and normally, these revived experiences
> and conflicts can be surveyed and reintegrated . . . prompted by the realization of
> approaching dissolution and death, and the inability to maintain one's sense of
> personal invulnerability. (p. 66)

Unlike Erikson's stage of older adulthood, Butler's phase of adult personality development is not unique to older adults approaching death, but can occur among anyone (regardless of age) who faces death from a terminal illness or societal condemnation.

McAdams, de St. Aubin, and Logan (1993) provide yet another perspective on adulthood. This research team proposed the onset of young adulthood to be between ages 22 and 27, suggesting that true adulthood begins during midlife (ages 37–42), and that older adulthood begins between ages 67 and 72. These stages echo Erikson's psychosocial stages of life and McAdams's theory of generativity (McAdams, de St. Aubin, & Logan, 1993; McAdams, Hart, & Maruna, 1998). McAdams, Hart, and Maruna defined generativity as "a person's desire for his legacy to live on (giving a gift to others), to defy one's own mortality, to express the need to be needed, to nurture, and to exert power and independence by creating a legacy that will live on into eternity" (1998, p. 10).

A person creates this legacy, in part, by formulating personal narratives of her life in relationship to societal expectations. Moreover, society shapes one's personal narrative in its definitions of economic status, occupational expectations, and ideological constructs. McAdams suggested that narrative construction actually begins in late adolescence, but is primarily created and maintained in midlife and older adulthood. Older adults create and share generative narratives "because stories are the traditional vehicle of choice" for people to make sense of their life actions in relationship to society and time (McAdams, Hart, & Maruna, 1998, p. 28). About his life story theory of adult identity, McAdams, Hart, and Maruna wrote:

> The modern adult defines himself or herself in society by fashioning an
> internalized and dynamic life story, or personal myth that provides life with
> unity, purpose, and meaning. The process of identity development in adulthood,
> therefore, is the gradual construction and successive reconstruction of a narrative
> integrating one's perceived past and present and anticipated future while
> specifying ways in which the individual fits into and distinguishes himself or
> herself in the societal world. (p. 12)

These developmental theories represent the foundation for understanding why adults choose to participate in musical experiences. Young adults might seek to belong to groups—perhaps musical ensembles—that help them develop their notion of personal identity. Thus, music educators' understanding and valuing extramusical reasons for participating in music experiences are essential in planning time in classes and rehearsals for social opportunities. For people in the middle adult years, musical engagement may provide an alternative to their primary focus on career. In addition, participating in continuing education music courses or ensembles models artistic values for family and friends, while also contributing to a larger community artistic purpose. The older adult might seek musical engagement as a way to reconnect with others and reconcile life's missed opportunities. Further, music participation might give older adults challenges that lead to their creating personal narratives of lifetimes of contributions to society and self.

It is imperative for undergraduate and graduate music education students to recognize diverse reasons for adult involvement in music learning as well as other forms of musical participation. Adults' goals may or may not coincide with those that teachers of children and adolescents have for their students. LaBelle (1982) suggested that children and youth engage in non-formal education that is "anticipatory" (p. 168); these students are engaged in learning information or a skill to use primarily later in life. Adult music education, by contrast, could be viewed as participation in musical experiences that are related to adults' current learning needs and interests—social relations, skill-building, and self-expression.

ENGAGEMENT IN LIFELONG
MUSIC LEARNING

The concept of lifelong learning emanated from the 1960s in response to the societal quest for educational change and equity among diverse populations of learners. Minichiello (1992) stated that "education for older people should be seen as a part of social policy, recognizing the lifelong right to education" (p. 403). Smith (2000) stated that lifelong learning can provide eclectic experiences throughout people's adult lives and is characterized by "the inclusion . . . of the widest range of types of learning, stemming from formal, 'age-segregated' manifestations to informal learning, and from learning that is planned, 'intentional' and curricular, to learning that is incidental and incorporated into real-time job aides, communities of practice and leisure activities".

Bowles (1991) reported: "prospective participants in adult music education are probably between 25 and 55 years of age, live in the city, and probably have higher-than-average incomes. They probably hold at least an undergraduate degree and may have a graduate degree" (p. 202). People in a retirement community were thought to be more apt to participate in music activities if they had participated in music as young adults (Wise, Hartmann, & Fisher, 1992). Adults who engaged in community music learning experiences also composed and arranged music, "jammed" with others, learned to play an instrument on their own, read about music, did independent musical study, bought musical recordings, and attended concerts (Bowles, 1991).

Some studies have examined the areas of music learning that are of greatest interest and enjoyment to adults. Adult who wish to continue music into adulthood tend to engage in music activities with which they have had previous experience (Bowles, 1991; Bowles, Duke, & Jellison, 2007; Roulston, Jutras, & Kim, 2015), and Bowles (1991) found they were most interested in taking piano, voice, or guitar lessons, singing with a choral ensemble, and participating in introductory music history and aural analysis courses. Cooper (2001) found that 75% of the adults in his study enjoyed taking private music lessons, and 78% enjoyed practicing. Of those adults who studied piano as children but quit temporarily, 44% resumed their study as adults; 68% of those who started taking piano lessons in adulthood continued playing. Cooper also reported that the primary reasons for adults' continuing their piano study were skill development, pleasure, relaxation, and means for self-expression. Adult piano students in one study described the benefits of studying piano as including gaining musical knowledge and technical skills, developing a sense of accomplishment, having fun playing, escaping a routine, and growing as a person (Jutras, 2006).

While developing piano technique and a body of musical knowledge were reasons for adults taking private lessons (Bowles, 1991; Cooper, 2001; Jutras, 2006), there were also extramusical reasons for engaging in musical activity. In a review of literature on music and the quality of life of older adults, Coffman (2002b) concluded that "musical activities (both music listening and music making) can influence older adults' perceptions about the quality of their lives" (p. 85). Older adults who sang in an intergenerational choir had more positive self-esteem, and they reported being more physically active than those who were not choir participants (Darrow, Johnson, & Ollenberger, 1994). Cohen (2005) found that, although the number of neurons in the brain decreases as people age, the number of neural connections (dendrites) actually increases between the ages of 50 and 70 if people are exposed to rich, stimulating environments.

In 2001, Cohen studied 300 older adults (mean age of 80), half of whom participated in community arts programs and the other half who did not. The study focused on the following factors: "sense of control and the immune system; social relationships and blood pressure/stress levels; aging and how the brain processes emotions; and aging and being able to use both sides of the brain simultaneously" (as cited in Boyer, 2007, p. 20). Cohen's findings showed that adult participants in community arts programs (1) used less medication; (2) had fewer doctor visits; (3) experienced elevated mood levels; (4) showed an increase in the level of independent functioning; (5) felt less depressed; and (6) exhibited more overall activity (p. 21). Coffman and Adamek (1999) found that older adults who were participating in band programs defined the quality of their lives by the quality of social engagement, their perceptions of well-being and accomplishments, and their involvement in recreation activities.

Music teachers play a critical role in the music learning experiences of adults. In a case study of older adult music learners in a rock band, Laes (2015) found that participants found value in learning music with the guidance of a music teacher. Some were focused on developing their skills and overall musicianship; others were less concerned with their musical development because of their age. Participants valued the music teachers for their music expertise as well as for their ability to provide emotional, pedagogical, and social support in the music learning setting that seemed to contribute to their musical agency and empowerment. In another study of adults learning to play instruments, participants were found to value working with a music teacher who understood their needs and supported their unique learning goals (Roulston, Jutras, & Kim, 2015). (Also see Myers, chapter 15; Dabback & Smith, chapter 16)

Preparing Music Educators to Teach Adult Learners

The term "music education" typically holds the connotation of music instruction that occurs in precollegiate schools. It should be no surprise that music pedagogies and pedagogical tools have mostly been developed for these students. Laes (2015) noted that a "globally established concept of music education for older adults does not yet exist" (p. 53). Our limited conceptions of music education no longer adequately embody the myriad learning possibilities that support and nurture active and lifelong music participation. The music education profession needs to rethink its program offerings, curricula, and field experiences in order to facilitate collegiate students' awareness of and perceived values for lifelong learning and adult musical engagement.

One avenue of change is to adopt an artist-teacher-scholar model of music teaching that could extend coursework in music learning and teaching to music performance and composition majors. This model assumes that all music majors should consider what it means to teach and to think about the responsibility they have to serve their community as community music leaders, studio teachers, chamber musicians, lecturers, members of outreach programs, or participants in partnerships. The reality is that most, if not all, music careers will include teaching of some sort and, for many, that teaching will be geared toward adult learners. Thus, regardless of anticipated professional goals, music students across all majors will do well to develop skills and understanding in teaching and become proponents of lifelong music engagement.

As all music majors are required to attend concerts/recitals and take courses in music history and theory, they might also be required at some point in their programs to participate in community music ensembles or classes, as teachers and/or performers. Such community engagement would likely help music teacher education students recognize the value of music in people's lives and serve as a place for them to hone teaching skills used with adult, nonprofessional populations. This community music experience, along with gaining knowledge of how to find and build community music organizations, is a first step in developing pre-service (and in-service) music educators' and performers' values and understanding of lifelong learning.

In addition to the traditional music education programmatic emphases (instrumental, general, choral music), teacher education programs should consider the viability of a community music track in music education. This approach would likely necessitate additional courses beyond the standard offerings geared toward teaching children and adolescents. Though current teacher licensure programs are intensive and demanding, a community track might be attractive to students wanting to emphasize teaching adults or extend their traditional school work to include church choirs, community ensembles, community music schools, and private studio teaching for adult learners. Such a track might also offer performance, theory, musicology, and composition majors a complementary set of courses that would prepare them for broadened marketability, education requirements associated with arts grants or performing organizations, and entrepreneurial music initiatives in their communities—and it might offer a foundation for eventual teaching in higher education. Such a track could be designed at the undergraduate level, though it might be most practical as a graduate program. Regardless, all music education courses, even those focused on preschool and elementary/secondary levels, can be designed to help music students recognize and value music learning as a rewarding lifelong pursuit.

Information on adult music learning might also be included in developmental psychology and educational psychology classes, educational principles classes, adult cognition studies, secondary school music methods, and introduction to music education courses. Initiating collaborations with professors in psychology or general education might yield benefits not only for music teacher education majors but also for other students who may be in a position to support the importance and advantages of music learning in schools and communities.

It is important to give the study of adult learning time in the curriculum in order for collegiate music education students to

- Eliminate ageist stereotypes about adult music learning
- Recognize the potential of adult music learners
- Collaborate with business partners, the medical community, and arts agencies to provide engaging music experiences that promote adult learners' physical and emotional health
- Design and implement music programs in response to adult learners' musical interests and needs
- Design and implement music instruction with an understanding of individual adult learners' challenges and abilities
- Facilitate community involvement in adult music learners' experiences
- Understand the aging processes and adult developmental trends

Adult music learners seek learning opportunities that are not passive, but rather engaging, empowering, socially satisfying, and intellectually challenging. Thus, instruction must be differentiated in ways that accommodate students' chronological and psychological ages. Pre-service teachers, especially, might need to gain perspective in realizing that adult music learners may be more autonomous, self-directed, practical, and goal-oriented than younger music students, though these characteristics are not universal in every learning situation, nor are they the case for every adult learner. Adult music students do bring many years of experience as learners in a variety of contexts, and as individuals with accumulated wisdom gained through their life's work, raising families, and simply having lived through more years and events than children and adolescents.

Following a network economy business model (Jongbloed, 2002), music teacher education programs at the undergraduate and/or graduate level might offer music methods classes that guide teachers' visions for adult programs. In conjunction with the artist-teacher-scholar model, portions of music education methods course content that would honor adult learner traits include:

- Designing programs for adult music learners (consumers) based on their articulated learning goals
- Envisioning a partnership between learners and teachers in determining music learning goals and experiences
- Providing programs of study (i.e., courses, lessons, ensembles, distance learning experiences) that require short timeframes, ready success, and few prerequisites in musical knowledge and/or skill within flexible schedules
- Creating learning networks, so that one learning site (e.g., a community music school, a classroom, or a studio) is not solely responsible for providing all of the educational and musical resources

- Facilitating self-reflection, reflexive thinking, goal redesign, and assessment of learning between the teacher and the adult learner

Another component of the methods course might be placing theory into practice. By having portions of introductory and methods classes devoted to laboratory teaching episodes, students could have supervised opportunities to interact with and provide musical experiences for adult learners. Examples of such field experiences might include (1) student teaching or supervised clinical experiences within community music settings, music settlement schools, and community arts schools; (2) having internships with symphony orchestra/choral/opera education programs; and (3) participating in music therapy programs at senior centers, nursing homes, and hospitals. Music education students might also experience leading or assisting intergenerational musical experiences, such as community choirs, ensembles with religious affiliations, and community bands.

Finally, graduate music education students might take classes or enter master's degree programs that combine their graduate music education work with music therapy–type experiences in adult healing. Examples of such programs in this area include the Master of Arts in Transforming Spirituality degree program at Seattle University and the Center for Spirituality and Healing at the University of Minnesota. (Also see Teachout, this volume)

A SAMPLE OF ADULT FIELD EXPERIENCE TEACHING OPPORTUNITIES

In this section, we explore adult music education programs, mostly in the realm of nonformal learning, that might provide field experience opportunities, and that could be infused into pre-service music education methods courses (prior to student teaching) as well as graduate courses related to adult music learning and/or community music. This sample of existing programs also suggests models for those undergraduate and graduate music students who wish to develop their own brands of music learning opportunities for adults.

Community Music Schools

Veblen and Olsson (2002) defined community music as "opportunities for participation and education through a wide range of mediums, musics, and musical experiences . . . [that] are based on the premise that everyone has the right and ability to make and create music" (p. 730). Because of the changing societal demographics, there are community music schools that serve as cultural centers for communities, especially in areas with arts programs missing from their public school systems. There are institutions of higher education that officially offer community music and lifelong music pedagogy alongside their traditional precollegiate student teaching and scholarship opportunities.

Community music schools typically provide cross-generational opportunities for private and group lessons and ensembles. They also offer music theory, history, and appreciation courses for learners who are homeschooled and those of any age who seek musical enrichment through participatory learning experiences. Community music schools may provide a rich array of opportunities, such as fiddling lessons, drumming circle participation, chamber music ensembles, rock bands, and folk dancing/world music performance.

New Horizons International Music Association

This association (http://www.newhorizonsmusic.org/) began in 1991 as an opportunity for adults 55 years and older to participate in a band experience. Roy Ernst, founder of the New Horizons movement, envisioned this musical opportunity as an "entry and re-entry" point for adults wishing to take private instrumental lessons and play in a community of peer-aged learners (Ernst, 2004). Philosophically, New Horizons bands foster nurturing, noncompetitive, and risk-free musical experiences during rehearsals and performances (Coffman, 2002b).

Several researchers/practitioners have studied New Horizons bands extensively (Coffman, 2002a, 2002b, 2009; Dabback, 2008; Kruse, 2009; Rohwer, 2005a, 2005b, 2009). Listening to participants speak of their New Horizons band experiences and observing the participants at work, Don Coffman (2009), founder-director of the Iowa City/Johnson County Senior Center New Horizons Band, found several common themes in his rehearsals. The participants are dedicated, use humor, enjoy socializing, demonstrate creativity, look toward a sense of musical mastery, and deal with health/life issues that can hinder their musical performance. Coffman routinely has his university music students conduct the band, and found that the adult participants were also gentle mentors for collegiate student conductors who led the group. Adults provided suggestions and feedback about what they needed musically and pedagogically in order to learn the ensemble literature. The older adults' life experiences and perspectives nurtured the student conductors as they learned to be leaders and teachers. (Also see Coffman & Higgins, this volume)

Levine School

In its mission statement, the Levine School in Washington, D.C., boasts that, as a community music school, it is the "region's preeminent center for music education, a welcoming community where children and adults find lifelong inspiration and joy through learning, performing, listening to, and participating with others in music" (Levine School of Music, 2009). The school serves a broad age range: four months through adulthood. In addition to offering private lessons and master classes for beginning adult students, the school offers instrumental and choral ensembles, jazz ensembles and theory classes, musical theater experiences, music theory, composition and history courses, world drumming, world music courses, chamber music experiences, recording arts courses, and a Suzuki parents course. The course offerings occur not only in the evening, for working adults, but also throughout the day for senior adults, who are retired. Further, ensembles are designed to be intergenerational.

ORCHESTRAL EDUCATION OUTREACH PROGRAMS

Many orchestral ensembles have developed education/engagement programs designed for school-aged children and adults. These programs often serve as both educational and advocacy tools, building future audiences and retaining those who already attend. Orchestras realizing the necessity and responsibility to develop interactive opportunities to engage with people (who might not otherwise attend concerts) in their own communities. The following represent only a sample of professional orchestras and their educational programming in the United States; we encourage readers to visit each organization's website for more detail.

Some professional orchestras perform "satellite" concerts in their surrounding communities, particularly in neighborhoods whose youth and adult residents are underrepresented in their concert hall audiences (e.g., Los Angeles Philharmonic, Fort Worth Symphony). The Milwaukee Symphony Orchestra (MSO) has "MSO-Me" side-by-side performing experiences for adults, 21 and older, and MSO musicians playing together in family/community concerts.

Preconcert lectures (e.g., Chicago Symphony Orchestra, Philadelphia, Baltimore Symphony Orchestra) continue their popularity with adults who seek to connect with music scholars providing information (sometimes accompanied by multimedia presentations) about the music subsequently heard in concert. These lectures give those who are interested additional depth of musical, historical, and cultural understanding of the performance literature immediately prior to the concert. The Annapolis Symphony Orchestra, on the other hand, offers "Symphony Study Courses," courses centered on their orchestra's concert literature, presented from an interdisciplinary arts perspective, but at times during the week that do not immediately precede a concert. The Milwaukee Symphony Orchestra offers "Friday Talkbacks" in which concert-goers meet with the professional musicians and soloists after Friday evening concerts for a question and answer session.

The Cleveland Orchestra offers adult preconcert lectures and "Music Study Groups in Your Neighborhood" that familiarize adults with repertoire one week prior to a concert. Learning activities include informal lectures, listening experiences, and discussions at predetermined sites. Group discussions are led by expert musicians/historians/educators in the comfort of convenient urban and suburban locations. This event is particularly appealing for older adults and working adults, since they need not travel far to engage in musical learning.

Road Scholar

Exploritas (Elderhostel), renamed in 2010 as Road Scholar, is a not-for-profit education program that has led the lifelong learning movement for the past 40 years. Road Scholar offers 5,500 educational travel excursions in the United States and in 150 other countries, specifically designed for adults to build skills and pursue topics of interest such as food, music, art, history, and culture. Musically, adults select music participation, music appreciation, and music festival experiences that bring together small groups of adult learners having similar musical, cultural, and social interests.

Church Music Settings

Participating in music within religious institutions can provide adults with meaningful musical experiences. Moore (2009) addressed the function of music beyond that of performance benefits in African-American gospel choirs in churches. She stated, "music functions as a means of communication to recount the tests and trials of life, to confess hope for deliverance, and to glorify and praise God" while also transporting people from their everyday lives to a spiritual connection (p. 279). Moore suggested that student interns in church music settings must respect cultural community connections and life experiences that adults bring to the music learning and performance process. Further, interns must be comfortable working within a religious musical setting and in some circumstances teaching through the oral tradition.

Alternative Adult Music Groups

Music in adulthood can be found in spaces and with participants that are less traditional than others. For example, Dr. Kimberly McCord, Professor of Music Education at Illinois State University, started the "Grannies Band U.S." Based on the original band in Helsinki, called Riskiryhma, the group exists for adult women who are widowed. Riskirythma, along with the 50 or so additional bands taught at the Resonaari Special Music School, using Figurenotes© software and adapted guitars. "Guitars have the top and bottom strings removed and the other 4 are tuned A, E, A, E. That way, barred power chords substitute for learning the more complex regular chords. Stickers of different colors and shapes correspond to pitch and octave. For example, middle C is a red circle. The stickers are put on the keyboards, guitars, and basses. Music written in Figurenotes© simplifies traditional notation. What the musician sees connects with the stickers on their instrument." (K.M., personal communication, 11/17/16). McCord and collegiate students serve as the mentor musicians.

Choirs and song-writing experiences for adult incarcerated people are also becoming more prevalent throughout the United States. Sample choirs include the Oakdale Singers (Mary Cohen, Director, Iowa City, IO), East Hills Singers (Kirk Carson, Director, Lansing, KS), Oberlin Music at Grafton Choir (Jody Kerchner, Director, Grafton, OH), The FSU-MTC choir (Judy Bowers, Director, Quincy, FL), MCI-Framingham and MCI-Norfolk choirs (Andre de Quadros, Director, MA), and UMOJA, UBUNTU, KUJI, and Hope through Harmony choirs (Catherine Roma, Warren, OH). These choirs exist for the conductors, volunteers, and incarcerated singers to explore common humanity and expressivity and facilitate rehabilitation and reintegration through music. (Also see Mota & Fiegueiredo, this volume)

Palliative Care

Music experiences occur in centers that provide music therapy for people with cognitive, behavioral, and/or physical challenges; for those undergoing posttraumatic stress disorder rehabilitation; and in nursing homes and assisted living and health care centers. This area of geriatric music experiences has become especially important as a means of cognitive and emotional therapy for adults with dementia and Alzheimer's disease. Researchers found that sound therapy, beyond mere stimulation, provides adults with these conditions pleasure from hearing familiar melodies and rhythms (Clément et al., 2012; Vanstone et al., 2012). In fact, research indicates that "younger adults, older adults, and individuals with midl to moderate Alzheimer's Disease had strong recognition of traditional (familiar) melodies," even if they could not recall information related to the context related to how, where, and when they learned the tune (Vanstone et al., 2012, p. 506).

Acknowledging that graduate and pre-service music teachers' experiences might be initially unsettling in this context, music teacher educators can assist students in appreciating observable and nonobservable effects during adults' music engagement and human interactions. It is helpful for the students to focus on the importance of human interaction—one spirit to another—through music, rather focusing on the older adults' disabilities and ailing physical bodies.

CONCLUSION

Music education is not restricted to formal school contexts. Anyone who is teaching, or who is preparing to teach, music in any context ought to know about, experience, and be prepared to work with music learners beyond the traditional years of schooling. Music teacher education programs in the twenty-first century should take the lead in preparing undergraduate and graduate music students to recognize, value, and develop skills for teaching learners across the life span.

REFLECTIVE QUESTIONS

1. In what ways do children, adolescents, and adults engage in music throughout the day? In what ways can music teacher education courses document and illuminate formal, nonformal, and informal musical engagement? What implications do these musical experiences have for teacher preparation curricula?
2. In what innovative ways might music educators ignite precollegiate students' flames for lifelong music learning and engagement?
3. How might music teacher educators and their collegiate students collaborate with community musical and arts organizations to promote lifelong learning and musical engagement?
4. What types of pedagogical experiences (i.e., collegiate course and field experiences) might *all* music students experience in order to prepare for teaching students from early childhood through adulthood and promoting lifelong musical engagement? Where in their course of study might this occur?

KEY SOURCES

Erikson, E. (1963). *Childhood and society* (2nd ed.). New York: Norton.

Kerchner, J., & Abril, C. (eds.) (2009). *Musical experience in our lives: Things we learn and meanings we make.* Lanham, MD: Rowman & Littlefield.

Myers, D. (2006). Freeing music education from schooling: Toward a lifespan perspective on music learning and teaching. *International Journal of Community Music, D*, 1–24. https://www.intellectbooks.co.uk/MediaManager/Archive/IJCM/Volume%20D/03%20Myers.pdf[accessed October 26, 2010].

REFERENCES

Bowles, C. (1991). Self-expressed adult music education interests and music experiences. *Journal of Research in Music Education, 39*(3), 191–205.

Bowles, C., Duke, R., & Jellison, J. (2007). Relationships between past and present music experiences of adult audiences. *Southeastern Journal of Music Education, 11*(1999), 149–161.

Boyer, J. M. (2007). *Creativity matters: The arts and aging toolkit.* New York: National Guild of Community Schools of the Arts.

Butler, R. N. (1963). The life review: An interpretation of reminiscence in the aged. *Psychiatry, 26,* 65–75.

Clément, S., Tonini, A., Khatir, F., Schiaratura, L., & Séverine, S. (June 2012). Short and longer term effects of musical intervention in severe Alzheimer's Disease. *Music Perception: An Interdisciplinary Journal, 29*(5), 533–541.

Coffman, D. (2002a). Banding together: New horizons in lifelong music making. *Journal of Aging and Identity, 7*(2), 133–143.

Coffman, D. (2002b). Music and quality of life in older adults. *Psychomusicology, 18,* 76–88.

Coffman, D. (2009). Voices of experience: Lessons from older adult amateur musicians. In J. Kerchner & C. Abril (eds.), *Musical experience in our lives: Things we learn and meanings we make* (pp. 331–346). Lanham, MD: Rowman & Littlefield.

Coffman, D. D., & Adamek, M. (1999). The contributions of wind band participation to quality of life of senior adults. *Music Therapy Perspective, 17,* 27–31.

Coffman, D. D., & Higgins, L. (2018). Community Music Ensembles. In G. E. McPherson & G. F. Welch (eds.), *Vocal, Instrumental, and Ensemble Learning and Teaching: An Oxford Handbook of Music Education.* (Vol 3, pp. 301–316) . New York, NY: Oxford University Press.

Cohen, G. (2005). *The mature mind: The positive power of the aging brain.* New York: Basic Books.

Cooper, T. (2001). Adults' perceptions of piano study: Achievements and experiences. *Journal of Research in Music Education, 49*(2), 156–168.

Dabback, W. M. (2008). Identity formation through participation in the Rochester New Horizons Band programme. *International Journal of Community Music, 1*(2), 267–286.

Darrow, A. A., Johnson, C. M., & Ollenberger, T. (1994). The effect of participation in an intergenerational choir on teens' and older persons' cross-age attitudes. *Journal of Music Therapy, 31,* 119–134.

Erikson, E. (1963). *Childhood and society* (2nd ed.). New York: Norton.

Ernst, R. (September 2004). Roy Ernst and New Horizons. http://newhorizonsmusic.org/dr-roy-ernst/

Furstenberg, F., Kennedy, S., McCloyd, V., Rumbaut, R., & Stettersten, R. (2003). *Between adolescence and adulthood: Expectations about the timing of adulthood.* Working paper supported by the Research Network on Transitions to Adulthood and Public Policy funded by the MacArthur Foundation Grant #00–00-65719-HCD.

Jongbloed, B. (2002). Lifelong learning: Implications for institutions. *Higher Education, 44*(3/4), 413–431.

Jutras, P. (2006). The benefit of adult piano study as self-reported by selected adult piano students. *Journal of Research in Music Education, 54*(2), 97–110.

Kruse, N. B. (2009). "An Elusive Bird": Perceptions of music learning among Canadian and American adults. *International Journal of Community Music, 2*(2&3), 215–225.

LaBelle, T. (1982). Nonformal and informal education: A holistic perspective on lifelong learning. *International Review of Education, 28*(2), 159–175.

Laes, T. (2015). Empowering later adulthood music education: A case study of a rock band for third-age learners. *International Journal of Music Education, 33*(1), 51–65.

Levine School of Music. (2009). Our mission and core values. http://www.levinemusic.org/about/mission-and-history

McAdams, D., de St. Aubin, E., & Logan, R. (1993). Generativity among young, midlife, and older adults. *Psychology and Aging, 8*, 221–230.

McAdams, D., Hart, H., & Maruna, S. (1998). The anatomy of generativity. In D. McAdams & E. de St. Aubin (eds.), *Generativity and adult development: How and why we care for the next generation* (pp. 7–43). Washington, DC: American Psychological Association.

Minichiello, V. (1992). Meeting the educational needs of an aging population: The Australian experiences. *International Review of Education, 38*(4), 403–416.

Moore, M. (2009). Creation to performance: The journey of an African American community gospel-jazz ensemble. In J. Kerchner & C. Abril (eds.), *Musical experience in our lives: Things we learn and meanings we make* (pp. 277–296). Lanham, MD: Rowman & Littlefield.

Mota, G., & Fiegueiredo, S. (2018). Initiating Music Programs in New Contexts: In Search of a Democratic Music Education. In G. E. McPherson & G. F. Welch (eds.), *Music and Music Education in People's Lives: An Oxford Handbook of Music Education.* (Vol 1, pp. 187–205). New York, NY: Oxford University Press.

Myers, D. (2006). Freeing music education from schooling: Toward a lifespan perspective on music learning and teaching. *International Journal of Community Music, D*, 1–24. https://www.intellectbooks.co.uk/MediaManager/Archive/IJCM/Volume%20D/03%20Myers.pdf

Myers, D. (2008). Lifespan engagement and the question of relevance: Challenges for music education research in the twenty-first century. *Music Education Research, 10*(1), 1–14.

National Institute on Aging and World Health Organization. (2011). Global health and aging (Publication 11–7737). Bethesda, MD: National Institue on Aging.

Rohwer, D. (2005a). A case study of adult beginning instrumental practice. *Contributions to Music Education, 32*(1), 45–58.

Rohwer, D. (2005b). Teaching the adult beginning instrumentalist: Ideas from practitioners. *International Journal of Music Education, 23*(1), 37–47.

Rohwer, D. (2009). Perceived instructional needs and desires of 8th grade and senior citizen band members. *Journal of Music Teacher Education, 18*(2), 1–12.

Roulston, K., Jutras, P., & Kim, S. J. (2015). Adult perspectives on learning musical instruments. *International Journal of Music Education, 33*(3), 325–335.

Shanahan, M., Porfeli, E., & Mortimer, J. (2004). What marks adulthood—subjective identity or demographic markers? *Network on Transitions to Adulthood Policy Brief, 7*, 1–3.

Smith, M. K. (2000). The theory and rhetoric of the learning society. *The encyclopedia of education.* Retrieved from www.infed.org/lifelonglearning/b-lrnsoc.htm.

Teachout, D. J. (2018). (V1, P1, Ch.34) The Preparation of Music Teacher Educators: A Critical Link. In G. E. McPherson & G. F. Welch (eds.), *Music and Music Education in People's Lives: An Oxford Handbook of Music Education.* (Vol 1, pp. 326–329) . New York, NY: Oxford University Press.

U.S. Census Bureau. (2015). *National Characteristics: Vintage 2015.* Retrieved from https://api.census.gov/data/2015.html

Vanstone, A., Sikka, R., Tangness, L., Sham, R., Garcia, A., & Cuddy, L. (June 2012). Episodic and semantic memory for melodies in Alzheimer's Disease. *Music Perception: An Interdisciplinary Journal, 29*(5), 501–507.

Veblen, K., & Olsson, B. (2002). Community music: Toward an international overview. In R. Colwell & C. Richardson (eds.), *The new handbook of research on music teaching and learning* (pp. 730–753). New York: Oxford University Press.

Wise, G. W., Hartmann, D. J., & Fisher, B. J. (1992). Exploration of the relationship between choral singing and successful aging. *Psychological Reports, 70*, 1175–1183.

CHAPTER 19

THE ROLE OF HIGHER EDUCATION IN FOSTERING MUSICALLY ENGAGED ADULTS

CHELCY L. BOWLES AND JANET L. JENSEN

In many countries, formal music education and the training of teachers have long assumed that music in higher education is for those pursuing music as a profession. Career-aspiring musicians, however, represent only one segment of the population of learners 18 years and older who may be served by higher education. This chapter examines the responsibilities and roles of higher education in fostering musically engaged adults by exploring three primary contexts: (1) the adult population within the university; (2) the adult population in the community in which the university resides; and (3) the interactive university-community adult population.

A primary term to define at the outset is "music engagement." It is our position that active music engagement should be interpreted broadly to encompass not only making and creating music, but perceptive music listening and philosophical and intellectual reflection about music. This position aligns with the notion of engagement advocated by the 1967 Tanglewood Symposium, a pivotal conference that evaluated the role of music in American society and education. The final report (Choate, 1968) recommends that "music should be offered to adults both for instrumental purposes, to satisfy psychological, religious, and vocational needs, and for expressive purposes, to help each individual find means for self-realization, either as creator or as participant audience" (p. 115). In *Vision 2020*, the report from the Housewright Symposium, Carter (2000) emphasized that "*any* involvement in music, not just classical music and other forms of the European tradition, can be meaningful and valuable . . . it is incumbent upon us in music education to find ways to help students, and then later, adults, find value in the many varied music experiences that are available" (p. 146).

Analyses of various arts participation surveys and results of skills and attitude surveys in the United States over the past three decades indicate that music is important in the lives of adults, and most adults are engaged in music in some dimension (see Myers, chapter 15). The myriad community music ensembles, schools, and workshops that provide opportunities to participate in and learn about music across a wide variety of styles and genres offer evidence of adults' avid interest in music learning and performance. In addition, partial documentation of the broad range of programs available for adults to study traditional music indicates that many societies assume responsibility for music education and engagement of adults to help preserve and develop culture (World Music Central, n.d.).

If adults *are* musically engaged, why is there concern about fostering music engagement? Adults possess a varied array of backgrounds and experiences, including music, that may support their own individualized learning needs and interests. Opportunities to further develop their goals, knowledge, and skills for enjoyment and self-expression are important in achieving full and meaningful lives. Referring to music learning beyond the school years, the final report of the Tanglewood Symposium (Choate, 1968) argued that "continuing education should offer an opportunity to move as far in depth or breadth as each [person] can, through a comprehensive program of music that will equip him [or her] to live in the modern world" (p. 115). If it is the belief of the music education profession that people deserve lifelong opportunities to be engaged in music, then it follows that it is a professional responsibility among music educators to offer adults ongoing and sequential instruction leading toward significant and rewarding progress in their skills and knowledge.

Among the range of institutions and organizations that may foster music engagement among adults, institutions of higher education are in a unique position for several reasons: (1) the population of the university itself comprises adults (defining "adults" as those 18 years and older); (2) the university is in the business of educating both adults and educators of children who become adults; and (3) the cultural landscapes of the university community and the wider community of adults within which it resides are frequently shared and interdependent. It is at the intersection of the university's expansive educational mission and resources and the development of specific skills and opportunities for meaningful lifelong music engagement that higher education plays a significant role.

DEFINING THE RESPONSIBILITY
OF HIGHER EDUCATION

The responsibility of higher/tertiary education to embrace the role of facilitating adult music engagement has been addressed by several international organizations.

UNESCO calls arts education a "universal human right" (UNESCO, 2006, p. 3). In "recognizing the role of Arts Education in preparing different sectors of the public" (p. 15), UNESCO recommended that educational institutions "encourage active and sustainable partnerships between educational contexts and the wider community" and that they "facilitate cooperation to develop Arts Education programmes, so as to enable communities to share transmitting cultural values and art forms" (p. 17). The International Music Council (IMC), founded in 1949 by UNESCO, is the world's largest network of organizations, institutions, and individuals working in the field of music. The IMC works toward the advancement of rights for all children and adults to express themselves musically in full freedom, to learn musical languages and skills, and to have access to musical involvement through participation, listening, creation, and information (International Music Council, 2005). The European Music Council (EMC), a regional group of the IMC, is the umbrella organization for musical groups based in Europe. The EMC's mission includes "enhancing the visibility of initiatives that help *sustain* people's participation in music and cultural life" (European Music Council, n.d.; italics added).

Under the IMC/EMC umbrella, the Association Européene des Conservatoires, Académies de Musique et Musikhochschulen (AEC) is a cultural and educational network representing institutions concerned with educating professional musicians: "Although the primary focus of the Association is on professional music training, the AEC supports the importance of music in all levels of education in our society, ranging from early childhood to higher education and lifelong learning" (Association Européene des Conservatoires, Académies de Musique et Musikhochschulen, 2005).

While all of the aforementioned organizations are powerful advocates and policy drivers, the National Association of Schools of Music (NASM) in the United States is an accrediting agency with a membership of over 600 public and private institutions. A primary function of NASM is to address the role of higher education in advancing a rich musical culture. NASM posits that "professional training institutions have a responsibility to place the specialization necessary for professional music activity in a context that produces a deep sense of concern and responsibility for the development of cultural values" (*NASM Handbook*, 2016–17, p. 240). Further, "institutions that train professional musicians have responsibilities for addressing issues of music in general education. NASM expects member institutions to make significant commitments to these efforts in both human and material resources" (p. 84).

The Adult Population
in the University

Considering that institutions of higher education (hereafter referred to as universities) are entirely populated by age-defined adults, every member of a campus community is incorporated into this population. This includes degree-seeking music and nonmusic students, music and nonmusic faculty and staff, and nontraditional returning and adult nondegree students. Though all of these constituents can potentially interact in some way with a music school or department, this chapter focuses on priorities, delivery systems, course content, and collaborations as they apply to those most directly associated with the music unit: music-degree-seeking students, students in music courses seeking other degrees, and music faculty.

Degree Students: Music Majors

In addition to specialized professional studies, the education of music majors needs to prepare them not only to remain musically engaged themselves, but to foster musical engagement among others. These are not mutually exclusive endeavors; however, they do require experiences, curricula, and faculty dedicated to helping students grow in multiple ways. In comparing objectives and outcomes of school music programs with university music programs, Carruthers (2008) asserts: "while human understanding, social responsibility and the like may be acknowledged as desirable outcomes, most university performance programmes focus on developing human capital—on creating better musicians—who may or may not be better people for it" (p. 127).

NASM recommendations for *all* music majors can be grouped into four general categories: (1) an orientation that develops understanding of the philosophical and sociological significance of the arts in American life and culture, and that provides opportunities to integrate music with other artistic, historical, and scientific disciplines; (2) the provision of service learning opportunities in the community, including community performances; (3) pedagogical preparation and techniques for discovering new ways of understanding and teaching music, including the importance of encouraging the musical amateur; (4) the development of entrepreneurial, leadership, advocacy, management, and audience development skills (*NASM Handbook*, 2016–17, p. 240).

These recommendations can largely be accomplished in extant degree programs and courses (see Kerchner & Abril, chapter 18). What is more important is that the nature of relevant experiences and their wider implications be overtly and purposefully addressed. Curricula and course content can be scrutinized for opportunities to better realize life-span-related goals of philosophical, sociological, and interdisciplinary musical understandings and can enhance the understanding that music is an act of sharing and communication, often with listeners and learners whose experiences differ widely from the experiences of those pursuing music degrees.

Increased emphasis on pedagogy based on a commitment to lifelong learning and infused throughout the curriculum has the potential to address multiple aspects of engagement and to serve as connective tissue for the preparation of professional musicians. Smilde's extensive work in lifelong learning for musicians (see Smilde, chapter 20) has implications for their professional and pedagogical preparation (Smilde, 2008):

> A curriculum emerging from the conceptual framework of lifelong learning is based on acquiring competencies, requires team-teaching and receives feedback from external partners. It values both tradition and change. It is reflective of the outside world and it re-evaluates existing knowledge. (p. 250)

Clearly, many performance majors will teach at some point in their careers. Every music department has experts in pedagogy, learning, and learners. Team teaching, as well as specialized pedagogy and music education courses, can provide a platform for fostering sentient and caring musicians who are conscious of the responsibility and privilege of teaching learners at all stages and ages.

Finally, if music students are themselves to remain professionally engaged and personally fulfilled in their own lives, they will likely need to be entrepreneurs, advocates (for themselves and for their art), leaders, and managers. They will need to relate to multiple audiences and market themselves and their art. They will have what Smilde (2008) calls "portfolio careers" (p. 243): having multiple simultaneous or successive types of employment across the lifespan. Programs addressing these needs are growing, also encouraged by NASM:

> Under economic stress there is a temptation to retrench and protect the status quo, yet those who position themselves well will choose to adapt and advance new causes to create new effects. Embracing an entrepreneurial mindset can afford both institutions and students alike a greater chance of success during this time of uncertainty. (National Association of Schools of Music, 2009)

Degree Students: Music Education Majors

Especially critical to fostering an engaged adult population are those individuals enrolled in music teacher education programs. In many countries, but particularly in the United States, most curricula for music teacher training programs have been developed on the assumption that structured experiences during the PreK to secondary school years will inspire and prepare people for a lifetime of music participation. However, Jellison's (2000, 2004) frank discussions of the failure of elementary music education to translate into musically capable adults parallels Myers's (2008b) similar conclusion related to secondary school music practices: "producing successful ensemble performances in school, while a worthy effort in some respects, does not necessarily instill skills and understandings that empower people to fulfill their music drives and potential over a lifetime" (p. 50).

In their presentation at the first American conference of the Society for Music Teacher Education, Bowles and Myers (2005) proposed that equipping pre-service and in-service music educators with a "lifespan perspective" take into consideration the nature of authentic, meaningful music participation and learning throughout life. Although many adults do what they are ultimately trained to do through school programs—play and sing in bands, orchestras, and choirs in which most decisions are made by a director—a majority of adults seek to engage in independent activities for which they most likely received no practice within the school curriculum.

Implementing a lifespan perspective in teacher preparation can also help music education students develop an enlarged sense of their roles as music educators. There is currently a rapidly increasing population of adults who may not have had school music experiences leading toward the ability to develop musical independence. Therefore, there is a need for music educators who are prepared to utilize strategies especially effective with adult learners who may be new to, returning to, or continuing their musical development. We can encourage music education students to explore careers beyond PreK–12 school teaching, and introduce them to opportunities with adult and intergenerational learners through pre-service experiences. In addition, expanding the scope of music teacher education programs to include specialization in adult learners may attract potential students who do not envision themselves in PreK–12 settings.

It is important that music majors in *any* specialization understand that fostering a musically engaged adult population is an investment in their own futures, and they must be equipped to envision and transition to futures beyond their existing university programs.

Degree Students: Non–Music Majors

NASM speaks unequivocally about the responsibility of higher education for non–music majors, those students participating in elective music opportunities, or in required music courses for humanities credit: "the institution should provide non-major students with opportunities to develop awareness and understanding of music as an integral part of the liberal education and the human experience" (*NASM Handbook*, 2016–17, p. 84). The document indicates that the music unit should actively promote participation in music studies and activities, including live performance whenever possible, as well as participation in courses for music majors for which they may be qualified. Furthermore, a variety of participatory ensemble experiences for amateur performers should be provided, with leadership being of professional standing, along with the management and support necessary to serve those ensembles. An effective program for building audiences among the nonmajor student population should be maintained, and opportunities should be provided for the participation of nonmajor students in activities involving visiting musicians (p. 240).

Historically, most discussion of nonmajors and elective music has focused on music in general studies, emphasizing musical perception and appreciation over engagement. Not as much attention has been given to the specific and unique needs of the nonmajor in performing organizations, in spite of the fact that these students have likely invested in performance since childhood and are more likely to continue in the future if helped to make a successful transition. Performance organizations

also offer interaction between majors and nonmajors, potentially a mutually beneficial collaboration, and may be the most cost-effective instructional setting for the
music unit, with an extremely high student-to-teacher/conductor ratio.

Where institution size and enrollment allow for performing groups composed
entirely of nonmajors, the opportunity is particularly rich for addressing their needs
and interests specifically and intentionally with regard to present and future engagement in music. Such an enrollment base allows the organization to be structured
according to the profiles of nonmajors (including accommodations such as scheduling, repeatable credits, credits earned, and recognition of academic conflicts) and
to serve as a bridge to lifelong participation, rather than as a training group or ensemble of lower rank. Conceived as a learning community, the nonmajor ensemble
provides opportunities for music majors to coach and conduct, thus giving them
experience in working with the diverse interests and achievement levels of beyond-
school populations they may encounter in their own professional lives.

With regard to non–music majors who choose music class experiences other
than ensemble performance, NASM states:

> The aesthetic products of human culture and experience, including music, are among
> the most significant human achievements. Therefore, all the arts merit reflective and
> technical study as subjects of intrinsic worth. Because of the connections of the arts
> to all human forms of life, studies in history, culture, language, and other such liberal
> subjects are incomplete unless attention is given to their aesthetic dimensions. When
> appropriately taught, reflective, technical, and interdisciplinary studies in the arts can
> promote and enhance the aesthetic appreciation and discrimination of students who,
> in turn, become audiences and provide leadership in the continuing and various
> processes of artistic creation, presentation, and education. . . . Such comprehensive
> understanding with attendant skills, attitudes, and aptitudes is the fundamental
> ingredient in a liberal education as traditionally conceived. The presence of programs
> in music in educational programs at all levels is thus an entirely appropriate
> educational objective. Initiatives in pursuit of this objective must, of necessity,
> originate from music units within educational institutions. NASM believes that these
> initiatives are essential to the continuing growth of the music culture in the United
> States. (*NASM Handbook*, 2016–17, pp. 238–239)

The realization of this objective, despite its challenges, may be the best opportunity
to cast a wide net of inclusiveness for both the present and future. Course content
needs to be both relevant to students and valid in terms of the music unit's disciplinary credibility. To ensure the integrity of delivery, teachers of such courses need
to be experts who also enjoy working with nonmajors, "respecting their general
intelligence rather than patronizing their musical limitations" (Willoughby, 1982,
p. 56). Adjunct faculty or experts from fields outside the music unit may be valuable
resources, though the teaching of nonmajors must be valued as professional activity
among full-time music faculty and administrators: "program structures should encourage faculty and administrative involvement in the education of non-majors.
Policies for promotion and tenure should recognize the significance of faculty
attention to music in general education" (*NASM Handbook*, 2016–17, p. 85).

Music Faculty

The greatest resource of the music school or department for enhancing music engagement is the expertise, dedication, and talent of its faculty. But faculty are also often constrained by a system that does not give serious consideration to, or recognition for, activities that specifically provide opportunities for adult learners. Though higher education generally, including research universities, has become more attuned to engagement as integral to its mission, outreach and service may often continue to take the position of a distant third in reviews of faculty qualifications for permanent tenure.

Faculty research efforts related to adult music teaching and learning should be encouraged and recognized as crucial to the understanding of how music is experienced across the lifespan, and methodology specific to the teaching of adult learners should be explored as aggressively and rigorously as it is for learners at young age levels. In a keynote address to the International Research in Music Education Conference in Exeter (UK), Myers (2008a) proposed that "the research community must seek to extract itself from the tendency to confirm the obvious and move towards an attitude of discovery that pushes the field forward, particularly with regard to the duality of lifespan engagement and relevance" (p. 5).

A final observation regarding the role of music faculty in promoting lifelong engagement is the importance of encouraging an *expectation* of lifelong music engagement among all students, both nonmajors and majors. Toward this goal, faculty can encourage their music students to view and analyze themselves as adult learners, and to inject into their terminology and methodology a lifespan perspective on their own music learning and engagement journey.

THE UNIVERSITY'S COEXISTENT
AND INTERACTIVE COMMUNITY

Beneficiaries of Community Adult Engagement

In contrast to notions of a "town-gown syndrome," in which a university and its community are in conflict, the university-community music relationship around lifespan learning may be symbiotic. While the community benefits culturally from the musical expertise, performances, and learning opportunities provided by the university, the university benefits from a community that supports the university by attending performances and classes, and by participating in a variety of events. In some cases, the community provides financial support crucial to the music unit's ability to offer a wide range of publicly available experiences.

An important consideration is the assumption that community adults will be the core audience for many university performances. Research indicates that adults who are currently engaged in one kind of music activity are more likely to participate in other music activities (Andreasen & Belk, 1980; Bowles, 1991; Cooper, 1996; Fink, Robinson, & Dowden, 1985; Mitchell, 1984; Waggoner, 1972). What does this mean in relation to building and maintaining symbiotic community-university relationships? If a desirable outcome of a musically engaged adult community is that the public will attend more university offerings, then the university might regard the provision of a variety of direct personal learning experiences for adults as a benefit to its own programs.

Given the range of expertise within a university music department, the provision of a rich array of adult learning opportunities, both in performing and nonperforming contexts, may promote the importance of music as a means of understanding and enriching one's expressive life. Providing quality experiences that foster enriched philosophical and intellectual engagement through music can in turn inspire increased participation and involvement that might extend to benefit both the music unit and the larger university in multiple ways.

Utilizing University and Community Resources

Universities have the resources—expertise, administrative and organizational structure, and facilities—to encompass a larger range of adults than those explicitly within their internal communities. If universities are to realize their potential as facilitators of a musically engaged adult population, they can start by committing existing resources to an expanded population of adult learners. Many universities already do this by making courses and degree programs available to non-degree-seeking adults on a reduced-fee basis. Music units can develop or consult in developing programs for adult learners that operate independently of degree curricula. They can also spearhead efforts to design learning experiences in which university students and community adults participate collaboratively. The university is in a unique position to cross boundaries—that is, the university walls need not be the boundaries of the university—and to broaden current offerings to include community learners and to utilize community expertise.

Organizing for Adult Learning in the University

Designated Units for Adult Learners

Internationally, various organizational models exist for universities to offer designated programs for adults. Distinct community or outreach units, which may or may not interact with the music department, may offer the kinds of learning opportunities suggested above. Ideally, such units are able to offer sequenced instruction and experiences across the spectrum of music disciplines. Models for such extensive programs might include music sections within larger university-wide programs (such as continuing education divisions) devoted specifically to continuing/community/adult education; community music schools; and programs within music departments devoted specifically to community outreach and education. These programs may be able to offer a wide variety of experiences serving diverse learner needs across multiple delivery systems (e.g., continuing and sequenced courses; workshops; lecture series; distance learning).

Within such organizational structures, the possibility exists of utilizing resident music expertise. Undergraduate and graduate students, for example, may gain valuable expertise (and income) and enhance their own learning and career development through teaching private lessons and music courses, and by directing and coaching ensembles. Such programs also afford opportunities for guided student internships supervised by faculty who have particular expertise and interest in adult music learners.

Restricted budgets are a way of life in the university context, and funding challenges can compromise even the most potentially valuable programs. However, programming for community adults affords the possibility of self-sustaining revenue. Adults, whether engaged in on-site instruction or distance learning, generally expect to pay for services. Careful attention in determining fee structures should be given to the inclusion of all costs, including those associated with program administration and teacher training. Though profit motive should not be the basis of offering programs, adult/community lessons and courses may provide sufficient revenues from those able to pay that scholarships and innovative learning experiences may be extended to those unable to pay for them. Adults within the university community may receive reduced rates or possible exchanges of service whereby they usher or provide other support to the music unit in return for learning opportunities.

Blending University and Community Adults

Given the fiscal challenges faced by university music departments, an efficient way to offer adult opportunities is to blend university and community learning. Creatively analyzing organizational structures and program needs for adults, along with music department curricula, expertise, scheduling practices, and facilities, may reveal potential for including adult learners with little or no increased funding. Blended programs may also give music faculty with interests in teaching nondegree adults a structure through which they can realize their commitments without expending excessive additional preparation and instructional time.

One of the more subtle outcomes of combining university and community populations is the opportunity for traditional university students to interact with adults who have more life experience, and who value music and continue to participate in it. Blended experiences overseen by faculty can provide opportunities for music students to work alongside adult learners, as well as to experience intergenerational teaching and learning. Such interactive programs might help foster lifespan perspectives and the vision of continued music engagement for all people throughout life.

Blended Programming

One common "blended" experience in music departments is the performing en-semble, where university students and community musicians may learn and per-form collaboratively. In addition to traditional orchestras, choirs, and bands, ensembles such as world/ethnic music groups may be opened to community adults. Opportunities may exist to expand the music curriculum by encouraging student participation in community ensembles exploring styles and genres the music unit might not have the financial resources or expertise to provide. With faculty facili-tation and supervision, these experiences can be recognized academically, and they may provide unique intergenerational and multicultural opportunities.

Other blended performance experiences might include community adults in foundational skill classes, such as those in piano, voice, or orchestral instruments. Such blended courses offer excellent opportunities for music students to gain ex-perience teaching adults with little or no music experience (as opposed to music-major peers), and could foster a lifespan perspective on teaching and learning. Master classes and workshops with guest artists might also expand to include ad-vanced community adult musicians.

Many academic music courses (i.e., classes not focused on excelling in perfor-mance) are ideal for blending university and community members. Offerings might include undergraduate courses on music theory topics, courses related to music history or ethnomusicology, and courses that offer general knowledge acquisition about music. There may also be knowledgeable community adults who are inter-ested in more advanced music topics such as those taught in upper level under-graduate or graduate courses. Not only would interested adult students benefit, but these sometimes sparsely enrolled courses would have greater chance of surviving with increased enrollment. The inclusion of adults in such learning experiences as lecture series or special seminars provides faculty and graduate students with an opportunity to share their scholarly work, and for adult learners to become more intellectually engaged with music.

Issues Related to Blended University and Community Adult Experiences

There are several issues to address when considering the provision of blended experiences for university students and community adult learners. Even taking into account the acknowledged benefits of blended experiences, there are important challenges to be addressed in order to facilitate quality experiences for both tradi-tional credit students and credit or noncredit community adults participating in the same music performance organizations or academic music classes.

Scheduling may be the most obvious challenge in facilitating blended experiences, especially when trying to develop opportunities for working adults. Though classes and ensembles scheduled during working day hours might be ac-cessible for adult learners with flexible schedules (other university faculty, staff, retirees), working adults on traditional schedules will require early morning, eve-ning and weekend learning opportunities. Instructional staff and university students must be willing to adjust their daytime course and work schedules in order to facil-itate an extended class day.

In addition to scheduling, there are issues related to having non-credit-seeking adults enrolled in classes that other students are taking for credit. Instructors may feel that the focus of goals and attention must be with the credit students, and that the inclusion of noncredit students is both a diversion from preconceived course goals and constitutes an increased workload in evaluating achievement. However, the long-range value of having traditional music students actively engaged in lis-tening and discussion with community adults can be considered when determining course goals and when devising the syllabus to accommodate diverse learning goals and needs.

Two related issues that might surface in blended contexts are (1) the ability of music department instructors to address the learning needs of non-degree-seeking adults, and (2) the readiness of affiliate community musicians or music students to teach adults. Musical expertise and successful teaching in tightly structured university classrooms may not necessarily translate to the more diverse audience represented in blended programs.

As suggested earlier, learning experiences for traditional music students, in-cluding all majors, should include pedagogical and developmental considerations related to learning across the lifespan. However, such inclusive teaching-learning experiences are rare in current music school curricula. Similarly, it cannot be assumed that community music experts recruited to lead formal learning experiences will have sufficient background for successful teaching, particularly in blended university-community contexts. A survey of experienced teachers of adult music learners clearly indicated that both career musicians and career music teachers desire training specific to adult learners (Bowles, 2010). The university is in a position to provide supplemental teacher training workshops and courses specific to the needs of those leading music experiences for adult learners. Such professional development opportunities may be led by those who have been adequately pre-pared systematically and/or through direct experience to work with adults. Veblen (2008) indicates that universities in the United Kingdom are initiating new training programs for community music workers, which may be a rich resource for models.

CONCLUSION

Adults whose lives are personally enriched through music engagement are likely to have the passion and the power to advocate for, and to facilitate, musical engage-ment for others across the lifespan. To date, the music education profession has focused its efforts primarily on developing musical skills and knowledge among children and youth, and on preparing educators to perpetuate this priority. In general, it has been assumed that music learning in youth will translate into the desire and opportunity to continue participation throughout life. Even if the translation were successful, we must acknowledge that many adults may have lacked the opportunity or inclination to engage in school music, and that music education during childhood and adolescence may or may not have been a positive experience. Research supports the general assumption that children whose parents are musically engaged are more likely to engage in music (Bowles, 1991; Bowles, Duke, & Jellison, 2007). If we are to realize a goal of a musically engaged adult population, it is critical to provide personal experiences for adults that capture, enrich, and extend their own expressive lives—a legacy that may ultimately transfer to their children.

An important outcome of providing meaningful experiences for adults can be a personal passion for music that can fuel political advocacy on behalf of music education initiatives for people of all ages. In "Freeing Music Education from Schooling" (2008b), Myers reminds us that

> even when music educators have embraced the importance of school-community
> integration, the profession has often managed, in its own inimitable way, to
> bifurcate the topics of adult and community music from school music. . . .
> As a consequence, we lose sight of things such as the crucial role of music
> in intergenerational cultural transmission, or how providing high-quality
> music education at any age benefits from knowledge of lifelong developmental
> contexts. . . . We also lose sight of the fact that building support for in-school
> programmes may be a matter of providing direct educational experiences for
> adults. (p. 54)

It is imperative that higher education embrace its responsibility and pivotal role in the musical life cycle. It must utilize its potential and existing resources in facilitating experiences for adult learners, and work to infuse a lifespan perspective across all of its internal and interactive constituent contexts.

REFLECTIVE QUESTIONS

1. When and where does responsibility begin and end for higher education institutions to advance musically engaging opportunities for adults?
2. What are, or should be, the aspirations of the music education profession for postsecondary students to be musically engaged throughout their lives?
3. What opportunities exist, or should exist, for adults who were not involved in typical school music programs to begin and continue developing musical skills and knowledge?
4. Within the higher education curriculum, how much emphasis should be placed on educating music professionals as opposed to those who have no intention of becoming music professionals?

KEY SOURCES

Choate, R. (ed.) (1968). Documentary report of the Tanglewood Symposium. Washington, DC: MENC.

Jellison, J. A. (2000). How can all people continue to be involved in meaningful music education? In C. K. Madsen (ed.), Vision 2020: The Housewright Symposium on the Future of Music Education (pp. 111–137). Reston, VA: MENC: National Association for Music Education.

Myers, D. E. (2008). Freeing music education from schooling: Toward a lifespan perspective on music learning and teaching. International Journal of Community Music, 1(1), 49–61.

NASM Handbook 2016–17. (2016). Reston, VA: National Association of Schools of Music. https://nasm.arts-accredit.org/accreditation/standards-guidelines/handbook/ [accessed November 23, 2017].

UNESCO. (2006). Road Map for Arts Education. http://www.unesco.org/fileadmin/multimedia/HQ/CLT/CLT/pdf/Arts_Edu_RoadMap_en.pdf

REFERENCES

Andreasen, A. R., & Belk, R. W. (1980). Predictors of attendance at the performing arts. Journal of Consumer Research, 7, 112–120.

Association Européene des Conservatoires, Académies de Musique et Musikhochschulen. (2005). https://www.aec-music.eu/about-aec/organisation.

Bowles, C. L. (1991). Self-expressed adult music education interests and music experiences. Journal of Research in Music Education, 39(3), 191–205.

Bowles, C. L. (2010). Teachers of adult music learners: An assessment of characteristics and instructional practices, preparation, and needs. Update: Applications of Research in Music Education, 28(2), 50–59.

Bowles, C., Duke, R., & Jellison, J. (2007). Relationships between past and present music experiences of adult audiences. Southeastern Journal of Music Education, 11, 149–161.

Bowles, C., & Myers, D. (2005, September 16). Toward a lifespan perspective in music teacher education. Paper presented at Symposium on Music Teacher Education: Revitalizing, Researching, Rethinking, Greensboro, NC.

Choate, R. (ed.). (1968). Documentary report of the Tanglewood Symposium. Washington, DC: MENC.

Carruthers, G. (2008). Educating professional musicians: Lessons learned from school music. International Journal of Music Education, 26(2), 127–135.

Carter, W. L. (2000). Response to Judith A. Jellison's "How Can All People Continue to Be Involved in Meaningful Music Participation?" In C. K. Madsen (ed.), Vision 2020: The Housewright Symposium on the Future of Music Education (pp. 139–152). Reston, VA: MENC: National Association for Music Education.

Cooper, T. L. (1996). Adults' perceptions of piano study: Achievement, experiences, and interests. Doctoral diss., University of Texas, Austin.

European Music Council. (n.d.). http://www.emc-imc.org/about/ [accessed November 23, 2017].

Fink, E. L., Robinson, J. P., & Dowden, S. (1985). The structure of music preference and attendance. *Communication Research*, *12*(3), 301–318.

International Music Council. (2005). http://www.imc-http://www.imc-cim.org/ [accessed November 23, 2017].

Jellison, J. A. (2000). How can all people continue to be involved in meaningful music education? In C. K. Madsen (ed.), *Vision 2020: The Housewright Symposium on the future of Music Education* (pp. 111–137). Reston, VA: MENC: National Association for Music Education.

Jellison, J. A. (2004). It's about time (Senior Researcher Acceptance Address). *Journal of Research in Music Education*, *52*(3), 191–205.

Mitchell, A. (1984). *The professional performing arts: Attendance patterns, preferences and motives*. Madison, WI: Association of Colleges and Community Arts Administrators, Inc.

Myers, D. E. (2008a). Lifespan engagement and the question of relevance: Challenges for music education research in the twenty-first century. *Music Education Research*, *10*(1), 1–14.

Myers, D. E. (2008b). Freeing music education from schooling: Toward a lifespan perspective on music learning and teaching. *International Journal of Community Music*, *1*(1), 49–61.

NASM Handbook 2016–17. (2016). Reston, VA: National Association of Schools of Music. https://nasm.arts-accredit.org/accreditation/standards-guidelines/handbook/ [accessed November 23, 2017].

National Association of Schools of Music. (2009, November). The entrepreneurial music school in a challenging economy. Conference materials at Pre-conference Session, National Association of Schools of Music Conference, San Diego.

Smilde, R. (2008). Lifelong learners in music: Research into musicians' biographical learning. *International Journal of Community Music*, *1*(2), 243–252.

UNESCO. (2006). Road Map for Arts Education. http://portal.unesco.org/culture/en/ev.php-URL_ID=30335&URL_DO=DO_TOPIC&URL_SECTION=201.html [accessed November 29, 2016].

Veblen, K. K. (2008). The many ways of community music. *International Journal of Community Music*, *1*(1), 5–21.

Waggoner, R. B. (1972). Factors relating to participation and non-participation in community performance groups on the adult level in Atlanta, Georgia. *Dissertation Abstracts International*, *32*(11), 6482–A.

Willoughby, D. (1982). Wingspread conference on music in general studies: Music programs exist for everyone. *Music Educators Journal*, *69*(1), 54–56.

World Music Central: Traditional and World Music Schools. (n.d.). http://worldmusiccentral.org/page/5/?s=Traditional+and+World+music+Schools [accessed November 23, 2017].

CHAPTER 20

LIFELONG LEARNING FOR PROFESSIONAL MUSICIANS

RINEKE SMILDE

In order to meet the challenges of rapidly changing cultural life in the twenty-first century, professional musicians need to be lifelong learners, drawing on a wide range of knowledge and skills. To be successful in a variety of roles, they require a reflective and responsive attitude to change.

This chapter addresses the concept and meaning of lifelong learning among professional musicians, as well as the ways institutions and teachers can facilitate attitudes and capacities for lifelong learning. Using biographical perspective as a lens, lifelong learning is viewed in terms of interconnections between musicians' personal and professional development. Lifelong learning in the aggregate complex of music education (i.e., educational organizations and learning environments, teachers, students, and graduates) is especially relevant. The chapter concludes with recommendations related to implementing lifelong learning in the education of professional musicians.

WHAT IS LIFELONG LEARNING?

Lifelong learning generally is perceived as a continuum containing all purposeful learning activity throughout a person's life (Fragoulis, 2001). Kohli (1985) observes that as the phases of the life course (which he considers to be preparation, activity, and retirement) are blurring in today's society, education is permeating all three. The role of education is thus no longer restricted to the first phase of people's lives, but is of importance throughout the life course. Maturing, in this sense, becomes a lifelong process (p. 24). Jarvis (2006) offers the following definition of lifelong learning:

> The combination of processes throughout a lifetime whereby the whole person—body (genetic, physical and biological) and mind (knowledge, skills, attitudes, values, emotions, beliefs and senses)—experiences social situations, the perceived content of which is then transformed cognitively, emotively or practically (or through any combination) and integrated into the individual person's biography resulting in a continually changing (or more experienced) person. (p. 134)

Lifelong learning may include formal, nonformal, and informal learning. In addition, definitions of lifelong learning generally incorporate the following characteristics: an emphasis on learning as opposed to training, including, for example, learning that is related to the context (such as the workplace, the orchestra, or the community setting); the combination of professional and personal development; and the use of context-related assessment. Interdisciplinary approaches and modes of learning that encourage learners to learn in an autonomous and creative manner are also important (Smilde, 2009a, p. 50).

In the context of lifelong learning, formal learning is generally understood to mean learning based on a structured curriculum, with specific learning objectives, duration, content, method, and assessment, aiming to develop skills and competences that are specifically relevant for the music professional. Nonformal learning can be defined as organized educational activity that contains learning elements outside the established formal system, for example a project done in collaboration with a partner in a music profession. Informal learning refers to learning that takes place in an implicit way without the intervention of a teacher, exemplified for instance by pop musicians who learn by listening to and imitating each other in garage bands. Green (2002) sees informal learning in music as a set of practices rather than methods.

Lifelong learning entails more than continuing education and broadening possibilities for employment. As Jarvis's definition suggests, lifelong learning also relates to people's biographical learning. In biographies, learning may be viewed as a (trans)formation of experience, knowledge, and action in the context of people's life histories and the world they live in (Alheit & Dausien, 2002). Biographical learning includes people's experience, knowledge, and self-reflection—everything people have learned throughout their lives and given a place in their biographies.

The importance of biographical knowledge and learning within the framework of lifelong learning is relevant in terms of Kohli's (1985) statement above that education is permeating all life phases. People learn throughout their lifespans, and they also learn through important transitions in their lives, whether on a personal level, for instance when going through divorce, or on a professional level, as when changing careers. The relevance of the role of biography is apparent in the important place that interconnections between personal and professional development hold as a feature of lifelong learning.

CHALLENGES FOR PROFESSIONAL
MUSICIANS IN THE TWENTY-FIRST CENTURY

Today's changing social-cultural landscape for music becomes evident in the expansion of new audiences, whether due to demographic change, the internet
and new technologies, or the ready availability of all kinds of music. This rapidly
changing cultural life is leading toward change in the music profession and professional musicians' careers, including those of performers, composers, educators, and
others. Increasingly, professional musicians are confronted with questions of how
to function flexibly and exploit opportunities in these evolving cultural contexts.

Musicians' careers in the twenty-first century are increasingly fluid, entailing
a decline in the numbers of opportunities for full-time, long-term contract work.
Rarely employed in one job for life, music graduates employ themselves more and
more as freelance artists, and their work is often project based (Smilde, 2009a).
This change in musicians' career patterns can be seen in what may be termed the
portfolio career, where the musician is increasingly an entrepreneur, having simultaneous or successive brief periods of employment, combining several forms of professional activities. Myers (2007) observes:

> The role of portfolio careers in sustaining the professional lives and energies of
> musicians carries important implications for lifelong musician education and
> learning. Moreover, the fact that at least a portion of these successful musicians
> has grown to see themselves as adding value to the larger society, rather than
> expecting society to sustain their isolated and detached musical prowess,
> indicates the need for early grappling with the question of what it means to be a
> musician in contemporary society. (p. 4)

The portfolio career creates a need for transferable real-world skills, such as self-
management and decision-making, as well as business skills. Rogers (2002) reports
that "being a musician today involves having the opportunity to take on a series
of roles, different from and broader than the act of performing and composing"
(p. 4). Professional musicians holding portfolio careers have to respond to the
variables within different cultural contexts, with roles that include those of performer, composer, teacher, mentor, coach, leader, and more. These diverse roles
require musicians to be innovative, reflective and responsive, collaborative and
entrepreneurial.

Though this complex of roles and skills is influencing the practice of traditional music careers, it is also exemplified in the relatively new career of community musicians and/or creative workshop leaders working in societal cross-sector
settings. The increase of musical and creative work in the community showed first
in the United Kingdom (Smilde, 2009a). Community musicians devise creative
workshops in health care, in social care, or in prisons, and this trend points to the
greater social and economic influence that music has on individuals in contemporary society (Rogers, 2002). Creative workshops are given by music leaders in these

very diverse venues, underpinned by the notion that the improvisational nature of collaborative approaches in creative music workshops can lead to people expressing themselves creatively, instilling a sense of ownership and responsibility both in the process and product, and exchanging ideas and skills as an integral part of the process (Gregory, 2005). Within this context, musicians may also be challenged to collaborate with practitioners in other arts.

In sum, the profound changes with which musicians are confronted present a major challenge to the increasingly international music profession as well as to institutions educating professional musicians. To this end, lifelong learning and its implementation are important to address. Lifelong learning is seen as a dynamic concept that responds to the needs generated by continuing change. Responding to change in society and the cultural environment must take place on the individual level of the professional musician, facilitated at the institutional level through education and professional development opportunities.

Toward a Conceptual Framework of Lifelong Learning for Musicians

Two major questions need to be addressed in order to define a conceptual framework of lifelong learning for professional musicians. The first is what knowledge, skills, and values are necessary for contemporary musicians to function effectively and creatively, and the second is how musicians actually learn, and in what domains.

From a biographical perspective, research into the interrelated development of the life, educational, and career spans of musicians provides important insights regarding these two questions. I investigated lifelong learning among professional musicians (Smilde, 2009a) through explorative biographical research that examined developments in the professional lives of 32 musicians. This work resulted in a collection of narrative learning biographies (Smilde, 2009b) that described critical incidents and educational interventions of exemplary value.

Findings gleaned from the evidence in the 32 learning biographies underpin the remainder of this chapter. The findings include the following:

- Changes in twenty-first-century cultural life were reflected in musicians' biographies, first and foremost among those musicians having portfolio careers.
- Those skills that enable musicians to respond to different demands and contexts in their professional lives had mostly been missed during their formal training as professional musicians; these skills included teaching skills, improvisation, and generic (life) skills.
- Three interdependent incentives appeared fundamental to the process of shaping musicians' self-identity: the first was singing and informal

music-making throughout childhood, the second was improvisation, and the third was engagement in high quality performance.

- Three highly interconnected conceptual facets of lifelong learning emerged during the analysis of the learning biographies. These included musicians' leadership skills, their varied learning styles, and their need for an adaptive and responsive learning environment within an institutional learning culture.
- Within the domain of artistic leadership, the concept of artistic laboratories that reflect the workplace, such as orchestras, or chamber or jazz ensembles, constituted the core. Generic leadership was frequently shown by the musicians in the ways they devised creative coping strategies for profession-related physical and psychological health issues. Educational leadership showed first and foremost in what one of the interviewees termed "holistic teaching approaches," encompassing roles of mentoring and coaching in the teaching process.
- Strong informal learning processes were observed within formal settings, sometimes within nonformal contexts. Musicians' artistic learning also often happened in informal ways, though such learning was underpinned, especially in the case of classical musicians, by formal, knowledge-based learning.
- Musicians functioned best when they had experienced an adaptive and responsive learning environment in their collegiate educations. This included having supportive, knowledgeable, and coaching teachers. Teachers were nearly always very important for the musicians. Both positive and negative experiences with teachers had long-lasting effects. (Smilde, 2009a, p. 257–258).

I now address these findings in greater depth related to the concept of lifelong learning.

SKILLS OF LEADERSHIP

Exploration of the question of what knowledge, skills, and values are necessary to function effectively and creatively as a contemporary musician led to the notion of musicians' multifaceted leadership. Musicians' leadership skills were evident in their capability to deal with change and create value and motivation while fulfilling the various roles required by rapidly changing professional demands.

Artistic leadership skills showed in the biographical research in the development of musicians' conceptual artistic thinking, where they showed artistry (Schön, 1983) and used tacit knowledge and understanding (Polanyi, 1966). An artistic laboratory, where relationships of trust among musicians were often perceived as a fundamental value, appeared conditional for the transfer of tacit knowledge. One of the interviewees, a cellist, discussed how an artistic concept can emerge while playing with other musicians. He compared what is happening on the stage with a (nonverbal) dialogue. Tacit knowledge and understanding are imperative in this dialogue, as we hear in the cellist's narrative:

> I don't talk anymore. I just play. And I notice that, just by playing, things will be added. . . . Words are phenomenal media, but not here. . . . We should maybe think or just feel or smell . . . when I explain what I am doing in rehearsal, I am not free anymore. (Smilde, 2009b, p. 71)

A substantial amount of research endorses the cellist's observation. Davidson and King (2004) discuss the general musical and social knowledge that underpin all types of performance. They address the specific moment-by-moment information that must be processed and responded to in an ongoing manner (p. 105) and point out that, indeed, too much talking can disrupt the flow in rehearsals (p. 111). Schön's (1983) concept of artistry, which he describes as the intuitive knowing of the practitioner that is "richer in information than any description of it" (p. 276), may be applied to this narrative. McPherson and Schubert (2004) address the dialogue as "engaging in musical conversation" (p. 69). They observe that superior coperformers can lift a musician to perform closer to her peak. This observation is corroborated by a number of the narratives of the musicians in my study.

The notion of the artistic laboratory also presents itself in the creative workshop. Gregory (2005) discusses "laboratory environments in participatory arts" (p. 282) and gives a beautifully broad definition of artistic leadership, saying "the key . . . is to lead by following and to follow by leading. Leadership is about listening and responding sensitively without negating one's own knowledge and expertise" (p. 293). Within an artistic laboratory like the creative workshop, the workshop leader needs to switch between various roles and know how to read a group, realizing participatory learning while facilitating the exchange of skills and ideas among the participants. In such artistic laboratories the boundaries between performing and composing disappear, giving way to shared leadership, both in an artistic sense and in leadership through example.

The latter form of leadership may be described as generic leadership. It includes the development of transferable life skills and social leadership. In the biographical research, there was an abundance of evidence regarding musicians' coping strategies and empowerment through learning brought about by major life events. Some musicians went through life-changing critical incidents that deeply influenced their life and career paths and often resulted in strong learning experiences.

In this context, the narrative of a female jazz singer (Smilde, 2009b) serves as an example of transformative learning (Mezirow, 1990). The singer suffered from severe performance anxiety, and at some point discovered its source, which was the fact that she had been severely bullied at school throughout her childhood, leaving her with low self-esteem. Her discovery led to important self-initiated interventions. Once she began to cope with her stage fright, the jazz singer became aware of the professional pathway she wanted to pursue, which was teaching:

> Already when growing up I used to think that I wanted to have work involving
> important social components. I find that more in teaching than in performing. . . .
> For me music is the means to be engaged in social processes that I feel involved
> in. Music is not an aim for me, but a means. That goes for teaching, but also for
> my own development. (Smilde, 2009b, p. 145)

Such learning can be considered transformative. Key to transformative learning is changing the frame of reference of learning. In the singer's case, reflecting on her biography was the incentive to let go of her insecurity, creating awareness of her desire for further personal and professional development. The biographical research revealed that the coping strategies musicians used for stage fright evolved more from transformative learning experiences emerging out of critical reflection, rather than from strategies such muscle relaxation, cognitive behavior therapy, or recipes like sedatives or alcohol, as they are described by Steptoe (1989).

Educational leadership is closely connected with other forms of leadership and addresses holistic teaching and learning as well as mentoring. The phrase "holistic teaching" was used by a concert pianist, who pursued teaching as a result of a critical incident at a later stage in his life. When he began to teach, the reasons were first and foremost financial, but gradually he developed strong motivation and became an effective pedagogue. Teaching was, as he termed it, "a voyage of discovery," and he found great fulfillment in the shared learning experiences with his students. As he described it, "working and growing together makes it an entity. . . . It is a two-way circle; the two are interdependent" (Smilde, 2009b, p. 108). There were more musicians in the study who taught in such a holistic way, taking on roles as facilitators, coaches, and peers.

MUSICIANS' LEARNING STYLES
THROUGHOUT THE LIFE
SPAN: INFORMAL LEARNING

Musicians I studied drew on a wide range of learning styles, and informal learning was especially important. Informal and nonformal learning were often present during childhood and throughout the life span, enabling musicians to gain personal ownership of their learning. Playing in an orchestra or wind band, often with siblings or other family members, or singing in a choir or at school were very important for most musicians and led to strong intrinsic motivation. These findings endorsed Sloboda's (2005) observations that occasions with significant meaning for young musicians were informal and took place in a relaxed, nonjudgmental atmosphere, often in the company of family and friends. One of the interviewees remembered vividly:

> When I was eight years old my father all of a sudden put a bugle in my hands and
> took me to the wind band. Actually I could hardly read music. The librarian of
> the band was handing out a march, he saw me sitting there and gave me a second

> bugle part. There I was! Then my neighbour W. whispered to me: "You come and sit with me, I'll teach you those notes." That's how it went. My siblings played in the same band. (Smilde, 2009b, p. 334)

This musician, who became the principal horn player in a world-famous orchestra, never forgot his incentives in childhood, saying:

> So at a young age I was in the situation where I am in now. . . . The heart of what I grew up with hasn't changed. It impressed me deeply at that moment. The playing and the conducting fascinated me. How could one man get such a big machine moving? (Smilde, 2009b, p. 333)

Musicians who in childhood learned music in an informal way alongside more formal instruction often continued to pursue such possibilities in later situations of formal learning. Even during the period of studies in music colleges, the musicians themselves often created interventions that provided opportunities for informal learning.

IMPROVISATION

Improvisation was of critical importance to musicians. Most of the musicians improvised spontaneously from early childhood. However, within their formal education, there was no attention to improvisation. Often teachers did not know how to respond to their pupils' eagerness to improvise, or worse, even forbade them to improvise. Musicians reacted differently to this, but the majority did not let go of the desire to improvise, as improvisation was close to their self-identity.

Kenny and Gellrich (2002) consider improvisation "a performance art *par excellence*, requiring not only a lifetime of preparation across a broad range of musical and non-musical formative experiences, but also a sophisticated and eclectic skill base" (p. 117). Throughout their development, improvisation served musicians in the study as an outlet for expressing their inner selves. Improvisation related to expressivity, communication and conversation, musical identity, social learning, motivation, ownership, and trust among musicians. These findings support Sloboda and Davidson's (1996) underlining of the importance of informal practice alongside formal practice, as well as of improvisation, for musicians to become motivated for life.

BIOGRAPHICAL LEARNING

The relevance of biographical learning showed convincingly in a substantial amount of musicians' biographies. This ongoing chain of various modes of learning from early childhood on included formal and nonformal learning alongside informal learning, as well as experiential learning, which is understood as learning in the context of earlier experiences and future opportunities for experience (Illeris, 2004,

p. 153). Wenger's (1998) four interconnected components of the community of practice came together convincingly in the majority of biographies: meaning (learning as experience); practice (learning as doing); community (learning as belonging); and identity (learning as becoming).

As briefly mentioned earlier, three interrelated incentives stood out as anchors for musicians' self-identity throughout their lives: informal music-making; improvisation; and high-quality performance. There was also a relationship to be found between substantial informal music learning and a decrease of stage fright. This could relate to musicians' sense of belonging in the community of practice (Wenger, 1998) where "legitimate peripheral participation" allowed musicians to learn and cope by trusting their peers, and where a sense of belonging and self-identity prevented or overcame the emergence of a sense of low self-esteem. Coping with performance anxiety in this way showed the "transformative practice of a learning community" (p. 215).

LIFELONG LEARNING IN THE EDUCATION OF PROFESSIONAL MUSICIANS

The features of lifelong learning described in this chapter remain marginalized in many institutions of higher education. Too often, lifelong learning is understood only as continuing education courses. Therefore, it is imperative to explore what needs to happen on the pivotal institutional level in order to make lifelong learning for musicians a given. How can concepts of lifelong learning inform educational approaches that define a reflective and responsive educational institution?

Professional musicians must respond to rapidly changing cultural contexts while fulfilling a variety of professional roles. If music colleges want to enable their graduates to enter the music profession with confidence and inquisitive and responsive minds, the concept of lifelong learning needs to be present in an organic way, permeating all aspects of an educational institution: curriculum, teachers, students, and graduates.

Any music college needs to fine-tune and adjust itself continuously to the needs of the profession. This requires ongoing responsiveness to the core business of today's world, where portfolio careers are increasingly typical among successful professional musicians. The development of educational practice should take place in association with professional organizations, and this joint practice must be relevant to the current and changing social and cultural landscape. In this way it is possible to foster an informed perspective that integrates with developments in the profession, including cross-arts, music technology, and a cross-cultural and cross-sectoral world (Smilde, 2009a, p. 251).

A responsive and adaptive learning environment requires approaches to teaching and learning that establish a strong motivation for lifelong learning among music students. The relationship between informal learning and strong intrinsic motivation has been shown frequently in research (Gardner, 1993; Wenger, 1998; Sloboda, 2005), and intrinsic motivation is essential for the development of effective practice strategies (Chaffin & Lemieux, 2004).

Musicians studied for the biographical research (Smilde 2009a, 2009b) appeared to need first and foremost an open learning culture, with space for their self-identities to develop. Such learning environments distinguish themselves by an atmosphere of trust, where students experience self-worth, excitement, and challenge. These environments feature holistic learning laboratories resembling Wenger's (1998) communities of practice, which are supported by a learning culture in a lifelong context, where transformative learning can evolve. In such laboratories, both experiential and formal cognitive learning can be underpinned by critical reflection and shared motivation within a group.

The dynamic synergy between the music college and the external world should be reflected in flexible curricula, providing a variety of learning pathways, based on the acquisition of competences and feedback from external partners. Entrepreneurship needs to be interwoven into such curricula, where one can find "a genuine thirst for learning of a kind that engages one's identity on a meaningful trajectory and affords some ownership of meaning" (Wenger, 1998, p. 270). Connecting to the context is key, where musicians are required to change their frame of reference, for example, when working in the community. Working with children, prisoners, or the elderly requires different frames of reference with which musicians need to connect, while at the same time leaving their individual artistic fingerprints on the creative work.

Curricula based on a conceptual framework of lifelong learning include the development of individual portfolios. Evaluation and assessment in such curricula need to be context-related and based on reflective practice, where an ability to reflect on the professional, cultural, and social environment at large is important. It is then of critical importance to ensure that the definition of quality is *not* a narrow one, limited to quality of performance, and failing to take into account a variety of contextual variables. In this sense, Gregory (2005) observes:

> The aim to develop a more "rounded" musician, fit for the challenges she or
> he will face in the twenty-first century, demands a framework and critical
> vocabulary for evaluating the quality of process, project and performance in a
> variety of contexts. This aim embraces an underlying commitment to widening
> participation, where diversity of skills, experience, needs and purpose are
> acknowledged as key components for a framework defining "excellent practice"
> through artistically driven education and community programs. (p. 20)

Teachers as Models
of Lifelong Learners

Implementing change that leads to an open learning culture must occur at both institutional and individual levels, and teachers play a pivotal role. Much depends on their mindsets, especially when taking into account the one-to-one relationship between many music teachers and their students. Without the good examples of their teachers in terms of attitudes and values, students are less likely to be motivated to become lifelong learners.

Ideally, teachers will be living examples of reflective practice and personal development. Teachers should be encouraged to be enablers rather than transmitters of knowledge, facilitating the growth of their students' artistic identities while acting as colearners. Teachers can touch the tacit dimensions of musicianship with their pupils through improvisation and high-quality engagement in musical performance, thus inspiring students' intrinsic motivation.

Teachers also must be able to take on mentoring roles. Mentoring plays a central part in the personal, artistic, and professional development of all musicians and can be defined as an approach to encourage critical reflection (Renshaw, 2006). Within the conceptual framework of lifelong learning, mentoring is fundamental for preparing students to enter the rapidly changing profession with confidence and understanding:

> By drawing out the interconnections between the musician's artistic, personal and professional development, fundamental questions regarding identity, motivation, meaning and personal creativity become the heart of a continuing reflective and reflexive dialogue. (p. 45)

Continuing professional development for teachers needs to be an integrated part of the learning culture in which they work. This goal can be realized through peer learning and comentoring of colleagues within the music college as well as within professional partnerships that require looking at the world from different perspectives and reflecting on change.

From the very beginning, music students need to be aware that they are part of a learning culture. A personal, individualized development plan should be central for students, leading to development of a portfolio, guided by their mentors. This plan should be one that can provide a basis for continuing career development beyond higher education.

FOUR RECOMMENDATIONS

To function in the rapidly changing music profession, lifelong learning needs to be the core business of educational institutions. Four recommendations suggest ways institutions can address this need in preparing aspiring career musicians:

- Create space for informal and nonformal learning in settings of a community of practice, with a fundamental role for improvisation.
- Consider music colleges holistic learning laboratories, reflecting the constantly changing workplace, including artistic, generic, and educational

knowledge and skills and entailing a strong integrated strand of continuing professional development for graduates.

- Ensure space for students' own interventions and leadership in relation to building their future careers.
- Enable critical reflection through comentoring as a means for broadening horizons, responding to globalization from the perspective of self-identity, and developing perspectives for change that encourage transformative learning.

REFLECTIVE QUESTIONS

1. Which different roles are you holding in your music profession?
2. When reflecting on your biography, how did you establish your career choices? and how are your personal and professional development interconnected?
3. After having read this chapter, how do you perceive your learning styles and what skills of leadership do you recognize in yourself?
4. When reflecting on your education, how would you regard the learning environment that you encountered in relation to your goals and motivations?

KEY SOURCES

Alheit, P., & Dausien, B. (2002). The "double face" of lifelong learning: Two analytical perspectives on a "silent revolution." *Studies in the Education of Adults*, 34(1), 1–20.

Jarvis, P. (2006). *Towards a comprehensive theory of human learning*. London & New York: Routledge.

Schön, D. A. (1983). *The reflective practitioner: How professionals think in action*. Aldershot, UK: Ashgate.

Schön, D. A. (1987). *Educating the reflective practitioner: Toward a new design for teaching and learning in the professions*. San Francisco: Jossey-Bass.

Wenger, E. (1998). *Communities of practice: Learning, meaning, and identity*. Cambridge, UK: Cambridge University Press.

REFERENCES

Alheit, P., & Dausien, B. (2002). The "double face" of lifelong learning: Two analytical perspectives on a "silent revolution." *Studies in the Education of Adults*, 34(1), 1–20.

Chaffin, R., & Lemieux, A. F. (2004). General perspectives on achieving musical excellence. In A. Williamon (ed.), *Musical excellence: Strategies and techniques to enhance performance* (pp. 19–40). Oxford: Oxford University Press.

Davidson, J. S., & King, E. C. (2004). Strategies for ensemble practice. In A. Williamon (ed.), *Musical excellence: Strategies and techniques to enhance performance* (pp. 105–122). Oxford: Oxford University Press.

Fragoulis, H. (2001). Innovations to address the challenges of lifelong learning in transition countries. In D. Colardyn (ed.), *Lifelong learning: Which ways forward?* (pp. 154–167). Bruges: College of Europe.

Gardner, H. (1993). *Creating minds, an anatomy of creativity, seen through the lives of Freud, Einstein, Picasso, Stravinsky, Eliot, Graham and Gandhi.* New York: Basic Books.

Green, L. (2002). *How popular musicians learn: A way ahead for music education.* Aldershot, UK: Ashgate.

Gregory, S. (2005). The creative music workshop: A contextual study of its origin and practice. In G. Odam & N. Bannan (eds.), *The reflective conservatoire* (pp. 279–300). London: Guildhall School of Music & Drama; Aldershot, UK: Ashgate.

Illeris, K. (2004). *The three dimensions of learning.* Frederiksberg: Roskilde University Press; Leicester: Niace.

Jarvis, P. (2006). *Towards a comprehensive theory of human learning.* London & New York: Routledge.

Kenny, B. J., & Gellrich, M. (2002). Improvisation. In R. Parncutt & G. McPherson (eds.), *The science and psychology of music performance: Creative strategies for teaching and learning* (pp. 117–134). Oxford: Oxford University Press.

Kohli, M. (1985). Die Institutionalisierung des Lebenslaufs. Historische Befunde und theoretische Argumente. *Kölner Zeitschrift für Soziologie und Sozialpsychologie, 37,* 1–29.

McPherson, G., & Schubert, E. (2004). Measuring performance enhancement in music. In A. Williamon (ed.), *Musical excellence: Strategies and techniques to enhance performance* (pp. 61–84). Oxford: Oxford University Press.

Mezirow, J. (1990). How critical reflection triggers transformative learning. In J. Mezirow & Associates (eds.), *Fostering critical reflection in adulthood* (pp. 1–20). San Francisco: Jossey-Bass.

Myers, D. (2007). Initiative, adaptation and growth: The role of lifelong learning in the careers of professional musicians. Keynote speech delivered at Trends in the Music Profession in Europe: Lifelong Learning & Employability. Groningen/The Hague: Lectorate Lifelong Learning in Music. http://www.lifelonglearninginmusic.org [accessed November 23, 2017].

Polanyi, M. (1966). *The tacit dimension.* New York: Doubleday.

Renshaw, P. (2006). *Lifelong learning for musicians: The place of mentoring.* http://www.lifelonglearninginmusic.org [accessed November 23, 2017].

Rogers, R. (2002). *Creating a land with music: The work, education and training of professional musicians in the 21st century.* London: Youth Music.

Schön, D. A. (1983). *The reflective practitioner: How professionals think in action.* Aldershot, UK: Ashgate.

Sloboda, J. A., & Davidson, J. (1996). The young performing musician. In I. Deliege & J. Sloboda (eds.), *Musical beginnings. Origins and development of musical competence* (pp. 171–190). Oxford: Oxford University Press.

Sloboda, J. (2005). *Exploring the musical mind: Cognition, emotion, ability, function.* Oxford: Oxford University Press.

Smilde, R. (2009a). *Musicians as lifelong learners: Discovery through biography.* Delft: Eburon Academic Publishers.

Smilde, R. (2009b). *Musicians as lifelong learners: 32 biographies.* Delft: Eburon Academic Publishers.

Steptoe, A. S. (1989). Stress, coping and stage fright in professional musicians. *Psychology of Music, 17,* 311.

Wenger, E. (1998). *Communities of practice: Learning, meaning, and identity.* Cambridge, UK: Cambridge University Press.

....

CHAPTER 21

AN INTERNATIONAL PERSPECTIVE ON MUSIC EDUCATION FOR ADULTS

....

JOHN DRUMMOND

It is never too late to start learning music. This idea lies behind the principles and practices of music education for adults. Adults become involved in music learning for many different reasons, and they access it in many different ways. Every adult who comes to music learning has his or her own story. Adult music education can be intracultural, in which the learner works within a known and familiar music, or it can be intercultural, in which the learner explores a new music, perhaps a folk or ethnic music. There may be the rediscovery of a childhood love for music, or of a family cultural heritage. The involvement may come about because of serendipity, or family opportunity, or social invitation. The mode of learning may be traditional, formal, or informal, or through contemporary technology. Often it takes place at the border between institutions and the community.

Adult music education is found in many cultures across the world, although not everywhere. In Fijian communities, for example, there is no need for it, since all children learn music from an early age as part of attendance at church, where everyone sings in the choir (Russell, 2002). In many parts of Africa, according to Nzewi (1999), all children participate in the community's music from an early age—"the encouragement of mass musical cognition through active participation" (p. 73). Fijian and African people learn their music while they are learning about the community they belong to, its structures, and its values.

However, many people around the world do enter into and engage in music learning as adults. This chapter explores music education for adults in terms of why and when adults participate in music learning experiences, and what, where, and how they study. A number of examples from various world cultures are discussed.

> Ms. A. always wanted to play the flute, but her family circumstances made it impossible. Through her married life she built up a collection of sound recordings of music. Now widowed, with her family grown and gone away, she has finally realized her dream, has taken up flute, and attends weekly lessons with a young teacher.

WHY?

Music learning in adulthood is undertaken by choice rather than under compulsion. The motivation is internal. Only rarely is the motive a desire to become a professional musician. In music practices where a very high level of professional training is required, such as Western classical music, learning to make music is unlikely to be undertaken by adults with the intention, or the hope, of reaching the heights of full professional performance. Adult music learners are more likely to think of learning music as a contribution to serious leisure (Stebbins, 2007), an activity more important than those undertaken for casual leisure and requiring greater effort. The level of commitment is high: there is a willingness to make the necessary sacrifices, to devote the appropriate time and money, and to persevere until the goal is achieved. What drives individuals to make this commitment?

Coffman (2006) investigated the reasons why individuals joined a community band in Australia and identified three: (1) the inspiration of a friend or participant; (2) the opportunity offered by a change of life circumstances; and (3) a social reason—an opportunity to meet others through a shared active experience. Underlying these reported reasons may be a deeper motive: learning to make music is important for personal well-being. It may bring the satisfaction of meeting a goal, or the rewards of social inclusion, or the emotional excitement that results from personal contact with music. One of Coffman's informants puts it simply: "it's a buzz" (Coffman, 2006, p. 17). Without the experience, one's life would be less fulfilling.

Southcott and Joseph (2010) interviewed the members of a Bosnian choir in Victoria, Australia, who agreed that increasing well-being was one reason for their participation (p. 22). A group almost entirely made up of refugees, the Bosnian Behar Choir also identified two other factors: developing a sense of community through singing together, and maintaining their cultural identity (Southcott & Joseph, 2010, pp. 22–24).

> Ms. B. has joined a Sweet Adelines group, but is having difficulty holding her voice part. She visits a music teacher each week for six weeks to learn how to do this.

Group music participation often leads toward a sense of common purpose and common values. The group develops its own culture—a set of attitudes and behaviors, protocols, and rituals—through which it identifies itself: the willing participant becomes part of that culture. The music may be part of a much wider culture, and participation may lead to a sense of belonging. Some adult learning is done primarily through one-on-one learning, and here the identification is likely to be with a wider culture, perhaps a dimly perceived and more anonymous community of musicians.

> Dr. C. played the piano as a child, and passed high-level grade exams, but couldn't
> find the time for piano during his medical training. Now he has retired, and
> wants to take it up again. He has found a teacher and has a weekly lesson.

The senses of well-being and of belonging are closely related to people's sense of individual and group identity. Parents everywhere encourage their children to learn the music that belongs to or defines the culture they live in and by. Adolescents in Western culture adopt the popular, mediated music of their generation as a way to belong to their international age group. When adults come to participate in music education they may do so because of music's ability to reinforce or change their sense of identity.

At times of crisis or significant change in our personal lives, such as the death of a partner or close family member, or retirement, or migration, we need to have our sense of identity repaired or strengthened. We need to be reassured about who we are and to what cultural community we belong. Music-making can help perform this function.

> When solo parent Ms. D.'s teenage daughter died in a car accident, she was
> distraught. A friend took her along to rehearsals of the local choral society. It was
> very difficult at first, but gradually the music exercised its healing powers.

An adult may have learned a particular music in youth but was unable to continue to practice it, or might have wished to study a music in youth but was prevented from doing do by circumstances such as lack of opportunity, financial constraint, or lack of parental approval. In later years, this deficit can be made up. The adult will seek out, or be inspired by friends to seek out, an opportunity to develop musical skills that reinforce her existing sense of identity, both on a personal level in terms of the accomplishment attained, and on a communal level in terms of belonging. In this situation, the choice of music will fall within the cultural background of the adult. The learning will be of what one considers to be, in some sense, one's own music.

Conversely, an adult may choose to learn music in order to modify identity. Perhaps there has been the discovery of other cultural identities besides one's own, and the desire has followed to come to know them better. The contact with the unfamiliar may have been through a travel experience, a sound recording, or a friend. It may have been quite accidental. In this situation the desire is to expand or broaden one's identity by finding out about a hitherto unfamiliar musical culture. What happens, frequently, is that music-making with a new community creates a strong identification with the group, and, as Coffman (2006) points out, the development of a new subcultural identity. To one's many existing identities (membership of a family, a locale, a sports club, a friendship group, a church) is added a new one: membership of a particular music group, or of the community whose music it is.

> Mr. and Ms. E. were shopping one day at the mall when they heard the distinctive sound of a gamelan orchestra performance. Enthralled, they inquired of one of the players and discovered it was a regular community music activity in a nearby town. They have joined the group and now learn to play gamelan every Wednesday night.

What adults can gain from their music learning, then, is an enhanced sense of well-being, either directly personal or indirectly through membership in a group identity. The learning may be of a familiar music or an unfamiliar one—it may reinforce an existing sense of identity or expand it.

WHO AND WHEN?

Adults of any age may and do take up music education. The New York Men's Choir in New York is made up of Japanese businessmen, including "bachelors and married fathers, retired seniors and teenagers" (www.pbs.org/previews/shallwesing). Adults at different stages of life may have different motivations and circumstances. For instance, young and middle-aged adults may engage in music learning activities as a result of peer-group or work-group pressure. Many older adults are probably retired from formal employment and have more leisure time to become involved in group music-making.

There may also be a connection between age and the kind of music adults choose to play. Some music has an association with high social status. As individuals in society develop wealth and status, their social identity may change, and they may adopt the music that goes with the new identity. They begin to feel it is "their" music. Others may have had a brush with Western classical music in their childhood and then, in their adolescence, chose a different music, such as rock music, that expressed their burgeoning adult identity. But as adults, they may come back to the music of their roots when they attain a certain age and position in the community. There may be deep psychological reasons for such changes across the lifetime. Perhaps the traditional music articulates or reflects some basic principles of the culture, which only resonate fully when the individual reaches a leadership age in that culture.

Music and Younger Adults

Many younger adults move into music learning situations as a result of invitation, inspiration, or pressure from a peer group or colleagues at work. Some are persuaded into it through a close personal or family relationship. A few are simply self-motivated, through a love of music that has not had the chance to be nurtured.

> Mr. F. is in his twenties. He has been a bedroom guitarist since his early teens, but never took lessons. Now he has a steady job, and is anxious to build his skills. He is following an online course of instruction and is progressing well, although he finds it challenging.

> Ms. G.'s office party at the end of last year was at a karaoke club. She was embarrassed when she found it hard to pitch the notes. She has found a singing teacher who can help her.

Migrants may carry their musical cultures with them, working hard to pass them on to their children. In some cases, such homeland music may become superseded by other musics in the homeland itself. Alternatively, the immigrant may abandon traditional culture and adopt the culture of the settler country, in order to achieve quicker assimilation. In this situation, it may be a later generation that rediscovers the family's roots and seeks to renew them. This may be more likely to happen to a younger adult still in the process of identity formation.

> Ms. H is an office worker in Sydney, Australia. Her grandparents moved to the city from Greece after World War II, but her Greek mother married an Irish father, and so Greek culture wasn't a big part of her upbringing. But now she wants to explore her Greek roots, and so she has joined a class to learn to play bouzouki.

Migrants, temporary or otherwise, may seek a way to join the musical culture of the host country while at the same time preserving something of their own. The New York Men's Choir of Japanese businessmen performs Western music in Western formal dress, but its website is entirely in Japanese. Two different threads bind the group together: its own language and the music of the host community. They need no teacher or director for their language, but they do need to be guided in how to sing Western music well.

Social relationships emerge from group music-making, but existing social groupings can also bring about participation in adult music education. Members of work-groups, such as those in an office community, often like to develop out-of-work activities in sports or the arts. Sometimes the activity is a musical one, either regular or occasional. The members may appoint a leader to guide their music-making—perhaps a music teacher or an animateur, a person who facilitates a group of musicians to achieve the goals they set for themselves.

The motivation for becoming involved in a music learning opportunity as a younger adult may be attributed to family or personal relationships.

> Ms. I. studied Suzuki violin from the age of six to the age of thirteen. Then, for over 10 years, she didn't play. But her current boyfriend plays in an Irish folk

band, so she has joined it as a fiddler, picking up the style and technique from the experienced fiddler beside her.

Ms. J. has always loved musicals. When her daughter was given a role in a local amateur production of *The Sound of Music* she applied to sing in the chorus and was accepted. Now she's sung in six productions and has joined the theater society. The music director is giving her some vocal coaching, and she intends to audition for a solo role in the next production.

Music and Older Adults

Fisher and Specht (1999) note that successful aging often includes creative activity, which encourages positive attitudes, personal growth, autonomy, and sense of community belonging. Retirement, and a move away from the direct responsibilities of parenthood, can liberate time and energy. Senior citizens who leave a workforce, particularly one they have been part of for many years, often find a gap in their lives: they need a new social environment, one that offers at least something akin to the challenges they faced in their working days.

> Mr. K. has joined SCORCH, the local older adults' orchestra, as a cellist. He used to play, in his youth, but he hasn't touched the instrument for years. He isn't taking any formal instruction, but he finds that rehearsals, and practice in between, allow him to recover some of his skills. He hopes he might advance a desk next season.

Many examples of adult music education are particularly provided for older members of the community. The members of the Bosnian Behar Choir are aged over 50. The same was originally true for the larger New Horizons International Music Association (NHIMA), begun in 1991 by Roy Ernst at the Eastman School of Music in Rochester, New York. Starting as a band program for people 50 and over, New Horizons serves people who either never had the opportunity to make music or learned at school and then had a period of inactivity. It has expanded to include orchestras and choirs, and most of the groups are now open to adults of any age. There are over 200 groups in the Association, including many in the United States, several in Canada, one in Ireland, and one in Queensland, Australia (www. newhorizonsmusic.org).

Don Coffman (who leads a New Horizons band in Iowa) surveyed 1,652 NHIMA musicians to learn about their experiences (2009). The survey included a question about the age and gender of the participants. Results showed that 90% were over 55, including 42% over 65 and 20% over 75. One of his questions was this: "Do you believe that playing an instrument in a New Horizons group has affected your health, either favorably or unfavorably?" Nearly 74% responded positively; 41% claimed increased happiness while 33% claimed an increased sense of purpose. Those claiming increased happiness used words such as *emotional health, well-being, quality of life, contentment, joy, uplifted, enthusiasm, energized, feeling younger, feeling new, laughter, calm, relief,* and *reduced stress.* Those claiming an increased sense of purpose used words such as *something to look forward to, being active, disciplined, busy, involved, learning new things, a creative or artistic or emotional outlet, increased awareness, self-esteem, self-confidence, self-worth, pride, sense of accomplishment,* and *being productive.* Nearly a quarter of respondents considered that involvement in a New Horizons group had improved their physical health, including posture, dexterity, muscle tone, flexibility, and coordination; and 18% spoke of social benefits such as a sense of belonging, camaraderie, and new friends (Coffman, 2009, pp. 383–384). Coffman's study is one of many supporting the emotional, social, and physical benefits of engaging in music activities as an older adult learner.

WHAT?

Learning about Music

Although the benefits of playing and singing music are widely recognized, many adults wish to become involved in developing their understanding of it. This is often the case where a complex, sophisticated music is involved, one with a lengthy history, internal rules of structure and theory and purpose, and a large repertoire or canon. Western classical music is an obvious example, although many East, South and West Asian court musics have the same characteristics. Western adults renewing their acquaintance with Western classical music, or with time to discover more about it, are commonly enrolled in classes focusing on knowledge about music. Many performing organizations (symphony orchestras, choirs, chamber music societies, and the like) offer preconcert study sessions or ongoing courses that seek to explain the music to potential audiences, thus deepening their understanding of the aural experience. Radio networks devoted to classical music may include similar informative programs. Television series on classical music and printed books as well as internet sites provide opportunities for adult learning.

> Mr. and Mrs. L. began attending concerts of Western classical music in their early fifties, initially because Mr P.'s firm was sponsoring a local orchestral concert, but thereafter because they enjoyed it. But they are aware that they know little about the music they are hearing, so they have enrolled in a course at their local university, in which music to be performed at forthcoming concerts is explained.

Learning across Cultural Borders

Though many middle-class Asian parents encourage their children to learn Western musical instruments, there appears to be less evidence of middle-class Western parents encouraging their children to learn Asian instruments. Including cultural diversity in formal music education for children and young people is a difficult matter, as numerous studies have shown (e.g., Campbell, 1991; Schippers, 2010). Questions relating to the importance of context, the difference between Western and local pedagogies, and the difficulty of appropriate assessment, all of which are complex matters relating to authenticity, can be seen as impediments to the inclusion of world musics in the Western formal school curriculum.

Such questions seem less critical in the context of adult music learning in more informal settings. Learning may or may not require formal assessment. Teaching is often undertaken by culture-bearers who themselves provide the cultural context and determine the pedagogical method. In this way, adult learners may well gain a more authentic experience of the music than do children in a school setting. This may partly account for the success of such programs and the consequent demand for them.

> All the members of the M. family are learning djembe in a small town in Sweden. The older son encountered it at school, and persuaded his younger brother, sister, and parents to come along to an open day. They enjoyed it so much that they have joined the community group, which practices on Thursday nights so it can play effectively in public spaces on Saturday mornings.

Gamelan and djembe are well established in many cities in the West, and sitar is also widespread, as is Latin American music. Folk and ethnic music of many kinds is attractive, it seems, to adult Westerners.

The Irish Academy of World Music and Dance is based at the University of Limerick in Ireland. As a University institution, it offers degree and diploma qualifications, but it provides a good deal more than this. Its Maoin Cheoil an Chláir Music School teaches both classical and traditional music side by side, and "because we believe it's never too early, or late, to start learning music we welcome students of all ages and stages of experience; toddlers, teenagers, and adults" (www. maoincheoil.com). The Irish Academy hosts a number of other programs for adult learners. The NOMAD project offers community music workshops in Traveller's Music. Sanctuary celebrates the musical traditions of refugees and asylum seekers in Ireland. Ionad na nAmhrán is dedicated to the performance and study of traditional song in both the English and Irish languages (www.ul.ie/~iwmc/).

During its summer session in 2009, London University's School of Oriental and African Studies (SOAS) offered the following musical practices, all open to the public: Afro-Brazilian music, Afrocuban batá drumming, Australian didgeridoo, Balinese gamelan, Bulgarian singing, Chinese kunqu opera, Cuban big band, Indian tabla, Japanese shakuhachi, Korean samulnori percussion, Mongolian overtone singing, mouth harps, Russian singing, Senegalese kora, South Indian violin and vocals, Tibetan music bowls, Ugandan music, Yiddish language and music, and Zimbabwean mbira. A course called "An Introduction to Middle Eastern Music" was also offered (www.soas.ac.uk/music/summermusicschool/timetable/). This range indicates not only the richness of the world's treasure-house of musics but also the demand for such courses.

Located in the hilltown of Valjevo, the Amala School for Roma and Serbian Music has as its mission "to open vibrant Serbian cultures to the world" (www.galbeno.com). Since 2001 the School has provided a series of short summer schools in gypsy music. Participants live in a Romani-Serbian household, eat the local food, and enjoy village life. The school uses traditional teaching methods, and all the students learn by ear. Music, dance, and language classes are organized for beginners and for those who already have some experience.

The World Music and Dance Centre at the Rotterdam Conservatoire in Holland offers teaching in five different musical genres: flamenco guitar; Northern Indian classical music; Latin, African-Caribbean, and Brazilian music; Argentinian tango; and Turkish (folk) music. While students may study formally for qualifications, there are also open workshops in which adults from the community can participate (www.codarts.nl/01_home/02_cons/05_AWM/index.php).

> Mr. N. learns a new music every year. Last year he took workshops in Jamaican metal band; this year he's taking *taiko* drumming; for next year he has Brazilian percussion in mind. He says it keeps him young.

The Tar School is a Persian Music Institute operating in several locations in northern California. It offers teaching, to pupils of all ages, in the six-string tar and the setar. Teaching is one-to-one and is backed up by workshops, which include classes on music appreciation and the history of Persian music and use a combination of traditional and modern approaches (www.tarschool.com).

The Amala School, the Tar School, and the World Music Academy, like the SOAS Summer School and other institutions of a similar kind around the world, primarily offer courses to those who wish to explore unfamiliar musics, or perhaps musics different from their own heritage.

> Mr. O. works in a firm in Oslo that employs Iranian refugees. During breaks he hears them listening to Persian music, and he has found the sounds fascinating. He has bought some recordings. He has also discovered that there is a traditional Persian performing group in the city and is plucking up the courage to ask whether he could join it.

WHERE AND HOW?

While often taking place in independent and informal community settings, adult education can sometimes use the resources of formal education, and interaction between the two is evident in many cases (e.g., Mumford, 2002; Conway & Hodgman, 2008). Music educators may work across sectors, teaching young people by day and becoming involved in adult music education at other times. In some school jurisdictions it is common to encourage the use of school facilities by members of the community (see Alfano, 2008). As school music-making practices and resources develop outside the norms of Western classical music, and often use external community expertise, it is likely that the barriers between formal childhood/adolescent schooling and adult music education will break down further.

A number of modes of adult music learning can be identified, many of which have been touched on already. At the simplest level, an adult may receive one-on-one instruction from a teacher on a regular basis. This is usually a contractual arrangement: the learner submits to the teacher's authority—although, as an adult, the goals can be clearly articulated by the learner and the terms agreed on by both. If the teacher's experience has been largely with young people, some adjustments in approach may be necessary. Printed teaching materials may be more suited to younger students than to adults, and additional resources may need to be sought.

Adults may choose to enroll in workshops or series of workshops, summer school, or music camps in order to learn a particular music. This mode of learning is the norm for ensemble music, from whatever musical culture. Learning is in a group situation, with lower levels of personal attention than in one-on-one instruction. However, many adults consider the benefit of social interaction to be sufficient compensation for lack of personal attention.

> Ms. P., a nurse, is attending a summer music camp at which she is learning scat singing. It's her second year, and she has made some friends there from the same town. They are talking about forming a regular group.

In intentional learning situations, the activity typically involves payment to the teacher. But there are other situations in which adult music learning occurs more indirectly, when a person joins a music-making group with a desire or expectation that musical skills will be enhanced. The initial reason for joining may simply be to enjoy making music, but then there grows an awareness of the potential—or the need—to develop more advanced skills. Many community music-making networks have a competitions system as a way of improving standards and enhancing commitment. Although music-making is primarily collaborative rather than competitive, competitions can offer an incentive to improve the music-making skills of the group and of the individuals within it. Often, some formal tuition (instruction) takes place, with a group leader or section leaders working with individuals, as with brass bands and Scottish pipe bands.

> Mr. Q. sang a lot as a young man, but had little time for it during his working years. Recently made redundant, at the age of 52, he has joined a barbershop quartet, which is being coached for participation in the statewide competitions next month.

Some forms of adult music education involve learning with or from written musical materials, such as notated music. Here the skill of music reading is necessary to make progress, although the particular notation to be learned will differ from music to music. Other forms do not require music reading, because the music itself has no notation, or because the traditional way of learning is through oral and aural transmission.

Kruse (2009) identified a disparity in some adult community bands between those who wanted clear direction and those seeking a more democratic way of learning. For some adults, learning is linked to their school experiences, in which they received clear direction. Others seek a more collegial approach.

> Mr. R. has undertaken genealogical research and discovered his family has Scottish roots. This has led him to a fascination with all things Scottish, and he has taken up the bagpipes. He learns through Skype from a distant cousin in Scotland.

Contemporary Information and Communications Technology (ICT) has transformed the ways people of any age can learn music. Courses on learning to play instruments are available to be purchased on DVD, or can be accessed on the internet. The Tar School, mentioned above, offers tuition through Skype. Music-making with others can also be undertaken through e-jamming sites. While older adults who have not grown up with these technologies may be shy to use them, it is clear that in the future more and more adults will be familiar with the opportunities offered by ICT to develop their musical skills.

The Christchurch School of Music (CSM) in New Zealand was formed in 1955 to provide teaching in Western classical music to young people outside the hours of formal schooling. It has enjoyed considerable success, providing a steady stream of players into the New Zealand Symphony Orchestra's National Youth Orchestra and into professional music careers. Working with the National Research Centre in Music Education and Sound Arts at the University of Canterbury, the CSM has developed an online, real-time distance-teaching program in instrumental music using the high-speed broadband facility of New Zealand's Kiwi Advanced Research and Education Network (KAREN). In 2007 the project was tested with four rural schools, and it now extends into 12 other schools and into universities across the country. The technology allows access to expert musical tuition by people who are otherwise prevented by location or other circumstances from acquiring it (www.csm.org.nz).

CONCLUSION

It has been argued that "adults who sing [in choirs] are remarkably good citizens" (Chorus America, 2009). The evidence at least indicates that most adults who learn music in group settings achieve a high level of personal well-being, physically and psychologically, partly as a result of interaction with the music, but also as a result of the social interactions involved. Social and cultural identities can be confirmed or expanded. Adults learning music do so for the same reasons anyone learns music: to find out more about themselves, and to develop their sense of identity in a familiar or unfamiliar community setting. The rewards are considerable in terms of achievement (because the motivation is strong and personal), in terms of enjoyment (because the goals are being met), and in terms of self-esteem (because the self-identity is deepened).

An increase in the average age of the adult population entails profound economic and social implications. Technology is transforming the way many people lead their lives and manage their leisure time. Adult music education will evolve as these external circumstances develop. At the heart of adult learning in music there lies a constant, however: the desire to make music, and to make it better, in order to nurture personal well-being. That is what music can offer to everyone, and there is every reason to suppose that it will continue to do so.

REFLECTIVE QUESTIONS

1. According to Chorus America, "adults who sing in choirs are remarkably good citizens." Is this because good citizens are likely to want to sing in choirs, or because singing in a choir might make you a good citizen?
2. Participation in music-making by adults would seem to bring benefits beyond purely musical ones. How important is this?
3. Learning a music, especially one other than your own, as an adult, can be challenging. Why bother?

KEY SOURCES

Campbell, P. S. (1991). *Lessons from the world: A cross-cultural guide to music teaching and learning.* New York: Schirmer.
Coffman, D. D. (2009). Survey of New Horizons International Music Association musicians. *International Journal of Community Music, 1*(3), 375–390.
Schippers, H. (2010). *Facing the music: Shaping music education from a global perspective.* Oxford: Oxford University Press.

REFERENCES

Alfano C. J. (2008). Intergenerational learning in a high school environment. *International Journal of Community Music,1*(2), 253–266.
Campbell, P. S. (1991). *Lessons from the world: A cross-cultural guide to music teaching and learning.* New York: Schirmer.

Chorus America. (2009). The 2009 chorus impact study. http://www.chorusamerica.org/ [accessed November 23, 2017].

Coffman, D. D. (2006). Voices of experience: Interviews of adult community band members in Launceston, Tasmania, Australia. *International Journal of Community Music*. http://www.seriousleisure.net/uploads/8/3/3/8/8338986/coffmanpaper.pdf

Coffman, D. D. (2009). Survey of New Horizons International Music Association musicians. *International Journal of Community Music, 1*(3), 375–390.

Conway, C., & Hodgman, T. M. (2008). College and community choir member experiences in a collaborative intergenerational performance project. *Journal of Research in Music Education, 56*(3), 220–237.

Fisher, B., & Specht, D. (1999). Successful aging and creativity in later life. *Journal of Aging Studies, 13*(4), 457–472.

Kruse, N. B. (2009). "An elusive bird": Perceptions of music learning among Canadian and American adults. *International Journal of Community Music, 2*(2 & 3), 215–225.

Mumford, M. (2002). Music ensembles: Making and maintaining effective, complementary, rewarding relationships. In J. Drummond & D. Sell (eds.), *Taonga of the Asia Pacific Rim* (pp. 274–280). New Zealand: NZSME.

Nzewi, M. (1999). Strategies for music education in Africa: Towards a meaningful progression from tradition to modern. *International Journal of Music Education, 33*(1), 72–87.

Russell, J. (2002). Sites of learning: Communities of musical practice in the Fiji Islands. In *SAMSPEL-ISME 2002 Proceedings 2002.* (No pagination). Bergen: ISME 2002.

Schippers, H. (2010). *Facing the music: Shaping music education from a global perspective.* Oxford: Oxford University Press.

Southcott, J., & Joseph, D. (2010). Sharing community through singing: The Bosnian Behar Choir in Victoria, Australia. In e-journal of *Studies in Music Education, 8*(2), 17–27.

Stebbins, R. A. (2007). *Serious leisure: A perspective for our time.* New Brunswick, NJ: Aldine Transaction.

Index